GUNSTOCK
Finishing & Care

A Textbook, covering the various Means and Methods by which modern Protective and Decorative Coatings may be applied in the correct and suitable Finishing of Gun and Rifle Stocks. For Amateur and Professional Use

by

A. Donald Newell

A Samworth Book on Firearms

STACKPOLE BOOKS

COPYRIGHT, 1949, BY
THOMAS G. SAMWORTH

All rights reserved. No portion of this book may be reproduced in any form without permission of the copyright owner.

Published by
STACKPOLE COMPANY
Cameron & Kelker Streets, Harrisburg, Pa. 17105

May 1969 printing

Printed in the United States of America
By THE TELEGRAPH PRESS
Harrisburg, Pennsylvania

Contents

	Introduction	ix
1.	Woods for Gunstocks	1
2.	Preliminary Finishing Operations	28
3.	Stains, Staining and Graining	60
4.	Drying Oils and Their Application	100
5.	Varnishes	136
6.	Lacquers	186
7.	Shellac	228
8.	Plastic Finishes	253
9.	Driers, Thinners and Solvents	262
10.	Waxes, Polishes and Rubbing Compounds	277
11.	Forearm Tips and Grip Caps	299
12.	Refinishing Operations	315
13.	Refinishing of Military Rifle Stocks	339
14.	Antique and Early Gunstock Finishes	366
15.	Auxiliary Equipment	387
16.	Laboratory Tests and Notes	409
	Natural Resin List	421
	Evaporation and Drying Time	422
	Standard Liquid Measure and Equivalents	423
	Glossary of Terms	426
	Sources of Supply	432
	Artificial Graining of Gunstocks	437
	Index	474

This book is dedicated to Audrey, *my wife, without whose tireless patience and fine cooking it would never have been written*

Introduction

ED FRUMPDILLY is in a bit of a quandary. He is just an amateur like the rest of us, but in restocking a rifle he has gotten down to the finishing operation and what to use on it.

Looking through the ads in *The American Rifleman* he spots a score or so of offerings by different concerns, but he is not sure just how good they really are and he does not want to experiment. He then digs into all the various gunsmithing textbooks available to him, but comes up with nothing but some ancient dope on rubbed linseed oil. You can take it from there. He probably ends up using the rubbed oil for lack of something better.

It was at just such a point that I found myself some many moons back. Having gone through just about everything I could lay my hands on in the way of information and finding nothing of real value I decided to investigate the entire field. Working as a technician in a paint plant certainly has its advantages at a time like this! The investigation consisted mostly of tests run by myself and of digging up facts previously known or published but which have received little popularization.

My purpose in writing this book was twofold. First; I have endeavored to give as much information as possible concerning materials used in wood finishing, both old and new. Second; I have attempted to uncover and rectify the many erroneous ideas, statements, and theories which have plagued the gunsmith for many years.

INTRODUCTION

The average gunsmith, amateur or professional for that matter, has no way of testing materials and methods of application unless he is in some way connected with a well equipped laboratory. Simple permeability tests, for instance, will require two hundred to three hundred dollars' worth of equipment.

In addition, much of the information given is common knowledge to the paint and varnish industry but this, too, is unavailable to the average man.

Because so much misleading and downright false information has been and is accepted as the truth I feel that the gunsmith and amateur is entitled to more of a break than he has been getting. This thought started research which eventually broadened out and resulted in this book.

There is no question that I shall meet censure from certain quarters. These quarters will contain advocates of the old school of thought which figures "what was good enough for Dad is good enough for me." There is always a certain amount of that sort of thing present no matter what the situation or subject so at least I shall be in good company.

Possibly this old school of thought is a stabilizing force and therefore pardonable, but when something provably superior is introduced it should then at least nod to if not bow to progress.

I have had several personal experiences with such men. They grudgingly admit the superior qualities of this or that relatively new product or substance, but can you get them to even try it? Not by a damsite. They stick to their old favorite and there is no budging them.

I do not like to think of myself as one of these "flash in the pan" boys who jump at everything new that comes out and condemns all the old tried and true principles which have been used so successfully for years. That is not true. But having been technically (and scientifically) trained, for my money a new idea of merit should be given its innings and fully accepted if it works out.

INTRODUCTION

No matter how much or how little equipment is available to us we are still free to observe the actions and properties of materials with which we have to work. We can improve many existing methods by simple shortcuts if only those shortcuts can be seen. I realize that the substances in use have certain limits, but those limits may be stretched considerably if we only realize what makes the things work the way they do. The explanation of those workings I have tried to put forth here.

Do not allow the things with which you work to dominate you! When something new is offered to the trade check up on it. Get some and try it out. Only in this way will you be able to advance. Investigate, experiment, and investigate again! Such investigation and experimentation has brought us as far, technologically speaking, as we have so far come and without it civilization would not only cease to move forward, but would recede and disappear.

It is not necessarily the boys in the big factories and labs who are responsible for such advances, though they have played a large part in it, but the small man with foresight and curiosity who found a little better way to do something did the ground work for most of the inventions. These inventions were in turn taken up by industry and improved to a point where they were made practical for everyone.

Do not think you are limited by what you have to work with. You are limited only insofar as you allow your intelligence and reasoning to do that limiting. Accept a narrow horizon and your work will reflect that thought, but by realization of the vast possibilities open to you your scope of operations will be broadened and your work will reflect that freedom of thought and action.

The observations and facts given in this book are not only those which I myself have found, but are also those of many qualified men in the industry. I am indebted not only to those publications given in the Bibliography, but also to the following persons who have given freely of their time and knowledge. To these people I wish to express my gratitude:

INTRODUCTION

Frank Bakos, Henry Miller, By Stephens, Ed Kabala, Jack Olson, Bill Ironsides, Wesley Wilbur, Mel Gerson, Lee McNally, Jim Murray, Walter Hall, and Vic Schwenke, all of the Ditzler Color Division; H. E. Esch, of the Electric Sprayit Company; W. L. Edmonds, of the Edmonds Engineering and Manufacturing Company; H. W. Martin, of the General Dyestuff Corporation; M. H. Boyce, of the duPont Company; John E. Rowe, of the Binks Manufacturing Company; W. E. Dremel, of the Dremel Manufacturing Company; F. L. Browne, of the U. S. Department of Agriculture, Forest Service; R. F. Buike, of Durez Plastics & Chemicals, Inc.; Mark K. Pinkerman, of Reichhold Chemicals, Inc.; C. A. Cosgrove, Jr., of Cosgrove's Magazine; William Millington, of Baker Furniture, Inc.; Mr. and Mrs. Arthur R. Newell for their faith and understanding; and last, but not least, Thomas G. Samworth for his much tried patience and guiding hand.

With my special thanks to Earl Pulve the photographer and to Roy Brown who made the sketches for this book.

In closing I would like to say that each and every material mentioned in the following pages is available if the proper source is tapped. The list of Suppliers has been given to expedite the reader's search for this or that basic material and it should be sufficient in most cases.

If the reader encounters difficulties along the line, either in procuring substances or in using them to give satisfaction, I will be more than glad to give him what help I can. Questions, suggestions and just plain exchange of ideas is all grist for my mill, located as I am in the position of trying to run down the whys and wherefores of wood finishing.

A. DONALD NEWELL

CHAPTER ONE

Woods for Gunstocks

SINCE the dawn of recorded history weapons and their accessories have been made of wood. It has played an important part in the development of civilization and the employment of the different kinds and types of wood has increased rather than decreased with the passing years.

A gunstock, if it may be classed as an accessory, is the most important factor in contributing to the beauty and utility of a firearm. The method of treating such wood will determine to what degree beauty and utility will appear. In order to develop these important characteristics, however, the proper type of wood must be employed. Too often a poor piece of wood will be worked on and sweated over by the stocker with totally unsatisfactory results in which case he will usually condemn the materials with which he attempts to finish the wood rather than the wood and himself.

Wood is composed of fibers of cellulose. The way in which these fibers develop, the degree to which they are packed together, and the alignment of the fibers will determine the properties and characteristics of the resulting mass which we call wood.

We make two broad classifications: softwoods and hardwoods. Each of these classifications will embrace a multitude of different kinds of wood, but the ones in which we are interested and which have been used traditionally for centuries are the hardwoods, and of those only a few.

Of the great number of different hardwoods available only

a few will be totally satisfactory. Some woods, while possessing excellent properties, will also possess other highly unsatisfactory properties which will rule the use of that wood out. While the field of gunstocking is allied to that of furniture making it is a highly specialized branch of the field and what may hold true in the one may not hold true in the other. Therefore, the woods that will be acceptable for furniture may not always be suitable for stock work.

DESIRABLE WOOD TYPES

Following is a list of the woods most often recommended for stock work together with some of the properties of each:

Ash: Different species of this wood are available such as white ash, black ash and green ash. The different varieties are grown in different parts of the country and some of the properties will differ in each one.

This wood is not heard from very much as being a stock wood because there are other woods so much better in regard to strength, color and weight. This may be used if nothing else is available, however, as it is strong and tough. The weight will vary from 33 to 40 pounds per cubic foot.

The specimens usually seen are rather light yellow in color and have fairly coarse grain.

This wood should be stained with a light brown or brownish-red stain and filled with a dark walnut colored filler. Then it may be varnished, lacquered, shellacked or oil rubbed.

It is possible to obtain sections of plank large enough for stock blanks.

Almond: At the present time most almond wood planks are obtained from Cuba.

It is a light colored wood varying from gray to yellow-gray. The grain is fairly fine, but very open necessitating filling. The figure of the wood is very good with wavy grain predominating. It is strong and will withstand the shocks of recoil and handling well. The weight of the wood is about 42 pounds.

This wood should be left as is or stained only a very light

brown. The only reason for selecting it as a stock wood would be to have something out of the ordinary and for that reason it would be unwise to cover the beauty by making it look like walnut or mahogany. Filling is necessary in most cases because of the open pores. A very light color filler should be used in order to keep the overall color of the wood unchanged. It may be desirable to use the finishing material as a filler in which case varnish, lacquer or shellac will serve very well.

Not much of this wood is seen on the market and it is hard to find.

Apple: This wood is obtained from either the wild or the domesticated apple tree of the United States.

The color is usually a light reddish shade though it is sometimes seen in gray or grayish-white planks.

This is very good wood for stocks, though the figure is sadly lacking. It is strong and withstands splitting well. The weight is about 46 pounds which makes it heavier than is desirable.

The very close grain makes filling unnecessary. Inasmuch as the color is so light it will be necessary to darken the wood with a light brown or brownish-yellow stain. This wood may be finished in any of the conventional finishes in which case the finish itself will be used as a filler. If a drying oil only is used a wash coat of shellac or varnish should be used to fill the minute pores before rubbing on the oil.

This wood is rather scarce at the present time.

Beech: A fairly common stock wood, especially before 1870.

This wood grows over a fairly large area of the United States. The color is light and no appreciable grain structure is evident except upon close examination.

Strong and hard, it resists splitting well and may readily be used if nothing else is available. Weight is about 41 pounds.

Filling is not necessary because of the fine grain. Staining should be done to darken the wood, in which case a brown or reddish-brown color to approximate walnut is desirable. Finishing may be done with any of the standard materials, though a rubbed oil finish will be the least **desirable** of all.

Some planks of this wood are on the market, though it is not as easy to come by as formerly.

Birch: A common furniture wood grown in the United States.

The color will be very light, almost white in some cases. Occasionally a stock with good figure is found, but usually there will be no appreciable beauty to the natural wood.

Birch is very strong and hard and works well with edged tools. It is very fine grained, resembling maple in this property. Weight is about 41 pounds for yellow birch, the most common type available.

Inasmuch as the pores are so minute no filling will be necessary in using this wood. The beauty will be enhanced by staining a dark brown or dark brownish-red to resemble walnut or mahogany. What filling is done should be done by the finish itself. Lacquer gives an exceptionally fine finish over this wood, though varnish of the non-yellowing type will also work very well. A plain waxing of the stained surface has been recommended by some authorities.

Cherry: This wood is generally cut from large trees in hardwood forests rather than from the small domesticated cherry tree. These large trees are called wild black cherry.

The color generally runs from a light red to a dark red-brown. The grain is very close and the pores small. The wood is strong and fairly hard and works well under tools. Weight is about 33 pounds.

No filling is necessary for this wood. Staining is not necessary usually as the natural color and shade is sufficient and it may be finished in any of the conventional materials. Lacquer or varnish rubbed to a dull sheen is especially good.

This wood is hard to find in pieces large enough for stock blanks. If one is found it would be well to buy it as there is a certain demand from antique collectors and refinishers for genuine cherry wood. The old flint rifles are especially suited for finishing in this wood.

Mahogany: This wood is usually called by the area from

which it was taken such as Honduras, Mexican, African.

It will range from light to dark red with shades of brown and yellow in between, depending upon the locality in which it was grown. It is fairly open grained and will require filling. It is fairly hard for the better grades of wood and works very well under edged tools. Weight ranges from 33 to 41 pounds, depending upon the species.

This wood should not be stained but should be filled with a dark brown or reddish-brown filler and finished in varnish or lacquer.

Mahogany is included in the list because it is possible that you may be able to obtain a blank or plank suitable for stock work. Generally the better grained woods will have been used for veneer and it is for this reason, mostly, that fine blanks are seldom seen.

Osage Orange: Often called "bois d'arc" from the extensive use for bows and arrows.

The color is normally an orange or light red. This wood is strong, tough, and takes an excellent finish. It is rather heavy, weighing about 48 pounds.

The wood is fine grained enough to be finished without filling. The color will usually be dark and deep enough so that staining is not required. Varnish and lacquer may be used as a filler-finish with good success, but wax alone has been used in the past.

It is possible to obtain this wood in large enough pieces for blanks, though it is used to a very great extent for archery supplies and posts. Possibly a dealer in such archery supplies could locate something for you.

Maple: The wood of this type which is most useful for stock work is called Sugar or Rock Maple. It is very heavy, 44 pounds. The soft maples are lighter, weighing about 33 to 38 pounds.

Hard maple is an extremely close grained wood which will take a very smooth surface under sanding. The color is white to red-brown and various figures such as bird's eyes, waves, or curls may be had depending upon the individual specimen and upon how the blank is cut from the log.

It is very difficult to work with this wood because it is so hard. Unless hand and edged tools are kept in the best of condition it will be discouraging to inlet a blank completely.

Maple may be sanded so smoothly that coats of protective films may have very poor adhesion. There is no great number of appreciable pores for the film to hang onto and the wood should be scuffed with fine or medium paper before finishing.

For good grained maple no stain is necessary or desirable. The color and figure of the natural wood should be left in and accentuated as much as possible. Filling is not necessary as there are no pores. Finishing should be done in varnish or lacquer with only a very thin coating being applied.

Very fine color and figuring may be brought out on this wood by the use of the Flame process described in Chapter 3. This is what Alvin Linden called a Suigi finish and is well suited to maple.

This wood was much used by colonial craftsmen for their better stocks and even today it is possible to find good pieces. This is the exception rather than the rule, however. Most of the good maple seen today will be hand-picked blanks and will cost a pretty penny.

Birch is sometimes substituted for maple, but a really good blank is impossible to duplicate by the use of any other wood. Inasmuch as the wood is so light in color it is not desirable to make all our stocks of them, but for an occasional stock or especially fine gun it will be very well suited.

Walnut: American walnut, sometimes called American black walnut, grows extensively in the United States and practically all of the stocks or blanks offered today are of this wood.

The color is generally of a yellow-brown shade with no especially fine figuring. The wood is one of the best for stock work being strong, light, and tough. It will stand the shocks of recoil and handling well and because it is easy to work with hand tools it has been the peer of stock woods for a great many years. The weight of the wood is about 35 pounds.

This wood is relatively coarse grained, but will take an excellent finish. It should be stained dark brown or reddish-brown if the natural color is not deep enough. A filler may be used of a dark brown color or, if desired, the finish may be applied to act as a filler. Walnut will take any of the conventional finishing materials well, though in using drying oils a filling coat of varnish or shellac is recommended.

Many stock suppliers offer different grades of walnut, depending upon the price you wish to pay. Low grade blanks may be had for as little as three or four dollars, but they will always be light in color, very open grained, and with little or no distinguishing figure. From there you can go on up to the 40 or 50 dollar mark in which case you will (and darned well should) get a very fine grade of wood with extremely fine figuring and close grain.

The use of the more expensive woods will not give you a better stock, though. True, the beauty of the rifle will be enhanced, but the durability of the wood and its handling will be no better than a standard five or six dollar blank.

English walnut: A very rare, fine wood for stocks, but it is seldom seen today. Even the English guns are stocked to a great extent with imported American black walnut.

Wood from mature trees has a rich brown tone with good grain markings. It is tough, fairly hard, and works well with hand tools. Weight is about 35 to 38 pounds.

This wood is finished and handled in the same way as American black walnut. It should be left in the original color unless not deep enough for the stocker's taste in which case it should be deepened with a brown or brownish-red stain. Filling may or may not be necessary, depending upon the specimen. If of a poor grade or exceptionally open pored a dark filler is necessary. Any conventional finish will work over this wood including the rubbed oil finishes. English walnut is highly recommended if available.

I understand that considerable quantities of domestic (American) grown English Walnut are available. Such wood is from English Walnut trees which are raised in this country, especially on the west coast. Not much of this wood has come to my attention, nor is it in general supply through ordinary stock wood channels. Possibly a letter to one or the other of the principal suppliers of such woods in this country would give you the desired information. See the Suppliers list at the end of the book for addresses.

Circassian walnut: This mythical king of the stock woods is usually a good, rich brown color with fine figuring. The better the grade of wood the finer will be the color and the figuring and the more you will pay. Even poorer grades of Circassian walnut are in great demand as they make into excellent stocks.

The properties of the wood are very similar to the other walnuts in that it will have the necessary strength, toughness, and workability to do the job.

Most blanks of this wood will have enough color and shading so that staining is not necessary in finishing. A particularly light grade of wood may need to be darkened slightly with the usual brown or reddish-brown, but generally this is not necessary. Filling is not recommended as a rule because in filling, no matter what the filling material may be, some of the delicate figuring is hidden or lost. Therefore any filling that may be required should always be done by means of the finish coat. While this takes a little longer the results fully warrant it.

Varnish, lacquer, shellac or wax will be suitable, but the wax may tend to pick up dirt a little easier than the other three, and will also hide the figuring to a certain extent, depending upon what wax is used and how it is applied.

Very few blanks or stocks of genuine Circassian walnut are seen nowadays. During the war shipments were greatly cut down or even entirely eliminated and that, together with the growing scarcity of good wood. explains why American walnut is about all that is offered to the market at the present time.

Italian walnut: This is another highly prized stock wood very similar to Circassian in color, figure, and other properties.

While one of the best woods for stocks in the better grades, the growing scarcity and deterioration of quality will greatly restrict its use. Very, very few blanks are seen and what is available is extremely high priced.

Handle in the same manner as Circassian for finishing.

French walnut: Another of the better woods, and though the color and figure of this wood are not as good as that of Circassian, the other properties are about the same.

This wood rates along with English walnut for figure though the color is usually lighter. Generally it should be darkened somewhat as the natural color of the specimens seen in this country is rather light. The usual brown or brownish-red stain is best to use, though that will be governed by the tints and shade of any individual blank.

Fill by means of the finishing coat as in the case of Circassian walnut. Blanks are rather easier to obtain than those of Circassian wood.

Spanish walnut: This wood resembles French walnut in all respects and it is very difficult to distinguish the one from the other.

The same remarks hold true for both woods as to color, figure, and finishing details.

Some of this wood is available, though the supply does not nearly meet the demand.

African walnut: A rather fine walnut with good figuring. The weight is less than for most of the other woods but the strength is about the same.

Inasmuch as this wood will have a light color to it, it is possible to deepen the color, but in most cases this is not recommended. The wood has a distinctive color which should be left as is. When a blank is obtained that stands out by itself it should be left that way. You can get all the American walnut you want, and if you have something a little different it is a form of sacrilege to try and make it look like the poorer wood.

We have always been accustomed to the use of the dark brown wood on our stocks, but that is no reason for destroying the beauty of a lighter wood. Therefore, I do not recommend staining this wood or filling it. Finish in varnish or lacquer and let the finish do the filling.

It is possible to obtain this wood by careful searching.

CUTTING OF STOCK BLANKS

There are two basic ways of cutting a log in order to produce the flat planks which are in turn cut into smaller pieces.

First there is what is called plain sawing. As shown in the drawing, this is with the grain lines running in a vertical direction. This sort of cutting will produce the most beautiful stocks with the finest figure.

When made up into a stock the warping tendencies will be in a side-to-side manner. Therefore the barrel will be pushed against one way or the other and thrown out of line. The lighter the barrel and the heavier the forend the greater will be this deflection. Such a stock will have great strength in the grip and the butt, however, and will not flake or chip away at the tang under the shocks of recoil.

The other general method is called quarter sawing. This blank will have the grain running in a side-to-side line and will not be as finely figured as a plain sawed blank from the same log.

The warping tendencies in this blank will be in a vertical plane. It will warp either up or down, and seldom in a lateral direction. Quarter sawing will produce a stock that is weaker in the grip and the toe of the butt than a plain sawed plank.

Great strength is not needed in the forearm because it is stiffened by the presence of the barrel. At the same time the grip should be as strong as possible because it must withstand the shocks of recoil. Also, the toe, or lowest point at the extreme rear end of the butt, must be resistant to chipping and splitting.

For all these requisites plain sawed planks will be best. However, the lateral warping tendencies that the plain sawed blank will give to the forearm are undesirable.

For a stock in which beauty alone is important a plain sawed blank will be best.

For a knock-about stock where strength of grip is important the plain sawed blank will also be required.

For strictly target work, though, I would place my money on the quarter sawed wood. This will eliminate any lateral warping and consequent changing of zero of the rifle from week to week. While there may be a slight upward pressure on the barrel in case of warpage this can be minimized by relieving the inside face of the barrel channel slightly. Also, moisture and waterproof finishes may be applied which will practically eliminate any warpage whatsoever.

Looking at a cross section of a quarter sawed stock at any point the grain should run as nearly horizontal as possible. This will always guarantee that the forearm will warp either up or down if it is going to warp at all. If this cross section shows a slight curve or bow you can figure that any warping will be done in the direction of the curve.

For example, if the grain shows a slight curve with the middle of the bow upwards then warping will be upwards, but if the bow swells down then the warping tendency will be in that direction.

The two places on a semi-inletted stock most suitable for checking this are at the butt and in the magazine well where the wood has been cut away to allow entry of the magazine and action.

Also, the line of the grain lengthwise on the stock should run either close to horizontal or slightly upwards. That is, if the line of the grain starts in the middle of the grip and drifts upwards so that it comes out the top of the blank somewhere in the middle or end of the forearm it will be a good, stable stock. If the grain starts in the same spot but makes a beeline toward either the top or the bottom of the stock along about the magazine well then that will be all right, too, but the grip will probably be less likely to split than in the first instance.

As long as the grain runs about straight or slightly upwards then you should have no trouble with that stock. But if it twists and turns every which way you may be in for serious trouble when a stretch of wet weather comes along and you have a long shot or a tight group to make.

EVALUATION OF BLANKS AND SEMI-INLETTED STOCKS

There are several organizations in the country today which offer stock blanks and semi-inletted stocks to the trade. They invariably advertise their stocks and blanks as the best that money can buy (for that price) and I am inclined to agree with them.

While there is no doubt that occasionally one will run into one of these stocks which is a lemon and should never have been allowed out of the factory, the great majority of the stocks which are offered are of satisfactory quality, are kiln dried to within usable limits of moisture content, and stand up well under the conditions that they are usually required to meet.

For the price (which is about eight bucks) you cannot expect to get the finest figure available, and there is no question that you do not. Unless you go into the 20 dollar bracket (for a blank) or above you should not figure on getting grain contrasts between light and dark and special wavy or curly crotch grain in the butt with straight grain in the forearm. There is a very large production of these stocks and blanks and the makers must use whatever wood they can lay their hands on to meet such a low cost figure.

The stocks, usually, are of American black walnut. For a consideration you can get mahogany and maple but this consideration runs pretty high.

For example, let us suppose you have a snappy Springfield you are just dying to put into civilian dress. You take your hard earned nine bucks (or whatever the price is) down to the post office and send off a special delivery order for the sooper-dooper semi-finished stock that was advertised in *The American Rifleman* last month.

For the next two weeks you rush home from work every day hoping the stock has come. If it hasn't you kick the dog, are grouchy to the wife, and the kids live in hell. Well, one day you come home and there is the stock!

Upon taking it out of the cardboard carton you think, "Doggone it, those crooks sent me the wrong stock. I ordered the grade with the special light and dark contrasts and the pink and gold grains (the ad said) and here I've got what looks like the same kind of wood that the box was made of that the ice-box came packed in."

Anyway, after looking it over you decide to keep it. The wood is not half bad at that. Once you get down to the actual grain structure itself through the dirt on the outside and the black gookum that they sealed the ends with you are a little more hopeful. You may not find the pink and gold grains, and the light and dark contrasts are not what you have envisioned, but there is still enough to make a good looking stock if you do your part.

The companies that are selling these things are usually reputable outfits and are seldom out to cheat you. Most of them will refund your money or give you a different stock if you are not satisfied. Besides, they must maintain a certain ethical level or *The American Rifleman* will not carry their ads when they start to get complaints from very bitter individuals.

On stocks which have been semi-inletted by these companies there is a considerable difference in workmanship. One outfit may give you a good, close cut in the roughing which will leave you with a very small amount of work to do for the final inletting. Other outfits may give you something which looks as though a disgruntled beaver with missing uppers has been chomping away at time and a half. The best bet is to do your buying through a local gunsmith who keeps a supply of these stocks on hand. You will then have a choice of stocks from which to pick, and it also gives the gunsmith a few extra pennies to buy bread for the kiddies. Believe you me, the average gunsmith can sure use your custom.

Incidentally, this average gunsmith is a combination metal worker, cabinet maker, philosopher, tool maker, wizard, and pretty good Joe who is in the racket for the love of it, not because he is getting rich. You can count the gunsmiths on the fingers of one hand and still have some fingers left over if you count only the ones who are stashing it away.

When picking out a blank or stock make sure that the grain runs fairly straight in the forearm. You can find them that have good curly or wavy grain there, but they are still in the showcase because the fellows that knew better discarded them for other plainer stocks. It is not that they did not have a sense of beauty, but only that the plainer stocks were the only ones present that had straight grain where it should be.

Wavy grain looks fine, but if it starts to warp it warps in about eight different directions at once. It may look nice to your relatives who have never shot a gun in their lives, but it may very readily knock your zero for a loop.

Straight grain will also warp, but it will warp in only one direction. Therefore it is easier to control in inletting the blank or stock. You can put a little "English" on the inletting if necessary inasmuch as you will be able to tell in what direction it will move if it is going to move at all.

Curly grain or figuring in the butt is okay. You do not have to worry about it doing any harm there and it looks real nice like.

STORAGE OF STOCK BLANKS

Let us say that you have been lucky and have been able to locate three or four extra fine blanks, but you have a use for only one or two at the moment. If you ever get this chance by all means buy the extra wood even if you cannot use it. You can always sell it to a friend who is in dire need of such finely figured wood and cannot locate one when he needs it. I do not recommend this sort of thing as a rule, but there are so few good blanks around that you can always find someone who will be very grateful for the chance to take them off your hands.

If you do much stock work yourself then you will have a use for the wood, that you know just as well as I.

Anyway, now you have two or three extra blanks on your hands and what are you going to do about them? You want to store them, but that can be a bit tricky at times. You do not want to stash them away in the basement because it is so doggoned damp down there that this dry wood will pick up an awful lot of water in a short time.

The best place to store them would be in the attic in the summer and in a closet of a warm, dry room in the winter. The little woman will raise the roof if she finds her best shoes parked on top of the "nasty ol' sticks" (the quotes belong to the little woman) but if you have no place else for them it will have to do. I am beginning to sound like a bachelor, but a box of candy or a new hat would do wonders in a case of this sort.

Anyway, be sure that they are kept away from excess moisture. The ends should be soaked in good spar varnish or sealed with paraffin wax to keep them from checking or cracking. After that wrap them in waxed paper and put them away. This wood is (or should be) fairly dry, and will absorb moisture from the air over a long period of time. The waxed paper will prevent moisture from entering the wood and undoing the job the steam kiln has done.

If you do have to resort to a damp basement or outhouse of some sort then seal the ends as mentioned above and wrap the stock in that same waxed paper. Make sure that you have several layers of heavy paper all around the wood, and seal the ends or flaps of the paper by pouring melted wax along them. When this hardens it will form a moisture proof seal which will be good for a couple years anyway.

Tag the packages with information as to the kind and quality of the wood and any special figuring that may be useful on a particular job. In that way you can inspect your packages without opening them and then necessitating repackaging if they are not what you thought they were.

LAMINATED GUNSTOCKS

The procuring of wood suitable for a fine stock may be difficult at times when all characteristics wanted must be of the best. This refers to strength, beauty of grain structure and natural color. If such a stock is needed and is unavailable then I would suggest you investigate the little recognized field of combination stocks.

I use the words little recognized because, while the laminating of wood to secure strength is common in industry, it seems to have been overlooked almost entirely in the gun field.

Some writers have furthered this work, but little popular interest has been raised. Inasmuch as the idea is basically sound and practically within reach of most of us there is no reason in the world why this sort of thing should not receive more public interest.

The basic idea is very simple. Thin sections of wood are securely fastened together to build up a large enough piece for a stock. These thin sections may be of different kinds of wood so that some of them will produce beauty and the rest contribute to strength and durability.

Woods available to the stocker include ireme, maple, cherry, mahogany, walnut, amaranth, ebony, holly, lacewood, rosewood, prima verde, satinwood and benin.

Any of the woods listed above will cost more than the average man could afford if pieces large enough for whole stocks were obtained. While even ½" and ¾" thick pieces will cost a great deal also, the combination of these pieces with walnut or maple will cut the cost considerably.

These woods may be secured in strips of any reasonable length and of widths running from 3" up. Inasmuch as the average stock should be at least 2½" from side to side, 7" from top to bottom, and about 33" in length (these figures are for the rough unshaped blank) three foot lengths of 7" × ¾" would do fine.

There are two ways in which a stock may be built up. One is to place the laminations in a vertical plane, and the other is to place them in a horizontal plane. That is, the strips will run either from the top to the bottom of the blanks or from side to side. Obviously the top to bottom system will require more individual strips, and the ones used must be thicker. The side to side system will require smaller (thinner) strips, and will be less in number.

The question of aesthetic appeal comes in here with the choice of the system to be followed. To me the stock made with the vertical laminations is much more pleasing to the eye than one which has the pieces laid one on top of the other. The ends of the differently colored woods will peek through the top and bottom of the butt and forearm and make a very attractive stock. Too much of the laminations appear in the other system and it looks like a piece of plywood (which it actually is) rather than anything else. But choose your own poison.

Strength of the finished stock is very important. Some woods tend to be brittle, lack splitting resistance, and are generally unsatisfactory for stocks, but when these woods (possibly chosen for great beauty) are sandwiched between other highly satisfactory woods they take on some of the properties (apparently) of these good woods and the overall effect is very good. Of course, proper gluing of the laminations is the big factor and if you muff that you are in for a disappointment.

Nearly any of the woods available to you will be satisfactory for use, primarily because they will be combined with other woods which will take the gaff and guff the discharge imposes upon them. When making a choice of woods you need be guided only by color and beauty requirements up to a certain point. That limit will be discussed under actual manufacture of the stock.

Inasmuch as the following woods are nearly all unobtainable in pieces large enough for complete stocks they were not listed in the woods section at the beginning of the chapter. They are listed here, though, as they will be obtainable in pieces or strips large enough for this use.

Amaranth: A purple colored, medium fine grained wood used primarily for cabinet work and inlays that comes from British Guiana. When exposed to the sun before using, the natural color turns a deep, fine purple. Use in small strips of not thicker than $\frac{1}{4}''$.

Avodire: A yellow-brown wood with medium pores from West Africa. Do not stain. Use in small strips not thicker than $\frac{1}{4}''$. This wood will be satisfactory but not as pleasing to the eye as holly or maple.

Benin: This is really African walnut and is a very good stock wood from West Africa. It is light brown in color and will make into excellent side facing pieces in the vertical system.

Bubinga: This African rosewood is a very finely striped or figured red-brown wood. Use for side pieces with maple or walnut centers.

Cherry: A domestic American hardwood which is covered in the section on stock woods. It is a reddish-brown wood which will do very well for side pieces as it is strong and works well.

Ebony: A jet black, or nearly so, wood from Africa which sometimes has stripes or streaks of yellow or orange through it. This wood may do for thin $\frac{1}{8}''$ or $\frac{1}{4}''$ center sections, but is not particularly recommended for laminated stocks.

Holly: A very light white-yellow American wood which is used primarily for inlays and cabinet work. This wood is very close grained and will be very pleasing for center or near-edge sections. It is too light in color to use for extensive side panels or pieces.

Kingwood: It is basically an orange or light red wood from South America with dark streaks shot through it. Good for center pieces.

Magnolia: An American wood which is light enough with dark figuring to give excellent contrasts with dark woods. This wood should be used primarily for center pieces.

Maple: This wood is discussed in the section on woods. It makes excellent side pieces or center sections as you desire.

Padouk: From Burma or the East Indies. This wood is a light yellow color with characteristic red and orange streaks. It is very beautiful and will do well for either center or side pieces.

Peroba: This is a very red or orange-red wood from Brazil. It will do best as a center piece.

Prima Verde: This is actually a white mahogany from Central America and may be used any place mahogany is used. It will be best as a side panel strip though the color is a little light for most tastes. It would be better to use straight mahogany here.

Rosewood: A beautiful orange wood interlaced with black or red stripes. This wood from Brazil is rather brittle and hard to work with. It can be used as a center piece, but is not especially well adapted for it; the cutting necessary in inletting would be too apt to chip it out at the edges.

Satinwood: This wood from the East Indies is definitely a golden yellow and should be very attractive used with amaranth or one of the darker woods. Use as a center piece.

Silky Oak: Sometimes called Lacewood, this wood from Australia reminds one of lace having a fine interwoven silky pattern. The color is usually reddish-orange. Will make a beautiful side panel, but may be somewhat delicate if any rough handling is encountered.

Teak: This wood from Burma and Siam is brownish with

dark brown or reddish-black stripes. It is heavy and tough, being used for marine work. Possible as side panels.

Tulip: This wood from Brazil is predominately orange with red streaks or stripes through it. It is a little too light in color for side panels and as center pieces its beauty would be hidden.

Vermilion: This African wood lives up to its name being a definite orange or red. The figure is good but not particularly distinct.

Zebra: An African wood of great beauty, it is seldom seen in pieces even large enough for laminating. The color is yellow or yellow-orange with dark or black streaks. Good for side panels.

Combinations of Woods for Beauty: Any of the woods listed above may be combined with each other or with any of the common stock woods mentioned at the first of the chapter. Obviously, the light woods will contrast with the dark ones or will blend with other light ones. The selection of different colors will determine the ultimate beauty of the stock depending upon the taste of the person looking at it.

Personally I think that some contrast should be effected, but this can be overdone easily. For example, suppose you made up a blank using a center piece of ebony (jet black) two pieces of bird's eye maple (one on each side) and side panels of amaranth (deep purple). This will certainly give high contrasts, but will it be pleasing to the average person, or even yourself? Maybe yes, or maybe no. This would be a little too much for me.

I would take something like the following for a contrasting stock: center piece of amaranth (purple), two adjoining sections of prima verde (light yellow), and side panels of cherry (red).

Possibly this would not suit you, and we are right back where we started. Anyway, all I am trying to get across is that different combinations will strike different people differently. The ideal thing would be to get small pieces of each of the woods available and place them together in a dummy stock (miniature) and see how they look. That is the only way to get a real picture of the color scheme.

Always bear in mind that the greatest show of grain or figure will be in the side panels and that the other will show only their edges. While this will produce color it will not give much chance for the figure of the inside sections to show. This, of course, depends upon the width of each of your inside sections. If you have ⅛" widths then no figure will show, but only color. However, if you use pieces 1" wide there will be a certain amount of the figure visible. This will determine the thickness of your choices. Finely figured sections can be used to a greater extent, therefore, than plain or dull woods.

Manufacture of a Laminated Blank: In considering manufacture of a laminated blank you must consider the use to which the stock will be put. If it is to be used for a show gun and will have little rough handling then almost any of the woods in almost any combinations may be used. If, however, you wish it to have not only beauty but also the ability to stand up under field use and repeated firing then it would be wise to use a known stock wood for the skeleton and fill in the rest with decorative pieces.

For example, in a stock which will see considerable field use I would make the side panels of walnut, maple or other common stock wood. Because the inletting will cut out all wood at that point except the thin walls (side panels) you want something which is going to take whatever punishment will be inflicted upon it. Actually most of the woods could be used without failure in the average gun because the barrel and action will do a great deal of supporting and stiffening from the magazine on out. But for absolute safety I would use walnut along the sides and the other decorative woods for the center.

Obviously, if you are going to use a horizontal layout (strips running from side to side instead of top to bottom) then all pieces will do a certain amount of work and it makes no difference where they are in the pattern.

The exception to that statement is that the piece which will eventually form the bottom of the forend (when the blank is shaped) should be a tough character because it will take a lot of grief from being rested on benches, fences, and miscellaneous surfaces in firing. This one should be walnut or maple.

First, all strips must be made as smooth and even as possible. This should be done by some local wood shop which has a jointer available and a workman who knows how to use it. You are not going to want to lose ¼" of each side of the strip just because some joker set the knives too high. You are going to have some ⅛" and ¼" strips to work with so a delicate operation may be necessary in these cases.

If you have a good belt or reciprocating sanding machine you may be able to do the job yourself. No matter how it is done the surface must be smooth and even.

Next, figure out the combinations of wood you want for the contrasting effects desired. If you are going to use two strips of one kind of wood in a stock (say, one strip on each side of the center section) it would be best to get the wood twice as long as you need and cut it in half. Then place the two strips so that the warping tendency of the one overcomes the warping tendency of the other strip. This is done by laying half of the strip in one direction and the other half in the other direction. For example of this see the drawing.

The laminations are then placed together and fastened with a good waterproof glue. These glues react chemically when mixed with water and when set up will give a good, permanent bond. Do not use fish or hide glue. They are not waterproof nor as strong as the chemical glues.

The strips are well coated with the glue and placed under as much pressure as you can bring to bear upon them. C clamps, weights, or parallel clamps will do if you have nothing else available. Place the clamps as close together as you can. Every four or five inches will be best if you have enough clamps. If not then place a stiff board or piece of metal on each side of the pile and secure the clamps to those. They will help to distribute the pressure.

Leave the pile under pressure for at least four days, though if you have a good, warm room (at least 75°) the setting will be hastened considerably. The longer you apply pressure the better will be the bond between the pieces of wood.

When you have removed the clamps you have a rough blank and may proceed as with a normal stock blank from that point. All shaping, inletting and finishing operations will be carried out normally.

Incidentally, in finishing a laminated stock you will not be able to do any staining. The wood sections were chosen for the natural beauty and color and there is certainly no point in changing that color when you have gone to so much trouble to secure it.

Whiskering will be advisable in all cases.

Filling will not be advisable because of the different colored woods you have used. Employ the finish as a filling agent when using varnish, lacquer or shellac. For more details about this process see the chapters on the different finishing materials.

Finishing should be done in a non-yellowing medium if possible. This will be a clear lacquer, bleached shellac, or guaranteed non-yellowing synthetic clear. If available methacrylate or chlorinated rubber will be satisfactory. The use of a marine spar varnish will be acceptable, but not recommended. These varnishes become yellow upon prolonged exposure to strong light and will hide the color of very light woods at times.

PRINCIPAL ADVANTAGES OF LAMINATED STOCKS

Besides the obvious beauty that such a stock will have, the resistance to warping will be greatly increased over a one piece stock.

The reason for this is that as shown in the drawing a long piece of wood is cut in half and folded back on itself, so to speak. This will make any warping tendency fight against itself and result in no warping whatsoever.

For example, suppose that one of the side panels tends to warp to the right, normally. The opposing side panel was reversed and now tends to warp to the left. This left versus right will add up to zero as the two pieces will have come from the same plank and will thus have the same force or power to warp, the one compared to the other.

If this principle is applied throughout the whole stock even the dampest weather will produce no appreciable change in zero.

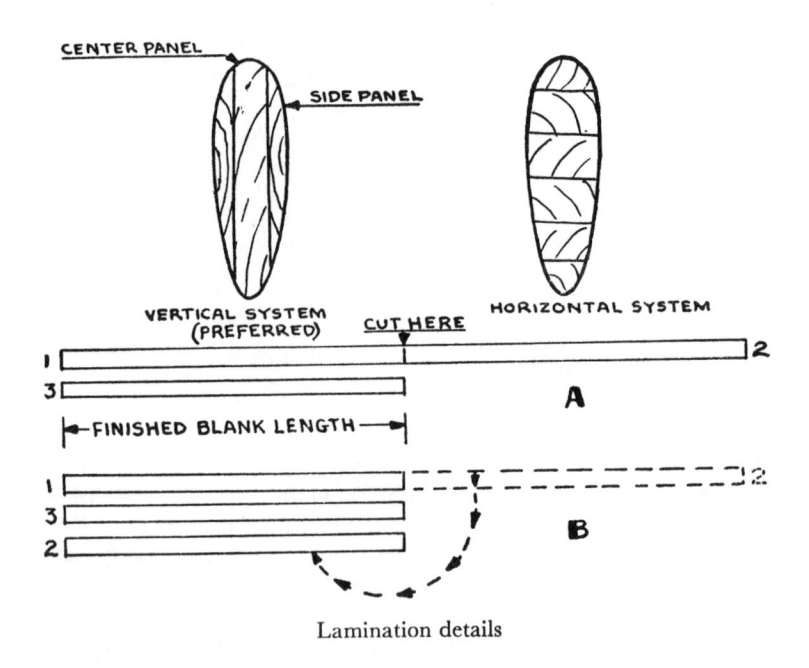

Lamination details

GENERAL CONSIDERATIONS

No matter what wood or woods are used to make a stock, no matter what particular system is followed in preparing and finishing the woods, and no matter what type of finish or degree of lustre is wanted certain basic facts must be recognized and taken account of to secure a satisfactory, pleasing appearance.

First of all, a secure surface must be given the wood. This will be the groundwork for satisfactory adhesion of the finish to the wood. Without this you have two strikes on you before you start. Obviously the finest and most durable finish in the world will not stay on a stock if it has been placed over a surface which will not allow that finish to stay put and, a more or less minor consideration, which will not allow the finish to take on its inherent beauty.

Secondly, the wood must be handled so that the color (which means shade or tint) is acceptable to the person viewing it. Even though you place on the stock a wonderfully lustrous film, if the color is repugnant or unpleasing the whole job will appear that way. The selection of color to be added or the treatment of the natural color (if no staining is contemplated) will determine this property. Your individual method of handling such a coloring treatment is more important than the color itself. Moderation is a great virtue and nowhere is it more necessary than when working with woods.

Thirdly, treatment of the stock to eliminate possible future trouble with moisture is as important as the actual placing of a suitable protective coating on the wood. This trouble may run all the way from trivial grain raising (whiskering) to actual warping or bending. The primary purpose of finishing a stock is to protect it from the elements (whether natural or man-made) and a finishing treatment which will not do this is worthless.

Last, but not least, the finish itself gives a "skin" to the stock and allows it to assume beauty otherwise lacking while at the same time it affords a measure (great or small) of protection against handling abrasion and destructive substances.

Each of these factors is taken up in detail as the book proceeds, but it is well to keep them in mind. They are the points upon which all wood finishing is based and the observance or neglect of them can and will result in either success or failure.

No substance can, of itself, do anything for wood. It is the individual who applies such substances that determines how successful the substance is in doing its job. Careful, intelligent reasoning and methodical application of that reasoning is the key to success at all times and under all circumstances. Blind following of rules or systems is the surest way to failure, though it may at times take a while for it to catch up with you.

All set rules and systems were formulated on a certain set of circumstances, and when those circumstances differ then the system may or may not still apply. This is where the reasoning comes in. When and if you encounter some change in conditions with which you are not habitually familiar weigh all the facts known to you, both of the wood and of the material you have to work with. The chances are that all facts necessary to get around the difficulty are plainly before you, but if you do not assemble these facts in proper order or if you ignore the need for such rearrangement of facts then you are stacking the deck against yourself, and it is ten to one that you will not be able to work the problem out to a satisfactory conclusion.

Speaking of facts, let us take known properties of finishing materials, for example. All materials discussed in this book have with that discussion as many details as possible concerning their behavior, manufacture, and possible uses. These details are based upon observations both in the laboratory and in the gunshop. They were examined, tested, and tried in practical applications. Thus you know what they will or will not do under the circumstances present in the shop and the laboratory.

Now, supposing you have the hypothetical case of a man who wants a spirit varnish base coating upon the stock, but over that he wants a French Polish. Such a case is seldom if ever encountered in life, but it could be. You have never done this sort of thing but if he wants it then you are game to tackle it. After all, never argue with a paying customer.

First, you assemble the facts known to you. You know that spirit varnishes are composed of this or that natural resin dissolved in alcohol (you know that because you've gone all the way through this little treatise by that time). You also know that French Polish is a special application of shellac, and that shellac is nothing but a spirit varnish, actually. Now put the facts together. Obviously if both materials are soluble in the same solvent they will have good adhesion, one to the other, and therefore the bond between the two will be good. Also, because the two are mutually soluble (or compatible) there will be no reaction to gum up the works.

With these known facts you can do the job with confidence that it will be satisfactory when completed.

Observe, you did not know at the start what the reaction of the two materials would be if placed one upon the other. But by taking known properties of the two and combining those properties (or assembling them to fit the conditions) you have been able to reach a conclusion which is vindicated upon practical trial.

It is doubtful that you will ever encounter a situation where the same sort of reasoning will not give you the answer you seek. Mind is more powerful than matter and the proper use of that mind will, in every case, give you mastery over the things with which you work.

Throughout the book you will find tentative time schedules given at the end of the larger chapters which may be followed loosely in calculating the time necessary to finish a stock. Obviously, such a time schedule will vary one way or the other depending upon the individual's working habits and the equipment available to him.

This will also depend a great deal upon the materials which he chooses to use and the number of applications necessary to give the finish needed. There is no way to cut down the time limit radically, but shortcuts developed by the stocker may pare an hour or so here and there from the tentative limits set.

CHAPTER TWO

Preliminary Finishing Operations

WITH the completion of inletting and shaping operations, remaining work on the gunstock will consist of preparing the surface of the wood to take some sort of a finishing material and of applying that material in such a manner that a smooth, protective film is built up.

In choosing and applying such a finishing material many factors must be taken into consideration. We must decide not only what sort of conditions the gun must meet, but also how we want to meet those conditions so that the stock will retain a satisfactory protective film. Different finishing materials will react differently to the same weather and handling conditions and how the film stands up will depend to a very great extent upon what care and foresight we have used in preparing the wood to take that film.

In order to have a satisfactory surface on which to apply our finish we must make sure that the wood is as smooth as we can possibly make it. Part of the beauty of wood lies in the fine, smooth, glossy finish which it invariably accepts. In order to have the finish smooth we must have the wood underneath smooth also. It will give us a good base upon which to lay the finish.

When you have completed shaping the stock to more or less exact dimensions there will always be tool marks left on the wood and these marks must be completely removed, as every little imperfection in the surface will be magnified and visible when the finish has been applied. Oil and coloring matter will lodge in the smallest of scratches and crevices and thereby render them visible. It is for this reason that the use of sandpaper is a must as a preliminary to finishing wood.

Before you attempt any actual finishing itself check once again for any necessary work which has been left undone. It is very simple to overlook some little item which, if it crops up later, will necessitate cutting and sanding to correct and which will tear up adjacent finished areas to a disgusting degree.

Has all fitting of the barrel and action into the wood been completed? Have you fitted the receiver sight (providing you intend to use one)? Has the butt plate, forend tip and grip cap been fitted and sanded to exact size? Is the cheekpiece deep enough for your (or your customer's) cheek?

When all these items have been checked and double checked you can go ahead confident that you will not need to come back later to do something you should have done now. You are ready to lay the groundwork for the finish.

SANDING

First of all, you must remove the tool marks mentioned above. The edges of plane and chisel cuts will not bother you to any great extent, but you must make sure that all tears from the teeth of coarse files or rasps are eliminated. These tools will wreak havoc even when all other principles have been observed. They will leave marks which may go down into the wood quite a distance if used incorrectly. I would stay away from the use of such rasps and their cousins when doing finish shaping, at least within the last $\frac{1}{8}''$ of finished shape. The reason for the avoidance of such tools is that under certain circumstances the teeth of the rasp will force the fibers of the wood to pack down upon themselves and compress the fibers underneath for quite a distance (relatively speaking). When the surface is then smoothed and finished, many times the crushed fibers will tend to stretch again and so will raise the surface in those spots.

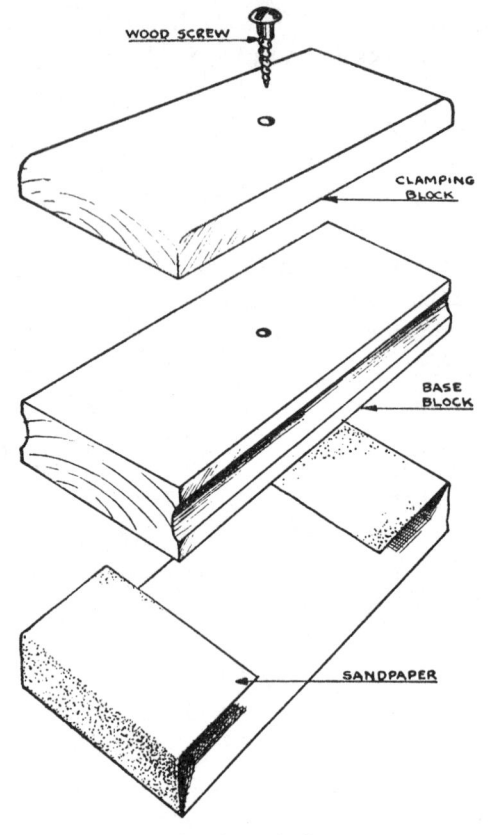

Sanding block

If you must remove wood quickly when so close to size I would definitely recommend the use of good, sharp chisels or other cutting tools. You can use straight chisels successfully on curves or rounded surfaces if they are properly ground and honed. They will do a much neater job than files or sandpaper and do it faster.

The removal of all tool marks should be done by the use of sandpaper. You should use the coarse grits to start with and then progressively finer grades until you are only burnishing the wood toward the last. Start with oo or o grit paper.

If you were careful in the shaping of the stock you will have very little work to do. Sharp tools will make the job much easier for you, not only in the actual shaping itself, but also in the elimination of sanding which would be otherwise necessary if the shaping was not skillfully done.

The sandpaper which you must use for all following sanding operations will come in many different grades. The designation by which the paper is graded will be a measure of the size of the abrasive grains on that paper. The following is a short outline of those grades which you will use:

Sandpaper

#3, 2, and 1½—very coarse. For paint removal, and such.
#1   —   coarse. For rough finishing.
#½   —   medium. For intermediate work.
#0, 2/0   —   fine. For finishing work.
#3/0 or finer —very fine. For finishing work.

Waterproof paper or cloth

20–40   very coarse.
50–100   coarse.
120–240   medium.
280–360   fine.
380–400   very fine.
600   polishing (similar to crocus cloth).

Sandpaper should be used only in conjunction with a sanding block. This sanding block may be of any size or shape which you desire, but generally the block should be about 3″ by 4″ by 1″ or 1½″. This size will fit the average hand well and will give a good grip. On the face of the block you should fasten (by means of waterproof glue) a ⅛″ or ¼″ sheet of felt or rubber. This facing will allow a certain amount of "give" to the sandpaper and will also prevent many a bad scratch or tear in the surface if the paper wears through under use. (I would not attach the felt or rubber with tacks because it is very easy for such tacks to work out under vibration and tear the wood.) Sandpaper is then fastened around the block or just wrapped around it and held by the hand.

Take whatever grit of paper you have decided to use and go after any marks or rough spots on the wood. Sand these spots out and in so doing remember that you must not allow any depressions or valleys to be formed. If you do have to go down deep into the wood in any one area then be sure you "feather" or blend this depression into the surrounding wood with long, gentle swells or sweeps. Any such depressions present at this time, even if so slight as to be virtually invisible, will show up badly under light when the smooth finish has been applied. These bad spots *must* be eliminated even if you have to sand vigorously over an area a foot long to cover up a spot which was originally a quarter of an inch long. Generally you need not worry about having to doctor up a spot in that manner if you were careful in the shaping and did not make a bad slip.

When you have gone over the whole stock with the very coarse paper change to a grade one or two grits finer than the first paper and repeat the operations. The reason for going progressively finer in grit is so that you will eliminate the scratches made by the abrasive on the paper preceding. As you go finer and finer each paper will leave scratches, but they will soon be so fine as to be invisible. You could have taken out the first scratches by the use of very fine paper without all the fuss or going from one grit to another, but these scratches will have been so deep that you will use a great deal of the fine paper before you get down to the bottom of them. It is quicker and more economical in the long run to have four or five grades of sandpaper and to use them all.

If at all possible you should obtain some waterproof sandpaper from your paint supplier. This paper is the type that is used by auto refinishing shops in wet-sanding automobile finishes preparatory to repainting the cars. It may be called under several different trade names, but I refer to the type called Wet-Or-Dry. This type of paper will not disintegrate when used with water as will the ordinary sandpaper. Such paper is classified by the number screen which the grains will pass in sifting. It may be as coarse as 180 which can be used for rough sanding, if desired, or it may go as fine as 600 which is so fine that it can be used for polishing the final finish. Such waterproof paper will be most useful when sanding between finish coats though it will be a trifle expensive to use for rough or coarse sanding.

You will never be able to achieve absolute smoothness on any wood. This is because the formation of grain in the wood will leave some small openings and these pores can never be eliminated no matter how far down into the wood we may go. There will always be some of them present. The coarser the wood the more open the pores will appear. In very close grained hardwoods such as some maple specimens the pores will be so fine as to be practically non-existent, but in the average walnut or walnut substitute which the stocker will probably have to work with the pores will be very much in evidence. These you can ignore at this stage of the game. We will take care of them later on.

When you have removed all visible sanding scratches from the surface go over the stock once again very lightly with a fine paper of about 360 or 380 grit. This will amount to a polishing operation and will remove most of the larger indistinguishable marks which will be there even though you may not be able to see them very well. At this point make a close, careful examination of the wood under strong light. Make sure that you have removed all of the scratches from the forend tip this time (if you have a forend tip on the stock). You are going to have to polish this tip sometime in the future and the more finishing you can do now the less you will have to do later when the finish is on. It will really break your heart to have to do any rough sanding on the tip then because every stroke you make will come dangerously close to the finished wood and if you happen to be careless and mark up the stock in any way you will have a tricky touch-up job on your hands. Finish that tip right along with the rest of the stock. From here on in it is an integral part of it and you should consider the one when you consider the other.

WHISKERING

We will assume that you have gone just as far as you can with sanding and the little walnut darling is as purty and smooth as a baby's cheek. But we have used up a whole evening getting to this point so let us just set it aside and wander upstairs for some shut-eye. Right after dinner the next evening we go down into the basement intending to get at the finishing, but when we pick up our pride and joy what do we find? We find that the moisture in the air of that damp basement has gone and raised up a million or so little grain ends, and the stock which last night was velvet smooth is now a mass of rough bumps which feels like your face after a week-end of not shaving.

The reason for this is that you have cut down into the wood by your planing and sanding and have exposed cut-off grain ends to atmospheric moisture. These grain ends then absorbed some of that moisture and have swelled. You will find that the swelling could be reduced by placing the stock in the sun for awhile or even by subjecting it to a slow drying process with artificial heat. But then the next time that the stock had a chance to absorb moisture there would be that swelling again. This swelling or grain raising is most noticeable (and most disastrous) when a well meaning individual has gone ahead and put some sort of protective coating on the stock immediately after sanding it. The grain would not have had a chance to absorb any moisture and it would appear to be all right. However, the first time moisture crept through the protective film that grain would just pop out through the film, probably ruining whatever finish he had placed there.

In order to remove all possibility of having the finished stock ruined by just such an accident we will have to raise all the grain we can *before* we finish the gun. The application of water and artificial heat will do the trick and raise it so completely that never again will this unpleasant habit bother us.

The photographs accompanying this chapter show the method I use to accomplish this "whiskering" or "dewhiskering," whichever you wish to call it. (The names are used interchangeably by different writers.) The stock is easier to manipulate quickly if placed in some sort of a holder. Usually an ordinary checkering frame will be highly satisfactory. Then a cloth or rag is soaked in water and squeezed as dry as the hand can get it. This will leave the rag in a fairly damp condition. This rag is then rubbed over the surface of the stock in a small area. *Immediately* the desired area has been moistened some sort of heat is used on the surface. I find that a Bunsen burner is most convenient for my use. This burner is played quickly over the moistened area in order to turn the moisture in the wood into steam which will then leave the surface. The action of the steam will force any available loose grain ends up where they will remain. Then go over the wood lightly with medium or fine steel wool. Many times you will find that sandpaper is recommended for cutting off the projecting ends, but in a great many cases these ends will be merely pushed down rather than cut off. The tangled fibers of the steel wool will loop themselves around these ends and pull them out rather than push them down and it is for this reason that I have found steel wool to be best.

Do not allow the flame to pause at any one spot. If it is allowed to come to rest you will burn the wood and the charred spots will then have to be sanded off. A light, quick pass will do the job. You can easily tell when the wood is dry by a lightening of the color. The moisture-laden wood will have turned dark, and as soon as that moisture is removed the wood will return to its natural color.

If you wish you can go over the whole stock with the water-flame operation before commencing to use the steel wool. This is a matter of choice and either way will be as efficient as the other. If you find that it is easier to steel wool an area before going on to another then by all means do so.

Depending upon the characteristics of the particular wood you have in the stock, you may have to repeat the whiskering procedure several times. I find that it usually takes at least two and sometimes four operations before no more grain is raised. As I say, it will depend upon your particular wood specimen.

When you have removed the protruding grain ends the stock will feel rather rough. Do not attempt to sand it smooth. If you do so you will recreate the exact conditions which made you whisker the stock in the first place. You will have to go down far enough to liberate more grain ends and you will be right back where you started. Even though you think the surface is rougher than you might like there is nothing you can do about it. The coarser the grain structure the rougher the wood will feel at this time.

Now that you have insured yourself against any grain raising no matter how much sweat or rain you may get on the stock in the future, you must be extremely careful in handling it. At this stage the wood is very, very delicate and even the mere laying of the stock on a rough bench may put an unsightly dent in it. After you have some sort of protective film on it, it will toughen up, but now guard it with your life. Here is where the checkering frame will come in handy! If you fasten the stock in that you will not have to lay it down nor handle it in any manner and that will be the best guarantee in the world that you will have an unblemished stock when everything is completed.

REMOVAL OF DENTS AND SCRATCHES

Let us suppose that you do become careless and toss the stock over on the bench for some reason. Let us also suppose that there happens to be a hammer laying on that same bench and the stock rested on it or fell against it in some manner. When you pick it up there will be a nice dent in the surface. Sure, I know you did not let it fall and were very careful about how you laid it down, but nevertheless there is the dent and what are you going to do about it?

About the easiest way to get out of this mess is to use the time honored method of steam raising. First, take a cloth and fold it over a couple of times to form a thin pad. Wet the pad well with water and squeeze it out so that it remains fairly damp. Place the pad over your dent and on top of the pad place a very hot metal object. An electric iron would do a fine job, or even a hot soldering iron would work. The heat from the metal will make the wet pad form steam. This steam will then be forced into the wood swelling the crushed fibers and returning them to normal, or nearly. You may have to repeat this process again in order to fully raise the dented area to the surrounding wood level.

This method will work only if the fibers are not severed. If they are cut there is nothing in the world that will do them any good. If the cut is deep at all possibly surgery with an inlay will be the only way out. Slight cuts or scratches could be successfully treated with the proper color gunsmiths' shellac.

At all times during the finishing operations the stock must be protected against accidents. The more or less delicate condition of the wood will allow such dents as I mentioned above and it is very easy to mark the surface badly by accidental scratching with the fingernails. If you do not have any kind of a gun cabinet in which you may store the stock while not working on it then I would suggest that you clear off a place on a shelf or under the bench, place about an eighth inch of newspapers there and allow nothing else to be stored in that spot. Even rough cuttings from the stock shaping operation can dent the wood if allowed to gather where the stock may be laid down upon them.

STAINING

When you have completed the grain raising now is the proper time to determine if and what staining is necessary. The use of the stains themselves will be taken up in a separate chapter, but now is the proper time to employ them, if they are to be used at all.

Just when stains or artificial coloring matter should be used is more a matter of personal choice than anything else. If you happen to have a blank which is composed of poor grade, swamp or low-ground walnut with a washed out color to it then I would advise you to go ahead and use a staining operation. Such wood will darken to a certain extent when the wood is impregnated with finishing material but the color will never change much. If you are more fortunate than many of us you may be able to obtain a piece of more or less highly figured, close grained wood which at the present time is seen mostly in what few imported blanks are available.

There is no hard and fast rule which determines when coloring should be added to the stock. I have found that, almost without exception, the stock finisher, both amateur and expert, will know just about how he wants the finished article to look. Perhaps he has seen a stock or a picture of one which is precisely what he would like to have on his gun. He can then determine just how far from that goal his present blank is and how far he must go in coloring to produce the approximate shade in that blank. This, too, is a matter of experiment. He can take a slice of the wood cut off from his blank and play around with it until he gets the color he likes. Then he can apply those same operations to the blank itself.

When working over a dummy stock in experimenting with color he must follow the same finishing steps that he expects to use in the finished stock. Many times certain types of finishing items will mask or change the color of the wood after being finished. This will not always be the case and in using clear lacquers will never happen. Some of the phenolic spar varnishes will change color when exposed to light, though, and will darken considerably. Also, some of the drying oils will darken the wood after application. Therefore, the safest bet is to complete the dummy stock finishing all the way through before definitely deciding upon this or that degree of color needed.

VARNISH SEALERS

After completing staining operations (if such are needed) you should now proceed to lay the groundwork for proper moisture resistance throughout the life of the stock. This is done primarily by use of one of the two following articles: the varnish sealer or the water repellent. I think it is safe to say that 90% of the professional stockers in the country have never heard of these substances. I have never seen an article in print which advocated the use of them and I have never talked to either an amateur or professional who even knew such materials existed. Undoubtedly there are *some* woodworking experts in this field who use them. In every field of endeavor there are some men who make a practice of keeping up to date and of using the best materials and systems that can be found. They are the conscientious ones who study any and all literature pertaining to their field and who, through this systematic study, advance to the position of recognized authorities and leaders in that field.

There is one gunstock supply company, which advertises consistently, that puts out a product which is actually a varnish sealer and they advocate its use as such. This is the only one that I know of that recognizes the importance of such wood finishing items.

Basically the varnish sealer and the water repellent work the same way. They consist of agents which have the properties of preventing the passage of moisture. The wood sealer is usually composed of very thin solutions of phenolic varnishes and drying oils (the drying oil is present only to a small extent). The solution is made thin in order to bring about maximum penetration of the sealer into the wood. The Forest Products Laboratory, of Madison, Wisconsin, reports that a very satisfactory water repellent may be made up of materials based upon paraffin wax and any of a number of different types of synthetic resins together with a small percentage of drying oils and a great deal of thinner. The thinner is to permit extreme penetration into the surface of the wood.

These two materials, the water repellent and the varnish sealer, must be used, either the one or the other, if maximum moisture resistance is to be given the gunstock.

As you read farther in this book you will note that I stress the property of moisture resistance in almost every other paragraph. Possibly *Ad Nauseum*. At the risk of boring you I would beg that you take this basic principle of mine to heart and never forget it! The introduction of moisture in any appreciable percentage will ruin most inletting jobs, when considered from the standpoint of accuracy of the rifle. The expert stocker as well as the more conscientious amateurs will know just how delicate is the foundation on which the continued accuracy of the gun depends. Tolerances are very small, and the best stocks are those in which the barrel channel is a snug fit to the barrel and the recoil shoulder and bore line are at precise right angles. When the stock is first inletted all points are close fits to each other. Many of you know just how the presence of even a thin shaving of wood accidentally introduced into the barrel channel will ruin the accuracy of the gun. It will shoot all over the place in most cases and, if it does not do that, it will have an entirely different point of impact than it had when sighted in with the shaving absent. This result is because the relatively springy barrel is forced out of line when the guard screws are tightened and this unnatural pressure forcing the barrel to one side or the other raises the devil with the normal vibrations the barrel sets up. The damped or changed vibrations will cause the barrel to be pointed at a different spot when the bullet leaves the muzzle than it would if that unnatural pressure were not present.

The same thing can happen if too much moisture is introduced in the wood after the inletting is completed. The presence of excess moisture will cause a certain amount of warping and this warping will play the same part that a shaving of wood would. In a great many cases the forend is warped from side to side, depending upon how the grain of the wood runs. If this happens, the forend pushing against one side or the other of the barrel will push the barrel out of line and again you have destroyed systematic accuracy. Even if the gun continues to be accurate it will shoot to a different point of aim when the amount of moisture in the forend varies much. This could very well happen if you subjected the rifle to a warm, sunny atmosphere after being in a cold, damp climate. The heat of the sun and air would force some of the moisture to leave the wood and the forend then tends to settle back to normal. This will not be particularly noticeable when the gun is used only a few times a year on the same range and in the same general climate, but if the rifle is used a great deal, as in the case of many of our small bore match rifles, then even the difference between spring and summer will throw your sight readings off a great deal.

Obviously the sealer and repellent are physical roadblocks to moisture. They prevent its entry by simply being in the way when it tries to plow on through. There is no chemical reaction or otherwise mysterious action generated.

Inasmuch as the great majority of water repellents contain non-drying waxes or greases I have never favored their use on stocks. While they may be a bit more efficient in stopping the passage of moisture the fact that these non-drying materials are present will interfere with adhesion of most finishing materials. Because we must have maximum adhesion I have always sided toward the varnish type sealers.

SEALER FORMULA

The home manufacture of sealer type materials is very simple. Procure the best grade of marine spar varnish that you can buy. If you have to pay a few cents more for a can of good stuff do so. The little that it will cost will be more than offset by the feeling of security that you will enjoy when the stock is finished and the gun meets foul weather.

Take a half pint bottle or can and fill it about a quarter full of the spar varnish. Then add enough VM & P Naphtha or white gasoline to make the mixture nearly as thin as water.

The amount of thinner that you will have to add will depend upon the viscosity or body of the unthinned varnish. The viscosity may vary from one make to another.

When you have stirred the mixture well you should have a clear liquid which contains no sediment. If some sediment is present it may mean that that type of varnish is not completely soluble in the naphtha or gasoline. If this is the case use whatever specific thinner is recommended by the manufacturer for thinning that varnish and proceed in precisely the same manner. The reason that gasoline or VM & P Naphtha is recommended is that these thinners will evaporate quickly. If you must make a choice of thinners other than the gasoline or naphtha take a little of each of the thinners you may use in the palm of your hand. The one that makes the hand coldest or which evaporates the fastest is the correct one to use.

SEALING THE GUNSTOCK

Take your thinned down solution and a clean brush or dust free rag. Dip the brush or rag into the thinned varnish and bring it out dripping wet. Transfer as much as possible of the dripping liquid onto the surface of the wood and spread it around. Cover the whole stock if you can and keep all surfaces swimming in the sealer. You must have a ready supply of sealer on the surface at all times for efficient penetration. Treat the end grain of the butt, the pistol grip and the cheekpiece at the same time. These areas where end grain is apparent will soak up the thin sealer as fast as you can apply it. After a minute or so the absorption will slow down and eventually this end grain will accept no more.

One of the most important places that you may forget is the inletting as well as the barrel channel. These places should be treated until they will not accept another drop of sealer. The walls about the inletting and barrel channel are very thin and will be easy marks for warpage. They must be protected at all costs because here is where the damage will take place if at all. If you do not plan on having a forend tip (which would have been fastened on by this time) be sure that this too is well soaked with sealer.

You will have to do a bit of fast work while applying the sealer. The relatively dry wood will drink it up very fast and the important thing is to keep all surfaces as wet and soaking as possible until all absorption has ceased. This point will be noted by the refusal of the wood to drink in any more of the sealer and any that you add will readily drip off onto the floor. The ideal thing in this phase of finishing would be to have some sort of a tank in which the stock could be submerged for ten minutes or so. However, this would be rather impractical for the average amateur. For the man who does even a few stocks a month or for a shop it would be an easy and inexpensive matter to have a tin shop bend up a piece of sheet metal roofing into a tank about 10" wide by 6" deep by about 40" long. This would take care of quite a few stocks at a time, though if you plan on doing any work on Mannlicher or full length stocks you had better figure on a 4½' tank.

The average sealer on the average wood may penetrate as much as an inch though it is usually quite a bit less than this. One coat will be sufficient as the synthetic resins in the sealer will harden up quite rapidly once they are in the wood and after that there is no chance for any additional penetration.

When you have soaked the wood for as long as you think it will take for the sealer to stop sinking in you should take a rag and wipe the stock as dry as you can, especially in the barrel channel and the inletting. You will have made these so they are a close fit to the metal and you do not want a thin skin of this varnish hardening in those spots to interfere with the proper seating of the action and barrel when assembled. The exterior must be also well cleaned of varnish. If it hardens on the wood you will have to sand it off before you can proceed with the finishing and it is a lot easier to take off when it is wet than after it is dry.

Now that you have sealed the wood against any attacks of moisture you can sit back a bit and relax. You probably know how even the moisture in the ordinary basement at times will warp or swell a stock between the time it was inletted and the time you get some protective coatings on it. Even the late Alvin Linden, one of the best in the business, warned about this in his booklet on stock inletting and he was a lot faster from start to finish than most of us ever will be.

FILLERS

Let us take a quick look at what we have now. We have our shaped stock whiskered and sealed. The whiskering, along with the natural open pores of the specimen of wood, certainly did not leave us with that smooth masterpiece we saw in our dreams! Not by a jugful. We now have a stock which is covered with very large pinholes and which, if we applied a coat of some sort of protective material, would allow that same protective agency to sink into the pinholes and leave us with a badly pitted surface. The thing we have to figure on now is to fill those holes up with something which will not let the finish sink into the pores.

For this we turn to what is known as a filler. A filler is usually a concoction which may be made up from anything as long as it fills the pore openings. Wood fillers are not brothers under the skin by a long shot. You can buy, without any searching whatever, plenty of fillers at fancy prices with fancy names and high-faluting recommendations at a buck a throw and many of them will prove to be "soft" and of no value or worse. They may actually louse up the works after you have spent 20 or 30 hours of loving care polishing, rubbing and sweating.

These "soft" fillers are usually thrown together by some Joe who needs a quick buck and figures, "What the Heck, I may as well take him as the next guy." So he gets himself a couple of gallons of boiled linseed oil, adds a little Japan drier for effect, and then tosses in all the cornstarch, whiting, or dust he can make the oil hold. Maybe he will put in some solvent or other to make the mixture brushable and go farther, and sells the whole thing for 1000% profit.

When you put this mess on your pet stock the fun begins. (It may be fun for the fellow watching, but it sure will not be any fun for you.) We will figure that you have gone through all the necessary steps such as raising the grain and sealing the wood, and then you make with the filler. You follow instructions to the letter by brushing it on and then scraping off the excess with a piece of burlap. It looks okay when it is

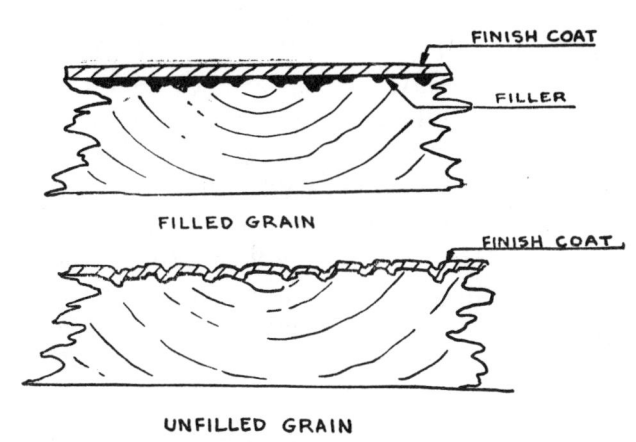

Finish coats over filled vs. unfilled wood

dried on the surface and maybe you even get so far as to apply a nice oil finish. But what will happen when you actually go to use the gun? Well, it is about like this. You notice after using the gun a few times that wherever you have touched it much (grip, cheekpiece) the finish is looking sort of seedy— as though it did not know whether or not it wanted to stay put. If you have used a good resin finish it will not be so noticeable for awhile, but if you have used the rubbed oil treatment the filler may actually be crumbling out of the pores. This will go on until the pores are completely innocent of any filling and the stock looks as though it has had a nodding acquaintance with nothing but sandpaper. The reason for all the trouble is that you have actually put nothing in the pores but good old putty, the kind that you put on the windows to keep the glass from falling out.

Let us suppose you were a little luckier in buying a filler. Let us suppose you got one made from a good grade resin solution (or varnish) and with a goodly content of silica. This will usually be carried in stock by the boys who want more out of life than wrenching your money out of your clammy little palm.

This product will be what I call a "hard" filler. I call it that simply because it will set up hard (much harder than the linseed oil-whiting mixture ever would) and will never crumble out of the grain. It will put its head down and hang on for all it is worth if you have done your part about giving it a good base to hold on to. These hard fillers are usually composed of a phenolic resin base with very fine ground silica (or silex) as the inert matter. The silica is so fine that it will not scratch the surface of the wood in applying the filler, and the chemical reaction of the varnish or resin solution which composes the liquid content will be so complete and efficient that it will not soften up under heat or abrasion.

There are a great many fillers on the market which will be of the hard type. They are not so listed, but most of the reputable gun supply outfits that carry restocking and refinishing supplies will have that kind. Do not buy what the old paint men call paste type fillers. These fillers are nearly always made up from the linseed oil and whiting base and, while satisfactory for some uses, will not be worth the powder to blow them up for our purpose.

If you cannot find anything on the market that you think will meet your purpose you can work on something of your own which will usually fill the bill and which will generally be as good as anything you can buy. Of course, you will not have the means to control your product as closely as the factory has but with a little fooling around with this or that varnish base to determine which seems to work best for you you can make up a good, durable filler.

Filler Formula #1

High grade spar varnish . . . . 10 parts by weight
Silica, finest grade 40   "   "   "
Mineral spirits . . . . as desired

Put the varnish in a clean, empty Crisco or Spry can. Add a little of the silica powder to the varnish and whip in well with an old spoon. Keep on adding a little of the powder at a time, stirring constantly, until all of the powder has been well mixed with the varnish. If you add too much silica at any one time you will find that it will tend to lump or stick together making dry spots in the mixture.

The reason for using the Crisco or Spry can is that it is deep with a large opening that you can put your whole hand into. This room to work is very necessary in order to do efficient stirring and pressing against the sides of the can. As the powder is added the mass will become stiffer and more heavily bodied until finally it looks more like putty than anything.

Keep at it. When you have all of the silica in the can then add a bit of mineral spirits or even turpentine. This will immediately soften the mixture and as you add more it will become more and more thin. Use only as much thinner in this manner as will give you an even paste. Then stop. Stir well once more and store the filler in a wide mouth jar (such as a Mason jar) with a screw top. Occasionally take the jar off the shelf and stir with a spoon or knife blade to keep the silica from settling too solidly to the bottom of the jar.

When you go to use the filler mixture, take whatever coloring matter you have on hand, whether it be plain burnt umber or some sort of an oil paint tinting base color, and stir well into the filler. You will be able to determine just about what color you will need from the color of the wood you will fill. Make the filler a bit darker in color than the wood so it will accentuate the grain structure.

When you have the filler to the color you desire then add more thinner until it resembles a liquid rather than a paste.

You must thin it so as to allow easy working into the grain.

Filler Formula #2

High grade spar varnish.......... 10 parts by weight
Silica, finest grade.............. 40 "   "   "
Boiled linseed oil................ 5 "   "   "
Japan drier (combination type)... ½ "   "   "

This formula is similar to formula #1 except that it contains boiled linseed oil to give a little more flexibility to the film and a little Japan drier to aid the drying of the linseed oil. You can do just as well by eliminating the use of the Japan drier. The boiled linseed oil will have some drier in it which will be sufficient.

The operations of preparing this filler are precisely the same as in #1. Be sure that the silica powder is added slowly with constant and vigorous stirring. This is the most important point to watch and is the keystone to a successful mixture.

Tint this filler before use with burnt umber and then thin to working consistency with mineral spirits or turpentine.

Filler Formula #3

High grade spar varnish.......... 10 parts by weight
Silica or asbestine, finest grade.... 40 "   "   "
Burnt umber................... 3 "   "   "
Mineral spirits................ as desired

This formula is handled the same as #1 and #2. The amount of burnt umber indicated may or may not be sufficient to color the filler just as you will need it. One or two trial runs on a scrap piece of walnut of the same texture and color as your stock will tell you whether or not you will need to add or subtract some of the pigment.

Thin this mixture with thinner before use the same as in the other formulae.

In all of the above formulae I have attempted to keep the mixtures as heavy bodied as possible right up to the moment of use. If you have ever purchased ready-made fillers of the liquid type and had them stand around on the shelf for a couple months before using you will see what I mean. The mixture is generally very thin in the manufactured product so that the user will not have to fool around with thinning it— just slap it on. But the solid matter in the mixture will not be dissolved, it will be only suspended in the liquid content. Therefore, over a period of time that suspended solid matter will gradually settle to the bottom of the container and if any great length of time is allowed before it is again stirred it will be so firm and hard that you will not be able to poke a knife blade into it to loosen it up. To eliminate this trouble I always recommend a low liquid content until the very moment of use.

When using these fillers, thin or reduce only what you are going to need or, at best, a little extra to allow you plenty of material to work with and no skimping. This practice will prevent you from throwing whatever is left over back into the container to avoid waste. If you do this enough times you will have in effect reduced the whole can and then it will settle out.

You should take whatever filler you intend to use, whether it be home-made or store-boughten and examine it carefully. Check the body by stirring with a blade or spoon and then lift the spoon out of the mixture and let some drip off. If it has been procured ready-made it should be a very thin liquid which flows almost like water. Poke around in the bottom of the can or bottle. If it feels mushy or sponge-like you can bet your boots it has settled, and the longer it has had to settle the harder that cake will be. If you do encounter this soft cake then pour out most of the liquid in the can (do not throw it away because you will be wanting it again) and loosen the cake up as much as possible by poking and twisting in it with a spoon. Usually this will loosen it enough so that you can pour back a little of the liquid and by vigorous stirring whip it back into proper condition. Do not be too vigorous with this stirring, though. It is awful easy to slop a couple of drops of that dark, brown liquid onto the cuff of that clean white shirt you are wearing. (It always happens that way. If you are dressed up to go out and are killing a few minutes while the wife is getting ready by fooling around in the basement then you will always spill something. If you are dressed for work in your overalls, though, you could not make that liquid splash if you threw the cat in it.)

At times you will find that such hard settling has taken place that there is not a chance in the world of loosening it up by stirring. Brother, in that case you have had it. You may just as well toss the stuff out and buy yourself a new can, this time making sure that you either shake the can every week or so or turn it over so that it is resting on what was the top. This constant turning end for end will usually keep the solid matter in a fair state of suspension. If you let it get settled too hard in the bottom, though, no matter how often you reverse it it will not go back into suspension.

Along with these varnish type fillers it is possible to obtain a type of lacquer-based filler which is known as a Lacquer Sanding Sealer. This material is fully covered in Chapter 6 on Lacquers, both composition and use.

METHODS OF APPLICATION OF FILLERS

The methods used to apply fillers are generally the same no matter what source of information you get them from. They are based upon the principle of getting as much of the solid matter as possible down into the pores of the wood and then removing whatever excess may remain on the surface.

These fillers should be of such consistency that they may be brushed on the wood freely. This, of course, means that they are thinned with some sort of solvent or thinner. This is the role that the mineral spirits or turpentine mentioned in the formulae will play. It will allow easy brushing.

When the material is thinned to the degree that you can easily handle it take a brush and load the bristles well. In this case it does not matter if you drip some of it onto the wood in passing over it. All that you are interested in is getting a very heavy coat of the stuff on the wood. Work the brush back and forth over the surface so as to work the liquid into the pores as much as possible. The more working in that you do the less chance there will be for some air bubbles to remain under the filler and show up afterwards as tiny holes or unfilled spots.

Take a small area at a time and make sure that that area is well worked over. Then go on to another area. Do not worry about any brush marks or laps which may be apparent at this time. They will all be removed in a very short while. Go over the whole stock in this manner until it is completed. At this point the stock will appear to have a brown overcoat. Now let enough time elapse so that the filler will partially dry or set up. This condition will be apparent when the coating takes on a dull or rather flat appearance. Then you can go after it with a piece of coarse rag. Burlap will work all right or any such coarse material. The reason for using this material is that it will tend to remove all filler material that remains on the surface. If you happen to use a fine piece of cloth it will merely polish the filler rather than taking hold of it with the coarse fibers and removing it.

With the coarse burlap (a piece of knitted wool sweater will work as well) rub *across* the grain. This will not only keep from pulling the filler out of the pores but it will also tend to help pack whatever remains down into the pores. Do not rub with the grain. If you do so you will remove nearly all of the solid matter that you originally packed in there.

Rub lightly at first. It is a more or less scraping motion rather than anything else. When you have removed most of what remains on the surface then you can work a little harder. If you have given the filler only enough time to dry slightly then it will be a fairly easy job. But if you have allowed enough time to elapse so that the drying has proceeded to a considerable extent then it will be rather difficult to remove. Judging this degree of drying is where a dummy piece of wood will come in handy. If you have familiarized yourself with the properties of your particular material then you will be able to figure when the right time has arrived to remove the excess.

If you find some spots or areas that look as though they might not be properly filled then you had better refrain from going at the rubbing of those spots or areas much. You can leave them until the filling coat has dried well for 24 hours and then see what the situation is.

When you have completed one filling and rubbing off process let the stock set for a day (or at least 18 hours). This will give time for the filler to harden completely and for all of the solvent or thinner to have escaped from the coating. Then take a look at it. You will probably find that the stock does not look nearly as well filled as it did yesterday. This is because of the shrinkage that has taken place when the thinners evaporated. Now is the time to take a bit of sandpaper and remove most of whatever remains on the surface. Do not bother taking it all off as you will have to apply another coat. If you do not like the idea of using sandpaper then you can take a piece of *smoothly* cut glass or a cabinet scraper and lightly scrape off the excess. You must be careful that you do not scrape down so far that you dig into the wood. If you did this the chances are that you would have to again touch up that spot with stain.

Examine the stock carefully. If the filling has been spotty or has not been complete (and it seldom will be) then you can go at it again with another coat of the filler. Pay special attention to the spots that looked the worst and make sure that those spots are well taken care of this time. Go over the whole stock in the same manner as you did with the first coat, brushing on the filler and working it well into the wood. When it has again taken on a dull or flat appearance go to it again with another clean piece of the coarse rag or sweater. This time try and get all of the excess off that you can. If you do not get it now you will have to later when it dries and that will entail using the sandpaper or the scraper. Of course, if you see that your coarse rag has removed a great deal of it from the pores in the wiping process, then it would be wiser to let most of it remain on the surface until it dries. In this hardened condition there will be no danger that you will pull any of it out of the pores. Take your choice of methods. You will work a little harder and a little more in using the scraper, but you will get more complete filling results. After all, that is what you are after here.

The amount of filling that you do now will depend to a great extent upon your choice of final finishing materials. If you intend to use an oil finish then you must see to it that filling is as complete as it is possible to achieve. The coats of drying oils that you will use will build up very slowly and it will take a great many coats to fill in and level off irregularities of the surface. As far as the average man is concerned there is no such thing as a filling process when using oil alone. It would take at least 15 to 20 coats as normally applied to do the slightest bit of building up and the average man (as well as the average professional) cannot possibly get that many coats of oil on a stock short of about a year's time. This is especially true when using raw linseed oil as so many of our people seem to do. The drying time of one thin coat will be at least a week and a half, with two weeks as a preferable minimum. Usually, however, the stock finisher will allow about three days between coats and when he has applied about five coats the stock will be so darned sticky, especially in hot weather, that he resigns himself to the fact that he has reached a maximum point in application and lets it go at that. When this happens he will have applied at the most about a quarter of a thousandth thick film and that will not do any filling at all as you can guess.

Let us suppose that you intend to use a good varnish or lacquer or even shellac finishing film. These items will do a lot of building up on the surface and you can be rather negligent in the original filling process and still make out all right. After about two coats of one or the other of these materials you will find that you have filled in whatever imperfections have remained after the filling. One or two coats will give you a film of about 1 ½ thousandths thick and that will do a lot of filling. That, of course, depends mostly upon how heavy you have applied the liquid coat and how heavy bodied that coat was.

PREPARING THE FILLED SURFACE

When you have filled the pores sufficiently you should see to it that all of the filler is removed except that which is actually doing the filling. I refer to any which may have formed a thin coat or film on adjacent surfaces. This excess filler coat will appear as a brown film due to the pigment which was used to color it. Inasmuch as it is so visible it will be no trick to use a little fine sandpaper on it until it is completely gone. There will be no deleterious effects if some is left on but it will create unsightly blotches.

When removing or sanding off this last trace of filler use only very fine sandpaper to avoid scratching the wood. It would be well to sand only in the direction of the grain for the same reason that we always do it that way—to avoid visible scratches. Obviously if the paper is coarse enough to remove the excess filler it will have some abrasive properties and these properties will also manifest themselves on the wood itself. If you travel only in the grain direction whatever scratches are inflicted will be invisible and will blend in with the grain structure. But if you sand across the grain whatever scratches are made will blend with nothing at all and will be emphasized greatly. Certain types of finishing materials will tend to cover or hide these faults, but will never do so completely. It will be much better to exercise a little care in sanding than to worry later about touching up and hiding these blemishes.

This is especially true when using an oil finish. Inasmuch as most formulae call for the inclusion of burnt umber or other kinds of coloring matter, this coloring matter will collect in the scratches during the process of hand rubbing and will magnify them. For final sanding of the stock after the filling process has been completed I would recommend that nothing coarser than about a 380 grit paper be used.

After you have done the final sanding and smoothing examine the stock under a strong light and with a magnifying glass. This magnifying glass will show you many defects which the normal, unaided eyes could not distinguish. You are looking for unfilled pores and pinholes in the filling. These will indicate that the filling has not been done properly and that there are small airholes in the wood. Unless there are many of them or what few there are are very large you can forget about them. If you figure on using a lacquer, varnish or shellac finish coat they will be well disguised and filled by those finishing agents. However, if you are going to employ a rubbed oil finish you will have to decide right now whether or not it is worth while touching up those faulty spots with additional filler. As I said before, if they are very few and very tiny you can get away with it, though with all the work you have put on the stock you should be willing to spend a few more minutes making a really good job of it. If the spots are large or numerous you better figure on a touchup job because the oil will not fill them nor will it cover them.

The touchup job will consist of going over those immediate areas with an additional spotting of filler in the same manner that the original filling was done. When the filler turns flat then remove the excess and when it is completely dry sand off those spots and check them again. This time there should be no unfilled points visible, even under the magnifying glass.

FINISHING FAULTS

Filler Turning White or Gray: At times, especially when using home made fillers, you may find that when the filler has hardened it will appear light colored. This will give the stock a dirty, muddy appearance.

This is because you have not used enough varnish vehicle in making up the mix. There will not be enough liquid resin present to bind the solid matter properly and as a result it becomes powdery.

The remedy is to experiment with a small amount of the mix while making it up. If it dries in this fashion then add a bit more varnish until such a liquid content is reached that will bind the silica properly.

The light color of the hardened filler could also be due to having insufficient coloring matter or pigment in the mixture. The remedy, of course, will be to increase the amount of pigment until the color desired is obtained.

Filler Crumbling Away: This fault will probably appear only if an oil finish is used. It may be potentially present when other types of materials are used, but they will mask this effect.

The cause may be insufficient varnish binder present to hold the solid matter together. If this is the case the remedy lies in increasing the varnish content of the filler.

If you are sure that you have sufficient varnish in the mix to bind the particles properly the crumbling will be due to poor adhesion which in turn will be brought about by having oil or grease on the wood before the filling took place. The remedy is to be sure, always, that you have not allowed greasy hands to handle the wood.

CHECKERING AND CARVING

It is very probable that the stocker will have a certain amount of checkering and carving in mind when making or refinishing a stock. The question arises "When is the best time to do this work, before or after the stock is finished?"

The answer to this question is optional, but a preference may be easily made. I would do this work before the stock is finished if at all possible. Of course, on a stock which comes into the shop for a simple checkering job the only possible thing to do is to work on the surface which is already finished, whatever the finish is.

But if a new stock or a stock on which the finish is to be removed preparatory to refinishing is the subject then you have this choice.

I understand that it is the general practise of professionals to do such decorative work after the finishing work has been completed. Here is where your choice comes in. You could work that way and have a fine job result. All that would be necessary would be to give the checkered or carved area a simple bath of varnish sealer to protect against moisture from the hands and then possibly a thin bath of tung or boiled linseed oil.

Personally I have found that just as good results are obtained by whiskering, staining and sealing the stock first and then checkering. After that the finish coat is applied as described below. You pays your money and takes your choice.

When the basic preparation of the wood is completed then do the decorative work. This will be done in the usual manner and no special precautions have to be taken.

Now you are ready for the filling and the finishing. If the finish is to do the filling, all the better. This is not only the best method to secure adhesion, but it is relatively more waterproof.

Using a piece of adhesive tape, Scotch transparent tape, or painters masking tape carefully go around the edges of the decorated area and completely cover them. The tape is to allow you to do a certain amount of dripping or splashing that is usually present, even with a careful worker, without the danger of filling up the delicate grooves and lines which you have spent so much time putting into the wood.

When the filling and/or finishing has been completed and is dry and hard soak the tape with alcohol or mineral spirits. This will allow the adhesive material holding the tape to the wood to be dissolved and the tape may then be pulled away from the wood easily without danger of ripping off any delicate points or edges. Clean the area with more of the solvent on a rag until no trace of the adhesive gum is apparent in the grooves.

Incidentally, if you have used a shellac finish do not use the alcohol. Obviously this would spot and soften whatever of the finish it came in contact with. In this case, or when using any spirit varnish, use some turpentine or mineral spirits. These will not dissolve the film and will leave it in good condition.

Now you will find that the checkering or carving has the bare wood staring out at you. Inasmuch as you did the staining before decorating the surface this area will now be considerably lighter in color than the surrounding wood. You should touch up the area now with thin solutions of the stain you used on the rest of the stock until the color is about the same. Do not get it too dark. If you do some of the detail and fine line work will be lost.

The sealing of the stock was done before, and the soaking of the sealer into the wood will have rendered the carved area more or less resistant to the attack of the stain, therefore you will not have a great deal of uncontrollable absorption into the wood and the end grain which will make up a great majority of the carved surface.

When staining is completed the decorated areas are ready for some sort of a finish. There are several ways in which this problem can be solved, and one way in which it must not be done.

Do not finish the surface in a varnish or lacquer and allow an appreciable film to build up. If this is done the checkering or carving will glint and glisten in the light and it will look like the devil. The reason for this is that you will not be able to get down into the fine lines and crevices placed there and remove the gloss from any hardened film which is built up.

In order to keep away from this shiny appearance you must either use a varnish with a high drying oil content, or a drying oil alone. If you think you are going to need maximum moisture protection at all points then I would recommend the following mixtures be used:

Formula #1

Marine spar varnish—2 parts
Boiled linseed oil —4 "

Mix the two together and rub into the wood with a rag. Allow to set for a half hour and then clean out as much as possible with a stiff toothbrush.

Formula #2

Marine spar varnish — 2 parts
Raw tung oil — 4 "

Use in the same manner as formula #1.

Formula #3

Marine spar varnish — 2 parts
Oiticica oil — 4 "

Use in the same manner as formula #1.

Formula #4

Oiticica oil — 3 parts
Turpentine — 2 "
(or)
Tung oil — 3 parts
Turpentine — 2 parts

Any of the above formulae will give you a coating which will be sufficiently protective, but will not be so glossy that it will reflect much light. The formulae with the tung or oiticica oils are preferable but if these oils are not available to you then the boiled linseed oil will do.

In all cases, though, the use of the toothbrush is necessary to keep a film from building up in the grooves or lines. Even if no light is reflected from such a film it will look messy and sloppy.

One or two applications of such a mixture will protect the wood sufficiently. The stock was sealed before so that even without the application of such materials moisture resistance will be good. This additional protection is merely an added safety factor.

CHAPTER THREE

Stains, Staining and Graining

THE word stain will cover a multitude of coloring agents which have been used singly or mixed together by woodworkers from the early days of history. The first means of coloring objects was by incorporating opaque earth pigments in some sort of vehicle or carrier. The first actual use of agents to change the color of an object without hiding it is not recorded, but the old violin varnish makers of the early 16th Century had a standard set of formulae with which to color their varnishes. The materials which were used to do this coloring consisted of natural dyes or stains from plants and roots such as madder, cochineal, lacdye, and logwood. In addition they used some natural resins which contained coloring matter such as aloes, dragon's blood and gum gamboge. These, of course, were in addition to the earth pigments such as the umbers and siennas.

The stains and dyes available today for our use include some several hundred synthetic coal tar products, many chemical stains, and many new pigments. They all have a definite place in our field and by combining several of them almost any shade or color can be imparted to wood or to varnish.

Different types of stains will have different fields of use depending upon the properties of any specific stain and also upon the conditions which the stained surface will have to meet. Some staining agents are much more durable than others, especially concerning the property of resisting fading due to strong light. (The stains which do not fade easily are called Light-fast and those which will fade readily are **Fugitive**.) Some materials used as coloring or staining agents will be relatively opaque and because of this will tend to hide the surfaces over which they are applied. Other agents will change the chemical structure of the wood itself and the compounds present in the wood.

All stains are applied in a liquid condition and as the base materials themselves are usually solid matter they are either dissolved in a suitable solvent or they may be suspended in a carrying liquid. The thinner a staining solution is the more it will penetrate, but the less coloring effect it will have. For this reason a balance must be found in preparing stains to insure effective penetration and still bring about the proper degree of coloring.

Inasmuch as there are so many new, durable compounds offered today it is almost foolish for the woodworker to attempt manufacture of his own staining agents. The sole exception to this rule is when a stocker wishes to duplicate exactly an old stock and wishes to use old time methods to do so. While the modern stains will do everything that the ancient materials did and more so even this would be unnecessary, but to satisfy a whim or to indulge in experimentation will furnish a satisfactory excuse if the stocker is looking for one.

Generally staining agents are called after the type of solvent which is to be used to carry that agent. The following list will cover most of the stains available today, but only in a general field. There will be specific materials and types which are too numerous to mention and which will come under one or more of the listed types.

TYPES OF STAINING AGENTS

Water Stains—
(1) aniline and coal tar dyes
(2) chemical (acid and alkaline)
Spirit Stains—
(1) aniline and coal tar dyes

(2) shellac stains
Oil Stains—
(1) aniline and coal tar dyes
Varnish Stains—
(1) aniline and coal tar dyes
(2) pigment color
Dyewood Stains—

CHARACTERISTICS OF STAIN TYPES

Water Stains—Aniline and Coal Tar Dyes: These materials number up into the hundreds and cover nearly every color and shade that can be imagined. They are the most important group listed and are used generally for fine work.

This type is very light fast, clear, transparent, cheap and will give brilliant colors besides having great penetration.

The disadvantages are that they will raise the grain of the wood upon which they are being used and it may be difficult for the novice to apply a water stain without showing laps where two stained areas join. This last fault can easily be corrected by a little practise.

These are sold in powdered form to be dissolved in water.

Following is a list of available water soluble stains put out by the duPont Company. Other manufacturers offer this type of material also, but these are representative colors.

Yellow
Tartrazine Conc.
Metanil Yellow Conc.

Orange
Orange II Conc.
Chrysoidine GN

Orange-Brown
Resorcin Brown 5G Conc. 200%

Brown
Resorcin Brown 3R

Red
Scarlet NS Conc.
Pontacyl Carmine 2G Conc. 150%
Pontacyl Rubine R Extra Conc. 125%

Blue
Pontacyl Fast Violet 10B Conc. 175%
Anthraquinone Blue SWF Conc. 150%
Pontamine Fast Turquoise 8GL Conc. 150%

Green
Naphthol Green B Extra Conc. 125%

Black
Pontacyl Blue Black SX
Nigrosine WSB Conc. Powder
Pontamine Black E Double

These colors may be combined in various mixtures to obtain a final color which will be suitable for any wood, depending upon the formula used to make that combination.

These materials are sometimes used in the so-called non-grain raising stains (NGR), but most of the time they are merely dissolved in water and used in that way.

Actually the non-grain raising (NGR) stains are the water soluble stains dissolved in certain organic solvents, such as Cellosolve, Carbitol, or others. The absence of water will guarantee that the grain is not raised and they will be as durable as the water stains, being composed of the same substances. The NGR stains are more expensive, though, and are no more satisfactory than the water type.

The following formulae may be helpful as a starting point for use of the staining agent:

Stain Formula #1, Maple

Tartrazine Conc.	— 1/8 oz.
Nigrosine WSB Conc.	— 1/8 oz.
Resorcin Brown 5G	— 1 1/8 oz.
Water	— 1 gal.

Dissolve the powders in the water and apply with a brush or rag.

This formula will give a light yellow-brown maple color and may be used on light or white birch or maple to deepen the color slightly.

Stain Formula #2, Light Maple

Tartrazine Conc. — ⅛ oz.
Resorcin Brown 5G — ⅛ oz.
Nigrosine WSB Conc. — ¾ oz.
Water — ¾ gal.

This stain is very similar to Formula #1 except that it is not as dark. It may be used over very dark woods where some lightening is desired. Very dark American walnut will take this stain well.

Stain Formula #3, Cherry

Scarlet NS Conc. — 1¼ oz.
Nigrosine WSB Conc. — ½ oz.
Water — 1 gal.

This stain is best used over light woods when a cherry or reddish tinge is desired. It will give richness to any wood if not overdone.

Stain Formula #4, Red Mahogany

Scarlet NS Conc. — ¼ oz.
Orange II Conc. — ⅟₁₆ oz.
Nigrosine WSB Conc. — ¾ oz.
Resorcin Brown 5G — ¼ oz.
Water — 3 qts.

This stain will give a darker color than Formula #3 and may be used to darken and redden light yellowish woods. Excellent for colorless (or nearly so) cheap walnut or ash woods.

Stain Formula #5, Brown Mahogany

Scarlet NS Conc.	— 1/8 oz.
Orange II Conc.	— 1/16 oz.
Nigrosine WSB Conc.	— 3/4 oz.
Resorcin Brown 5G	— 1/3 oz.
Water	— 3 qts.

Similar to Formula #4, but of a deeper, yellower shade. Excellent for deepening light woods.

Stain Formula #6, Dark Walnut

Orange II Conc.	— 1/10 oz.
Nigrosine WSB Conc.	— 5/8 oz.
Resorcin Brown 5G	— 3/8 oz.
Water	— 3 1/2 qts.

Similar to Formula #5, but lacks some of the reddish tinge. Will work very well over light, cheap walnut or other woods needing color.

Water Stains—Chemical (Acid and Alkaline): Chemical stains are those which are composed of some of the more common chemicals and are always dissolved in water for use. Many of them are in liquid form when procured from the chemist or supply house.

The colors produced by this material will be extremely light fast as the action of the chemical will change the composition of the wood itself or of compounds present in the wood and the new substance produced will never go back to its original state.

The chemicals commonly used are:

Acetic acid	Potassium hydroxide
Chromic acid	Lime (calcium oxide or hydroxide)
Hydrochloric acid—brown	Pearlash (potassium carbonate)
Nitric acid—brown	Sodium carbonate
Picric acid	Potassium bichromate
Pyrogallic acid	Potassium permanganate—red-brown
Tannic acid—brown	

Sulphuric acid—yellow-brown
Ammonia (ammonium hydroxide)
Sodium hydroxide

Copper sulphate—gray
Manganese sulphate
Potassium chlorate—gray-black
Copperas (ferrous sulphate)

All of the above chemicals have been used successfully in coloring wood though some are much more effective than others. All must be handled with caution as the majority are poisonous to some extent and some are dangerous to handle, especially some of the stronger acids. Those which I have used personally and which do a good job are noted with the colors that they have produced for me on my particular jobs.

These chemical materials will give differing colors depending upon the strength or density of any particular solution and upon the wood on which it is to be used.

When first applied chemical stains will appear much darker than the finished color actually will be. This is until the wood has dried. When the wood dries then the color will probably be lighter than the finished wood because many of these materials take some hours to develop their full color. It is better to wait until that full color has developed than to take a chance and add more stain only to have the final shade much darker than was intended.

If a combination of stained colors is desired you should make sure that you do not mix an acid and a basic or alkaline material together to get that color. This mixing will result in the one neutralizing the other and you may end up with no color change whatsoever. Only acids and acid base substances should be mixed together and alkalies and alkaline base materials the same. Acids will always react with alkalies to produce something entirely different from either of the two.

For example, suppose you wished to get the color that hydrochloric acid will give and at the same time you wish a tinge of the color produced by sodium hydroxide. If you mix the two together to produce a simultaneous reaction you will end up with only a water solution of table salt. This is because the acid and the base (alkali) will react with each other and the products of that reaction will be sodium chloride (table salt) and water. It would be best in this case to apply the alkali first, let it dry, and then apply the acid.

For dissolving or diluting any chemical stain the ideal solvent is either distilled water or, if that is not available, then snow or rain water. This type of water will contain no contaminating agents and if you have any left over you can always use it in the battery of the car.

These chemicals will almost always attack metal containers and contaminate the contents. For storing or even just working with these solutions the only thing you should consider is glass. An old glass tumbler or fruit jar will do if nothing else is handy, but under no circumstances use an iron or copper container for the acids and definitely never use any aluminum ware for working with alkalies such as lye and lime.

To dissolve solid chemicals it is best to use warm or hot water. When diluting strong acids or alkalies you must *never* add the water to the chemical. *Always* add the chemical to the bulk of the water instead. This is because adding water to the chemical will nearly always produce heat and if the chemical is strong enough that heat may turn some of the liquid to steam and the resulting explosion may throw acid into your eyes or face. Adding the acid or alkali to the water will not produce this much heat and should always be done.

Spirit Stains—Aniline and Coal Tar Dyes: These materials are from the same basic substances as the water type aniline and coal tar dyes but they will be soluble in alcohol. Alcohol has long been known as Spirit and it is thereby the name originated.

These stains and dyes have the property of drying very quickly because of the rapid evaporation of the alcohol solvent. Inasmuch as there is no water in the solution the grain of the wood will not be raised.

The advantages of this type are quick drying and brilliant and transparent colors.

The disadvantages are rather poor penetration because of

the rapid drying and great fugitivity (poor fading resistance).

These stains are good for touchup work because of the rapid drying rate but overall jobs will be apt to fade out quickly upon exposure to light.

The duPont Company has a selection of spirit stains, so called because they are soluble in alcohol, but they are not particularly fugitive. When covered by good varnish or lacquer they will be sufficiently light fast for stock work.

Following is a representative list of stains available:

Yellow
Luxol Fast Yellow G
Luxol Fast Yellow T

Orange
Luxol Fast Orange GS
Luxol Fast Orange R

Brown
Luxol Fast Brown G
Luxol Fast Brown K

Red-Brown
Luxol Fast Brown R

Red
Luxol Fast Scarlet C
Luxol Fast Red B
Luxol Fast Red BB

Blue
Luxol Fast Blue AR
Luxol Fast Blue G
Luxol Fast Blue MBS

Green
Luxol Brilliant Green BL
Luxol Fast Green B

Black
Luxol Fast Black L

These coloring agents may be dissolved in alcohol or cellosolve. The alcohol will evaporate rather quickly but the cellosolve will not. Therefore for more penetrating stains the use of cellosolve or methyl cellosolve will be best as it will not leave the stain as quickly.

Stain Formula #7, Maple

Luxol Fast Orange GS — 1/3 oz.
Luxol Fast Brown K — 1/8 oz.
Luxol Fast Black L — 1/50 oz.
Cellosolve — 1 gal.

This stain may be used on light or white birch or maple to deepen the color. Cellosolve is recommended here because alcohol will evaporate too quickly to allow penetration. If desired, a quarter of the cellosolve may be replaced by alcohol.

Stain Formula #8, Light Maple

Luxol Fast Orange GS — 1/3 oz.
Luxol Fast Brown K — 1/8 oz.
Luxol Fast Yellow T — 1/16 oz.
Alcohol — 3 qts.

This stain may be used on dark woods to lighten them. Very good on porous, dark brown walnut where a rubbed oil finish will darken the wood too much.

Stain Formula #9, Light Maple (#2)

Luxol Fast Orange GS — 1/3 oz.
Luxol Fast Brown K — 1/8 oz.
Luxol Fast Yellow T — 1/16 oz.
Luxol Fast Red BB — 1/32 oz.
Alcohol — 3 qts.

This stain is similar to Formula #8 except that it will add a touch of red to the wood. Excellent for lightening dark woods

Stain Formula #10, Cherry

Luxol Fast Red B	— 1 oz.
Luxol Fast Black L	— 1/20 oz.
Alcohol	— 1 gal.

This stain will give a deep reddish tinge to the wood. Excellent for walnut or mahogany with good figure but little or no color.

Stain Formula #11, Brown Mahogany

Luxol Fast Orange GS	— 1/20 oz.
Luxol Fast Brown K	— 1/3 oz.
Luxol Fast Red B	— 1/4 oz.
Luxol Fast Black	— 1/8 oz.
Alcohol	— 3 qts.

Excellent for deepening the color of any medium dark wood. Works well on walnut. Gives a good brown color with a touch of red.

Stain Formula #12, Dark Walnut

Luxol Fast Orange GS	— 1/10 oz.
Luxol Fast Brown K	— 1 oz.
Luxol Fast Red B	— 1/12 oz.
Luxol Fast Black L	— 3/8 oz.
Alcohol	— 3 qts.

Gives a good dark brown color on all woods. Excellent for deepening the color of normally light walnut stocks.

Spirit Stains—Shellac: These are the spirit stains which are dissolved in shellac for touchup work.

Oil Stains—Aniline and Coal Tar Dyes: These materials are usually soluble in some sort of oil or hydrocarbon solvent such as hot linseed oil, toluol, solvent naphtha, xylol, mineral spirits or benzol.

They are extensively used as they are easy to employ, dry slow enough to eliminate lapping, have fair penetration, and are fairly light fast except for some of the red stains.

The disadvantages to these materials are that they will not penetrate as far as water stains and they may tend to "bleed through" varnish coats applied over them giving a rather muddy appearance to the finish. This bleeding may be overcome if a thin glazing coat of shellac is applied over the stain.

The oil soluble stains on the market are listed in the representative list below. They are soluble in toluol, xylol, or benzol.

Oil Yellow
Oil Yellow N
Oil Orange
Oil Brown N
Oil Red
Oil Black BG

Stain Formula #13, Maple

Oil Yellow — 2 parts
Oil Brown N — 20 "
Oil Black BG — 1½ "
Solvent — 50 "

This formula may be used for deepening the color of light birch or maple. It gives a decided yellow-brown tint.

Stain Formula #14, Light Maple

Oil Yellow — 3 parts
Oil Brown N — 15 "
Oil Black BG — ½ "
Solvent — 35 "

This is similar to Formula #13, but is lighter. It will be best as a lightening stain for very dark woods.

Stain Formula #15, Light Maple (#2)

Oil Yellow — 3 parts
Oil Brown N — 15 "
Oil Black BG — ½ "
Oil Red — 1 "
Solvent — 35 "

This is identical to Formula #14 except that it will give a slight reddish tinge to the wood being lightened. This will furnish a richness in most cases which overcomes the dominant yellow cast.

Stain Formula #16, Dark Walnut

>Oil Orange —1 part
>Oil Black BG—5 parts
>Oil Brown N —4 "
>Solvent —30 "

This formula will darken light woods sufficiently for most users. Very good on light walnut, though not very good on the birch and maple woods where it will give too dark a color.

Varnish Stains—Aniline and Coal Tar Dyes: These are made by adding oil stains to proper types of varnishes. This may be done as the oil soluble substance will dissolve in the thinner which the varnish carries. For application see the last section in this chapter.

Varnish Stains—Pigment Color: The coloring materials in this type of agent are usually the opaque earth type pigments. They will be the least transparent of any stains but will be the most light fast. They will never fade out under the strongest light.

The substances used are:

>Black: Drop black
>Bone black
>Carbon black

>Brown: Van Dyke brown
>Raw and burnt umbers
>Raw and burnt siennas
>Bismarck brown

>Red: Red iron oxide
>Turkey red
>Vermilion
>Chinese red

>Blue: Prussian blue
>Chinese blue

Such pigment colors are invariably ground or mixed with a varnish or oil to put them in a state of suspension. These are what the paint supplier carries under the name Paste or Tinting colors. While they are used mostly for tinting paints they can be thinned down considerably with a suitable thinner and used directly over wood. As mentioned before, the penetration will be very slight but the following coats of protective oils or varnish will keep them from being worn away.

Dyewood Stains: These materials are among those which the old violin makers used to prepare colored varnishes for use on their masterpieces. They are composed of roots, herbs, and special resins which will impart color to the solvent used to steep them in.

Some of the great number of basic substances are dragon's blood, gum gamboge, aloes, madder, brazilwood, logwood, sandalwood, saffron, kermes, cochineal, lacdye, or alkanet root. Inasmuch as very few of any of these dyewoods are available to the average experimenter (and even if they were they would not be as good as any of the synthetic stains easily procured) there is no point in going into the subject too deeply. Many times you will find modern formulae giving alkanet root as a coloring agent. While it has its place, at times, you will do much better by resorting to one of the water or oil soluble synthetic (aniline) substances.

COLOR COMBINATIONS

No matter what make or type of staining or coloring matter you have to work with, there are certain basic combinations which will produce certain overall colors. It would be wise to keep the following in mind, rather than try to remember any certain or specific formulae, though specific formulae have their place.

Combine	To Get
Yellow and blue	green
Red and black	brown
Red and yellow	orange

Orange
Brown
Black.......................maple or oak

Yellow
Brown
Black.......................light maple or oak

Scarlet
Black.......................cherry

Orange
Black
Brown......................walnut

Orange
Black
Brown
Red........................mahogany

Any of the above basic combinations may be changed or modified by the addition or elimination of some constituent, and such a modification, even in small quantities, can change the shade to a great extent. It is only for specific, reproducible colors that formulae are necessary and are so used.

PREPARATION OF WOOD

Wood surfaces must be in the final stages of finishing before stains are used. This is because many staining materials will not penetrate well and any succeeding sanding which may be done could very easily cut through the thin coats of color and bring out the uncolored wood underneath. If this happens you will have a touchup job on your hands. It would be much simpler to do any sanding necessary before applying stains.

If you decide to use some sort of a varnish sealer on the stock before final finishing you must determine just what sort of stain you intend to use. If it is of the penetrating type (water stain or oil stain) then you must stain the wood before this sealer is applied. The presence of any sort of oil, shellac or varnish on the wood will prevent any penetration from taking place. If you are figuring on using some sort of a pigment or surface stain then you can use the sealer before staining. Inasmuch as you do not intend to have penetration take place anyway you may as well get the sealing over with. Occasionally the solvents in the sealer will tend to dissolve or float away such a surface stain and then you might have to go back and touchup the job.

The rule to follow is: for non-penetrating stains seal the wood first, but with penetrating stains stain the wood before sealing.

APPLICATION OF THE STAIN

Make sure that all sanding has been done before staining.

If the staining agent is in powdered form follow the directions given by the supplier or those on the container. The proper solvent to use will be indicated as will the approximate amounts of that solvent for normal use. The degree or depth of color (light or dark) which the wood will assume will be determined by the wood itself. If it is a softwood of some sort the color will usually be deeper than if the wood is a hardwood.

If you have considerable end grain showing in the stock it may be advisable to put a wash coat on the stock. The reason for the wash coat is to control the degree of penetration and thereby the amount of darkening of the wood. The wash coat may be a very thin solution of shellac (about a 2 pound cut); a couple of thin coats of drying oil previously worked into the wood; or it may even be a thin coat of varnish. No matter what you intend to use as a wash coat it must be thin in order just to seal the pores of the wood against stain penetration without building up an appreciable film or coating.

Water stains should be applied hot to allow maximum penetration into the wood. If you have used a wash coat this penetration will not be very great but you should attempt to secure as much as possible.

Stains are best applied by using a wide brush, though they

may be readily worked in with a pad of cloth. Dip the brush or cloth into the staining solution and allow just enough to soak into the bristles or cloth to give a wet effect. If too much is used then you may accidentally drip some on the stock in passing over it to get to the area you are working on and if these drops are not noticed and cleaned up immediately they will produce a spotted effect on the finished stock. Once they have penetrated the surface there is nothing you can do about them.

Bring the wet brush to the wood and brush well. It will amount to working the stain into the pores and crevices so that all parts of the surface get an equal bath. It is better to apply the stain too thinly than in too heavy a coat. Thin coats will allow lapping to take place without the laps-sections showing. Heavy coats will darken the wood wherever applied and when the adjoining area is wetted then some of that heavy coat will run over onto the previously wetted surface and a definite line of demarcation will appear wherever two such areas meet. In the case of the water type stains the surface may be lightened considerably by going over the still wet surface with a wet or damp cloth. This will lift some of the stain from the wood. This process may be definitely helpful in cases where laps may be showing. The water in the cloth will help blend the two areas together and thus cover the lapped lines.

If you find that a particular specimen will not take stain evenly or readily you can help the situation by first dampening the wood with a wet rag. The dampening will allow the stain to wet the wood evenly when it is applied.

Here a question arises. All along I have warned against the dangers of allowing any amounts of water or moisture to come in contact with the wood and here I reverse my stand and tell you how to use stains that are about 90% water base. The question is, do I follow my first warnings or do I disregard them and use the second suggestion? The answer is more simple than you may think. I do both.

The way in which the two are brought together is to use the water stain as a grain raising agent and thereby kill two birds with one stone. Granted, we may not get quite as much penetration as we normally would but inasmuch as all sanding and cutting of the surface has been completed by this time we will not need much depth to the coloring.

In this system you use the stain instead of just plain water and proceed with the normal whiskering (or dewhiskering) operations. You use the same tactics that I recommended back in Chapter 2 exactly. The stain coat is applied to the wood with a cloth using only enough stain to wet the cloth well. When the surface is well dampened then pass a flame over the wood in such a manner as to drive off all free water present but not so as to char the wood. When you have removed with steel wool whatever grain ends that have raised up repeat the process until no more grain raising is apparent after wetting and heating once more. If you find that the color is not yet deep enough continue the wetting and heating process until the desired color has been attained. Once you have gotten to a point where the grain ceases to raise you will not need to use the steel wool any longer. From now on it is merely a true staining operation. When the last coat of stain has been applied go over the stock once more with steel wool to make sure that every bit of protruding grain has been removed and you are through. Now you can go ahead and use the varnish sealer if you have a mind to!

As far as I am concerned this is the only way that water stains may be used safely. The heat of the flame passed over the wood immediately after it has been wetted will insure the water present passing off in steam rather than soaking down into the heart of the stock which is so sensitive to that water.

In staining on end grain the color may darken very deeply even with the small amounts of coloring matter which will be taken into the wood by this process. Here you must be very careful not to allow the color to become so deep as to appear black.

Precisely the same rules should be followed when using the chemical stains as were (or should have been) followed with the water stains. Inasmuch as the chemical stains are water solutions of different common chemicals they should be used as grain raising agents during application.

These chemical stains should, for safety's sake, be applied while wearing rubber gloves if you are going to use a wad of cloth to apply them. If you intend to use a brush then the gloves will not be necessary unless you are sloppy and splash quite a bit.

The big difference here is that, unlike the aniline water soluble stains, chemical stains may take a period of some hours or minutes to develop the final color. If you are not sure just how deep the final color will be with the strength solution you are using I would apply two coats with the recommended heating to drive off water, whisker the grain ends with the steel wool, and then set the stock aside for several hours to see what develops. If you still need more color put on another coat or two and repeat the heating, whiskering, and waiting process. In this way you will insure yourself from going too far and maybe even getting a color that is doggoned near black rather than the delightful nut brown you had envisioned. If you reach the color you want before the whiskering operation has been completed finish that up with pure water.

In applying oil or spirit stains the danger from moisture will be nil. Because the stain contains no moisture you need not worry that penetration of the solvent will damage the wood. This solvent will evaporate from the stock quickly.

Methods of application of such materials are the same as for water type stains except that no heat or flame is necessary or even desirable. Most of the liquid content of such materials will be very inflammable and the presence of a flame could ignite the stock. When I spoke of methods of application I referred to using a brush or pad of cloth. Many of the oil stains and all of the spirit stains will dry very quickly because of the volatile thinners contained therein. This rapid drying will increase the danger of having lap marks show at the end of the operation and decrease the effective penetration of the stain. Inasmuch as you will have a good protective film over the stain you will not need extreme depth of color as pointed out above. The greatest disadvantage to using such items is that in some of the red shades the color may soon fade out from the effects of strong light (ultra-violet content of sunlight, for instance). The oil stains, being much more stable in this than the spirit stains, are therefore preferable when a choice is possible.

The use of varnish and pigment type stains has long been advocated by many who should make it their business to inquire more deeply into this angle of stock work than they evidently have. However, while these materials have many disadvantages they also have qualities which make them desirable in many cases.

Pigment type colors are nearly always insoluble particles which must be suspended or carried by heavy vehicles in order to make them workable. The very fact that they are solid, insoluble materials will make their use undesirable on the better stocks. The solid particles will tend to gather together in the pores under the influence of the applicator pad or brush. They will never penetrate the wood at all but will remain on the surface where the slightest scratch or abrasion may rub through them into the uncolored wood beneath and thus leave an unsightly mark.

Stocks which are to be colored with this sort of stain must be sealed before coloring. If the stain is applied before the sealing the thinners which will be in the sealer will dissolve or float away the pigment.

As mentioned before, these materials may be best purchased from a paint supply store under the name of Paste colors, or Tinting colors. In this form they will be very heavy, semi-solid pastes which must be diluted with varnish or some sort of thinner to be workable. If applied in the form in which they are purchased they will only leave a nasty smear on the wood. Add enough thinner (the kind recommended by the paint supplier) to make them rather runny. Or, preferably, add varnish of the type you intend using to finish the stock (if you are going to use a varnish finish). In this mobile condition they may be rubbed on and worked into the surface until the desired shade is obtained. Then allow the stock to dry completely for 24 hours.

Shellac stains used for touchup work are regular spirit or alcohol soluble stains with the shellac resin present to act as a glaze coating. These items will be rather fugitive and are not recommended. If you do find it necessary to use them they may be thinned as desired with pure grain or denatured alcohol to give whatever degree of coloring is desired. They should be used with a thin striping brush for touchup work and allowed to dry for at least an hour.

STAINING OLD VARNISHED SURFACES

If you ever have occasion to stain old finished surfaces the old finish, whether it be in good condition or badly damaged, must be removed as completely as possible. Any small amounts of such previous finishing materials will prevent the stain from "taking" at that particular point and will result in a spotty appearance. This warning applies especially to old varnished wood.

The proper way to remove such an old finish is by means of one of the varnish removers sold by paint suppliers or by making some yourself from one of the formulae given in Chapter 10. I would not advise ever buying paint or varnish removers which contain wax. Many of them do, but the wax will invariably remain to a certain extent in the pores of the wood and will prevent effective adhesion of following coats of finishing materials.

You may use sandpaper in removing such finishes, but that will entail a considerable amount of elbow grease and wasted time. Besides, you will not be able to get down in the pores and clean them out if you use sandpaper and this is necessary in staining. You might be able to get away with it if all you wanted to do was to take the varnish off the surface so you could put other varnish on. In that case the old stuff in the pores would act more or less as a filler and that would be okay. But for staining it would be a very sloppy way to do business.

PREFERENCE OF STAINS FOR STOCK WORK

While most of the materials given above will work well under different conditions of use I prefer to use the water soluble type aniline stains on most work because of its great durability. It will be a trifle more difficult to use when applied as a grain raising operation, but the fine results which may be secured together with the wide range of colors available place it first on my list.

Secondly I recommend the oil soluble aniline stains. These will have sufficient durability and light fastness for all practical purposes and the ease of use is certainly a point in its favor.

The chemical stains, while definitely durable, will depend to a great extent upon the specific wood specimen for the resulting color and will be at times a bit dangerous to work with. They are fine for experimental work, but for the man who does not have the time nor the ambition to fool around with chemicals until he hits upon a good concoction I would say that they are nowhere near as desirable as either the water or the oil stains.

Alcohol and spirit stains are completely out of the picture because of the lack of resistance to fading. Who wants to make up a good stock and then have the color disappear after a few hunting trips? They remain the quickest way to touch-up any bad spots or scratches, but for overall work I definitely do not like them.

Pigment stains are another fine experimental item, but for the average stocker who needs a stain right now and has not any prepared they will be useless. Of course, if you have mixed yourself up a batch of stuff that seemed to fill the bill for that last stock then I would say that you would be perfectly justified in using it. Remember, they will be as durable, or even more so, than the water stains. Always remember, too, that the pigment stains will partially hide grain structure because they are extremely opaque.

STAINING VARNISHES

The old tried and true method of coloring wood by staining it directly is by far the most popular method. In fact, many men have not even heard of the method of staining a varnish rather than the wood itself.

This system was used by many of the old violin makers way back when and it has always given fine results when handled carefully. It is not as resistant to abrasion as normal coloring methods, but if care is taken of the wood finished in such a manner then great beauty may be brought out which by other systems may be hid.

The procedure is to use a stain which is soluble in the varnish or finishing material you intend to employ. This may take a bit of trial and error, but usually oil stains will be dissolved easily and completely by any of the varnishes you will get. Of course, if you intend to use shellac, either brushed on or in the French Polish method, then an alcohol soluble stain will be necessary because of the alcohol solvent in shellac. If you intend to use lacquer probably most of the oil stains will dissolve readily in that also, though you better check on that with an experimental mix. It will depend upon the individual lacquer used and upon how much of the stain you want the lacquer to carry.

When you have your materials at hand place a bit of the stain in a saucer. Add some of the varnish, shellac, or lacquer to the saucer and mix well. Make sure that all of the stain dissolves completely for if some undissolved particles are left floating around in the mixture then there is a fine chance that those particles will show up on the finished stock as tiny, colored bumps or pin points. When the stain and varnish (or shellac or lacquer) have been well mixed pour out a little of the solution (mixture) into the container with the finishing material. Stir it well so that the stain is evenly dissolved through the whole can and brush out a little on a piece of wood the same color as the stock. If the color does not seem to change any, or very little, then pour a bit more of the base stain mixture into the can, stir well, and try another spot on the piece of wood. Continue this until you find you have enough color in the varnish to approach the color you want on the stock. Do not get the material so dark that one coat will give you the depth of color you will finally want. Remember, you should put on at least four coats of the varnish or lacquer and that every coat you add will bring that much more color to the wood.

It would be much better to stay on the light side and have to add more coats of finish to get the color. In this way you can control the shade and sort of slide up to it gradually rather than to hit it all of a sudden and go on past before you can stop. Of course, if you do this there is always the sandpaper handy with which you can lighten it in a hurry, but the more careful workers would frown upon this, I am sure.

If you intend to rub the final finish to bring out a certain degree of lustre then that rubbing will lighten the color depending upon how much you rub. Coarser compounds will cut rather quickly and will therefore take off some of the color. Effective use of such compounds, whether coarse or fine, will serve only to smooth the surface and not to do any appreciable cutting. You need not worry about how much lighter the stock will be after rubbing if you do not lay on the rubbing pad with all you have got.

Inasmuch as such a finish would have dissolved coloring matter in it that finish will be totally transparent. If a sensible choice of colors was made then that finish will be strictly out of this world. Let me warn you this will be a little tricky at first and will call for a bit of common sense in judging when to stop adding color to the varnish. However, anyone who has enough interest and ambition to read a book such as this will have enough in the upper story to carry out such a staining process successfully.

ARTIFICIAL GRAINING OF GUNSTOCKS

Many times stocks are encountered that have very little character or figure. It is possible to improve the appearance of such wood by artificial graining. Actually it is not graining that we do, but the system leaves the stock with light, dark, and variously colored streaks or areas which will give "life" to the wood.

There are several ways in which this operation may be done. We may use a stain of some sort, we may use a pigment in oil, we may use flame, or even a common acid.

Inasmuch as this process must be done at the time staining is carried out it is best discussed at this point.

First of all, what makes beauty in wood? Grain or pattern of the fibers for one thing, but even more than this beauty is brought about by contrasting streaks or spots of light and dark. From a distance the grain structure of a stock is invisible, but one stock will catch our eye because it has these contrasting spots and areas while another which may have better structure will appear flat and lifeless because it is a uniform color overall.

It makes no difference what material you use to bring out these contrasts, but it makes all the difference in the world how you use them. For example, take a piece of walnut. Using almost any staining agent dip a brush in the stain and slop some of it onto the wood. Brush it out evenly over the whole section of wood and let it dry. Now, at the same time, dip the brush into the stain again, but on a second piece of walnut sort of dab or spot the stain on the wood. If you wish flick the brush at the wood without actually touching it with the bristles. Some of the stain will fly from the brush and land on the wood in spots which will partially resemble bird's eyes when dried.

When both pieces of wood are dry examine them, first closely and then from a distance of a few feet. The first piece of wood will have good overall color but will still appear drab. The second piece, however, will have a little life to it because the slight contrasts give that appearance.

By using a combination of shades and colors even a well figured piece of wood may be made much more attractive. The old Kentucky rifles sometimes were finished with flame and acid or herb stains. They took on the tiger-tail or flame patterns with attractive coloring by this method.

First of all, we shall take up the lightening and darkening of the stock to give contrasts. Later the coloring will be discussed. First things first, Joseph.

Flame Graining: Alvin Linden took up the subject of flame treating when he talked about his Suigi finish. This was nothing more than the surface charring or darkening of the wood by means of a flame. Of course, it is not quite as simple as this, but that is all it amounts to.

The Suigi finish (with your permission I shall retain the old Japanese name for an old Japanese system of finishing) works best when applied to wood of a naturally light color and which has grain or figure of a curly or wavy nature. This will refer mostly to maple and birch, the two most common light-colored stock woods.

For such a finish on good wood (wood with good figure) the necessary tools are a gasoline torch, a Bunsen or Meker burner, or hand blast torch of some sort. We need plenty of heat with no free carbon liberated. If the flame shows yellow or smoky then it will mean incomplete combustion of the gas and this smoke or yellow, luminescent flame will deposit soot or unburned carbon on the wood. This is an undesirable condition. Have whatever flame you use blue or nearly colorless. This will insure you getting maximum heat from the flame and also you will not soot the wood where you want it burned.

When I speak of burning the wood you need not worry

about it going up in flames. This burning is merely the darkening of the surface. Never allow the flame to play on one spot long enough to char it black like a young bride's roast.

The stock that is to be figured or receive this Suigi finish must be free from any finish whatever. If it is an old, finished stock then go after it with the varnish remover and the sandpaper until it is entirely innocent of finish. Get right down to the bare wood. All sanding, cutting, and shaping must have been done previous to this coloring. It must be ready for the finish.

Now place the stock in the ever present checkering frame. Make sure that it is secure enough so that it will not slip, but that it turns freely enough for easy handling. Take the torch (whatever kind you have available) and set it going.

With the flame at least two to three inches long sweep the flame over the surface of the wood. Return slowly and repeat until the wood takes on a dark enough brown to show up whatever figuring will come out. Turn the stock slowly as soon as one area has been completed and continue the turning and the flame treating until the whole stock is covered.

Incidentally, the figure or waves which are in the wood will be brought out very strongly because the wood in those spots will be more dense, or harder, than the surrounding areas. These dense spots will not burn or brown as easily or as quickly as the softer portions. By leaving the flame in one spot too long you could burn the entire surface black, but this is not what we are after. Just enough darkening or browning to bring out the waves in bold relief is our aim.

Be very careful around any corners and edges, such as on the cheekpiece and the edges of the inletting. These very delicate corners will char black at the drop of a hat. When you come to these places turn down the gas and sharpen the flame as much as possible. Then go very lightly and very cautiously after the corners and edges. If you are careful you can darken these just the right amount. Practice will give you the knack.

When the stock is completely **browned** **then** turn off the heat and pick up the sandpaper block. We must go after any actual charring of the surface and remove that. Not enough to remove all color from the wood, mind you, but only enough to remove loose, burned surface fibers.

Never, under any circumstances, use sandpaper backed only by the fingers. The darkened wood will come off easily and the chances are a hundred to one that you will make that stock look like it has a myriad of ups and downs. This is because you will have the ups and downs. They will be made by the removal of the surface fibers over the softer spots, and the waves, or dense areas, will not come away so readily.

I do not want to give the impression that wood which is just turned brown can be abraded away easily—it cannot. But it can be torn off more easily than the unheated waves of the figuring. And sandpaper unsupported by stiff backing will do just that.

When you have smoothed the surface sufficiently then thin a little linseed oil with turpentine and soak the stock with it. You need not worry about leaving undried oil in the stock because maple or birch are so close grained that very, very little oil will penetrate. The reason for the oil bath here is that there is something about linseed oil that does things for wood. It will bring out the beauty of the wood as nothing else can. Just one thin bath will do it, though.

When the surface of the wood has absorbed as much of the oil as it is going to then wipe off all that you can remove with a dry rag. We do not want to leave any of it on the surface. Whatever has gone into the skin of the stock will serve our purpose and more than this will be undesirable.

Allow the stock to dry for a couple of days, and then apply whatever finish you intend using. Make sure that the surface of that wood is not sticky. If it is then it will mean that there is an appreciable amount of the linseed oil left on the wood and it is not yet completely hardened. Wipe the stock again as clean as you can and wait until all stickiness has disappeared. Then go ahead with the finishing.

If you apply a finish over the sticky coating of linseed oil the finish will not have any adhesion when dry, and the chances are it will be very flat or dull.

Suppose you do not have any appreciable figure or waves in the wood. Suppose you have a perfectly plain piece of birch or maple and you want to make something out of it. By following the general principles in the above charring process we can make some waves or curls.

As with the first stock this one should be all ready for finishing. Place it in the checkering frame or holder and turn up the flame. Now play the flame *crosswise* on the stock. That is, from top to bottom and port to starboard. Inasmuch as most stock wood is cut in such a manner as to bring natural waves in this direction then our homemade article should resemble the natural product.

First use a broad or "brush" flame. Every inch or couple of inches brown a streak with this broad flame. Then cut down the flame so it is more or less needle pointed. Take this and go between the large, broad flame marks and make a series of interweaving or over-lapping flame marks. If done artistically you will have a fine wavy maple stock when you finish up.

If you wish you may make a tiger-tail pattern, the same as some of the old Kentuckies had on them. This is done in the same manner as above, but use only the needle flame. Make definite, well defined paths with it every inch or so, or maybe every inch and a half. You may make your own patterns, if you wish, but do not make them too even or with precise distances between each path. Nature never gives us this sort of thing, and you definitely wish to give a natural appearance to the stock.

When you have the pattern you desire then use the linseed oil bath and finish as you desire.

A twist to this system is to use a little moisture on the surface of the wood before applying the flame. Dampen small areas of the wood with a rag, or sprinkle the stock with drops of water. Then immediately apply the flame and you will find that wherever the water or moisture has been the wood will be lighter in color. This will give you a bird's eye or spotty appearance which, if properly done, will be very attractive.

The flame treating of wood may be done successfully only with the light woods, such as birch and maple. It may be done with dark walnut and mahogany, but you will get only overall darkening of the surface without the attractive figure waving. It would be much better to grain or figure such dark woods with stain or acid.

Color Graining: Let us suppose that you have paid your seven bucks and received through the mail a stock which is entirely lacking in figure. Even though you paid only seven bucks you can make something out of it.

First of all, let us take the case of stain graining. Of course, the stock must be inletted and finish shaped and sanded. Once we work on the surface we do not want to have to come back and sand out the beautiful (you hope) figure that you have given the wood just because you forgot to raise the grain or left a dent in the wood which you intended to fix up but forgot about.

Place the stock in the checkering frame and get out your supply of stains. You have a fairly decent overall color on the wood, let us say. It does not have to be deepened at all. Okay, that is one thing we do not have to worry about.

Take a stain or mixture of stains that will give you a fairly good contrast when applied to the wood. For example, on a light brown wood a dark red-brown stain will give the stock richness if not overdone. Or maybe the wood is rather dark brown. In that case a reddish-yellow stain will lighten the wood enough to give it life.

Take a piece of cloth and douse it with very strong stain solution. The solution should be strong, rather than thin or reduced, because you want the worked over areas to stand out fairly well against the deep background color. Now wipe or skim the stock here and there with the rag. The wood should take on enough of the stain to take the color well, and the haphazard skimming will give a rather natural effect. If you apply the rag in precise, ordered lines then the natural look will vanish and it will look like you have stained the stock with a rag. (That is just what you have done, you know.)

It is much better to have less color imparted to the stock and have it look natural than to make the color deep and artificial looking. The only sure way of working this system is to use a flock of scrap pieces of wood and practise until you get what you want. You can do it on stocks if you wish, but be prepared to throw out the first ten that you work on.

The color that you will get should be most apparent on the butt and grip of the stock. That is where the eye looks in most cases. The forend should be worked over, too, but it is not as important as the butt.

The lines or streaks that you place on or in the wood should be thin rather than thick or heavy. You can run several thin streaks almost together and it will look very well. A heavy or thick streak or line will take on an artificial look unless expertly applied and blended in with the background. Speaking of blending, the edges of the streaks should be feathered or smoothed into the background, also, immediately after application. This is necessary because if you wait until the stain is well soaked into the wood or until the solvent has evaporated you will not be able to do any appreciable blending. In that case you will have to use a thin solution of the stain and wipe or feather the edges of the streak so that they are not so obvious.

The whole effect should be that of gentle blending rather than abrupt streaks.

Besides using the graining or streaking system with a rag it is possible to use it with a fine striping brush. The same procedure is followed as with the rag; that is, the brush is dipped into the stain and quickly flipped or skimmed across the surface of the wood.

If done in a systematically haphazard manner the streaks or figures which will result will take on a natural appearance.

Again do not allow the lines or streaks to appear in a precise or ordered manner with each the same distance from the other.

It is possible to obtain from dealers in automotive refinishing supplies or art supplies what is called a graining comb. This is a rubber affair having teeth cut into it just like a hair comb.

Such a comb is used for graining instrument panels and window moldings of automobiles, but it can be used successfully here. The comb is dipped into the stain and drawn lightly across the surface of the wood. Wherever the teeth touch the wood they will leave a trace of the stain and the overall effect will be that of actual grain. Of course, the teeth are set in the comb at set distances from each other, but if a wavy path is drawn across the wood with swirls or twisting now and then the effect will be excellent.

The rubber teeth will not absorb much or any of the stain so it will be necessary to redip the comb at frequent intervals. If done carefully the grain line may be made continuous and the points where the teeth were taken away and then returned to the wood will be unobservable.

Almost any of the stains may be used for this process, but the following will be a guide for experimental mixtures. These formulae may be varied as the basic color of the background wood varies, but you can observe just which general formula gives you the best effect on any color or shade of wood.

Graining Formula #1, Cherry

To be used over light brown wood.

```
Scarlet     —   1.3 parts
Blue-black—     .6   "
Solvent    —100.0   "
```

This mixture will result in a cherry color. It will give reddish or pinkish shades to the grained areas and is very attractive.

The solvent will be either water, alcohol, or toluol, depending upon the composition of the stain and the solvent recommended by the manufacturer of the staining agents.

Graining Formula #2, Red Mahogany

To be used over light brown wood.

    Scarlet — ¼ part
    Orange — ⅟₁₆ "
    Black — ¾ "
    Brown — ¼ "
    Solvent — 100 "

This will give you a dark or red mahogany cast to the grained areas.

Solvent is that recommended by the manufacturer and will be on the container. May be water, alcohol or toluol depending upon the composition of the agents.

Graining Formula #3, Maple

To be used over dark woods for lightening effects

    Yellow — 1 part
    Black — 1 "
    Brown — 11 "
    Solvent — 500 "

This color will be lighter than that of the dark background wood. Solvent is recommended by the manufacturer.

Graining Formula #4, Dark Walnut

To be used over light walnut or ash wood.

    Orange — 1 part
    Black — 6 "
    Brown — 4 "
    Solvent — 500 "

This formula will give dark brown coloring. The contrast will depend upon the shade and color of the background wood. Solvent as recommended by the manufacturer.

PIGMENT GRAINING

Besides using ordinary staining agents for producing grained effects, the use of earth pigments is also a definite possibility.

In this system the use of the rubber graining comb is definitely of help and probably will be more satisfactory than the use of a rag or pad. Because the pigments are carried or suspended in an oil medium rather than dissolved in solvents there will be very little penetration into the wood, but the very fact that little penetration is achieved will make the graining stand out better.

Formulae are given for various colors but they are all handled in the same manner. The pigments are ground or stirred into oil or varnish with a spatula or knife blade. They are then thinned to a workable consistency with turpentine or other suitable solvent and applied.

The use of varnish is recommended because of its considerably faster drying time. Oil will work, but will take several days to dry and harden and this is very undesirable.

When the formula is made up the application is done by means of the rubber comb or matted fiber. This fiber may be excelsior, coarse steel wool, rug padding (the coarse fibrous pad which is laid under rugs to preserve their life and resilience), or very coarse burlap.

The coarse fibers should be worked between the fingers until a wad or pad is formed which may be held between the fingers. The pad thus formed should be lightly dipped into the thinned mixture and wiped or swept lightly across the surface of the stock. Use circular as well as straight motions to duplicate swirls or waves in the natural wood. Allow just enough of the mixture to remain on the wood so that well defined lines or figures are obtained. If too much is accidentally placed and left on the wood then all that will appear will be blotches.

If you get too much on the stock then you must take some thinner and completely wash that portion of the surface clean. The mixture will be opaque and will not take kindly to smearing around in attempts to redeem a faulty job of graining.

Graining Formula #5, Dark Walnut

>   Burnt umber—2 parts
>   Varnish   —1 "
>   Turpentine —1 "

Mix the umber into the varnish stirring well with a spatula.

Then thin with the turpentine by stirring and use immediately. If allowed to stand for any length of time the umber will settle out and must then be restirred back into suspension.

This formula works best on fairly light or medium dark woods where contrast is wanted.

Graining Formula #6, Light Walnut

>   Raw umber —2 parts
>   Raw sienna —1 "
>   Varnish   —1 "
>   Turpentine —1 "

Mix the umber and sienna into the varnish and then thin with the turpentine.

This formula works well with fairly dark woods and, while not giving great contrast, will add life to the wood if applied in wide blended streaks or areas. This will lighten the wood somewhat but not a great deal.

Graining Formula #7, Dark mahogany

>   Burnt umber—3 parts
>   Vermilion —½ "
>   Raw sienna —½ "
>   Varnish   —1 "
>   Turpentine —1 "

Mix the pigments with the varnish and then thin with the turpentine.

This formula will work best over light or medium dark woods. The vermilion will add redness and richness to the color and the sienna will give enough yellow to tone down the redness.

The coloring may be varied according to the background color of the wood and the effect desired.

Painter's Oil Tinting Colors: The following formulae are based upon the tinting colors which may be purchased already mixed from paint supply houses. They need be thinned only. Inasmuch as there is such a great selection of colors available possibly these formulae will be more popular.

Graining Formula #8, Dark Walnut

    Van Dyke brown—2 parts
    Turkey red   —2 "
    Washed ochre —3 "

This formula should be thinned with turpentine until of the desired consistency. It will give good coloring over light or medium dark woods.

Graining Formula #9, Mahogany

    Turkey red   —2 parts
    Toluidine red—¼ "
    Raw sienna —2 "
    Burnt umber —1 "

Thin with turpentine to desired consistency.

This one may be used over either light or dark woods, though the lighter the wood the greater the contrast will be.

Graining Formula #10, Cherry

    Turkey red   —2 parts
    Chrome yellow
      medium   —¼ "
    Burnt sienna —3 "

Thin with turpentine as desired to work well.

This one will give cherry or reddish tints to the wood. It would be best to apply this formula in very thin splotches or areas so that only a suggestion of the color is left. Do not allow this one to build up on the surface much. Thin until about the consistency of water and rub in well.

ACID GRAINING

The use of acids or chemicals to give life and color to wood is very old. The old timers used it along with the flame method.

Personally I would recommend the use of a true stain for graining operations, but inasmuch as this has been used successfully it should be brought up at this time.

The acid is used in the same manner as the stains given previously. A rag or pad or cloth is used to spread the chemical or a fine brush may be used.

Graining Formula #11, Mahogany

    Potassium permanganate—1 gram
    Water   —5 grams

Heat the water and dissolve the purple crystals. When completely dissolved apply the solution with a rag.

This solution will turn the wood a violet color at first, but it will then change to a dark brown when the chemical reaction is completed. This may take a couple of hours.

This stain is most useful on light colored woods. It will not show up too well on dark walnut or mahogany.

Graining Formula #12, Dark Brown

    Nitric Acid—3 parts
    Water   —1 "

Apply this in the usual manner with a fine brush or rag. It will turn most woods a dark yellow-brown.

STAINING CHECKERED OR CARVED AREAS

When refinishing old stocks that have been decorated with some odds and ends of checkering or whittling you may find that these decorated areas will tend to darken much more rapidly than the surrounding areas of solid stock. This will be because there is a great deal of end grain exposed by the cutting of the surface. The sides of the pyramids in checkering and the sides of the slopes and valleys in carving will be composed of all end grain and this end grain will absorb staining solution as quickly as a blotter would because of the fine pores and capillaries present.

In working with such end grain it would be desirable to use some sort of a glaze coat to prevent such rapid absorption of the staining liquid. This may consist of a very diluted shellac solution or even some plain, ordinary linseed oil (boiled) worked in by the finger tips and a toothbrush. Do not use very much or the presence of this glaze coat or oil will prevent the stain from taking at all. I would favor using the shellac if possible and not too much of that.

Brush it on very lightly and when it is dry try a very diluted solution of the stain to see just how much the glaze coat will keep the stain from penetrating. It would be very much better to have to use four very thin solutions of stain than one heavy one and have the color get away from you and darken the checkering beyond all hope.

If you are using a water or chemical stain be very careful in applying the heat to raise the grain. The fine points and edges here will be very easy to burn or char. Use just enough heat far enough away from the stock to evaporate the water. Four passes of the flame six inches away from the stock will be much more satisfactory than one pass with the flame brushing the wood. The use of the finest grade steel wool will be indicated to remove any raised grain ends. In checkering this raised grain will not be very noticeable to the hand, but such a condition on or in a carved section can be easily felt, especially if the slopes or valleys are shallow.

BLEACHING THE WOOD

Many times in the refinishing of wood it is found to be highly desirable to lighten the wood for some reason. Perhaps the stock has darkened greatly through excess handling, or perhaps some sort of stain has been applied previously that is now undesirable. Whatever the conditions may be which cause the wood to be too dark, bleaching of that wood may be easily done.

Wood may readily be bleached almost white. This, of course, will be much too light for the average stock but then it is very easy to come back with a stain to give the stock whatever color you desire.

There are several ordinary materials which may be used for such bleaching action and they include household laundry bleach, calcium hypochloride (chloride of lime), hydrogen peroxide (in the stronger solutions), and oxalic acid.

Of all of these I personally find the oxalic acid to be best. It is easy to work with, does a first class job, and leaves no destructive residue behind if properly handled. It is used in the following manner:

Take a half pint of water and heat it almost to boiling. Then dissolve in the water as much oxalic acid crystals as you can make it hold. Brush this solution on the wood while it is still hot and allow it to dry. When it has dried you will find that the stock is covered with a white powder. Brush as much of this powder away as you can with a stiff bristle brush. Then take some water which has had a little ammonia dissolved in it and rinse the stock. You do not have to soak the wood, but use the brush again with this water-ammonia in it. That will not only dissolve what remains on the wood, but it also will neutralize whatever acid crystals may be down deep in the pores.

Now the wood should be a great deal lighter than it was when you put the oxalic solution on, though if you wish you may repeat the process if it still is not light enough in color.

The degree of lightening which you will get will be dependent upon the strength of the solution. If you wish very little change then you can make the solution much weaker; that is, dissolve less crystals in the hot water.

Now that we have gone over the complete operation let me say something. I have never yet seen a stock on which I would use a bleaching solution. The reason is that you are defeating the main purpose of having a stock finish. Any finish is formulated primarily for protection against moisture and secondly for looks. By soaking that stock with water in the bleaching process you are loading it with the moisture that is so dangerous. The water that you put on the stock will very quickly soak down into the sub-surface of the wood and from there gradually be absorbed into the heart of the wood. This is what we are trying so doggoned hard to avoid!

If I have a darkened stock to work over I always use sandpaper to get down to the untouched layer of wood underneath that darkened skin. In most cases a very thin skin is all that is necessary to remove. Some cases will be a little more reluctant than others. In these tough situations I soak the stock with a lot of varnish remover or plain toluol or xylol in order to remove oxidized oil and varnish which may have collected dirt. This will generally remove enough coloring substances that, together with a light touch of sandpaper, I have a light enough wood to work with. This I would recommend as being far and away the best method to change the color.

The only reason I even mentioned the bleaching of wood was that somebody will write and ask me about it anyway, and I may as well be as complete as possible here, even though I do not like it.

CHAPTER FOUR

Drying Oils and Their Application

D**RYING** oils are natural oils, obtained from the seeds and nuts of trees and plants, which will form hard, tough, protective films on surfaces over which they have been spread.

HISTORY

These oils, or films, have been known and used from the very early ages. While certain agents such as egg albumin, honey, gum arabic, and treated beeswax gelatin were used by the Egyptians and other ancients as vehicles or carriers for pigments in paint they were not especially durable when subjected to weathering of any sort. The reason that much of the Egyptian art is available to us is that not only was the climate dry and hot but also whatever still remains was invariably concealed in tombs and closed places so that no moisture or cold got to it.

Galen, A.D. 131–230, left us the first known written record of the possibilities of the use of drying oils when he suggested the use of nut, hempseed and linseed oils for protective purposes.

Actius, A.D. 540, mentioned the use of linseed oil in the arts because of its drying properties.

It was not until the 13th and 14th Centuries, however, that the value of drying oils as a protective measure was generally known in England, France and Germany.

In the 15th and 16th Centuries a fuller knowledge of the behavior of oils and the use of driers was gained. From this time until the beginning of the 19th Century no greater advances were noted in the use of such materials.

The greatest advances in this field have been in improvements in methods of processing and refining the raw materials to eliminate some of the more undesirable properties. Prior to the 19th Century the general theory was to use nature's gifts just as nature gave them to us. It was decided that the Lord's gift to men was meant to be used as is and that any attempt to improve or change such materials bordered on blasphemy. Also they had no idea what made the stuff work like it did and therefore had no way to improve it even had they wanted to. Probably their pious attitude was merely an unconscious attempt to excuse the technological ignorance of that day and age.

From the very earliest times linseed oil was the king of drying oils. It was used more than any other oil because it was the only easily procurable one which exhibited practical drying qualities. Other oils were used, it is true, but none then available came up to linseed in all-around properties. The use of perilla, soybean, tung, fish and oiticica oils belongs to the 20th Century for the most part. The properties of these oils were known for quite a while before this, but they were not in general use.

At the present time most drying oils are used in their natural state, except for filtering to remove any suspended foreign particles. Little or no heat treatment of any sort is employed, except in the case of the manufacture of boiled and blown linseed oils.

The mechanism by which all such oils harden or dry is still in the state of theory only. No positive, unimpeachable theory has been recognized, though the general principles are definitely known. Only details are still lacking. The basic, proven mechanism is the absorption of oxygen from the air into the wet film of oil. By reacting chemically with this oxygen the oil will produce certain substances which form together in small bands, or groups. Then these groups join together to form an over-all hard mass which is the finished, hardened film. This whole process takes place over a period of some hours and is extremely complicated, but the key to the whole situation is the original combination of the oxygen of the air with the body of the oil.

PROCESSING

As mentioned before, natural drying oils are obtained from the seeds and nuts of trees and plants. The seeds or nuts are collected and are then pressed or crushed to remove the oil. Many different systems of pressing are used, depending upon who does the pressing. If the oil is obtained in a raw state from some far flung outpost of civilization the only methods which have probably been used were those of backward peoples calling upon tradition as their engineering guide. Crushing in crude stone mills is still practiced in some places, and in others wooden presses are the thing, employing screw type hand presses. The early Chinese, in the extraction of tung oil, would place the nuts in a hollow log with wooden plugs or spacers at intervals. Then wedges were driven between the plates expanding them and forcing the oil out. The oil was then recovered and placed in containers to be carried to the nearest place of commerce, unless they wanted to use it themselves.

As time went along the hydraulic press was invented and improved upon from time to time.

Modern presses consist of several rollers, between which the seed is forced. These rollers force the oil out and at the same time grind the seed to a fine meal or powder. The meal is then cooked and pressed to remove all traces of oil remaining, after which it is bagged and sold as stock feed or mixed in with other livestock and dairy feeds.

The oil, after being filtered, is known as the raw commercial oil. The oil which was recovered before the cooking of the meal is known as Cold Pressed Raw linseed oil, a type of drying oil the stock finisher will use little of.

REFINING

The manufacture of drying oils, which includes both the pressing of the oil from the seed and the refining of it, is a very important point in understanding the why and wherefore of finishing materials.

It is often said, especially by the old-timers, that "the oil you get nowdays sure is not what it used to be. We used to get linseed oil you really could work with." Well, I will agree that the oil is not what it used to be, but for a different reason than the old timers gave. The oil you get now is a lot better than what they knew. Maybe the curtain of time has come down on their memory and blacked out everything but what they want to remember about it. At any rate, this angle of it is just what the chemists had to put up with when they first started to invade the paint industry. The dyed-in-the-wool old varnish men would not have a thing to do with them. The old ways were good enough for their fathers and good enough for them. Besides, the presence of the chemist would bring out the varnish maker's secrets into the open so that they would not be the number one important specialist they used to be. The varnish makers (and oil makers too, I suspect) carried their secrets with them and they and they only knew how to make the product satisfactorily. They were top man in the plant and knew it. If they were angered at something and walked off the job the plant just folded up until they could find another such magician who would condescend to come in and make their varnish for them. But the chemist wrote down what he found out about whatever it was he was investigating and passed the information on so that another chemist could work with it and perhaps add something to his findings.

It was only after science came in that the paint industry really found out what it was doing. It found that batch after batch of a product could be made with no apparent difference from one to the other and that real quality and uniformity resulted. This, of course, was most important in varnish making, but the oil maker also benefited by it. Now the boys in the know can give you oils the properties of which were not even dreamed of 50 years ago.

The methods of refining of oils determines their properties as differing from the properties of the raw oils.

During the 15th Century refined oils were produced by heating with heat treated bone particles and pumice stone. The oil was then skimmed off and treated with white copperas and allowed to stand in the sun. The end product of this treatment was pale and clear and dried much more quickly than raw oil, primarily because of the metallic manganese content of the copperas which was taken up by the oil. Of course, they did not know just what part the copperas played in this reaction—they just knew that it was necessary to add it if they were going to get the quick drying of the finished product.

From that time until the early 1800s the production of refined drying oils consisted mostly of heating the oil with metallic salts and bleaching in the sunlight.

Gower, in 1792, described a process of refining oils by means of sulphuric acid. He secured a patent on this process and basically it remained the same up to the present day. This method consisted of treating the oil with amounts of strong acid. The acid reacts with impurities in the oil and causes them to separate out from the rest of the oil and settle to the bottom of the container. This mass settling downward also carries some of the other impurities which the acid did not act upon, but which were nevertheless removed by this means.

The same effect is produced in our modern method of refining oil by means of caustic soda. The impurities are also acted upon in the same manner and settle out. The mass is then washed with water to remove the soaps which are formed from the alkali-oil reaction.

After the oil is chemically treated it is bleached. This was first done by means of sunlight as noted above. However, inasmuch as this light bleaching was necessarily slow various chemicals were eventually tried. At one time peroxides were used but they had such an undesirable effect upon the oil that the method was abandoned.

Present day means of bleaching are mostly the use of activated charcoal and fullers earth. After bleaching the modern oils are then refrigerated to remove grease and wax components which are among the non-drying "foots" present in the raw oil. This refined, bleached, refrigerated product is known as Alkali or Acid Refined linseed oil.

TYPES OF TREATED OILS

In order to make the present day boiled oil the above refined material is heated by means of steam for short periods of time. When the oil has reached a certain temperature it is held there for awhile, certain driers are added and the oil is then allowed to age. This is the boiled oil of commerce.

You will note that no mention is made of actually boiling the oil. This is never done. The old time formulae for boiled oil (and many formulae given today by those who do not know any better) insist that the oil be brought to a boil for certain lengths of time. This will effect no desirable properties other than slightly bodying the oil, or making it a little thicker. The reason for boiled oil's use is because it will dry faster and better than true raw oil. The only thing in the oil that makes it dry faster is the presence of metallic salts (driers) and simply boiling the oil without adding some of these salts will not increase the drying rate.

Contrary to popular belief, the presence of the driers in the oil film will not have any deleterious effect on the durability of the film. Of course, excessive amounts of such driers will certainly do the film no good, but the makers of such oil see to it that only enough drier is added to give increased drying and never enough added to injure the film in any way. If your boiled oil is purchased through a reputable dealer you need not worry that it will not stand up.

There is a certain class of individuals who occasionally crop up in this business. They will take a barrel of raw or refined oil (it is usually raw as the refined will cost more), draw off a little of the oil and then add some Japan drier through the bung hole. This oil is therefore called Bung Hole Oil and is sold as genuine boiled oil for a goodly profit. The majority of the boys will not have anything to do with this stuff and you will not run much danger of getting it for the real article if you patronize somebody you know is on the up-and-up or a reputable supplier. Inasmuch as the bung hole oil has not had the drier properly incorporated you will not get proper drying from it. There is also more than an even chance that much too much drier was added in the process and that your final, dried film will be very poor in many qualities.

Besides the raw, refined, and boiled oils there are many other forms of linseed oil used by the industry. Usually the other forms will have some special qualities such as unusually light or heavy viscosity, or color. These special oils are neither of interest nor are they available to the average citizen.

One other form which may possibly be used in place of or in conjunction with boiled oil is what is known as blown oil. Blown oil is produced by passing finely divided bubbles of air through the oil for considerable periods of time. This tends to oxidize the oil to some extent and thus produces quick drying films. The viscosity of this blown oil is much greater than that of either raw, refined or boiled oils. There is no particular advantage in using this oil when boiled oils are available. The drying is no faster usually and the finished, hardened films will have about the same properties. Besides, there are very few retail or even wholesale sources of supply that will even know what you are talking about.

The above processes of refining oils are in common usage today, but are nearly always limited to linseed oil. Except for filtering, the other oils used by the paint industry will be used in the raw state.

TYPES OF DRYING OILS

Drying oils encountered by the hobbyist or amateur may

not always be true drying oils. By this I mean that some of the oils often recommended by various and sundry authorities fall into the semi-drying or non-drying classification. These three classes (drying, semi-drying, and non-drying) may overlap at times, depending upon the technical definition of the class involved and also upon the technical generosity of the authority defining the classes. At the end of the chapter will be found a more or less complete listing of the various oils under each classification. However, some of the more well-known members are given below followed by as much general information as possible.

Drying Oils
Chia seed oil
Dehydrated castor oil
Hempseed oil
Linseed oil
Oiticica oil
Perilla oil
Poppyseed oil
Safflower seed oil
Soybean oil
Tung (china wood) oil
Walnut oil

Semi-Drying Oils
Cottonseed oil
Sunflower seed oil

Non-Drying Oils
Castor oil, raw
Olive oil
Palm oil

Any oils or waxes listed under the non-drying class will be just that. They will never dry to a good, hard film and to all intents and purposes will remain wet for so long that they will be totally useless for anything upon which we may wish to use them.

Oils listed under the semi-drying class will probably remain wet and tacky for periods up to several weeks, though in many cases the drying time will be considerably less. Those oils which may be close to the drying classification will probably set up to a more or less dry film even as quickly as four to five days, but they are rather rare. Even though such oils may have a definite drying time most of them will not harden well to a usable film. The resulting film will stay soft and jelly-like and will be almost as impractical for our use as the non-drying oils are.

True drying oils will harden fairly well, but even these may have drying times which will stretch over a period of a week or so. The use of oils listed as drying types will be a matter of availability and experiment. It is highly possible, if not probable, that you may not be able to obtain many of the oils listed and which may be recommended at times by this or that writer. In that case obviously you will not be able to do any experimenting with it. If you are in a position where you can get at least small samples of any of the oils in which you are interested I would advise running a few sample blocks of wood of about the same texture and grain structure that your stocks will have. You will be able to determine just which will meet your needs, and if any are worth while for you it would not be a bad idea to lay in a small stock of the stuff against a day when you may not be able to get any for a particular job. Even the best of the drying oils will keep well in storage over a period of several years if the containers are filled to the brim and no air space is left above the oil level.

The oils which are hereafter listed are those which I have found will be most nearly available to the experimenter or which will have properties most practical for his use. I do not recommend them all but they are surely items of interest since each one has, at one time or another within the past twenty years, been mentioned as distinct possibilities for the stock finisher.

Linseed Oil: One of the first known drying oils, linseed oil is obtained from the seed of the flax plant, *Linum usitatissium*. The oil content of the seed varies from about 32% to 43%, the quantity and quality depending upon the variety of seed, the locality in which it is grown and the climatic differences of that locality from year to year.

The plant is grown mostly in the northwest of the United States, Burma, India, Russia, Uruguay, and Argentina.

This oil is satisfactory for wood finishing either in the raw or the refined state. The raw oil contains quantities of mucilaginous matter such as waxes and greases which will tend to make it non-drying. As a matter of fact, the mucilaginous matter (foots, as it is called) will never dry. It is for this reason that pure, raw linseed oil will remain relatively wet for long periods of time and is never used by the experienced wood worker unless for some highly specialized purpose other than for its drying action.

One of the most satisfactory forms of linseed oil for use either by the painter or the gunstocker is boiled oil. As mentioned above, this oil is not actually boiled, but it is heat treated with added driers so that the drying action is considerably faster than that of raw oil. Also, there is reason to believe that properly prepared boiled oil will give more moisture resistant films than will raw oil, primarily because the non-drying constituents have been removed by refrigeration.

Blown or heat bodied oils are available which will be more efficient than raw oil, but which are not as satisfactory for use as the boiled material.

When properly applied to wood surfaces and correctly handled this oil will give a surface film the beauty of which cannot be touched by any other drying oil. For this reason, and also because it is the only oil which many wood finishers, past and present, have had access to, linseed oil is known the world over as the finishing oil without peer.

It is acclaimed by most every writer, gunsmith, and furniture man as the only medium worthy of the fine works upon which it is to be placed. That, of course, is strictly a matter of opinion—the other guy's opinion I might add. Every man is entitled to his opinion and I would be the last one in the world to say he is wrong or set myself up as the highest court of appeal, but I do say that my ideas on the subject do not precisely coincide with a lot of others which have been floating around loose these past few years. 'Nuff said.

There is no doubt that this item (in the boiled form) will give extremely fine finishes and for strictly showcase stocks is indeed something to be considered seriously for fine work.

My whole case against it, therefore, is built around the relatively low moisture resistance which the final film exhibits. It does pass moisture very freely. As a matter of fact, this property of permeability to water is one of the chief reasons why linseed oil is used to such a great extent in outside house paints. It will allow any moisture which may be in the wood to pass outward through the film almost unobstructed. Therefore it prevents continual blistering or bubbling of the film which a less-permeable film would develop. This is because all wood, especially new or "green" wood used in construction of buildings, contains a certain amount of natural moisture. When the wood is exposed to the sun or to warm weather, such as in the summer months, the moisture is forced out of the wood and must have someplace to go. It goes toward the exposed surfaces, and if these are covered with resistant or impermeable films it makes no difference. The pressure of the moisture against that film will break it loose in every case, unless the film is porous enough to allow the moisture to pass *through* it. This is what happens when linseed films are used. It allows that moisture to go right on through just as though there was no film there at all.

The same thing can happen on a stock. Only in this case, the moisture from humid atmospheres will go through *into* the wood just as easily as it can pass out. If the wood is easily warped then you have not a chance in the world of keeping the wood from warping and when that happens you may as well toss the stock out and build yourself a new one.

This is the reason that I condemn linseed oil as the *only* finish for stocks which may possibly have to meet severe weather conditions, or even storage in damp basements. It may be used as a *final* finish as long as you have a good waterproofing varnish sealer under it. Even here I would keep that stock away from the rain. It is strictly an interior item and there is no use kidding ourselves. Sure, we all have seen stocks that were finished in linseed oil and which were carried through rain, snow, and sun for years and still that gun shot as true and purty as a picture. Well, in that case all I have to say is that either it was a lever type gun in which the stock plays no part other than a handle to hold onto, or the owner had some well placed grain in the stock which would not have warped even if he had left it bare and dunked it in a bucket of rain water every week.

Aside from its use on wood which will meet severe moisture conditions linseed oil is perfectly satisfactory for the average stock. Inasmuch as you may not be able to obtain any other oils, and you may not like to dabble with varnish and lacquers, or have not the time to do so, then I would say that you can count on this item to give you a fine finishing job, one of which you may be very proud, providing you do your part.

Tung (china wood) Oil: This item is less well known than linseed oil, but one which deserves a great deal more attention than it has received in the past. It may be a bit hard to come by, but almost any of the larger paint companies throughout the nation will have a supply on hand and a courteous letter to the sales department will nearly always procure some.

Tung oil is a relatively new oil. By new I mean it has gained its popularity in the paint industry since the turn of the century. The qualities which it possesses have made it the darling of the varnish maker, though. It will contribute extreme water resistance, fast drying, and hard though flexible films.

It is very seldom used alone in any industrial capacity, though the Chinese have used it for centuries for waterproofing their boats and buildings and it was actually used considerably for making the buildings and walls by mixing the oil with binding materials and allowing it to harden.

Tung oil is obtained from the nuts of the tree, *Aleurites fordii* which is cultivated extensively and almost exclusively in China. Recent plantings in the southern portion of the United States have had a certain success, but the bulk of the oil is still obtained from China.

The nuts from which the oil is pressed contain about 50% oil.

Tung oil is much faster drying than linseed oil. In fact, where refined linseed oil will dry hard on a glass plate in about 72 hours tung oil films will dry to the same degree of hardness in about 18 hours. This fact is one of the reasons for the growing popularity of this oil in stock work.

The other and more important reason for its popularity is the fact that films of dried tung oil will be extremely impervious to the passage of moisture. Reports to the contrary notwithstanding, tung oil films will allow less than half the moisture to pass that linseed oil will.

The big disadvantage to the use of tung oil is that the dried film will be very flat with many minute wrinkles attending the drying process. When such oil is used on a stock the finished surface will reflect no appreciable light and the wood will appear to have a coat of velvet attached to it. Even rubbing and polishing will not bring the lustre up to any great extent. This effect may be partially overcome by mixing tung oil with linseed oil or other drying oil. I would say that you must have at least 50% of the mix be linseed oil in order to have any lustre at all. This linseed content will, of course, reduce the moisture resistance of the finished film but there is no help for that.

This oil may be used with a varnish instead of the linseed oil in order to cut out much of the flatness. This will be perfectly acceptable and in many cases desirable.

Raw tung oil never has drier added. It is not necessary and only increases wrinkling.

Oiticica Oil: This material is very similar in appearance and properties to tung oil for which it has been used as a substitute a great deal. It will dry nearly as fast, and its moisture resisting properties approach those of tung oil.

It is obtained from the nuts of the tree *Licania rigida* which grows over a wide area in the north of Brazil. The nuts contain about 60% to 65% oil.

When oiticica oil was first introduced to the industry it was looked upon with suspicion at times. Some shipments would arrive with the oil in a semi-solid condition. The increasing demand for this material has brought about improved conditions under which the oil is produced and that together with increased knowledge as to technology involved in handling and using it has eliminated all opposition.

Films of this oil will dry to the matted, wrinkled surface which is also characteristic of tung. With proper handling this wrinkling may be overcome to produce smooth, glossy varnish films.

As with tung oil, the only way to prevent the raw oiticica oil from forming a lustreless film is to combine it with other drying oils which will not wrinkle, such as linseed.

Driers are not needed, nor are they ever used, in working with this oil. The drying time on a glass plate is about 18 to 20 hours which is sufficient for most of us, and the driers, if added, will not speed up this drying time much. They will only tend to accentuate the wrinkling of the surface film.

Perilla Oil: This material is obtained from the seed of the plant *Perilla ocymoides* cultivated in India, Korea, Japan and China. The seed contains from 35% to 45% of oil with an average of about 38%.

The raw oil is a bit slower drying than linseed though it is reported to have a greater resistance to moisture passage.

It has possibilities for use in stock work, especially with hand rubbed finishes. I have never used it because it is relatively unavailable and other materials to be discussed give me more than satisfactory results. The drying time is too slow to suit me.

Soybean Oil: This oil is obtained from the seeds of the plant *Soja max* which has been cultivated in Africa, Australia, Europe, India and the United States. It is native to China and Manchuria, however, where it has been used for food for centuries. The seed of the plant contain from 16% to 20% oil.

The raw oil is considerably slower drying than linseed and

does not seem to have any properties which would recommend it to the gunstock finisher. Drying time is about 120 hours on a glass plate and puts it about two to three times slower drying than the different types of linseed oils.

Poppyseed Oil: The seeds of the plant *Papaver somniferum* furnish this oil. The plant is cultivated in Europe, China and India.

The oil film will dry more slowly than that of linseed.

There are no special properties which will be useful to us, though it has been recommended from time to time, especially by some of the old-timers who ought to know what they are talking about. I would advise using this only as a last resort if nothing else were available, or as a matter of experiment.

Hempseed Oil: This is obtained from the seeds of the plant *Cannabis sativa* which is native to many parts of the world. The seed of this plant contains from 32% to 35% oil.

This oil dries more slowly than does linseed oil. I can find nothing to recommend it to your use.

Chia Oil: The seeds of the plant *Salvia hispanica* contains this oil. Such seeds contain about 34% oil.

It is similar to perilla oil in most properties, especially drying characteristics. Not especially recommended.

Safflower Seed Oil: This oil comes from the seed of the plant *Carthamus tinctorious*, cultivated in India, Egypt, and Turkestan. The seeds contain from 24% to 36% oil.

This material dries more slowly than linseed oil and is not particularly to be desired by the stock finisher.

Sunflower Seed Oil: From the seeds of the plant *Helianthus annus*, cultivated in Russia, China, India, Argentina, and the United States. The kernels contain from 22% to 32% oil.

The properties of this oil are very similar to those of soybean oil which does not make it especially desirable for use.

Walnut Oil: From the tree *Juglans regia* which grows extensively in Europe, China, and the United States. The nuts of this tree contain about 65% oil.

This oil is one of the very early drying oils used in varnishes and has properties similar to linseed oil. If available it may be of interest to the experimenter, but contains no especially desirable properties not found in linseed oil and is considerably more expensive.

Dehydrated Castor Oil: The raw oil is obtained from the seeds of the plant *Ricinus communis*. The raw oil is entirely worthless for drying purposes, but after it has been subjected to chemical treatments it does have drying characteristics which fall near those of linseed oil. In other words, this chemical brother to castor oil might be worth investigating.

Unfortunately, such chemically treated oil is unavailable to the great majority of us. Perhaps some of the larger paint plants would be able to get some for you.

Fish Oils: Normally fish oils are non-drying or semi-drying liquids which have very undesirable odors.

It is possible to obtain certain oils from menhaden, sardine, and pilchard which, upon refining, may be used with no ill effects. Even these especially refined oils will dry slowly to tacky films which will not be satisfactory for our uses.

Except as an experiment I would turn thumbs down on fish oils in any form.

Japanese Wood Oil: This oil is produced in Japan from the tree *Paulownia imperialis*. It is very rarely seen on the market and hence is not available to most of us.

It has properties very similar to tung oil and would be well worth investigating if available.

Cottonseed Oil: This oil is listed under the semi-drying classification. It is obtained from the seeds of the cotton plant.

Dries slowly and is not recommended.

Experimental Synthetic Oils: In addition to the above listed drying oils, some synthetic oils have been produced from petroleum products which have very desirable properties for stock work. Unfortunately, these oils are definitely not available to the average consumer and even very few technicians in the paint industry have had any such petroleum oils to work with. These synthetic oils are actually liquid drying resins rather than oils.

By special chemical treatment linseed oil may be given extremely quick, hard drying properties. This oil is another of the laboratory's babies which very few are privileged to observe. Possibly in the near future they will be made more available for general use.

The laboratory has also produced certain forms of soybean oil which it has been able to convert into a drying oil which rivals linseed oil in properties.

The special chemical forms of petroleum, linseed, and soya oils are the outcome of efforts by the industry to obtain substitute oils for those which were in short demand during the war years. While they certainly have succeeded in their efforts the cost of such oils is out of the question and they will therefore remain more or less industrial curiosities unless some special use is found for them or the cost of production is brought way down.

For many years now industrial uses have included very little drying oils used by themselves. Other than to make some types of outside house paints these oils are invariably incorporated with some form of resin. Of late the resins have been of the newer, synthetic type rather than the natural resins formerly used in spirit varnishes. No matter whether the use calls for natural or synthetic resins, however, the oils will be mixed with them by means of heat. The resin constituent in the mixture will impart certain properties that the oil alone could never give, and it is for this reason that the oil is now considered a lesser, if not a minor, partner in the union.

Nearly all forms of protective coatings use oil in some form and to some degree. Varnishes and enamels contain considerable amounts, while lacquers contain less; the purpose of the oils in both cases primarily is to impart flexibility and resistance to cracking and checking.

Some plastic materials used as protective coatings also contain oils to some degree, some much more than others, depending upon the properties of the plastic itself and the end use desired.

USE OF DRYING OILS FOR STOCK FINISHING

As most of you know, the use of one oil or another has been recommended by authorities for stock finishing. But which oil to use, and the best way to use it for finest results are details which have been kicked around hither and yon for years and which nobody knows for sure.

As with everything else in the gun business (and other businesses too, I am informed) the best results for *you* are invariably determined by the way you work and not by what you have to work with. Any of us could take the best materials available and by being careless and negligent in the application of such materials could turn out a job which we would be ashamed to show anyone. Conversely, even though we have mediocre materials for use we could, by careful and painstaking effort, turn out a stock that would rank with the best of them for beauty and utility. Personally I think that there is no one best item, or even type of item, for stock work. There is one best item, or type of item, for your method of operation, though. Those last two sentences, while seemingly contradictory, are only complementary. You and you alone by the way you work and by the care which you use will determine whether or not any given item will be satisfactory. You have probably all attempted to use one sort or another of formulae which have been acquired from another person, either by word of mouth or by reading. Possibly the formula which you have used has proved to be highly successful for you, but the other chap who used the same one found that he had something when he finished up that was worse than before he started. This last lad is the one I give you as an example. There was something which he did not do, or some condition which he lacked that made his job turn out a flop. In his case he must now go ahead and work out a variation in that formula which will work for him.

The second fellow will probably tell his pal, Blevitch, how lousy the oil is that he used and will attempt to steer Blevitch away from using it, while Blevitch, having used it once and finding it to work for *him*, will immediately tell him he is full of hot air and another fine argument is launched. It is just that sort of thing that prompts all the sniping back and forth at gun club meetings and which, I am happy to say, almost always ends happily with each of the boys using his own system and condemning that of the others. Actually these arguments are a pretty good thing as it prompts the fellows to use a little initiative in their stock work in order to prove the other man wrong and thus very often leads them on to find something new which is certainly worthwhile.

To get down to the actual finishing operations, it will be up to you to determine how you want to go about these operations. The choice of oils or other materials is strictly up to you. I know that many of you will use nothing besides raw linseed oil. That has been bandied about for a great many years, and if you like it there is no reason in the world why you should not use it. Personally I prefer the boiled linseed oil as it will give me much quicker drying, will be just as easy to apply, and will allow my stocks to be used dry between applications of the oil, rather than the tacky, sticky finish which raw oil will leave for days at a time.

In order to finish any piece of wood, whether it be gunstocks or furniture, you must have the wood in condition to receive a finish. Obviously you must have all of the cutting and sanding done as you will only tear up a perfectly good oil finish if you find some part of the wood later that needs smoothing down with sandpaper. You must have raised the grain of the wood (or whiskered it, as it is called). This will be doubly necessary with an oil finish as some of the oils you may elect to use will not be particularly moisture-proof and the first really damp or wet day that the stock sees will pull any loose grain ends up where you can feel them. You must have stained the wood (if any staining is deemed necessary).

No matter what type of stain you intend to use it will not penetrate an oiled wood surface. All these things must have been done before any kind of finish whatsoever is allowed to touch the wood.

Before you actually intend to slap some oil on, how do you figure on using this particular stock? As with varnish and lacquer finishes the final use of the wood should determine what sort of finish you apply. I have mentioned this before, but it should be firmly fastened in the back of your mind that plain oil will not stop moisture from creeping through into the interior of the wood, no matter what kind of oil it is. Even the renowned tung oil will not do a complete job.

Assuming that you are going to use the stock out where the weather can get at it for long (more than a day or so) I would suggest you investigate the field of spar varnishes, at least for an undercoating. This is the only most nearly moisture-proof material that I know of for use on stocks.

However, if you are like so many of the rest of us, your gun will see very little outside use. If you are the fireside type of hunter (by necessity rather than desire) you can rest assured that a good oil finish will be perfectly satisfactory. You will not encounter enough weathering to bother a correctly applied finish and that is about the only thing that you will have to really consider when it comes to stock protection.

Now is the time to decide whether or not you are going to use a filler on the stock. Fillers were discussed awhile back in the book and you may have some definite ideas by this time as to whether or not you want to experiment with them. There are some fellows in the game that would not touch a filler with a ten foot pole. They are invariably the ones that have been stung sometime in the past with a gooey, messy linseed oil and whiting mixture which somebody or other foisted on them. As mentioned in the section on such concoctions you can get satisfactory items even if you have to make them up yourself. There are some mixtures offered by people in the gunstock finishing game that seem to work fine and if you do not care to fiddle around with homemade articles I would recommend one of them, especially one of the many which are advertised in the pages of *The American Rifleman*. The lads who put out that little gem of wisdom do not allow misrepresentation in their ads and if they do find such is taking place then the advertiser is in for a rather difficult time, believe you me!

Using some sort of oil film alone for finishing purposes will almost necessitate the use of some sort of filler if you desire to have any sort of a first-rate appearance to the finished stock. Oil films will not build up a coating of more than about a half a thousandth unless the operations are stretched out over a much greater length of time than any I have ever seen. Therefore the final coating will not be thick enough to fill in and build up the low spots in the pores of the wood and consequently any pores present will appear on the surface after the oil finishing has been completed. This may be all right for some of the rustic types of furniture, but it does not go over in a big way with the gun expert (aesthete, that is). He likes his stock to be smo-o-o-oth with every little indentation and pore totally filled in. This can only be brought about by the use of some material which will fill those indentations and pores.

As you may have gathered by this time, my opinion is that filling is necessary when you are using oil films. With varnish and lacquers you have a different proposition, but here I see no way out of it.

Assuming that you decide to side along with me and have eliminated the pore openings (Chapter 2 on Fillers will give you an idea of how to attack the problem) you will be ready to start to work with the oil. In order to be able to control the materials that you are working with it will be necessary to know something about their properties. If you have not had a great deal of experience with the particular material you have chosen you may be in for trouble by just plunging into the job not looking either **way**!

There are one or two little, simple tests that you should make at this point which will be very helpful. The first test consists of pouring a little of the oil out into a cup or beaker. Now roll it around the sides of the container. How does it look to you? Is it thin and watery or is it rather heavy-bodied and viscous? The reason for this check is that a very heavy-bodied liquid will have considerably less penetration into the surface of the wood than a light, thin oil. If the particular material you wish to use is of the heavy, thick type then you must be sure that you do not flood the stock with it on the first few applications. Such thick oil will only flow into corners and depressions and stay there, oxidizing on the surface but never drying completely all the way through the film, primarily because the film will consist, practically, of a pool of oil. You must have thin films for efficient drying. On the other hand, if your test shows the oil to be thin and runny then you can figure you will get a bit more penetration and the first few coats can be so liberal that they will warrant the name of a soaking operation. Of course, even with the thin oil you cannot allow wet coats to build up in low spots. Even thin oils must be applied in thin coats.

Along with this improvised viscosity test you should test the drying time on a glass or metal plate, preferably the glass. It is possible that in using a metal surface some oxide will be present and it will act as a drier and give you a false reading. Even a piece of broken window glass or the bottom of a pickle jar will be satisfactory. It must be clean however.

Flow out a thin film of the oil onto the glass surface and set it aside where dust cannot collect on it. Every so often check it and see if it is still wet and sticky or if it has dried up into a hard film yet. When you find that it has hardened enough not to feel tacky, or sticky, to the finger then you can figure that the time it took the film to reach that stage of oxidation will be a good measure of the drying time of that type of oil *in your particular atmospheric conditions.* I stress this qualification because that same oil from the same container will dry differently in the summer than it will in the winter. It would be best to make this check every time you have a stock to finish. Perhaps the humidity and temperature are very much different from those the last time you used that oil and it will take longer on this job. The most important reason for this test is that you must not, *never*, throw on another coat of oil before the preceding one has dried. It is perfectly possible for a coating of drying oil on wood to feel dry to the touch, but down in the depths of the film there is still some of the oil which is not completely oxidized as yet. If you do happen to apply a second and then a third or more coats over these partially soft coats the undercoatings will practically never oxidize the rest of the way. They will stay in that soft, jelly-like condition for months and perhaps up into a year or longer. While they are in this condition they will feel sticky in hot weather, will pick up grit and dirt readily, and will not polish well if at all. Also, a more important point, they will not develop maximum moisture resistance until fully dried.

Before attempting to do any oil finishing of a stock, be sure that the stock is completely sanded. Make a close examination of the wood under a strong light. Check to see that no appreciable sand scratches are present and that no marks from cross grain sanding show. If you do find these faults present take some very fine sandpaper and remove all evidence of them. Under no circumstances should you sand across the grain. If you do so, no matter how fine a grit paper you have used, some scratching will show through the final finish.

After you have completed the drying oil tests on the glass plate you are ready to go ahead. Now that you know just what to expect from the oil you can give it a chance to do its best.

A little oil should be taken into the palm of the hand, a few drops at a time, and applied to the surface of the stock with a vigorous rubbing motion. Bear down fairly hard and work the oil *into* the wood rather than just on to the surface. These first coats must penetrate as completely as possible in order to give the next coats a good, firm foundation to hang on to and one that will be imbedded deeply enough into the wood so that handling of the stock later will not tend to loosen the film. As you proceed with the rubbing of the oil into the wood you will find that the palm becomes unpleasantly hot at times. This is a good sign that you are using enough energy and elbow grease to really work the oil in where it should go. The warming of the oil and the stock by the hand will not serve any purposes of increased drying of the oil but it will show that you have your heart in your work.

Proceed to work over a small area at a time, using a few drops of oil over any given section. By concentrating on such small areas you will be sure that all sections are correctly covered. When the wood feels hot and more or less dry from the heat of rubbing it will indicate that the oil has been worked into the surface sufficiently. Then you may go on to another part. Repeat the rubbing process here and on all parts of the stock until the whole thing has had one bath of oil. *Then stop!* Do not go back and apply another shot just because the wood feels rather dry. You must now allow that first application to dry as hard as it is going to. And that is where the drying time test comes in. Allow the stock to set for as long as it took the oil film to dry on the glass plate, and then add 24 hours. You can then be pretty sure that almost complete oxidation has taken place and that the finish on the stock will not gum up on you when a good, hot spell of weather hits it.

Occasionally during this drying period it will not hurt a bit if you take the stock out of the rack and give it a good massage. It will help to work any still wet portions of the oil deeper into the wood.

When you figure the film is now dry repeat the first oiling procedure. A few drops at a time, remember, and a small working area will pay big dividends later on. This is the only positive method by which you can be sure that all parts of the stock have had equal amounts of oil applied and this oil equal opportunities for penetration.

You will find that the portions of the stock representing open grain (where you have applied a filler of some sort) will not seem to take a finish well. No matter what kind of filler you have used (unless it be an impermeable film of varnish or lacquer alone) the filler will seem to soak in some of the oil and will appear to be much flatter or duller than the surrounding wood. You need not be concerned about that condition. After you have applied enough oil coats the surface of the filler will accept the oil in the same manner that the wood itself does and the dull areas will disappear leaving a uniform appearing finish. When this point is reached you can figure that any succeeding oil coats you apply will be so much gravy. You can stop right there, if you wish. If time allows, however, it would be wise to add at least two more applications before polishing with rottenstone. This extra thickness of hardened oil will be so much insurance that constant handling of the wood does not wear the film away down to the surface which will then look like something the cat dragged in.

POLISHING THE OIL FINISH

After you have as much oil on the wood as you think will meet your needs or desires you should consider polishing the final finish. It could be and often is left in the condition it was when the last coat of oil dried, but polishing will tend to increase whatever doubtful lustre the finish may have had at that time. A well oxidized, polished, rubbed oil finish has something about it that has fascinated men from the time that this finish was first known and used. An old stock or piece of fine furniture which has seen the passage of a great number of years will have a beauty about it that it is impossible to achieve with the best of modern finishes. There is no doubt that a great deal of that sense of beauty emanates from the dignity of age which only age itself can bring forth, but there is also a depth and mellowness about such a finish that age alone is not responsible for. Undoubtedly this is due for the most part to the entirely completed oxidation and polymerization which the oil has undergone and which will give the film the property of taking on and holding a degree of soft lustre otherwise unobtainable. You will be able to approach such a lustre by the proper use of oil such as linseed (which is what the old masters used to a great extent in their oil rubbing).

The polishing of oil films is a very old and well known process and one which has not varied a great deal for many, many years. The substances used are precisely the same now as then and certainly the hand polishing which you will use was the only thing available in those days.

Obtain a piece of felt about a quarter of an inch thick. This may be purchased from some of the gunsmith suppliers around the country. It comes rather high in price, at first glance, but you can use a piece of it over and over again so that the end cost will be very little. When you have the piece of felt (about 3″ x 4″ is a good size) fasten it to some sort of a sanding block or even just a plain block of wood in such a manner that the whole one side of the block is covered. We do not want part of the block to hang over and maybe dig into the wood at a crucial point, so all sections of the rubbing face *must* be completely covered. You can glue the felt to this block, but if that is done be sure that you use a waterproof glue. The felt is at times dipped in water (depending upon your personal preference) and if this is done you must be sure that the block and the felt cover do not part company in the middle of a stroke which is the best way to ruin absolutely a good stock finish. If it makes you feel safer you can tack the felt to the rubbing block making sure that there is no chance for the heads of the tacks to come in contact with the stock while polishing.

The only abrasive substance which will be suitable for

the actual polishing operation is rottenstone. This may be purchased from nearly any paint dealer in half pound containers. A half pound of the stuff will last you from now 'til Hector, the pup, has great grandpuppies playing around under the kitchen stove. It is a dirty brown color and will feel soft between the fingers. This softness is due to the extremely fine granulation of the powder and to the form of the individual particles, but it will be sufficiently hard and abrasive enough to knock off the uppermost layer of oil and any irregularities (microscopic) thereon.

Spread out a thin layer of rottenstone in a cigar box or a saucer. It does not really matter how much you use and most of what you pour out will be eventually poured back again into the can with the rest of it. The saucer or box must be shallow and wide enough so that you can freely dip the rubbing block into the powder. When you have everything ready you can go to work.

There are two schools of thought at this juncture. Some say that the best way to work with the rottenstone is to have the rubbing block wet with water and the other school says that the best (though more messy) way is to use everything dry. Personally I have found that a wet block will transfer enough water to the abrasive to make it cake rather badly unless you use an excess of water. While it may do the job, the presence of a great deal (or even a little bit) of water on the stock will immediately attempt to work its way through the oil film and get into the wood. This will be no chore for the water if you have raw linseed oil on the wood. Therefore I prefer to put up with powdery dust than to take a chance that some of that water goes where it has no business going. Your stock is going to be hard put to shed moisture from the air without giving it the additional trial of a soaking in water before it even gets on the gun.

But whether you vote the wet or the dry ticket the polishing is done in the same manner. The block is dipped down into the rottenstone container so that a thin film of the abrasive adheres to the face of the felt. Then the block is applied to the stock just as you applied the oil. Rub lightly at first, always with the grain, and take a small area at a time. Even such a fine powder as we now have will leave some scratch marks if worked across the grain. Definitely do not rub in a circular motion. Always use long, even strokes and when you think that particular section of the stock is sufficiently rubbed then transfer to another section, continuing this until the stock has been covered from forend to butt. You will find that constant dipping of the block into the rottenstone to insure sufficient abrasive action is necessary. The time that it will take you to complete a stock is dependent upon the care which you use in polishing. Continue the operation until the smoothness and lustre of the finish does not seem to increase to any extent. When you have reached that point you are through.

It is possible to apply a machine buffing to the polished stock. This buffing should be done only by a fine, soft sheepskin buff as any other kind of material will readily scratch the oil film and you will be worse off than before you started the polishing. In buffing you may use a dry buff on the hand polished stock to bring out the last little bit of lustre. I would not apply abrasive to the stock and then the stock to the rapidly moving buff. This sort of thing can easily result in bad streaking. If you must use some rottenstone at this time apply a small amount mixed with paraffin oil or water to the face of the buff in a very thin coating. Work it well into the buff and allow the motor to spin it for a minute. This whirling will free the wheel from all excess material and what little is left will be enough to give the finish that final touch. I would not stand in direct line of wheel travel while it is spinning, though. Even a thin paste of water and rottenstone can sting you pretty badly if you get hit in the face with it. The stock should travel as much as possible in a motion paralleling the grain of the wood. This is to eliminate any possibility of cross grain scratching which even a sheepskin buff is capable of at times. Use the periphery of the wheel as much as possible, even on flat areas such as the face of the cheekpiece. The buff will flatten out under pressure so that it will not leave streaks where one polished area overlaps another.

When you have completed the machine polishing you should have a stock which leaves nothing to be desired. If you have done your part correctly you will be perfectly justified in feeling mighty darn proud of yourself.

VARIATIONS IN FORMULAE

While the average amateur will have little to work with other than genooyne raw linseed oil (of dubious quality) you can improve upon such a material considerably by the introduction of other substances. First of all make sure that your oil is the best that you can get. Secondly, be sure that you get real honest to goodness boiled oil (which really is not boiled at all) from a reputable dealer who carries quality goods. You will have two strikes against you from the start if even good quality raw oil is used. As far as I am concerned this stuff is not even in the picture. The drying time is ridiculous and even after it dries the presence of the foots will render it rather softer and more permeable than boiled or refined oils.

Formula #1

Boiled linseed oil	4 oz.
Tung oil (raw)	1 oz.
Turpentine	1½ oz.

Mix the linseed oil and the tung oil together. Then add the turpentine stirring well. Use in the standard manner rubbing in well with the palm of the hand until hot and dry. Continue the applications until a good film has been built up which does not flat out over filled pores and then polish with the rottenstone treatment.

The addition of the tung oil will increase the moisture resistance of the resulting film and give it greater durability. Such a small amount of tung oil will not be sufficient to cause a wrinkled, flat appearance.

The addition of the turpentine is for reasons of viscosity. Tung oil is a very heavy, viscous liquid and the addition of it to the already more or less viscous boiled oil will result in a mixture which will be rather difficult to work with. The presence of this solvent will also allow more penetration than ordinary. It will evaporate slowly. More coats of this mixture may be necessary than when using straight boiled oil because the turpentine constituent will leave the film upon evaporation and thus cause some shrinkage.

Formula #2

| Boiled linseed oil | 8 oz. |
| Burnt umber | 1 teaspoon |

Place the burnt umber in a saucer and pour into it a little of the oil. Stir the two together well making sure that no lumps remain. When the two are well mixed pour the oil-umber mixture into the remainder of the oil. Stir vigorously and use immediately for the umber will quickly settle to the bottom of the container. This is not a true solution but is what is called a suspension. This is because the particles of umber are only suspended in the oil and will settle out as quickly as the friction generated by the tremendously large surface area will allow. Most of it will be on the bottom of the can in a couple of days time.

The purpose of this formula is to add some color to the wood. The brown particles of umber will darken the wood, and that which collects in any open pores will accentuate those pores and thus apparently bring out the grain of the wood.

This mixture is used in the same manner as oil alone. The umber will necessitate no differences of application or handling. Unless a considerable number of coats of this mixture is applied, however, the darkening effect will not be apparent.

Formula #3

Boiled linseed oil	4 oz.
Turpentine	4 oz.
Beeswax (melted)	6 oz.

The beeswax is heated until it melts, then the heat is turned off. The linseed oil is added to the wax with vigorous stirring. If the oil is cold enough to solidify the wax it is permissible to preheat the oil to prevent this. As soon as all the oil is dissolved in the wax (or vice versa) the turpentine is added.

The resulting material will be a semi-solid mass. This type of finishing material is of doubtful value because the wax will allow little or no adhesion of the oil to the wood, and will prevent the oil from drying normally and in some cases from drying at all. I do not recommend this formula for use and included it only as a representative formula which is often seen from time to time and of which I have had inquiries.

For use the mixture is applied in the same manner as any other oil, that is, by taking some in the palm of the hand and rubbing vigorously. If desired it may be placed on a cloth for rubbing. The friction will heat the mixture sufficiently to allow a limited amount of penetration and a surface film may be very quickly built up by its use. As mentioned before, the presence of the wax will prevent efficient drying of the oil and the film will remain relatively soft for long periods of time. If such a waxed surface is desired I would prefer to build a base coat of drying oil alone and then wax the surface as mentioned under the chapter on waxes and polishes.

Formula #4

Boiled linseed oil	4 oz.
Ester gum solution	4 oz.

If you have available a source of supply of ester gum (such as a paint manufacturer or raw materials supplier) this formula may prove to be of interest.

The two liquids are mixed together with stirring and then applied in the standard manner. You will find that the ester gum will set up very quickly and that the overall drying time of the mixture may seem to be decreased tremendously, say to a few hours. Actually the linseed oil will not dry any faster, or as fast, as when used by itself, but the presence of the rosin derivative will mask most of the wet, tacky feeling of the unhardened oil.

This formula will give you more gloss than the other oil formulae but no increase in durability. Moisture resistance will be increased to a small extent. While the ester gum will be very brittle by itself the presence of the oil will plasticize it (reduce brittleness) and thus the two will help each other.

The ester gum solution may be unavailable to you in which case formula #5 will be your best bet.

Formula #5

Boiled linseed oil	4 oz.
Spar varnish	3 oz.

The two constituents are merely mixed together. Standard rubbing application, the same as for the other formulae, should be used.

The presence of the spar varnish will increase the water resistance of the final film to a great extent. Inasmuch as these varnishes normally are not brittle adhesion will be satisfactory. Excellent lustre will be obtained from the use of this mixture and resistance to handling will be much greater than that of oil used alone.

Personally I do not see the value in using drying oils with varnishes. If you wish the lustre of the varnish then use it alone as mentioned in the chapter on varnishes. Great lustre obtained from the use of such varnishes may easily be cut down by the use of abrasives and rubbing compounds.

The above formula may prove of greatest value when used in this manner: following the procedure for applying varnish finishes you will build up the base and finish coats with spar varnish alone. When you have sufficiently built up the surface then use formula #5 with the standard hand rubbing process. The presence of the varnish will provide maximum adhesion to the under coats and you will get the effect of the hand rubbed oil finish because of the presence of just such an oil finish.

SUITABILITY OF DRYING OIL FINISHES

In the light of information given concerning the varnishes, lacquers, and waxes the use of drying oils is not especially recommended.

As a top or additional film to cut down the lustre of some of the other materials it is okay. But for a protective coating by itself it lacks durability, moisture resistance, and building or filling qualities which are necessary to give a pleasing appearance to a finished stock.

I do not recommend the use of these items for stock work.

CLASSIFIED DRYING OILS LIST

True Drying Oils

Alfalfa seed oil
Afzelia seed oil
Arara nut oil
Bagilumbang oil
Black walnut oil (from *Juglans nigra* tree)
Cedar nut oil
Chia seed oil
Cockle burr oil
Croton seed oil (not Croton oil)
Dehydrated Castor oil
Funtumia seed oil
Grape seed oil
Gynocardia oil
Hemp seed oil
Japanese wood oil
Kentucky coffee nut seed oil
Kickxia seed oil
Lallemantia oil
Linseed oil
Lumbang (candlenut) oil
Manihot (Ceara Rubber) seed oil
Manketti nut oil
Mercuriales seed oils
Mexican rubber tree seed oil
Niger seed oil
Nsa-sana oil
Oiticica oil
Osage orange seed oil
Para rubber seed oil
Perilla oil
Pimento seed oil
Poli oil
Poppy seed oil
Po-Yoak seed oil
Rabbits' fruit (nut) oil
Safflower seed oil
Salvia sclarea seed oil
Soybean oil (Soya)
Stillingia oil
Tung (china wood) oil
Walnut oil (from *Juglans regia* tree)

CLASSIFIED DRYING OILS LIST
Semi-Drying Oils

Ajowan seed oil
Anise seed oil
Apricot kernel oil
Beechnut oil
Brazil nut oil
Bryony seed oil
Cantaloupe seed oil
Cape chestnut seed oil
Caraway seed oil
Carrot seed oil
Cayete oil
Celery seed oil
Ceratotheca sesamoides seed oil
Charlock oil
Chinese colza oil
Cherry kernel oil
Colocynth seed oil
Coriander seed oil
Corn oil
Cottonseed oil
Croton oil
Cumin seed oil
Curcas oil
Dill seed oil
Egyptian lettuce seed oil
Eruca sativa seed oil
Fennel seed oil
Garden chevril seed oil
German sesame (Cameline or Dodder) oil
Grape fruit seed oil
Hollyhock seed oil
Hubbard Squash seed oil

Ivory wood seed oil
Jamba oil
Jute seed oil
Lemon seed oil
Lime seed oil
Madia seed oil
Mlenda seed oil
Mustard seed oil
Narras seed oil
Oat oil
Orange seed oil
Parsley seed oil
Peach kernel oil
Pine nut oils
Plum kernel oil
Prickly Poppy seed oil
Princeps seed oil
Pumpkin seed oil
Radish seed oil
Rape (colza) oil
Ravison oil (Black Sea Rape)
Rice oil
Rye oil
Sativus oil
Senat seed oil
Sesame oil
Spurge nettle seed oil
Sunflower seed oil
Tomato seed oil
Unicorn (Devil's Claws) oil
Watermelon seed oil
Wheat oil

CLASSIFIED DRYING OILS LIST

Non-Drying Oils

Allanblackia seed fats
Almond oil
Andiroba (crabwood) oil
Apeiba (Burillo) oil
Atta (Owala bean) oil
Avocado oil
Bacury kernel oil
Baobab oil
Bayberry tallow
Bey bean butter
Borneo tallow
Cacao butter
Cashew nut oil
Castor oil, raw
Carpotoche oil
Cay-Cay fat
Chaulmoogra oil
Chinese vegetable tallow
Chufa oil
Crotalaria oil
Cupu seed oil
Da (Ambri hemp) seed oil
Dumoria oil
Ergot (Secale) oil
Gemsbok bean oil
Gorli seed oil
Hazel (Filbert) nut oil
Hydnocarput oils
Indian kapok oil
Inoy kernel oil
Kapok oil
Katio seed oil
Koeme (Jiconga) seed oil
Kurrajong oil

Laurel (Bay) oil
Locust (Carob bean) seed oil
Lupu seed oil
Macadamia (Queensland) nut oil
Macasser (Kussum) oil
Mafura oil
Mammy apple seed oil
Maroola nut oil
Niam (Meni) oil
Neem (Margosa) oil
Ochna Pulchra oil
Okra seed oil
Olive oil
Oncoba klainii (*caloncoba glauca*) seed oil
Oncoba welwitschii seed oil
Palm oil
Palm kernel oil
Peanut oil
Pecan nut oil
Pili nut oil
Pistachio nut oil
Pitjoeng (samaun) oil
Pongam (Hungay) oil
Pracaxy oil
Sequa oil
Shea nut oil
Soap tree oil
Spinosa oil
Sterculia oils
Tea seed oil
Ungnadia (Mexican budkeye) oil
Zachun (Hegli) seed oil

DEFINITION—DULL LONDON OIL FINISH

The Dull London Oil Finish is a term applied to a type of oil finish which has a certain beauty long sought after by gunstockers. This finish is seen only on some of the works of the old masters and refers primarily to stocks on firearms though I assume that it was at the same time used on furniture. It is supposed to have originated with some of the London gunmakers and, if you listen carefully, you will find that a great many of the boys today figure it is a lost art, one of the secrets of the ages, and so on and on.

Excuse me if I stick my neck out, but there has been so much loose talk around lately about the way to secure the Dull London Finish that I feel I am entitled to give my idea on the subject.

Take a fine piece of walnut. Smooth it well by rubbing with sand and a flat piece of bone. Stain it with logwood solution to darken it. Then rub in about fifteen coats of poor grade raw linseed oil with all the foots left in it. Rub it from time to time for the next one hundred years with some soft cloth. Place the name of a famous contemporary on it and arrange to have one of your descendants place it in a museum.

Thus and only thus can the genuine article be secured.

CHAPTER FIVE

Varnishes

I WONDER how many of you are familiar with varnish as it really is? Naturally, a lot of you think of it in terms of the glossy, glassy, shiny finish we all associate with the early, cheap, single shotgun. Actually this class of finishing materials is one of the best, if not the best, for our particular needs.

A great many of the boys who should really make it their business to know better will condemn a varnish-finished stock without looking at it or inquiring into the whys and wherefores of its use. It is varnish and that is all they have to know—"the hell with it." But why do the lads in the know quietly use it at times on some of the best stocks they turn out, even though they would not admit it to their best friend? Naturally, if the friend blabbed it around town the loud-mouthed opposition would jump all over the stocker and give him what-for for turning out such a poor piece of goods. (At least, they would think it was poor. The poor old gunsmith knows better but he cannot convince anyone else of it.)

The only way to let you see what I am talking about is to give you all the facts (not as I see them, but as some of the best authorities and scientific labs in the country have discovered).

Pigs is pigs, they say, but then there is a lot of difference if you will only look twice. I suspect that they have personalities of their own that sets each one apart from his pen pal, and it holds true with varnishes also.

Of course, it is only lately that that has been so.

HISTORY OF VARNISH

During the early era the Greeks and Romans used egg albumin, honey, and a few other items of lesser importance for binding their paints. They had no clear varnishes, as such, but incorporated pigment in all of their finishing materials. At that time wax and pitch were used for the bottoms of their ships, and what oils and resins were available were used more for the therapeutic effect than anything else.

Perhaps I should digress a moment and explain just what we mean when we talk about Varnish. Webster describes it as "a viscid, resinous liquid, used for giving a gloss to wood or metal work." Of course, that does not give the whole picture by a long shot. Most varnishes can be, and are, used to bind pigments or coloring matter to make what is known as Paint. Very simple—without color it is varnish, and with color it is paint. Of course, not all of the resinous clear liquids that are used to bind pigments are used by themselves as clear finishes. So, to clear things up as much as possible and to avoid any confusion with those of you that may be technically trained enough to call any pigment binder or paint vehicle a varnish, let me say that from here on in when I refer to varnish I refer to the liquid which is used by itself, without pigment, as a finishing material.

Known Oriental vehicles for paint and varnishes, were generally shellac, waxes, gum arabic, and tree saps in their fresh form. The closest thing they had to what we know today as varnish was the sap of the Varnish tree which the Japanese used for water-proofing drinking vessels and armor.

We know very little more about such substances until about the 11th Century when Theophilus, one of the more practical monks of that day, gave the first known description of an honest-to-goodness varnish. This formula of his is doggone close to what was in general use at the beginning of the 20th Century. It consisted of heating certain oil, or oils, with water and combining the resulting substance with certain natural resins. These resins were heated (or "run") before incorporating with the water-oil material. Very little attention was paid to this dreamer, evidently, for there is no record of his invention ever having been used during that period.

As near as can be determined, some of the finest violins of all time were finished in a special varnish consisting of linseed oil, Greek pitch (from the fir trees of Calabria), and pine resin all boiled until the whole mass was very thick and viscous. This was about the year 1564.

A few years earlier than this Cennino Cennini had described the "running" or heat treatment of rosin and sandarac, and mastic. These varnishes were to be used for armor and weapons, and were generally applied with a sponge.

It is believed that Jan van Eyck, a noted 15th Century artist, used either oil and resin varnishes as a base or glazed the finished painting with such a material. His works are remarkably durable, which would indicate his use of something entirely different from his contemporaries. These other boys, incidentally, generally used a base material of egg-white or albumin.

Cuyp and Rembrandt definitely employed such oil-resin varnishes containing amber resin.

Shortly after this time Alberti, of Magdeburg, described the use of thinners for oil-resin varnishes. The use of thinners had been entirely unknown up to this time.

Driers were used considerably, but were thought to be dehydrating agents, which we now know is false.

Inasmuch as all varnishes were manufactured by the individual for his own use their quantities were limited. The average size of a batch was about six ounces. These individuals also experimented considerably with different resins and oils, and the resins of greatest importance for them were dammar, kauri, copal, congo, east india, and amber.

A little after the Rennaissance the use of linseed oil in preparing rosin, amber, and sandarac varnishes increased. The use of thinners and driers was increasing and the bleaching of the oil to be used was done with water.

At this time the usual procedure in making varnish was to heat the natural resin to be used until it foamed up in the kettle. At this point the heat was removed. The heating was necessary to bring about certain chemical changes in the resin to make it soluble in the oil which was to be added later. After cooling the resins were dispersed in oil.

At the time of the American Revolution copals and amber were the principal resins used. They had been found to give the best results with the oils and equipment available in those days. The oils were linseed, walnut, hemp seed, and poppy seed. Turpentine was the principal thinner employed.

Watin, in 1773, first described the proper methods and procedures for the paint and varnish industry, and his book was the varnish makers standard text until about 1900. Between 1736 and 1900 his book was reprinted 14 times, and if the early boys did not have Watin's little treatise on the shelf they just were not in business.

About the year 1803 there were only five classes of varnish available: two spirit varnishes (resin dissolved in alcohol); one turpentine varnish; a soft copal varnish; and an oleoresinous varnish containing copal, amber, linseed oil, nut oil, poppyseed oil, and turpentine.

Up to the beginning of the 20th Century everything went along just as Watin said it should. Nobody knew just why things happened, but they did their best. They consulted their little black book because there was not anything or anyone else to consult. If something went wrong with the batch they fixed it by guess and by golly. If Grampa had used half a pound of cat's whiskers in such a situation they, too, went out and gave the grocer's cat a rough time of it.

MODERN VARNISHES

This sort of thing came to an end about 1910, however, when science stuck its nose into the picture. When this happened the little black book was doomed, and was destined to be hung alongside Sears-Roebuck's catalog in the old two-holer. (The same catalog that Grandma used the pages out of the gun section and Grandpa used the pages out of the latest fashions pages. And did they used to get mad at each other!)

Now, to get along with what we started on, the varnishes in which we are interested fall into several different classes. About the easiest way to clear up the whole thing is to start at the beginning and work down the list.

Probably the most basic breakdown that we can make is by method of hardening, or drying.

1) **Solvent release types:**
    Any material which is liquid and which sets up or dries by the evaporation of the thinner, or solvent only. These items are composed of resins (natural, mostly) merely dissolved in a volatile thinner. They are invariably fast hardening or drying. Good examples are shellac and lacquer.

2) **Oxidizing types:**
    Any liquid material which will absorb oxygen from the air and by doing so will condense into hard films. All drying oils such as linseed and tung are of this type. Some of the synthetic (man-made) resins are also of this type, such as alkyd resins.

3) **Polymerization types** (See Webster for pronunciation):
    This type of liquid will react with and within itself to form hard films. The reaction is extremely complicated but the easiest way to describe it is to liken the many small molecules composing it to a swarm of elephants in a circus. Nothing happens until the ring-master blows his whistle—this whistle blowing corresponds to the spreading of the liquid on the surface to be finished. Then the elephants in the yard all line up nose to tail with the trunk of one grasping the tail of the other, thus making a number of long chains. So, too, when the varnish is spread out in a thin film the innumerable small molecules connect or bind themselves together

nose to tail, so to speak, and thus form long chains or groups. This forming of the long chains from many small individual units changes the physical characteristics of the varnish and it now becomes hard and tough. Examples of this type material are many of the phenolic based varnishes.

Many modern formulations contain more than one of the above types of basic materials. They may contain all three types, but probably the majority of varnishes will be based on the oxidizing reaction, while the so-called spar varnishes for marine use will be almost exclusively of type Number 3.

SPIRIT VARNISH TYPES

Very often you hear the term Spirit Varnish. This will have a different meaning to you, depending on where you first heard it.

In Europe, resins cut or dissolved in alcohol or any other solvent without the presence of a drying oil will be termed a Spirit Varnish. But here in the United States resins cut in alcohol alone are known as Spirit Varnishes, and resins cut in any other solvent whatsoever are called Volatile Oil Varnishes.

Probably the most commonly known varnish resins met with in speaking of spirit varnishes are shellac, dammar, mastic, and sandarac. Of these four resins probably the best known clear finish is produced by shellac, followed closely by dammar films.

Dammar clears, or varnishes, dry rapidly, leave glossy surfaces and give moderately hard films. However, these films are not as brilliant as those of shellac or as durable as drying oil films.

Mastic resin, which comes from Chios, in the Aegean Sea, produces very soft films and is used primarily by artists to give lustre to paintings. It may at times be combined with dammar and other resins to give elasticity and toughness to the films.

Sandarac is completely dissolved in alcohol and is therefore sometimes mixed with shellac as it imparts toughness, hardness, elasticity, and great lustre. It was at one time used over brass and other bright metals to prevent tarnishing.

Shellac is a very versatile substance. It has been used for countless years as a finishing agent and well deserves the name it has built up for itself as an all-around varnish. It is the best known of all the spirit varnishes. It forms hard, waterproof films (I will bet I hear from a lot of you about that statement. But it is true, so help me) and has great lustre. In Chapter 7 on Shellac it will be taken up in greater detail and its application and handling covered.

Among the natural resins the following have been used extensively, but probably are not as well known to the average man.

Congo resin, one of the hardest of the natural resins, was not used extensively when first introduced. This was due to the insolubility of the resin in nearly all solvents then available. However, the correct method of heat processing was found and it then became one of the most valuable basic substances available. It was especially useful in varnishes containing quantities of drying oils.

The resin comes from Belgian Congo, whence it gets its name, and is collected by the natives. Inasmuch as it is a fossil material and is buried underground the natives collect it by digging immediately after the annual flood waters have receded, but before the ground has had a chance to harden.

This resin has been found to be greatly improved by the chemical process called Esterification, after which it has such improved properties that even the best synthetic resins science can produce have not displaced it for some interior finishing jobs. This improved material is called *Congo Ester Gum*.

Next to Congo resin the old timers used *boea resin* for their oil varnishes which they wanted to have good weather resistance.

This resin was sometimes known as Soluble Manila Chips.

Elemi is one of the softest resins available. It was until recently used extensively as a plasticizer in decorative coatings.

Kauri is another of the fossil resins which was looked upon with great favor by the early varnish makers. It could be run, or heat treated, and then incorporated with drying oils easily and gave varnishes which had good durability and were very elastic.

Pontianak is a semi-fossil which has been used considerably in true spirit varnishes, being soluble in alcohol and turpentine. It has been used also for oil varnishes in the past.

The East India resins (both Pale and Black) were commonly used in oil varnishes as the solvents that the early varnish makers had available to them would not ordinarily dissolve these resins.

The use of the above mentioned resins in either spirit varnishes or in oil varnishes is dying out, due to the extensive use by the industry of the newer synthetic resins. Shellac and Congo are still holding their own, however, and as yet science has found nothing that will supersede shellac satisfactorily. Many substitutes were introduced during the war, but none came up to shellac in all-around properties.

SYNTHETIC VARNISHES

The modern varnish maker has a host of synthetic, or man-made, resins available to him with which to work. They have such a variety of properties, depending upon how they are handled, that the formulator can literally pick the properties that he wants out of the air and discard the ones that he deems undesirable in his particular case. It may not be quite as easy as that but it comes mighty close to it.

There are thousands of varying formulae in use today, each one representing a slightly different end use, but in every case the basic material that is used will come from one or more of the following resins listed. They form the background upon which the paint and varnish industry of today is founded.

Obviously, to go into extreme detail concerning these resins would require somewhere in the neighborhood of two to three thousand pages, and would serve no useful end. Therefore, I shall try to limit the discussion to facts which are pertinent to the subject.

The following list includes every important resin used today by the industry. These resins are combined with varying amounts of drying oils, thinners and driers to form every varnish and oleoresinous paint vehicle on the market today.

1) **Pure alkyd resin (drying type):**

   Produced by chemically reacting certain organic acids or anhydrides with a special class of alcohols.

   The drying type contains certain amounts of drying oils, such as tung (china wood) oil, linseed oil, perilla oil, or oiticica oil. When large amounts of drying oils are present the resins are used in brushing finishes. Resins containing smaller amounts of the drying oils are used primarily for spraying application of baking enamels.

2) **Pure alkyd resin (non-drying type):**

   The same basic materials as above but which contain quantities of non-drying oils such as castor oil or cottonseed oil.

   They are used primarily in lacquers to produce elasticity and to reduce brittleness. This action is called Plasticizing and the material producing it called the Plasticizer.

3) **Rosin modified alkyds:**

   Alkyd resins containing amounts of rosin or rosin derivatives. This type usually contains small amounts of oils in addition to the modifying agent.

   The rosin constituent makes the resin set up or dry faster and harder, gives good gloss, and increases adhesion to whatever surface it is applied. However, the rosin will tend to make the film considerably less resistant to weathering, depending on how much rosin is present. The more rosin the less weather resistant the finished product will be.

This type of material is used mostly in gloss interior finishes, either with or without pigment, and in floor varnishes.

4) **Phenolated alkyds:**

Alkyd resins which are modified by (or contain) derivatives of the phenol family. The resulting product is very hard and will resist water and alkali very well. This resin is used in furniture and general purpose varnishes.

5) **Pure phenolics:**

Resins which are derived from the phenol family by reacting phenol and formaldehyde together. If made without modification of any sort the resulting resin is known as 100% phenolic.

The 100% phenolics are extremely weather resistant, and will have exceptional resistance to water, alkali, chemicals and alcohol.

This type of resin is used exclusively in the marine spar varnishes where high resistance to water and moisture is necessary.

Varnishes made with these resins will tend to yellow and darken upon prolonged exposure to strong light. This yellowing and darkening will not be severe and will be noticeable only when used over stock woods of a very light color.

6) **Modified phenolics:**

Phenolic resin containing percentages of various materials to lower the cost of manufacture when the exceptional properties of the pure phenolic varnish is not needed.

These resins are satisfactory for general interior use, such as floor varnishes, rubbing and polishing varnishes.

7) **Penta resins:**

Hard resins of the natural type chemically treated

with a substance called Pentaerythritol.

These resins give excellent drying properties to a varnish and have good water and alkali resistance. They are used mostly for furniture and general purpose varnishes.

8) **Ester gum:**

This is the trade name of a chemically treated rosin. This resin is a good general purpose material for interior varnishes and is sometimes used in lacquers. It does not have good resistance to weathering.

9) **Congo copal (fused, or heat treated):**

One of the natural fossil resins. This substance is heated to a point at which a chemical reaction takes place after which the resin is highly soluble in certain solvents and oils.

This resin gives good "depth" to varnishes, and is hard, tough, and has excellent gloss.

It is used primarily in rubbing and polishing varnishes.

10) **Congo copal ester (fused and esterified):**

The same resin as in #9, but which is, in addition, chemically treated.

This treated resin gives excellent gloss to varnishes, exceptional hardness, extreme toughness, and has good water and alcohol resistance. It has considerably improved properties over the untreated Congo but is used mostly in interior finishes.

Floor, rubbing and polishing varnishes are the principal end uses.

11) **Phenolated copal:**

Natural Congo copal resin which is combined with a percentage of phenolic resins.

This material has extreme hardness and good water alkali resistance.

Used primarily in rubbing and polishing varnishes.

12) **Coumarone-indene resin:**

Produced from compounds distilled from coal.

VARNISHES

It is inert toward water and moisture and has been used considerably in combination with beeswax, candelilla, carnauba and some of the synthetic waxes. Recently it has been used considerably in anti-fouling paints.

Some of these resins are what will compose the stuff that you get from the hardware store, Sears-Roebuck, Montgomery-Ward, or the local paint dealer when you go in and lay down some of your hard-earned shekels and get back a can marked "Varnish."

Varnishes are usually classified as Long Oil, Medium Oil, or Short Oil Length. This refers to the amount of oil that is present as compared to the amount of resin. The usual limits for each class are as follows:

Short oil length — 5 to 11 gallons of oil per 100 pounds dry resin
Medium oil length — 12 to 24 gallons of oil per 100 pounds dry resin
Long oil length — 25 to 50 gallons of oil per 100 pounds dry resin

Generally speaking, the more oil a varnish contains the softer and more elastic it will be after drying. Usually a greater amount of oil will produce higher water resistance also, but in the case of the pure, or 100%, phenolics a long oil varnish will be *less* water resistant than one with a smaller oil content.

SELECTION OF VARNISH TYPE

It is rather difficult to find out from either the dealer (who invariably does not know) or the manufacturer (who invariably will not tell) just what is in the particular can of stuff you get. However, unless you are very exacting in your requirements, or have a very special purpose for it, it will not make too much difference. The type of use for which your particular varnish is intended will be marked on the container.

It will probably say Spar Varnish, Marine Spar Varnish, Floor Varnish, or some other such designation.

The manufacturer will have used the best sources of information available to him which, in most cases, will have been his own technicians. He will have been able to determine just what the best materials are for the use marked on the can and then will have used those materials. You need not worry that the mixture will not live up to your expectations if you buy stuff from a reputable manufacturer and then use it correctly.

Of course, there is always some fellow around who makes up a company name on the spur of the moment, mixes the stuff in his garage (and he will not have any equipment to test the stuff to see how bad it usually is), and then peddles it. If you get stuck on some kind of a deal involving this type of junk then you have absolutely no chance of satisfaction.

Your best bet is to buy products of a well known company, whether it be large or small. Any reputable outfit will back their products to the hilt. If something goes wrong and it is traceable to you and not the product then, of course, you should not expect any consideration. But if the varnish itself is faulty then these outfits will bend over backwards to give you satisfaction. That will range anyplace from returning your money to giving you a new batch of stuff which they know is good.

Of course, as I mentioned before, if you slap some floor or woodwork gloss varnish on the storm windows and expect it to hang on for very long you are in for a disappointment. It just is not designed for that sort of treatment. Perhaps I had better say right now what I was going to save for a little later.

If you intend to use varnish for any exterior use, whether it be storm windows, the side porch floor or the garage doors you better get only the marine spar varnish type material. This stuff was designed for exterior use and it will really stand up to the elements. It is the same kind of finishing material that they put on the wood sections of the snappy station wagons which are so popular now.

However, even with this highly durable material you had better figure on revarnishing whatever the item is at least once every six months. That is about the longest that any manufacturer will guarantee a varnish to stay put and still be good looking. After that length of time, especially in very sunny climates, the lustre starts to fade out and the finish gets hazy. About that time it is looking pretty sad. If you catch it before it gets much farther than this all you need do is to throw on another coat of the same kind of varnish. But if you let it go so long that the varnish actually peels off the job then you have a situation which will call for considerable sanding. So to make it easier on yourself in the long run, when it starts to look bad, a few minutes will be enough to put the finish back into first class shape.

Let us say that you are at a point in your stock work where you figure you better start looking around for the stuff that you are finally going to use. So you traipse down to Uncle Ed's place. He carries rather a complete line of paint supplies so you figure you probably will have some choice in the matter. Looking up at the shelf you see that he has a goodly selection of cans marked Varnish. But getting them down where you can read the fine print on the label you find a myriad of uses on some of the cans, others will have only one or two uses listed. For general all around varnish you will do better with the kind that offers a broad field of use.

Some of the different names you may run into are exemplified by the following imaginary trade names found in my imaginary hardware store: Elias' Spar Varnish, Golden Oil Floor Varnish, Happy Days Rubbing Furniture Varnish, Pete's General Purpose Varnish, or maybe even Marine Spar Varnish.

Regardless of what the trade name is, the designated usages will be on the can in small print. Possibly it may read something like this for Elias' Spar Varnish: "This varnish is made from the finest materials obtainable. Specially selected oils and resins have been combined to produce the finest, purest, most durable product available. This Spar Varnish may be used on furniture, floors, woodwork, screens, storm doors, boats, garden tool handles, skiis, toboggans, and dog houses.

"This product need not be thinned, and should be applied with a clean brush.

"Will dry hard in four hours to a gleaming, hard surface."

That is a pretty good example of what you may find on a great many of the containers, depending on who makes it.

Or, if you buy the Marine Spar Varnish the directions may read somewhat as follows: "This Marine Spar Varnish is formulated to meet extreme weather conditions. Boats, storm sash, and any wood surface exposed to the weather will be protected perfectly if directions are followed.

"Three coats of this varnish should be applied.

"1st coat: Thin two to one with turpentine and allow to penetrate.

"2nd coat: Brush without thinning and allow to dry two days.

"3rd coat: Same as second coat.

"For best results the exposed object should be revarnished every six months."

You can use your own judgment as to what type of material to buy. It all depends on what use you are going to put the stock to, and also on what is available at the time.

The list of basic types of resins and their properties will be of little use to you at this stage of the game. This, of course, is because there is absolutely no way of your telling what product has any one or two particular materials in it. Probably you had better remember simply that if the object is to be used where any appreciable amount of weather can get at it you will be much better off with a strictly durable varnish, in which case you had better forget some of the properties that you had in mind for the ideal finishing material.

To elucidate, perhaps you thought that you would like to have the satin finish associated with a fine rubbing and polishing varnish. But in looking over the resins mentioned a page or so back, you see that the resins adapted for this type of finish are not recommended as having very great outdoor durability. And at the same time you think of the hunting trips you have planned and on which the rifle will be a constant companion. If you are very fortunate you will be able to be out in the woods or hills several months of the year, and some of that in the winter. (Not all of us are anywhere near this fortunate. Maybe we get one week each year for our little trips and that is all. And some of us do our hunting in front of the fireplace with a map, a book, and a gun cabinet as our equipment.)

Anyway, to get back to the lad who has more money and opportunity than 99% of the rest of us, he knows that his gun will have to take at least a little rough treatment, and considerable dousing with rain and snow before he gets home again. So he weighs the chances and wisely figures that he will do best with a finish on the stock that will really protect it, not just smile at his friends from the gun case. So he picks a good phenolic marine spar varnish that can really take it. And that varnish will, in all probability, be labeled Outside Spar Varnish, Marine Spar Varnish, or possibly 100% Phenolic Spar Varnish on the can.

The other side of the picture is the run-of-the-mill sportsman that at the most gets his one week vacation in the woods (and maybe half of that time will be on the road getting to his hunting grounds). The rest of the year will be spent polishing the stock, looking at it with loving eyes, and beyond all doubt slightly enlarging on his experiences to the rest of the lads who occasionally drop around in the evening for a glass of brew and a chance to enlarge on *their* experiences.

This dyed-in-the-wool sportsman will do just as well to pick one of the more delicate materials, such as the rubbing and polishing furniture types, or even the floor or general purpose spar varnishes. These items will protect very well for all of the moisture the wood will encounter (providing it does not stand year in, year out in a very damp basement without a dehydrating agent in the cabinet with it). There is no doubt that they will give a more beautiful finish than the phenolic types of marine spars. This rubbing and polishing type can be gone after in such a way that it shines like the old blue serge suit even in the crucial area after three years wear at the office.

After selecting the type of materials that you plan on using I would suggest that you take it down to the basement, open the can and swab some of the stuff on a clean, freshly sanded pine board. A test of this kind will let you become familiar with how it handles; is it thick and heavy or is it thin and runny; how quickly does it dry; how much does it tend to sink into the wood; and how hard is the resulting film after it has been allowed to set around for a day or so? All these items may seem minor at the time, but believe you me, brother, they will mean a lot later when you actually get around to using it on the refinished Enfield.

You may as well forget all about doing any stock work if you do not know how your varnish or lacquer or shellac is going to act. Become familiar with the materials. You can master them easily, but it is also a very easy matter to allow them to master you, and then you are sunk, but good.

VARNISHING THE GUNSTOCK

We will assume that you have gotten to a point where you are all ready to apply the finish. You have finished the actual preparation of the wood which will include the cutting and smoothing of the surface to the final shape desired, you have raised the grain as explained in Chapter 2 (and if you have not you may as well stop right here and go back to that information and study up on it. You will have neglected one of the very important steps and you will surely regret it sooner or later), and possibly you have stained and filled the wood also. If you want to use the finish coat itself as a filler you may do so and more power to you.

Again let me say that right now is the best time for that handy little moisture-stopper, the wood sealer. While I may be repeating myself it will be worth the effort you put forth to read it again. This step is just as important as raising the grain of the wood and may be more so! While the grain raising process is merely for sake of beauty and comfort, the use of the moisture-sealing or resisting preparation is vital to the non-warping characteristics of the finished stock.

Everything seems to be in order so let us go to it!

Open the can of varnish. Make sure that it is in good condition. There should be no "skin" or film hardened or formed on the surface, or in the process of formation around the rim of the can. If there is evidence of this condition take the stuff right back to the dealer. He will (or should) give you credit for the stuff (if he can see you have not used any of it out of the can and then let it stand around open for any length of time) or furnish you with another can. This time open it in the store in front of him. If his system of stock rotation is poor, or non-existent, this one will probably be in the same condition. In that case I would advise you to go elsewhere.

While we are on the subject let me say that it will probably pay you to get a small can of the stuff. If you buy a large size container and only use a small amount, the next time you open the can (which may be anywhere from two weeks to two years afterwards) it will probably be skinned over badly or even solidified entirely, right down to the bottom. If you have only a couple of stocks to finish the whole job will probably take not more than a few ounces of material from beginning to end.

Of course, if you do have a sizable stock business and must keep a goodly supply of your "special resin solution" on hand at all times then you would be perfectly justified in getting large amounts from the standpoint of economy if nothing else. In this case you can keep your material in first rate condition by getting a small quantity of fraction-sized cans at the same time you buy the varnish and transfer the liquid to the small containers. That stuff will keep almost indefinitely if kept from the air. *Keep the can full.*

Let us say you buy a gallon of Sooper-Dooper Marine Spar Varnish for your shop. You have twenty or so stock jobs lined up ahead of you but you know that it will take you a couple of months to do them because of the other jobs that come in such as blueing and sight mounting. You know that if you use the varnish from the gallon can by the time you are down to about the halfway mark in the can you will start getting small skins built up. Rather than risk this danger you buy 16 half-pint cans from the same dealer when you make your purchase. By transferring the gallon of liquid to the 16 half-pint cans (a half-pint is one sixteenth of a gallon or 8 liquid ounces measure) you have good, clean, fresh varnish to work with all the time.

Now that we have assured ourselves of first-class material we can go ahead with the work. You must make sure that you do not allow even the smallest amount of dust, dirt or other foreign matter to fall into the can of varnish as you work with it. It takes only an unbelievably small amount of such contamination to really louse up a job, and once a can has dirt in it the only possible salvation is to strain it all through a fine cotton strainer. And sometimes even that precaution will not remove all of the very tiny particles which will be present from there on in. If that proves to be true you may as well give the whole shebang to your father-in-law (unless you happen to like him) or use it to waterproof the legs on your bench, and they sure could use a coat of finish if they are like mine. If you find it necessary or desirable to strain the varnish then I would advise storing the strained material in a new, clean can. The old one will have some of the dirt left on the sides when you pour it out prior to the straining process.

VARNISHING EQUIPMENT

Next to the actual varnish itself the important items are the equipment with which you intend to apply the varnish. This will include brushes, rags or cloths, or spray outfit. Any or all of these should be as free from lint and dust as possible. Rags to be used during any part of the process should have been freshly washed and stored in a closed container or box to eliminate dust and dirt settling on them.

Brushes: The subject of brushes to be used is rather more inclusive. There are many different kinds of brushes, almost any of which will do. The average man may have two or three miscellaneous brushes around the basement left over from last summer when he painted the back porch. In most cases the brush will have been put into a can of synthetic paint thinner or turpentine to soften them and then forgotten altogether. Or if not forgotten then they were just plain neglected. These brushes will have hardened paint in the "heel" of the brush and they will invariably have bent bristles from resting on the bottom of the can for so long.

If you happen to run across this situation under *no* circumstances be tempted to wash the brush out and use it for delicate varnishing. The paint will *never* be completely removed from the brush, no matter how long you wash it or how thoroughly. There will always be tiny particles of this hardened paint present which will work its way into the varnish and will eventually show up on the varnished surface as tiny, highly unsightly bumps or bubbles. These bubbles cannot be removed short of washing off the entire coat of hardened resin and starting over. This working of foreign matter down into the bristles will be greatly expedited by the unfortunate habit of scraping or stroking the brush across the rim of the can each time you take up some varnish. (If you must do this then get another can to do your scraping into. In this manner you will prevent any of the old paint from being introduced into the full container of clean varnish. Of course, your stock job will probably still be ruined, but at least you will not ruin a full can of varnish at the same time.)

To get back to the actual brushes that may be available to you, they come in many different sizes and shapes. They did before the war, that is. I am not sure just what is available at the present time, but there is little doubt that you will have a satisfactory supply to choose from. The standard selection ranges about as follows: semi-oval, oval, and flat varnish brushes. Of course, you have the small, flat sash and bronzing brushes which may be used just as well. Most of the brushes which we could use will range from about an inch wide to three inches wide. I find that an ideal width is two inches, but even that is too wide for many spots and too narrow for others, such as on the wide open areas of the buttstock.

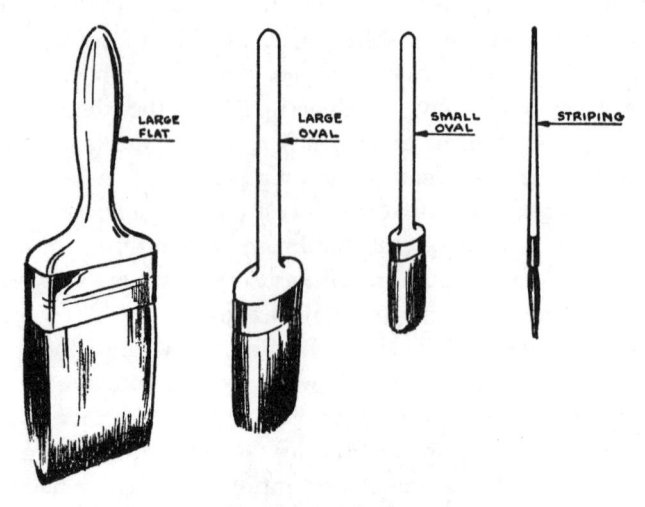

Varnish brush types

If I were to choose a selection of brushes for stock work I would list the following: oval varnish brush, size 2/0 (1 5/8" x 1 7/32"); oval varnish brush, size 12/0 (2 5/16" x 1 13/16"); oval sash brush, size 2 (1/2" x 1 1/32"); flat sash brush, 1" width; flat varnish brush, 2" width. The figures given for the oval type brushes are the approximate dimensions of the oval at the bristle ends.

Next to having clean equipment with which to work you must be certain that you do not pick up dirt and dust from the air, from the floor, from the bench and from the actual stock itself.

If you can possibly do so have a separate room in which you can do your stock finishing. Do nothing else in there, not even sanding between coats. Use it only for the application of the varnish or shellac or lacquer. Of course, with lacquer and shellac the drying time will be a matter of minutes so you do not have too much to worry about if the room is even reasonably clean.

But let us suppose you are like the rest of us. You have either a shop where innumerable other operations are being carried on at the same time that your stock work is being done, or maybe you have got the family basement to work in. There will always be a certain amount of dust floating in the air and it is this that you must guard against. As I said, the use of shellac, lacquer or any other rapid drying material will reduce the danger of a spoiled finish. But the use of a slow drying varnish will necessitate some precautions.

Be sure that the floor is well washed down (and dried) before varnishing. I would not sweep the floor, even with sweeping compound. I would wash it down with water. The sweeping would raise a tremendous amount of unseen and unsuspected dust particles which would float around in the air for days before settling. If you can wash the particles down the basement drain then you have saved yourself a lot of trouble. You should be sure that the floor has fairly well dried before attempting to work on the stock. The presence of any large quantities of moisture in the air will have an adverse effect on the drying and moisture resistant properties of the film, and a simple washing of the basement floor will liberate a great deal of moisture into the average sized basement, especially if the basement is warm.

Be sure that the rafters and beams supporting the ceiling are well brushed. A wet cloth on the end of a broom will take care of that pretty well. Of course, if you have your ceiling insulated or covered with one sort or another of ceiling tile or wall board you have nothing to worry about.

Make sure that your bench is clean and has been dusted with a damp rag. You do not want to raise a storm of dust just from the simple act of laying down a sheet of sandpaper or breathing hard on it.

Once you have these precautions pretty well taken care of you can go ahead and place your stock where you want to work on it. I invariably use a homemade checkering frame, fastening the stock between the centers with a rubber or composition pad or buffer to keep my forend tips from being marred by contact with wood or steel. There are many different designs given in the various books on gunsmithing, but they all work on the same general principle. A good example is illustrated, but you can use your own ideas in producing one.

There are two items in the way of equipment which should be investigated thoroughly by the professional or semi-professional. For the amateur who does maybe one stock a year they will probably be out of the question.

First, there are on the market several small electric sanders which cost in the neighborhood of $15.00. The majority of them are rotary types. That is, they employ a disc or wheel which revolves. They will be all right for buffing, but for sanding they are not too good. The reason for this is that they will leave very apparent marks because some of the sanding motion will be across the grain. To eliminate this cross grain marking the Dremel Moto-Tool people put out a reciprocating sander. This machine also costs about $15.00, but it sands in a back-and-forth manner just as in hand sanding. This machine is just what the doctor ordered for finish or fine sanding and I recommend it wholeheartedly. It is not sturdy enough to do extremely rough work, but for finish work it does the job. It may also be fitted with sheepskin pads for rubbing and polishing work.

The second piece of equipment may be made at home and is very useful. It consists of a cabinet or box with a heating source. A stock may be placed therein and the heat turned on. This will not only keep dust and dirt off the wet coating, but the heat will cause the coating to set up and harden or dry in a very short time. If the heat is controlled so that the temperature in the box remains at about 130°, varnishes may be hardened enough to be recoated in about an hour. Lacquer of course, will harden in this heat in about an hour or so, but for rubbing or sanding should remain about three hours more.

This box is further described in the chapter on equipment.

Once the stock has been placed in its holder, whether it is a checkering frame or some other type of holder, it should be touched and handled as little as possible (aside from the actual handling necessary in the finishing operations, of course). A single slip of the hand may easily put a fine scratch in the still-soft varnish, even after a drying time of 24 hours has elapsed, and a scratch of this sort is very difficult to cover so it will not be noticeable later on.

The stock should be well cleaned and dusted with a damp rag. Or if you want something easier to work with and immeasurably more efficient you can get a Tack Rag from your paint dealer. This tack rag is a piece of coarse cotton which has been saturated with a relatively non-drying varnish. After the cloth has been treated it is squeezed fairly dry and it is then ready for use. The purpose of the non-drying varnish is to pick up anything on the surface of the wood, whether it be lint, dust or dirt. The cloth is not wet or sticky enough to leave traces of impregnating varnish on the surface over which it is wiped, but it will be tacky or sticky enough to pick up these foreign particles and hold on to them. These rags will cost only a few cents, so little in fact that it is certainly not worth your while to bother trying to make them. The varnishes that will be available to you will be too fast drying and the homemade rag will stiffen or harden to such an extent that it will be useless after about 24 hours.

The tack rag will keep best between usings if you wrap it in waxed paper to keep the dust off it.

An additional extra precaution to avoid spoiling your primary supply of varnish would be to pour out a small amount of varnish into a clean dish or saucer. This is to insure that if you accidentally get something into the varnish supply from which you are working you can toss that away and use another saucerful without ruining your whole half-pint can. Pour out enough into the saucer so that you can be pretty sure it will last you through the whole session. One or two attempts will let you become very accurate in estimating just how much material will be required for any one coat. If you accidentally happen to pour out too much under no circumstances pour what remains back into the large can. There is too much danger of contaminating your primary supply with whatever may have fallen into the saucer in the course of the evenings work.

Application: In using a brush to work over the stock be sure that it is clean and dirt-free. Dip the bristles into the varnish allowing just enough to soak into the brush to saturate it about halfway up. Do not allow it to become so soaking wet that the liquid drips freely from the brush when it is withdrawn from the can. This will allow you to flow too much on the surface at any one spot and then you will be in trouble. If this excess is not worked out over a large area it will be too thick, or heavy, and then there will be great danger that one very thick spot will not dry hard or that you will produce "sags" if the surface is vertical before drying.

Flow the varnish onto the surface in a free, sweeping motion. Use long sweeps, the length of the area that you are going to cover with that brushful. Short, jerky movements will show laps when it dries and you may also possibly produce tiny bubbles from any suspended air bubbles that remain on the bristles.

When you feel that you have reached the limit that the brushful will cover then repeat the procedure. In blending one varnished area into another it is best to do most of your brushing from the area you are working on to the area you have already covered. This is to eliminate as many brush marks as possible. In some of the quick drying varnishes you will find that after about five minutes the varnish has already set up enough to be more or less tacky, rather than free flowing as it was when freshly applied. If you apply a brush to these tacky materials you will find that the bristles will leave

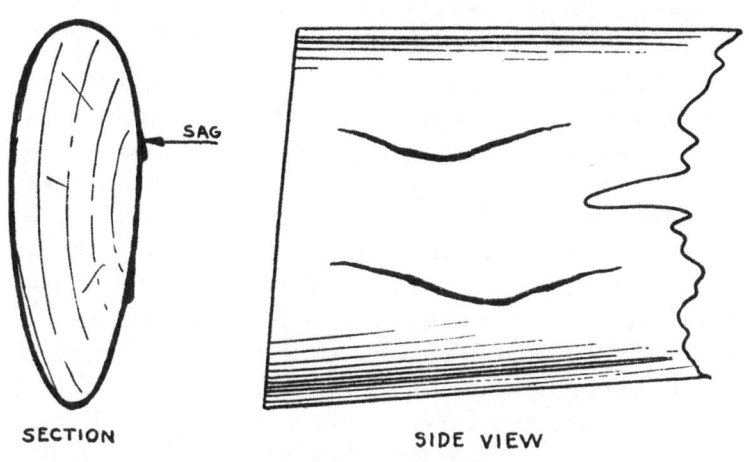

"Sags" on vertical surfaces

a definite mark that will never flow out of itself. The only way to eliminate these marks in that case is to sand carefully after the coat is dry, or to apply very carefully a thin coating of solvent, such as naphtha or turpentine (depending upon what thinners are recommended for thinning that varnish) and letting that solvent dissolve the partially dried varnish enough to flow out the surface at that point. All this is very risky, especially in working with the last couple of coats. The most practical way of circumventing these difficulties is to be careful in the first place so that it will not be necessary to touchup the bad spots later.

The principle that we wish to follow here is to allow the brush to act as a carrier for the varnish only, not a spreading medium. A little judicious handling of the brush will produce a fine surface.

It is best to apply the varnish in too-thin coats and use more of them. Of course, you cannot get your varnish too thin or it will be impossible to work with it and get any kind of a lustrous surface. Just enough varnish to cover the wood will be best, and this will be found by a few practice coats applied to a dummy blank, or even just a piece of scrap wood for which you have no other use.

Each coat must be done right. If you get a bad spot (and after a little practice you will be able to distinguish these bad spots as soon as you have made them) remedy that situation immediately before you apply any more liquid to the wood. Possibly the best way to take care of it would be to use a clean cloth and wipe that spot pretty well dry. Then go over it again, taking care to blend in the edges of the already varnished areas. Each blemish or imperfection will show through the dry coating, and in most cases will be greatly magnified. This is especially true of dust and air bubbles. If you let a bad spot go, either because you did not notice it or because you were too lazy to fix it right then you will have to go after it when it is dry. This will require sanding right down through the coat until the source of trouble is removed. Then you will have to take pains to build it up again on the next coat so that the very minute depression thus made in the finish coat does not show through. Any small spot caused by too much sanding will show up under reflected light as a shallow "valley." All these "valleys" must be eliminated one way or another. Of course, there is more than one way to skin a cat.

If you think you are really through and then inspect the stock very carefully, turning it this way and that under a strong light, and find a number of places where the shadow indicates you have done too much sanding you can fix that up by using your rubbing compound. With a coarse grit you can knock off the lustre and make the whole job into a lustreless, or satin, finish. With no fairly glossy surface to reflect light these low and high spots will not show up. After all, they will be in the neighborhood of one or two thousandths deep and with those kind of dimensions you sure will not be able to feel them.

That method I frown upon, as will any workman who takes pride in his work. It is a very sloppy way to achieve perfection and conscience, if nothing else, should be an important factor. If you have done a good job on the stock all the way along and then foul up the works like that it certainly will not be to your credit. Be careful and do not become too anxious at any point. A little undue haste here can spoil the finest job of restocking that was ever turned out. And the boys who have built themselves reputations certainly have not done it on those grounds.

Mistakes are bound to happen, that is for sure. But admit your mistakes and then try to correct them. You will have much more respect for yourself and your customers will have both respect and confidence in you. Naturally you do not have to point out your mistakes to anyone, but if they do happen and you are both qualified and willing to admit them and rectify them then you have nothing to worry about. You will do fine as an artisan.

If we can find our way back from this long-winded dissertation maybe we had better get along with the stock.

VARNISH AS A FILLER

At this point the question comes up about using the finishing varnish as a filling medium. I talked about it when discussing the subject of fillers and now some of the lads who took me at my word want to know how it is done. It seems that they are varnishing their stocks according to my ideas and they want to know what is going on. Their stocks look like the devil with all that open grain staring them in the face.

Now that you have already got a coat of varnish on the wood you have made a good start. Let that first coat dry good and hard for at least 24 hours. At that point the stock will look more or less beat up. Every tiny pore will be showing and there is certainly no semblance of filled grain at this point.

The idea is that you are going to use the varnish substance itself to do the filling. Instead of a doubtful, doughlike material we want to use something that we are sure will never crack open or fall out of the pores. The reason for using the varnish itself in such a role is that it will remain elastic (to a certain extent) and it definitely will have tremendous adhesion of coat upon the preceding coat. In fact, there is no process or treatment that I know of that will remove such a filling coat short of a bath in strong, hot lye. And even this will take some time to accomplish. Compare this with the easily removed filler preparations on the market. Those fillers may be knocked out of the wood by exposure to extreme sunlight over long periods of time. They may be removed by exposure to much moisture over the same long period of time, and there is no question that some of them (the oil and whiting variety) will actually prevent the top coats from adhering to the wood correctly.

By this time we will assume that the first coat has well hardened. Now take some of that old standby Wet-Or-Dry sandpaper of about 240 grit and dampen it well. Using a sanding block with a soft face (to avoid digging into the wood in case of slips) go after your varnish. Take that builtup coating right down to the wood, or maybe just a hair's breadth from it. Keep the sandpaper wet at all times. The water keeps the paper from clogging by washing the particles of wood and varnish away as they are released from the surface, it lubricates the surface and cools it, and it allows much faster removal of the material from the surface.

Be careful while you are sanding. Do not allow the sanding to proceed so fast that you dig down into the wood before you know it. We only want to remove the excess varnish which has hardened above the wood. If you have used a stain and that stain has not penetrated very far it is very easy to dig down past the stained area and then the unstained, light colored wood will show through. In that case you must do a job of restaining at that point.

Keep the stock wiped off with a rag while you are sanding. As you finish one section wipe it fairly dry before going on to another. We will admit that you have a good sealer in the wood and that should protect you against any of this water from getting down where it will do any damage, but there is no use in tempting fate. Get rid of that water as soon as you have no further need of it.

Allow the stock plenty of time to become perfectly dry after the sanding. It will turn white, or light colored, due to dust-like particles of varnish which have been torn off the surface and then lodged in the still open pores and in the sandpaper scratches. Remove this white dust with a clean cloth and then go over the stock again with your tack rag. This wood must be bone dry on the surface before it is safe to revarnish. Any water or moisture left on the wood will interfere with the drying of the following coat.

At this point the stock should have a myriad of glinting spots. These glinting spots are the pores which have had a thin layer of shiny varnish deposited in them and into which the sandpaper has been unable to reach.

Now repeat the varnishing process exactly as before. These first few coats will serve to fill the pores and crevices and bring the level of them up to the level of the surrounding wood. Very probably you will need to go through the varnishing-sanding procedure at least three times and possibly as many as five times before proper filling has been done. It all depends on how open grained your particular stock is and how deep the pores go. Naturally if your pores are only a half a thousandth deep you will need to put in less varnish to fill them up than if the pores extend downward for one or two thousandths.

Continue the filling and sanding operations until you find that upon sanding there are no glinting spots. This will indicate that you have brought the level of the varnish in all places up enough so that the sandpaper has been able to cut off the shiny surface. At this point you can start to work on the real finish.

The method of approach is the same now. You must be doubly careful, though, that you do not get sagging or dust bubbles. You will not be removing a great deal of varnish each time you sand from here on in. All that the sanding will accomplish now is to smooth up the surface and roughen it enough so that the succeeding coats will have good adhesion. Once the filling has been completed I find that 360 grit sandpaper is not too fine, and possibly 400 grit is better. The coarser the grit the more chance you will have to cut down deeply into the builtup coats. That is highly undesirable—it will only mean that you have to buildup these areas again. So take it easy at this stage of the game.

Once you have reached the point where you are actually building up the surface it is advisable to wait 36 hours after varnishing before sanding. The varnish must be very dry and very hard for best results. The harder it is the finer finish and polish it will take, and if you cover one coat of material before it is completely dry it will remain soft for a long, long time. Then, no matter how hard the top coat is, this very soft undercoat will tend to make the top coat rubbery.

It is even more important now to be sure that the surface is free from moisture before applying any more varnish. If you are really rushed for time you can use a gas flame, the same as in the whiskering operation. Of course, you must be extremely judicious in the use of such a device. The varnish will be fairly inflammable and you run the risk of charring the wood, especially at thin edges and corners. It would be much better to set the stock over or next to the hot air register in the living room for awhile (if the little woman does not object). Placing it in the sun will also be a very good way to dry it off quickly, but many of us must work on our guns at night and that would be out of the question. No matter what system you use be sure that you do not handle the stock any more than necessary. It will be very easy to scar badly at this point when the varnish has not completely hardened.

It is a matter of personal taste and judgment as to how many coats of varnish must be built up. I have found that the most durable coating will be not more than about fifteen thousandths thick. A heavier or thicker coat than this will be an invitation to chip readily. Probably the average thickness of coating which I apply on most of my stocks will run about ten thousandths of an inch and I have never had a stock chip or peel, even when run through a barbed-wire fence (I do not say it will not be scratched under those circumstances. It sure will—and how!) In terms of coats of brushed varnish I would say ten thousandths would be reached after about three to four coats. Naturally this will depend upon how much varnish is applied per coat. But for the average stock and the average brush hand I would say that, after you have filled the grain, four coats would be the desirable median.

Upon applying your last finishing coat let it dry for 48 hours. During this drying period you shall have to decide just what kind of finish you have in mind. From the standpoint of appearance, that is. Do you want a high gloss, a satin sheen, or a dull rubbed effect? This will probably depend on what you are going to do with the gun. If you figure on using it very much for hunting you will do better with a very dull effect. This will minimize the effect on the stock after being dragged through brush, snow, and maybe stepped on once or twice by some tangle-footed lunkhead in your party. Of course if it is strictly for show or even occasional trips to the range you will be just as happy with a satin type finish. This has all the class of a slinky movie-star draped in ermine and is not nearly as expensive.

RUBBING AND POLISHING

No matter how you want the finished product to look you are now at the crossroads where you must decide what direction you are going to take. If you decide on the high-gloss finish (which I do not particularly care for on any firearm) you are practically there right now. The only good thing that I can see about this high-gloss set-up is that it can be quickly made into the satin finish I mentioned above. That, brother, is the finish par excellence in my book!

Of course, this high-gloss finish is seen on the best furniture, but what the heck, you are not going to sit on the gun. When I speak of a high-gloss finish I am referring to the glassy smooth surface that will blind you if you look at it in the light. Cut down just a little, the lustre will still be up there fighting, but then it will resemble the fine hand rubbed radio cabinets and end tables for which they soak you up into the hundreds of dollars. As a matter of fact, that is exactly what it is—fine hand rubbed wood. The only difference is that you will not get a hundred bucks for it. Far from it! The guy that wanted it put on his pet smokepole will raise the roof if you ask him for more than about twenty bucks for the whole job, not including inletting.

Incidentally, this shiny, glassy finish of the non-rubbed finish is precisely what downed the lads on varnish in the first place. And a great many of them would not recognize a rubbed varnish finish as such if they saw it lying dead in the street. To them any glass-like, glinting surface has varnish on it. Without the glint it is not varnish.

I remember one of the first stocks I ever finished for anyone. I had a really good rubbed varnish finish on it and it looked like a million bucks, if I may say so. There was an overcritical lad who strayed in and saw it and he let me know that "that sure looks a lot better than those *"$%&# varnished stocks you had in here a while back. What have you got on that one, anyway?" At that point I casually mentioned something about a "special resin solution" and let it go at that.

Which reminds me—there is a swell out for you if you ever need it. Varnish is actually nothing but a solution of resin and oil, but who knows that besides you and me? The next time you have such a stock and do not dare admit it is varnish just tell the lads what I told the well meaning guy who liked what I had when he did not know what it was. I will lay you five to one that he would have turned his nose up at it if I had even mentioned the word varnish.

That is the way it is with everything, I guess. When they build up prejudices against something for Heaven's sake do not tell them they are wrong. You will get nothing for it but a punch in the nose. Give the rose another name and it will smell much sweeter to most of them. I am not advocating backing down from what you believe just because Joe does not like it. Far from it! But I do think that there could be a lot more tact used in many instances.

A RUBBED VARNISH FINISH

To get back to the lustre problem, this satin, rubbed finish is best achieved by using fine pumice stone (powdered) and water or rubbing oil. Pumice stone is the abrasive par excellence for rubbing. It has been used for many, many years either alone or in combination with other materials (as in prepared rubbing compounds). It is a natural stone which is pulverized and graded according to the size grit obtained from crushing. Different suppliers and manufacturers grade the product differently but the grits run about as follows:

        FFF grade—very fine
        FF
        F
        O
        I—coarse

The more Fs there are the finer will be the granulation. You will do best by consulting your paint supply store and actually getting samples of what he has to offer. At the same time you should investigate his supply of prepared rubbing compounds. They will give you the same effect that pumice will and you will not have to fool with the loose powder.

At any rate, whether you use the compound or pumice the

procedure will be precisely the same.

You should have a rubbing block to work with. You can use the sanding block by attaching a cover of quarter inch felt to the rubbing surface; if you do not have a block available then a plain pad of cotton cloth will serve the purpose. The felt or cloth pad is wet with water, or whatever rubbing lubricant you plan on using, and the surface of the varnish is also dampened with the lubricant. The purpose of the lubricant is to cool the surface, to wash away particles of varnish which will be removed from the surface, and to keep the rubbing pad from becoming badly clogged. If you wish you may use paraffin oil, linseed oil, sweet oil, or mineral oils. They have all been used very successfully. Or you can buy specially prepared rubbing oils which I think are not one bit better than any of the above.

After the pad and the varnish are dampened with the lubricant dip the pad into the powdered abrasive and, always rubbing in the direction of the grain, bear down fairly well at first. You should employ a more or less sliding motion in long sweeps, never short, jerky motions. Go over the whole surface, never staying in any one spot for any length of time and always traveling with the grain. Any cross grain motions you may make will be seen afterwards by a series of nasty scratches.

Dip the pad in the lubricant from time to time in order to wash away any caked abrasive and varnish which may have built up during the rubbing process. Never add new pumice or abrasive to an already rubbed area. This is because the pumice powder will grind itself smaller and finer during the rubbing and any new pumice added will show up as coarse scratches. If pumice is rubbed over any area long enough it will grind itself fine enough to give a polished effect. When moving over to a new area, however, you may add fresh pumice to the pad inasmuch as this area has not been worked over by the now finely ground abrasive and scratch marks cannot show up.

Leave the sludge or paste which forms from the rubbing on

the surface. This sludge will contain large quantities of extremely minute particles which will assist in polishing rather than cutting the varnish. When you have rubbed sufficiently this sludge should be removed by a clean cloth dampened with the lubricant you are using. The cloth is to be drawn over the surface in the direction of the grain, just as in the actual rubbing operations. Even now you can scratch the surface badly if careless about cross grain movements.

Inspect the surface carefully in a good light. Bring your eye down to the level of the wood and allow the light to strike the surface at a very flat angle. You will be able to tell just where you have missed proper attention to any places and where you have gone too deep. Scratches will show up as shadowed lines and insufficient rubbing will come out as glossy spots or areas. Then change your angle of inspection and look directly down at the wood from a vertical angle. Here is where you can tell best of all about spots missed completely. The high-gloss of such spots compared to the dull appearance of the rubbed areas will be immediately apparent. Go back over these glossy points with some of the finely powdered pumice on the ball of your finger. Make sure you do not take off enough to develop a definite low spot, but you must have all points equally dull.

When you have treated any such bad areas take a finer grade of pumice on the rubbing block and repeat the process over the whole stock. You must use each succeeding finer grade of abrasive to remove completely any and all scratch marks resulting from the preceding coarser grade. When you have achieved this uniform result you will be ready for a polishing operation.

THE FINAL POLISHING

The amount or degree of gloss or lustre you achieve in the polishing will depend entirely upon the roughness of the finish. That is, the fineness of the previously used pumice will determine just how smooth and glossy the final stock will appear. Obviously, if you have used a coarse grade of abrasive and thus scratched the varnish considerably (relatively speaking) no amount of polish and elbow grease will eliminate those bad scratches and the accompanying roughness of the surface. All polishes will do very little actual abrading of the surface. They are designed to clean up any particles and tiny points and edges which may remain from the pumice operations, but you could work for a month of Sundays without removing an appreciable amount of material from any surface with them. Of course, that will depend solely upon the constituents which go to make up the polish. If you happen to get one which contains pumice (though I know of no polish which does so) then you are going to get real honest cutting action. I know of none, however, which contains anything more harsh than rottenstone.

Rottenstone, another natural product like pumice but infinitely more fine and soft, has been the gunstocker's polishing agent for as long as books have been written on the subject. There is not one authority which has not gone on record as having recommended this material as the final polishing agent for stocks. There is every reason for these authorities to have done so. But I do not necessarily agree with all of them as to the state in which it should be applied. You can do a bit of experimenting yourself to determine how you like to use it, or you can use it in one of the concoctions given under the chapter on Polishes and Waxes.

I personally like to use it dry. It always seems to me to cake and become exceedingly gummy when using it with a wet felt rubbing pad. It has worked best for me by spreading some in the bottom of a cigar box or in a saucer. Then I take a piece of felt, about 2" x 3", place a piece of soft wood or even rubber behind the felt as a backing and dip the felt into the powdered rottenstone. A thin powdery layer of the abrasive will adhere to the felt and I then proceed to work over the stock, traveling with the grain at all times. While this material is exceedingly fine there is still a chance you may get some scratching if applied across the grain. The felt is redipped into the rottenstone from time to time whenever I think I am running out of it.

In this manner you will accumulate a considerable layer of powder over the checkering frame, bench, yourself and the surrounding area.

If you wish to do so you can use the polishing agent with either water or oil. The system is the same with both and consists primarily of impregnating your felt rubbing pad with the liquid you intend to use. Then spread the rottenstone on the pad by dipping the pad into the container of abrasive and coating it lightly. The rubbing and polishing procedure is precisely the same as given above. Always travel in straight lines and try to avoid a circular motion if possible. This circular motion will have the characteristics of a cross grain action and you will get scratching.

If you happen to have a polishing head or grinder in the shop (and there are not very many of us that do not) it might prove worth your while to invest in one or two sheepskin polishing buffs. These buffs are tops when it comes to applying the final polish to the finish. There are a few precautions to use, however. Do not use any of the pumice or coarse abrasives with a wheel of this type to cut down on the hand work. You will find that you will literally cut the finish to pieces if you do so. These buffs should be for the final polish *only*. Do the normal work up to and including a preliminary rottenstone polishing. Then place the stock against the buff and lightly run it to and fro, always in the lengthwise direction. Even this soft material will leave its marks on the finish. I would advise using only the outer inch and a half or two inches of the wheel. This narrow area of the wheel will give the same effect as a rubbing pad traveling lengthwise. If you do happen to get the stock down where nearly half the area of the wheel is working on it you will find that the forward half of the wheel will be running upwards and the rearward half running downwards and the combined vertical motions will give you the same effect as though you had rubbed the stock against the direction of grain travel.

If you are careful about using this narrow recommended rim of the wheel you can cut down the polishing time considerably, and in addition the final lustre will be much greater than if only hand work was done.

We will suppose, though, that you do not care for a high sheen on the stock. You can cut down on this by eliminating most of the rubbing with very fine pumice. A little experimenting will be necessary to determine just what you can get with what you have to work with. Certain varnish materials will take polishing easier than others and the type of varnish as well as the grade of powdered abrasive will determine the results. It is an easy matter to go from one degree of lustre to the other, though. If you find that you have overdone the polishing and the gloss is too high for your personal taste you can come back with a bit of coarser abrasive and cut down on that gloss. Or you can eliminate the polishing altogether. This polishing is what gives you that last bit of sheen. By stopping just short of where you would normally commence polishing, and instead merely give the stock a good rubbing with dry felt, you can achieve that very dull rubbed look in short order.

OIL RUBBING A VARNISHED STOCK

Maybe you want the old Dull London Oil Finish which has been so long admired and so seldom produced. This can be effected over the fine, durable varnish base by actually using oil. The big difficulty in the past has been that it took so doggone long for the oils that are normally used to dry (and they never did dry completely through) that 99 men out of 100 quit working on it long before they ever attained their goal. This merely means that they were not able to build up enough of a film on the wood to give them the effect that they were after. Well, we have that problem licked right now. We built up our primary film when we built up the varnish coating on the wood. All we need do now is to take it from there.

Once you have gotten this builtup varnish base take a boiled linseed oil (you will notice that I never recommend raw oil for anything for which reasons see the chapter on drying oils) and spread a little on the stock. Then, using the palm of your hand, really go after it. Rub as hard as you can and as fast as you can. Spread the oil completely over the stock in a very thin film until that film is so warm and thin that it seems almost dry. You will not need more than about ten drops of the oil to completely cover the stock. Set the stock away in a fairly warm place for 36 hours, or until the oil seems to have completely dried. You can tell this point as the oil will remain tacky or sticky while unoxidized. As long as the stock has the least little bit of stickiness to it forget about putting any more oil on it. You can rub it from time to time while it is still wet but that is all.

When the oil has dried examine the stock. It will not have taken on the appearance you want, but it will be a start. Go after it again with another treatment of the boiled oil, rubbing hard and fast all the time. It will take about three treatments to give you what you are after. You will find, however, that the stock takes on the rich, rubbed appearance of the true Dull London Oil Finish that no other treatment will bring out. When your final coat of oil has been applied and has hardened well you can then polish with the rottenstone and felt.

FRENCH POLISHING A VARNISHED STOCK

I see that I have neglected you boys who were interested in the application of the varnish by the French Polish method. The general principles are the same, except that you substitute a cloth rubbing pad for the varnish brush. Incidentally, I would apply my filling coats of varnish with a brush to get the greatest filling effect in the shortest period of time. After you have filled the pores then you can change over to the rubbing pad.

Your rubbing pad will consist of a piece of clean, freshly washed cotton cloth, about eight inches square. Fold it over in half one way and then in half the other way so that you have a pad about four inches square. Into this is placed a wad of cotton batting, enough so that when it is compressed with the fingers it will be about the size of a walnut.

Saturate the cotton batting with varnish, thinned down if you like, and squeeze out most of the varnish against the sides of the can. Then place the cotton wad into the center of the folded cotton pad and bring up the sides in your fingers. You will now have a small cloth bag, in the center of which is the varnish-impregnated cotton wad. The varnish will immediately begin to seep through the cloth and by lightly running the bag over the surface of the wood a thin, uniform coating of varnish will adhere. When the bag seems to become dry a light pressure with the fingers will squeeze more liquid out onto the surface where it can be spread around. You will find that this method of application will give considerably thinner films than by brushing. Consequently, the films will dry much more quickly and harder than corresponding brushed films. However, the fact that the films are so thin will require more coats and therefore more time.

You will eliminate danger of brush marks, but by careless handling of the bag with too much varnish applied to the wood you can get the same bad effect. Therefore, you must be very careful that you do not allow the cotton wad to be placed into the cotton bag while dripping wet. This will allow too rapid emergence of the liquid and consequent heavy coatings in spots.

The main advantage of this French Polish method of application is that it allows application of extremely thin films which will harden better and faster and therefore will tend to increase adhesion of one coat to another. The fast drying time will also decrease the danger of trapping lint and dust from the air in the sticky film.

No matter how you put the varnish on the wood, the method

of polishing is the same. Just be a little more careful with this last method. The chances are that your film will not be any too thick and it is very easy to cut right through the varnish down into the wood, especially on corners and edges.

VARNISHING WITH A SPRAY GUN

For those of you who intend to use a spray gun or an air brush the very same rules apply. The important thing for you fellows is to remember that on such an odd-shaped object as a gunstock it is very easy to get too much on in any one spot. That applies particularly to the corners and sharp curves of the cheekpiece, or the grip. The material to be sprayed will have been thinned down or reduced considerably in order to get it to work well through the gun and therefore you can possibly develop overloaded areas before you know it. But you will sure know it after they develop! They will start to sag and run like all git-out and there is not a thing in the world you can do to stop it. Nothing, that is, except to remove the entire coat you have just applied and start over. If you try to clean off that one heavy area and spot it in later you are out of luck. With varnish that is one thing that cannot be done very well. You would be better off to wait until it hardened and then go after it with sandpaper.

HOT APPLICATION

There is one little system that was developed during the war which I think is well worth looking into. That is the method of Hot Application of varnish (and lacquers, too). The problem on many fast moving production lines was to get efficient application of protective coatings on many items, aircraft included. With the normal method of operations the coatings were applied in several stages, allowing one to dry before another was applied. This took time and space. It was found that heating the liquid coating materials would make them thin enough in body to be used in the spray apparatus and therefore would reduce the amount of thinners required in the paint or varnish. By reducing the amount of thinners the time required for the coating to dry was cut way down, and at the same time it was found that more actual paint was applied to the surface.

We can do the same thing, even with brushing, by heating the varnish or lacquer to about 200° Fahrenheit or so and then quickly applying to the stock. The easiest way (and only way for the great many of us with no special equipment) is to place the finishing material (unthinned) in a beaker or metal can over a shielded flame. The flame must be shielded because the liquids that we are going to use are extremely inflammable and will flash at the drop of a hat. The hotter the liquid is the more of the volatile thinner is released and the temperatures we shall have to employ are way up above the flash points of any of the materials (except the resins themselves) that will be present.

I would recommend a hot plate (electric) every time. Even with that type of heat source you may occasionally get a flash fire, but the danger is much less than if you used an open flame such as a Bunsen burner or gas plate. However, whichever heat source you use, be it electric or gas, you should use a sheet of asbestos, thin sheet iron or other shield at least a foot square to prevent the fumes liberated from the hot varnish from drifting down into the flame and flashing back to the liquid source. Of course, even though the can should flash into flame it would not be highly disastrous. It will scare the living daylights out of you when it lets go with a resounding *poof* but quickly placing a cover of some sort over the can will immediately smother the fire. Have such a cover handy. Invariably the little woman will wander downstairs at this point in search of something she has forgotten and you then catch Holy Ned for smoking up the place. Other than that there is no particular disadvantage from trying this little trick.

On the advantage side of the ledger you will find that the varnish applied by this hot method will dry much more

VARNISHES

quickly, will collect less dust from the air and will allow the job to be done in less time than normally by building up the film much more quickly.

Assuming you want to take a flier at this Hot method we will assume that you have your little can of stuff stewing over the protected heat source. It will be moving around in the can

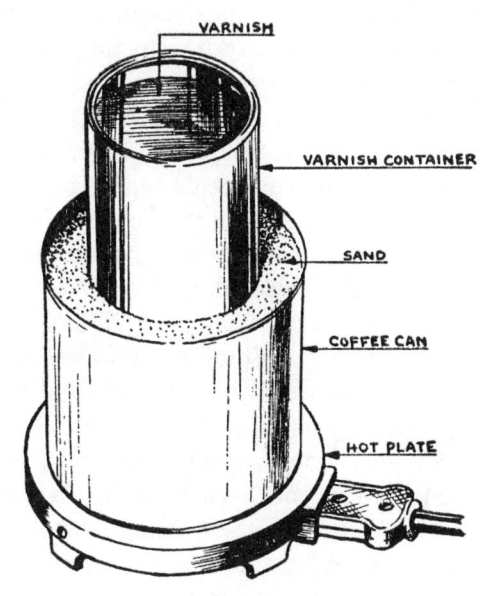

Hot application equipment

in slow swirls and maybe even bubbling the slightest little bit. After you get it as hot as you think you want, take a stick or blade and check the apparent viscosity by dipping the blade down into the varnish and lifting it up free from the surface. Observe how thin the liquid seems. If it is rather heavy, or flows from the blade in a more or less slow stream then continue the heating. You are not at the point yet where you will get any advantage from the heat. Allow it to simmer until it reaches a point where the liquid flows from the blade like water, or nearly so and then shut the heat off. The can of varnish will retain the heat long enough for you to work with it. You do not want to overheat it as every second the heat is on, it is driving thinners from the varnish. A little thinner loss goes a long way. If you lose too much thinners by evaporation the varnish will get too thick to pour when cold.

Dip the brush into the hot varnish and quickly flow it onto the surface of the wood. You must work fast as the varnish will cool very quickly when exposed to the cold wood. You will have very little time to do much rebrushing so use long, quick strokes of the brush. It will be to your advantage to use too little varnish at each dipping of the brush. If you use too much at one time you will run the danger of building up very heavy coats in spots and these heavy coats will not harden properly. Thin coats will allow you to brush over laps without them showing in the dried film.

This Hot system was really designed for use with a spray gun. The same general principles are followed as in normal spraying with reduced varnish but the heat will allow you to spray without reducing or thinning and here the advantage comes in. As explained above, you will be able to apply more solid varnish constituents per coat of finish. When you have completed one sprayed coat then change cups and spray a very thin "mist" coat of pure thinner over the freshly applied varnish. This thinner will tend to make the surface flow out and to promote great lustre of the hardened film. Be sure that you do not put on so much thinner that it actually reduces the varnish and starts to sag or run.

HUMIDITY WHEN VARNISHING

There is one point which I think should be emphasized again and again in wood finishing. That is the warning concerning the application of finishing agents, whether they be varnishes, lacquers or shellac, in atmospheres containing large amounts of moisture.

The actual amount of moisture which may be present and still allow satisfactory finishing depends a great deal upon the type of materials that are being used. No figures or statistics are available but a few general ideas might well be given.

If the little woman has just finished the week's washing and has the basement full of wet stuff that flaps against the back of your neck every time you look up from what you are doing then I would advise you not to proceed with any stock finishing that evening. You can polish or rub all you want, but I sure would not advise throwing any varnish or lacquer on the stock at that time. Or maybe you have a couple of rifles you just blued an hour or so before and you figure you will put another coat on the stock before quitting for the night. If you have open tanks for your boiling (or even closed tanks for the hot dip process) I would forget about it for awhile. I have had the basement, and even the kitchen upstairs, full of steam from my tanks and it would be plumb death on a finish to put on any at a time like that.

The reason for all the hullabaloo is that shellac, varnish and lacquers are sensitive to water and moisture while in the liquid state. With too much moisture deposited in and on the semi-dry material that same moisture will react with the constituents in the material and cause the finish to dry unsatisfactorily, or if it will dry at all it will be deficient in water resistance, gloss, and a few other minor properties. In the case of lacquer this excess moisture will usually cause blushing, or whitening of the film. In the case of shellac the water resistance will be lowered excessively.

About the most that can be said in the way of explicit warning concerning moisture content is that if the relative humidity is high enough that the air feels muggy, especially in summer, I would wait until the humidity drops. You will not have too much trouble during the winter and fall as long as the air temperature is high enough to be comfortable without a sweater.

Another very important point is never to mix different types or makes of varnishes, especially phenolic spar varnishes, with other types or makes. In many cases the resins in the one kind will not be completely soluble in the thinners of the other and you have what is called "throw-out." The resin that is not completely soluble will precipitate out of the solution, sometimes taking a period of several days to complete the process, and you will end up with a slimy, jelly-like mass in the bottom of the can. In this case you may as well throw the whole mess out and start over, this time not mixing the liquids together. If you are ever in doubt as to just what kind of material it is that you have in that unmarked can on the shelf do not take a chance and toss it in with some good varnish just because you do not want to waste it. The chances are it will mix all right, but there is also a good chance that it will not and the entire can will be ruined.

Certain types will be apparently soluble in other types and will mix well. But come back in a few days and take a look! You will find that the resin has slowly worked its way out of solution and is now settled on the bottom of the can.

SELECTION OF FINISHING VARNISHES

It is very certain that you will not be able to determine what varnish has which resin in it nor will you be able to ask the supplier for varnish containing alkyd, phenolic, or ester gum resins. He will not know and the manufacturer will not tell.

Therefore, for any particular finishing job I would make a choice of varnish types as follows:

If available, buy what is called a Synthetic Clear Enamel for a finish to give good wear resistance and excellent lustre. This may usually contain an alkyd resin which is the most desirable for general work. It will not be as water resistant as the phenolic varnish.

For finishes which are to take a maximum of wear and tear and water soaking buy the marine spar varnishes. These will contain the 100% or pure phenolic resins. The varnish will not rub or polish as well as the alkyd-containing Clear Enamel, but will give somewhat more protection under rough usage.

VARNISHES

For finishes to give beauty alone with no particular thought for abrasion or weather resistance any of the rubbing varnishes will do.

TIME OF APPLICATION OF VARNISH FILMS

The time that it takes for a stock to be completely finished in varnish will vary with the system used. The schedule given below is tentative but fairly accurate.

Non-Professional

Application of filler	— 30 minutes
Drying of filler	— 18 hours
Application of varnish	— 10 minutes
Drying of varnish	— 20 hours (minimum)
Sanding of varnish	— 15 minutes
Application of varnish	— 10 minutes
Drying of varnish	— 20 hours
Sanding of varnish	— 15 minutes
Rubbing and polishing	— 30 minutes

Total — 59 hours, 50 minutes

The above schedule is based upon using a filler and two coats of varnish. If filler is eliminated and varnish is used for the filler then an additional three coats should be figured.

Professional
(complete tools and facilities)

Application of filler	— 5 minutes (spray gun)
Drying of filler	— 3 hours (drying cabinet)
Application of varnish	— 2 minutes (spray gun)
Drying of varnish	— 1 hour (drying cabinet)
Sanding of varnish	— 5 minutes (electric sander)
Application of varnish	— 2 minutes
Drying of varnish	— 1 hour
Sanding of varnish	— 5 minutes
Rubbing and polishing	— 15 minutes (electric buffer)

Total — 5 hours, 34 minutes

FINISHING FAULTS

No matter how careful we think we are there are times when the job goes bad and we cannot figure it out. There are hundreds of reasons for bad results, but the following list may give you a hint if you are ever in a bad spot.

Wrinkling of Varnish: This fault will take the form of a very fine puckering or many fine waves or folds on the surface.

It is caused mostly by having too heavy a coat of material which dries too quickly. It may be brought about by very hot weather, humid atmospheres, wax or oil on the surface before varnishing or too much drier in the varnish. Some of the boys add Japan drier to everything they use just on general principles. This practise should be discouraged. In nearly every case where drier is added by the user this extra drier will be in excess of what the resin solution will tolerate and wrinkling will then occur. The manufacturer has put in what has been scientifically determined as the most efficient amounts of driers and unless the varnish has been kicking around in the garage or basement for three or four years that amount will be sufficient to bring about proper drying.

Wrinkling may also be caused by applying a coat of finishing material before the preceding coat was completely hard and dry.

Sagging or Running: This is invariably caused by applying too much of the liquid to a surface in a vertical position, or one which is later placed in a vertical position before the varnish has hardened to any extent.

Bumpy, Seedy, or Sandy Surface: If the varnish used is too cold it may develop this appearance. It can be brought about by having the varnish stored in an outside place at freezing or near-freezing temperatures. If this is the case the only resort is to strain it through fine cloth after bringing the temperature up to normal. If the "seeds" are very tiny, and they will be in most cases, you may not be able to remove them entirely. In this case you had better throw that stuff out and plan on keeping your new supply in a warmer spot.

The seeds or bumps are most often produced by allowing the varnish to become contaminated with dirt and dust from the air or from having a dirty brush dipped into it. Straining will nearly always remove this type of "seed."

It is possible that the varnish left the factory in this seedy condition. If you are sure that you have not allowed dirt to enter the can and that it has not been stored in very low temperatures then possibly the paint dealer from whom you purchased the varnish will allow you credit on that can.

Pitting and Pinholing: This fault is most often seen when using a spray gun. It is caused by moisture from the air or from water or oil in the air lines.

Sticky, Non-Drying Film: This may be found when wax or mineral oil remains on the uncleaned surface of the wood. It may also be caused by extremely high humidity and low air temperatures. Wrinkling may accompany this effect.

Very few completely non-drying films will be encountered. Usually the trouble will be confined to a very slow, long drawn out period which may extend over several days.

Alligatoring: This fault takes the form of deep, wide checks or cracks. It is caused primarily by applying a finish coat over an incompletely dried undercoat.

Checking: Similar to alligatoring but not so severe. The causes are the same.

Curtains: Another name applied to sagging or running. See Sagging.

Flatting (Flattening): A fault wherein the film loses its lustre or gloss upon drying. It may be caused by excessive moisture in the air, by application of a coat over an incompletely dried undercoat or by oil and wax on the surface over which the varnish is applied.

Sweating: A streaked appearance to the surface. Usually appears only on varnish coats which have been rubbed or polished. It is caused by rubbing or polishing before the varnish is completely dried. The remedy is to allow a longer drying time before polishing.

CHAPTER SIX

Lacquers

THE word lacquer today, especially in the countries where modern industry has gained a foothold, is a more or less standard name for a more or less standard substance.

It was much less so a definite designation in the past, however.

HISTORY OF LACQUER

The word lacquer originally referred to certain natural products used by the Orientals and to varnishes composed of solutions or cuts of resinous materials in volatile solvents. The very early Chinese and Japanese had a material that they called lacquer, but which was produced basically from the sap of a tree similar to the Varnish tree, *Rhus vernicifera*. This sap was put through an elaborate process to produce a compound which was used extensively to decorate their personal objects of art. There is no doubt that they used it for other objects, but the workmanship which must be put on a finishing operation was so painstaking and so time consuming that the common things would have gotten only a lick and a promise.

This lacquer substance dried slowly and hardened best in a cold, damp, dark atmosphere. Some of the more precious pieces which were to be done in this manner required a period of years to complete the job.

As the knowledge of effectively finishing and decorating objects traveled westward, more and more substances were found and used and a great many of them picked up the title of lacquer along the way.

The European conception of lacquer for a great many years was a shellac base material applied with the addition of heat.

As a matter of fact, the name lacquer is derived from the Hindustani name *"lakh"* whence shellac also gets its name.

Just what the difference is between shellac varnish and shellac lacquer is a moot point, but I rather suspect that the method of application, rather than the substance itself, differentiates between them.

COMPOSITION

Up to the early 1900s there was still a class of finishing materials which were termed lacquers and which certainly did not resemble each other in properties, other than that they would all dry to a hard film under certain circumstances. However, in America and Europe the word came to mean the so-called pyroxylin finishes late in the 19th Century. They were basically solutions of nitrocellulose in volatile solvents with the addition of camphor at times. The introduction of this pyroxylin, or nitrocellulose, gave us what we know today as lacquer.

These early solutions were made from primarily the same things that our present day lacquers are composed of, except that then they were in the very early stages of development and a great deal of work had to be done to overcome the serious shortcomings which then characterized them.

Nitrocellulose is a chemical combination of the atmospheric gas, nitrogen, and the building block of the universe, Cellulose. This cellulose is what composes all vegetable fiber. Cotton, wood, fibrous vegetable matter (such as the stalks of plants) and paper are common examples.

Cotton linters, the source of the cellulose in this case, is cleaned and then introduced into a mixture of sulphuric and nitric acids. The nitric acid (source of the nitrogen) combines chemically with the cellulose and the resulting substance is called nitrocellulose, or nitrocotton. This material is then well washed, carefully dried and held for further processing. At this point the nitrocellulose looks just about the same as the original cotton linters before nitrating. But what a chemical difference! Just touch a match to it and see what happens. It disappears before your eyes. The reason is that the chemical reaction with the acid has introduced nitrogen which combines with the cellulose in a very unstable bond. The presence of a flame, or even just plain jarring, will cause the combination to break the unstable bond so quickly that what is termed an explosion takes place. If the material is unconfined then only a flash of burning results. In fact, the burning is so fast that you cannot see it. Now it is there—now it is not. However, if the nitrocotton is confined then a true explosion takes place and in most cases whatever is confining the substances will be blown to bits. It is for this reason that dry nitrocellulose is extremely dangerous to handle or even to have in storage. The presence of moisture on the surface of the fibers will greatly reduce the tendency of the material to react and it is invariably shipped and stored wet for the sake of safety.

To make pyroxylin this nitrated cotton is dissolved in a very special mixture of organic solvents. In this form it is not dangerous, though it will still burn furiously if exposed to a flame. It will not explode from shock, however. The early celluloids were made from just this material, with the addition of camphor. Maybe you will remember how the old camera films and celluloid collars would burn if you put a match to them.

To make lacquers of this stuff the early lacquer formulators used the same process that they did for making the stiff collars, but they added enough solvents to produce a solution. The resulting film was exceedingly hard, very brittle, and took a great many coats to build up any kind of a surface. The reason for so many coats was that when you got enough nitrocotton in solution to make an appreciable film upon drying, the solution was so thick and heavy bodied that it could not be sprayed or even brushed. And if they thinned it enough to spray or brush then there was not enough solid material left to give a good film in a few coats.

They played around with the problem for a period of years, finding an answer or two from time to time. Eventually they discovered a way to allow enough cotton to be dissolved so that a good film could be built up quickly and still be thin enough in solution so that it could be sprayed.

Today the lacquers contain, besides the nitrocellulose, materials which will allow the film to remain hard, yet flexible. These agents which produce flexibility are called Plasticizers. They are composed for the most part of non-drying substances such as castor oil, dibutyl phthalate, triglycerly phosphate and some of the modified alkyd resins. When such alkyd resins are used as plasticizers the resulting film has the properties of both a lacquer and a type of varnish. Present formulations contain an increasing amount of alkyd resins modified, or combined, with coconut oil or semi-drying oil fatty acids.

Along with the cotton and the plasticizers certain resins are added to improve adhesion and other properties. Many modern formulae may contain several kinds of nitrocotton, resin, plasticizers, solvents and thinners.

SOLVENTS AND THINNERS

Of course, one of the most important constituents in the modern lacquer is the solvent and thinners. These materials allow the lacquer to remain in solution, but when spread out on a surface they will evaporate very quickly and leave the solid mass behind to form a film. As issued, the normal lacquer, whether clear or colored, has a percentage of very fast thinners in it. These fast thinners will evaporate so quickly that the film will form and harden well in a matter of 15 or 20 minutes, in most cases. These solvents and thinners are very much more volatile than any used in any varnish found today. The exception to this statement will be in the case of the so-called shellac varnishes. These shellac varnishes contain alcohol which will also evaporate in about the same length of time.

While we are on the subject perhaps it would be advisable to clear up the situation with a description of the field of lacquer thinners and solvents.

All the way through the chapter you will notice that I have differentiated between thinners and solvents. I have done that for a very good reason. Principally because the two are separate materials. In the case of varnishes almost anything you can thin them with will actually dissolve them and so the two words can be used there interchangeably. But in the case of lacquers some materials can be used to thin the liquid without actually acting as a true solvent. Confusing, but true.

Lacquer thinners are liquids which are used to reduce the viscosity or body of lacquers. Lacquer solvents are liquids which are used to actually dissolve the basic nitrocellulose in order to make a solution of it.

If you ever had any lacquer around the house or shop which you tried to thin down or reduce with turpentine or any other varnish thinner you will know the grief that can be caused by using the wrong thinners. Almost without exception the can of lacquer which a moment before was a heavy bodied, smooth mixture is now a mass (or mess) of tiny threadlike particles which under no circumstances will stir back into the smooth mixture it once was.

This is because the nitrocellulose component in the lacquer is not soluble (will not dissolve) in the hydrocarbon type varnish and enamel thinner you have no doubt used. Incidentally, all varnish and enamel thinners will be of this lacquer-insoluble type. The second that the thinner hit the lacquer it "threw out" as it is called. It is precisely the same thing that happens when you get too much water in shellac varnishes. The shellac resin is not soluble in the water and the presence of the water precipitates the resin.

The principal material that the nitrocellulose will dissolve in is a type called an ester. Lacquers will also dissolve as well in ketones (of which acetone is a good example). Therefore, the True Solvents for lacquers will be of the ester and ketone types. Invariably these solvents will be water clear, pungent, aromatic liquids. Their main role is to dissolve the nitrocellulose and to hold it in solution.

Differing chemically from the esters and the ketones we also use what is called a Latent Solvent in the lacquers. The latent solvent usually is one of the family of alcohols, or possibly even more than one may be used in any given formula depending upon what properties the lacquer is desired to have. The latent solvent has no direct solvent power upon the nitrocellulose. In the presence of some of the true solvents (esters or ketones), however, these alcohols will take on the property of allowing more nitrocellulose to be dissolved than the true solvents alone will permit. Thus the presence of a latent solvent will permit more actual solid material to be present in the lacquer. Also, the latent solvents may be an active solvent for whatever resins or gums are included in the formulation.

The last component in the mixture will be the Diluent. This diluent is very generally a kind of hydrocarbon (varnish type) thinner which, while definitely not capable of dissolving the nitrocellulose, will help to give workability to the film, will help to lower the cost of the finished lacquer by replacing some of the more expensive true solvents, and in many cases where lifting or softening of a previously applied film is undesirable it will tend to prevent this lifting or softening effect.

While the latent solvent types of liquids will be tolerated to a considerable extent in a lacquer the diluent materials must be closely regulated. If the percentage of the diluents is too high then the nitrocellulose will precipitate out of solution entirely. This is precisely what happens when enamel or varnish thinner is added to lacquers by mistake. The amount of hydrocarbon type thinners will then be considerably more than the limits which the nitrocotton will permit and the entire nitrocotton content will "throw out."

In formulating the complicated combination of different types of thinners and solvents for a satisfactory mixture many factors must be taken into consideration. The formulator must consider cost; if he uses a very large percentage of ketones and esters (true solvents) which impart high solvent power to the mixture then the cost of the mixture will be prohibitive. He must consider rate of overall evaporation; if the solvents all evaporate too fast moisture will be condensed from the air into the still wet lacquer film and "blushing" will result. He must consider amount and type of diluent; if he uses too much and they are slow evaporating then the more quickly evaporating true solvents and latent solvents will leave the film first and the nitrocellulose will then precipitate out in the resulting high percentage of hydrocarbon thinners in which it is insoluble.

It generally does not pay to attempt to make your own lacquer thinners. Unless you have a proven formula to work from you are just looking for trouble and usually find it!

The following formula I have found very successful in converting a normal spraying type lacquer to a brushing type material. Nearly every lacquer on the market today has been formulated for application by means of a spray gun. Of course, you can buy brushing lacquers but you are very limited in choice of materials, especially if you wish a colored lacquer for some particular job. Some slight changes may be made in this formula but, unless you are an experienced lacquer technician, I would not advise fooling very much with this combination.

Formula #1

Ethyl Cellosolve	10 parts by volume
Normal Butyl Alcohol	15 " " "
Toluol	15 " " "
Xylol	40 " " "
Normal Butyl Acetate	20 " " "

This thinner should be added to your lacquer until the lacquer is about the same viscosity as a good brushing enamel or varnish. Inasmuch as many lacquers differ in viscosity from each other there may be a difference in amount of thinning or reduction required one from the other. But there is no question that they all will require a goodly amount of the thinner to bring the heavy bodied mixture down to where it will brush easily. Possibly you may even have to add enough thinner to make a 1 : 1 mixture of the thinner and the lacquer, and sometimes even more will be required. A little experimentation is the only way to determine proper amounts in a case like this.

VISCOSITY

As with the varnishes, probably the only way you will be able to determine relative viscosities will be by means of a stick or knife blade dipped into the lacquer. When the lacquer runs off the blade at about the same rate that a brushing varnish does then you can consider that the viscosities are nearly the same. Let me warn you, though, that it is tricky trying to work it out this way. Be very alert. In cold weather, especially, and with fairly heavy bodied materials it is sometimes difficult to differentiate between medium and heavy viscosities.

For those of you that may be extensively equipped, or even for those of you that may have a speaking acquaintance with the owner of an auto refinishing shop there may be available to you the well-known #4 Ford Viscosity cup. It is a copper, cup-like affair that measures viscosities by measuring the length of time it takes a given amount of paint to flow through a standard sized opening. I do not think many of you will be interested in buying one, though—the usual price for this piece of laboratory equipment is about $95.00.

Further on in the book, under Miscellaneous, is a diagram for a homemade viscosity cup that will take only a few minutes to make and will cost only about eight cents. If any of you intend to work very much with finishing materials I would certainly advise you to make up such an item. Detailed instructions are given with the diagram as to the use of this cup.

Incidentally, turpentine is sometimes used in lacquer thinners. I definitely would not advise using it alone to thin a solution. As a matter of fact, I would stay away from it entirely unless it happens to appear in a published formula or is present in a prepared thinner you may purchase through a reputable dealer.

One more thing about terminology. It is perfectly acceptable to use the word thinner when speaking of a prepared mixture of solvents to be used to reduce lacquers. However, when speaking of any one specific liquid such as Ethyl Cellosolve or acetone the term generally used is solvent, latent solvent or diluent as the case may be for that particular item's properties.

Most lacquers, whether they be clear or colored (pigmented) will dry fairly hard within a few minutes, as opposed to varnishes which take hours to dry. Some lacquers will harden to a usable point about 20 minutes after application. At this time it will be satisfactory to rub or polish the film, if desired, or to apply another top coat. As a rule, however, lacquers should be allowed to stand for 18 hours before rubbing to be sure that all of the thinner has escaped.

EQUIPMENT

Invariably in the factories where it is used as a finishing material lacquer is applied by means of a spray gun. This is the easiest, fastest and most satisfactory method of application available.

Many of us cannot afford the equipment necessary to utilize this means, however. When you think that at today's prices a spray gun alone will cost from $17.00 up, and the compressor and motor about another $75.00, even for a small outfit, you will realize why the average man is entirely ignorant of the possibilities of this type of equipment.

When I first figured I needed something of this sort I went down to Sears-Roebuck and looked around. Surely they would have something in my class (which at that time was limited to about a maximum of $30.00). But I turned right around and came home. So I looked around for what I could pick up to make. (Go ahead, call me a cheapskate. If you ain't got the dough you just ain't got it, Brother, and that is all.) Eventually I located a secondhand refrigerator compressor that my brother-in-law had stashed away in the basement. I traded an old bike my wife had before we were married (and which he wanted for his little girl) for the compressor, put another five bucks in a secondhand ¼-horse motor and I was practically in business! Then I shopped around and located what must have been the first model spray gun DeVilbiss ever put out. It is certainly an antique and it looks like it has been in a wreck but how it does put out the paint! It is the cat's pajamas for putting paint on the screens and the back fence, and for finishing a few stocks now and then it cannot be beat. Incidentally, the gun cost me two bucks. Eight feet of air line and a safety valve for the air tank set me back another three dollars and I was all set.

Of course, the compressor will not give me enough air volume to operate a larger gun (maybe I get a couple cubic feet of air a minute) and I have to keep down below 40 pounds air pressure or I think I will blow the head off the little air tank I have, but I only paid $15.00 for the whole works. It works fine if I use my head and do not get my varnish or lacquer too heavy bodied.

If any of you can locate such a refrigerator compressor you can make a fine little outfit for home work. Sure, you will not be able to go into the automobile refinishing business, maybe, but you will have more than enough equipment to do anything you will ever need to whether it be painting the screens or working over a stock.

Before I got my spray gun I fiddled around with some brass I had in my junk box under the bench and made a fairly decent little gun. It is certainly crude and to stop it from spraying you either had to lift it out of the paint container or shut off the compressor motor. That could be easily fixed by some of you bright lads who like to tinker. The accompanying sketch should give you the general idea, though you may have to fool around a little to get your air and material openings precisely as you find they work best. Incidentally, the smaller you make your openings the less volume of air and air pressure you will require to make the gun work well.

I understand that you can do about the same thing with an old vacuum cleaner blower. I have never tried this, and I would think that the pressures developed by such a piece of equipment would be so small as to be worthless, but I pass the suggestion on to you for what it is worth.

Just one other suggestion. Somebody once told me that you could spray satisfactorily with a Flit gun. Never tried this myself, either, but when you are in need of something you will try anything. Personally I would think that it would work out okay if you are sure that the varnish or lacquer is well thinned. Maybe I will look into it as a matter of information the next time the wife is away from home.

To get back to methods of application, if you just cannot manage to make or buy any kind of spraying setup the next bet is to resort to the brush. This will present a few problems and take a little looking into. There are many people who will tell you that it cannot be done and still have a decent job result. Well it can, but you must regulate the solvents in the lacquer to do it right.

BRUSHING THINNERS

Formula #1 that I gave a few pages ago will be a fine starting point for you in converting a spraying lacquer to a brushing type. As I mentioned then you must experiment a little to determine just how much of this reducing thinner will be needed for your particular make of lacquer. Add the thinner slowly, a little at a time, stirring well all the time.

Occasionally check the viscosity with the stick or homemade viscosity cup to see that you have not gone beyond the limits that you set for yourself. If you happen to reduce the lacquer too much you will find that it will go on the stock like water and will run all over the place, leaving you with many unsightly sags and runs.

The purpose of using the given formula is to introduce slowly evaporating thinners into the lacquer so that it will not harden

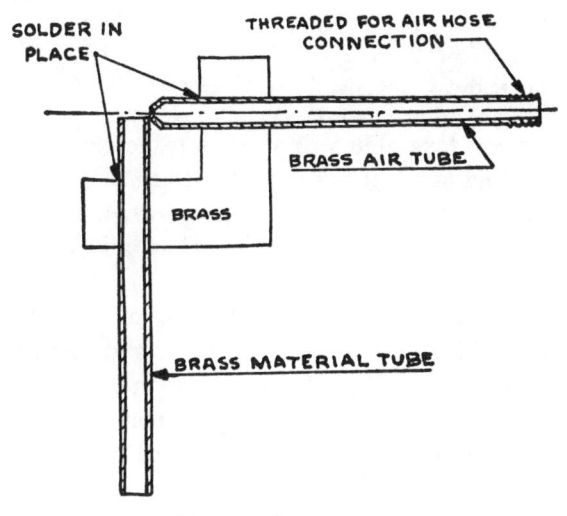

Homemade spray gun

up before you have time to brush it out correctly. Reduction, or thinning, with a normal lacquer thinner will give you such a fast evaporating liquid that you will be unable to do a good job of brushing.

In case, for some reason, you find that you do not like the first brushing type thinner formula given, here are others that you can try. They are all based upon the same principle—the introduction of slowly evaporating thinners into the lacquer so that it will dry slowly.

Formula #2

Normal Butyl Alcohol	15 parts by volume
Xylol	35 " " "
Normal Butyl Acetate	35 " " "
Butyl Cellosolve	15 " " "

Formula #3

Butyl Cellosolve	10 parts by volume
Normal Butyl Alcohol	20 " " "
Toluol	20 " " "
Xylol	10 " " "
Isopropyl Acetate	30 " " "
Normal Butyl Acetate	10 " " "

Any of these formulae will work satisfactorily if they are made according to the formula and not just slopped together. Be as careful in this as you are of any other detail in your finishing work and you will have very few failures.

When working with a lacquer reducer remember that the more thinners, especially the slow ones, that you have the longer it will take the lacquer to dry and the more time you will have to work with it. But you must also remember the very important point that the more thinners you have in the lacquer the thinner the dried film will be, thus necessitating more coats.

FINISHING LACQUERS

In the field of finishing lacquers you will find several types available. There are alcohol proof lacquers which I would advise most wholeheartedly. You can never tell when you are going to spill something containing alcohol on the stock of your pet firestick. Many so-called powder solvents contain alcohol or substances allied to them chemically, and they sure can raise Old Ned with a beautiful finish. Sometimes a little beer or White Lightning will soften the surface enough to allow fingerprints to be permanently placed therein. Naturally none of you would have any of the stuff around, but there is no telling when the other guy might be carrying some in his canteen—it is amazing the bad company you can get into unknowingly!

Besides the regular gloss type finishing materials on the market there are certain Semi-Gloss or Satin finish lacquers for sale. They are merely the regular gloss type materials which have had added to them stearates, or sometimes inert pigments to cut down on the gloss of the hardened film. They are excellent for many types of work and I would advise your trying one or two of them if you so desire. They might just be what you are looking for to cut out some of that laborious hand rubbing so often mentioned in these pages. Personally, I prefer to do my own flatting or gloss reducing by means of the pumice or rubbing compounds. This way you can choose your own poison and if you do not like what you finally get you can come back with a little polishing and bring the gloss right back to where it was in the first place.

But that is a matter for personal taste. A little experimenting never hurt anyone and in most cases will give experience which can be gotten in no other way.

SANDING SEALERS

You will find mentioned at various times throughout this book a material called lacquer sanding sealer. While not misnamed, this item may very readily be confused by the average wood finisher with the varnish type sealer, also mentioned throughout the book. The properties of the two materials are entirely different as is the designated end use.

Primarily, the varnish type sealer is formulated and used in such a manner as to permit deep penetration into the pores of the wood and prevent the passage of moisture whereas the sanding sealer made from a lacquer base is used to fill the pores of the wood *on the surface only* and thus to build up a smooth even surface which may be readily and quickly finished. As you can see from this, the lacquer sanding sealer acts more as a filler than anything else. In fact, that is precisely what the original formulator had in mind. These two materials will be called either a varnish sealer or a lacquer sanding sealer wherever referred to and it would be well to keep the distinctions in mind in order to avoid confusion and, at times, actual disaster which is what will take place if one is used where the other is specified.

Allow me to elucidate on this last statement. Let us assume that you have used a varnish sealer on a stock where the lacquer sanding sealer was intended. What will happen? Generally this—inasmuch as the average lacquer sanding sealer will harden within 20 to 30 minutes to a point where it may be coated, or recoated, with a lacquer finishing material and you have allowed this much time for the *varnish sealer* to dry (remember, you have made a mistake and used a varnish sealer where the lacquer sanding sealer was intended) you go ahead and either spray or brush on your desired finishing coat of lacquer. As soon as the solvents and thinners in the lacquer mixture hit the still wet varnish sealer (though it may have penetrated so well that the surface *appears* dry) these solvents will immediately tend to dissolve and swell the varnish which is present. The swelling will allow the varnish to loosen its hold upon the wood and when the film is dry it will have extremely poor adhesion to the wood, if any at all. This is because the base coat of varnish has no hold on the wood (due to the swelling and loosening) and it will never refasten itself to any extent, even when dry. Many times the swelling, or lifting, will be so severe that it will appear on the surface of the lacquer film and will look like areas of wrinkling or crinkling. If you ever see this on your stock you may as well prepare to remove the entire finish right down to the bare wood for you have done something mighty wrong somewhere along the line. Even if you think you may be able to cover up this fault by sanding slightly or rubbing you will never be able to repair the damage caused by the lacquer solvents swelling the still soft undercoats of varnish.

Maybe poor adhesion does not mean anything to you when

you hear it mentioned. Well, allow me to say that the subject of adhesion is one of the basic principles upon which the whole field of wood finishing is based. No matter what protective agent you may use over your wood it will be of absolutely no value to you if it does not stay where it belongs. The finest paint in the world will not stop any moisture if it is lying in a fragmentary heap at the bottom of whatever it was supposed to protect.

Now that we have lightly touched upon the case of the use of varnish sealers where lacquer sanding sealers should have been used let us look at the other side of the picture.

Here we will assume that you are using a lacquer sanding sealer where the instructions called for a varnish sealer. Inasmuch as the lacquer based item is nearly as thin as the varnish sealer should be you may not suspect a thing for awhile. After the film has had a chance to harden, however, you will find that you have your open grain and pores nicely filled and now you will not have to use that filler you were thinking of. Surprised, aren't you? But let us also suppose that you are going to use this rifle in lots of nice wet, rainy weather and had counted on the varnish sealer to buckle down and repel all that moisture which will undoubtedly try to seep into the wood over a period of time. Surprise again! When you have used the rifle for a few weeks in such weather you notice that you cannot keep the blamed thing shooting straight. Your zero is gone with the wind and every change in the weather from stormy to sunny makes the dratted barrel shoot to a different spot. Maybe you do not suspect it, but the whole thing is brought about by the finish allowing excessive moisture to creep into the wood and warp the stock. This warping will, of course, be greatly accentuated by having curly grain in the forend, or grain which runs off at an angle to the bore, especially if the angle is horizontal. When such wood warps it will bear harder against one side or the other of the barrel and force it to shoot to one side in direct proportion to the amount that the warped wood pushes against it. In dry weather the wood may be allowed to relax a bit and thus allow the barrel to return toward the true zero line (in relation to the sights). Thus more moisture in the air will make the barrel shoot wide of the point on which the sights are aligned and a drier atmosphere will shift the point of impact back toward the place it should be. This shifting around will play the devil when any long shots are required and it causes more otherwise good match rifles to be looked at askance than you can shake a stick at.

This whole nasty situation could have been easily corrected in the first place by reading the full name and designation of the particular item you are using to see if you have the right thing or only think you have the right thing.

MOISTURE RESISTANCE OF LACQUERS

While we are on the subject of moisture let us take a look at the whole field of lacquers. Lacquers, no matter what their composition, are not famous for their resistance to the passage of moisture. By themselves they are relatively permeable and it is only in conjunction with other products that they would be safe to use where extremely adverse weather conditions are to be expected.

Let us see what happened a paragraph or two back when we had nothing but the lacquer sanding sealer and lacquer based finish coats on the wood. Under the conditions that were described (wet, rainy weather) obviously the relative humidity was about as high as it could get. Also we have assumed that the stock is about as dry as the normal stock will ever be. Thus we have a great deal more moisture outside the stock than we have inside. Therefore, because of physical phenomena that I will not bother detailing, the high moisture outside the stock will be under great pressure to get into the dry wood until such a degree of saturation is reached in the wood that satisfies the physical laws by which the moisture was induced to enter.

Under these conditions lacquer definitely will not prevent

any great amount of moisture from entering the wood. Not only will it go right through the finish wherever it encounters it, but it will also rapidly penetrate through any end grain that it may find, such as unprotected butt ends, and interior inletting. (By unprotected I mean not especially prepared with a good moisture resistant compound.)

Now that the moisture has traveled fairly freely through the finish into the wood suppose the warm, sunny weather we talked about came along. Under these weather conditions the relative humidity in the air will be low and the moisture inside the wood will then tend to force its way *out* into the dry air. When this happens the moisture attempts to leave the wood faster than the permeability factor of the lacquer finish will allow. Consequently the moisture will force the integral film out in spots and form blisters or bubbles, if it does not rupture the film first. This is the same thing that happens on houses that were painted in cold, damp weather. The paint will always blister in spots and for the same reason that the lacquer did on the stock.

On the average stock under average conditions this blistering will not be especially noticeable, or it may even be nonexistent. But the special case is what we are interested in for the moment—the case in which severe moisture conditions are met.

There are two ways in which this blistering may be eliminated. The first is the easiest, and consists of not using lacquer on the stock at all. But perhaps you desire the especially fine finish which lacquers will give you when handled properly. In that case I would definitely recommend the use of as much waterproofing as possible both before and after applying the lacquer film.

The waterproofing of which I speak is the use of a varnish sealer directly on the bare wood. Such a sealer and its use are covered in the chapter on sealers and fillers. Ah, ah, before you speak I know what you are going to say. You intend to point out to me in no uncertain terms that I just got through telling you about the evils of using such a material under lacquer because of the lifting tendencies.

You are right—I did just get through telling you that. But the big point I want to stress is that if that varnish sealer is well dried and hardened then you will have no trouble with lifting. If you will remember the warning had to do with using a lacquer over fresh, wet varnish sealers.

By well dried and hardened I mean a sealer that has stood for about 18 hours. This period of time will give the sealer a chance to polymerize well on the surface but it will not be so doggoned hard that the lacquer will not bite into it a bit and get a good hold. This is a very important point. The varnish sealer must be at least 18 hours old, but no older than 36 hours if satisfactory adhesion is expected. Between these time limits you will secure maximum adhesion, minimum lifting and generally best all around results by using lacquer over varnish sealers.

As long as the subject has been mentioned, perhaps a further glance at lacquer sanding sealers is in order.

SANDING SEALER COMPOSITION

As has been mentioned, the designated use of this material is primarily that of a filler. It is nearly always a semi-clear, thin liquid which will have a tendency to settle slightly. By that I mean that some of the constituents are held in suspension in the liquid and over a period of time in storage these suspended particles will gradually sink to the bottom of the container. It is always wise to shake and stir well before using in order to put the settled particles back into proper suspension.

The usual lacquer sanding sealer is composed of a metallic stearate suspended in a clear lacquer solution. These stearates are what will settle upon standing. The purpose of the stearate in the sealer is to impart good sanding properties to the clear film after it has dried or hardened. Actually the film will not be clear. It will be somewhat cloudy, but upon coating further with a finishing material the cloudiness disappears and the entire film seems transparent. Usually the stearates which are used are zinc or calcium stearates.

A good formula for a homemade sanding sealer is as follows:

> Clear Lacquer............... 1 gallon
> Calcium Stearate............. $\frac{3}{16}$ pound

The calcium stearate is to be well worked into the lacquer by whipping or stirring vigorously. I would use calcium stearate rather than other metallic stearates because it is rather easy to work into suspension and will work very well. The other metallic compounds will have to be mixed in a type of grinding mill in order to make sure that no lumpy material remains in the mixture.

In selecting the clear lacquer to be used in making this sealer you should specify that a clear lacquer containing hard resins, or one which will give a hard film when dry be used. Soft specialty lacquers will not work nearly as well as a harder product, primarily due to sanding difficulties.

Application of Sanding Sealer: Lacquer sanding sealers are applied in precisely the same manner in which you apply any of the other finishing materials. If you have access to a spray gun you should surely use that means. If you have only a brush then they may be applied by that means. If using a brush, though, you would be wise to thin the sealer with the same type of slow, brushing thinners that you would use for the actual finishing coats. Even though you do not require the fine flow which the finishing coats need, the sealer must be worked in with the brush to a certain extent, and the longer you will have to work with it the better job you will do.

Application of the sealer presents no particular problems. Inasmuch as it is a filler no prefilling of any sort will be necessary, as it may be in the case when using a varnish finishing system.

Possibly you are wondering why the use of different types of filling agents? When do you use the paste type fillers rather than the lacquer sealers and vice versa? It is all a question of choice, and the choice is based upon convenience in most cases. If you are using a varnish sealer for moisture resistance and you intend to use a varnish type finishing film then I would definitely recommend that you use a varnish, or paste, type filler. In all cases where possible the desirable thing is to use all materials of the same base. It is unwise in many, many cases to sandwich a lacquer sanding sealer between two varnish based coats, mostly from the adhesion standpoint. Conversely, when you figure on using a lacquer finishing material then I would use the lacquer sealer where possible. This, too, is from the standpoint of adhesion.

I do not say you cannot use the varnish and lacquer materials indiscriminately, but I do say that the experienced wood workers stay away from it wherever possible. In the large furniture factories, in their finishing departments, they use all one system. Lately they have been straying toward the all-lacquer systems, mostly from the time saving angle. But you will not find them mixing their finishing items, even though time might allow them to do so.

ENHANCING THE GRAIN STRUCTURE OF THE WOOD

Before application of the sanding sealer you will have seen to it that all preliminary work has been done. The grain has been raised with water and heat (dewhiskering), if staining was needed that has been taken care of, and there is nothing left now but to go ahead. Wait just one moment, though, if you please. How about the grain structure? Do you feel that you have the basis for a beautiful stock if you could only make the grain stand out? In a great many of the domestic walnut stocks which are commonly seen today you will find by careful observance of the grain that it really is finely figured, but when finished merely in a clear system the grain structure is hidden, as it were. It does not stand out at all. Therefore, our problem is to make it stand out so that it can be seen and admired. Obviously the only way to do that is to provide some means of contrast between the pores and the high points of the surface.

I have found that an excellent method is to tint the filler or the sanding sealer (whichever I intend using on this particular job) with a little burnt umber or burnt sienna. When this is rubbed into the open pores those pores stand out from the lighter, uncolored areas and really show the true structure of the wood. A great many times a dull, uninteresting piece of wood may be turned into a section of finely figured walnut which always commands admiration.

Most of the fillers and the formulae for fillers now available indicate the use of such a coloring agent. This color is invariably the same, however. This accentuation of grain structure may be greatly enhanced by the use of the proper pigments. If the wood is dark to start with, or it has been stained so, then you will need a relatively darker graining pigment. If the pigment used is as light or lighter in color than the surrounding wood the effect will be that of a very dirty, muddy piece of goods. Always the graining pigment should be darker than the wood. Not too much so, though. If a soft effect is desired the pigment may be chosen so that the color is but little darker than the base wood. Or if a high contrast is wanted then the pigment should be as much darker than the wood as it is possible to obtain.

The use of different colored pigments is most easily accomplished by visiting the local paint supply store. They may be able to obtain for you samples or portions of different kinds of umbers and siennas, both burnt and raw. A selection of five or six different materials should allow you a wide range of pigment colors from which to choose.

The pigments can be mixed into the filler or sealer by simple stirring. This stirring must be complete, however. If any lumps are left in the mix you may find unpleasing dark spots on the wood due to the pure pigment lump being ground into the raw wood.

Once you are ready to apply actual finishing operation

to the wood you will find that the lacquer materials will be a little harder to work with than were the varnish items. This all boils down to the fast setting up or hardening of the film due to the volatile solvents and thinners. It is easy to get the hang of it, though, and once familiar with the feel of lacquers you will find that they can be brushed easily and with excellent results. This, of course, assuming that you use a brushing type thinner.

I guess we have fooled around long enough with discussions —let us really start to work.

LACQUERING THE GUNSTOCK

Take your thinned down sanding sealer (assuming you are going to use one) and dip the clean brush in it. As with varnishes, you must see that the bristles pick up only enough liquid to hold it without much excessive dripping. Again, the brush will act only as a carrying agent for the liquid. When you feel that you have enough and only enough sealer in the bristles for the brush to carry comfortably, transfer the brush to the surface of the wood. Again you must allow the sealer to flow onto the wood almost of its own accord. Do not attempt to force the liquid out of the brush by pressing hard on the wood. If you find that you have not enough sealer to work well with then quickly return to the can and pick up a second load of liquid and flow it onto the margin of the first application.

You will find the most satisfactory results are obtained from flowing or spreading out gently just as much of the sealer as the brush will carry in one load and spreading it out as thinly or as heavily as you will find will work best for you. Probably one brushful will cover an area about 3″ x 5″ very well if you have a 1½″ flat brush. An oval brush or one of greater dimensions will, of course, carry a greater load and will allow you to cover that much more area.

While you are covering this one small area make sure that you do a little working in with the brush. This is especially necessary on the first coat. Many times air bubbles will remain under the sealer if the first coat is not well worked into the wood. By working it into the wood I refer to the process of brushing back and forth over an area several times in rapid succession. This brushing and rebrushing will dislodge the undesirable bubbles in most cases. Naturally, there may be enough elapsed time during which the process is being carried out to allow the sealer to start to harden. In this case you will be apt to find considerable brush marks present in the film after it has completely hardened which may take 30 minutes or so. Do not worry about these brush marks in the sealing coat. You are going to sand it down to the wood anyway in order to apply the second coat and then the marks will have all been eradicated.

After working over one area you will then have to go on to the adjacent surface. Here, too, laps will show because the film on the first area operated on will have started to harden by the time you finish the second spot. These laps are of no importance for the same reason we ignored the brush marks. The sanding operation will eradicate them, too. The important thing here is to make sure that all spots have been covered well with the sealer.

When a half hour has passed since the stock was completely covered you can go back to it with some of the Wet-Or-Dry sandpaper and water. Use the sanding block to make sure that you do not dig into the wood in places and sand the coat of sealer completely off, right down to the wood. If you wish you may refrain from going all the way down. You can take off just enough to level the surface and do away with any objectional marks which may have been left there from the brush or from lapping over from a fresh area to a partially dried one.

While you are sanding you may notice that the sandpaper will accumulate a white layer. This is due to the ground-off particles of sanding sealer which you have removed. This layer must be kept to a minimum by dipping the paper and block into a can or bucket of tap water which you should have present for just this use. If you do not allow the layer to build up too heavily just a dipping of the paper and block into the water supply will wash it away and the paper will then be clear again. This is the main advantage of using this kind of sandpaper. The ordinary stuff that you buy in the hardware store will simply dissolve and float away if it encounters water.

Continue sanding over the whole stock. You will find that the sealer is very easy to remove and that it does have good sanding properties. Sanding this kind of film is really a pleasure. As you finish one spot and go to another have a rag handy so that you can remove any water remaining on the wood where you have sanded. You probably will not get any through the film and into the wood in this short exposure, but it is best not to take a chance. Anyway, you are going to have to wait for the stock to dry before you can go ahead with anything so you will save a little time by drying it off as you go along.

After you have sanded the entire stock take another dry rag and go over the wood again. This rag should be as dust free as you can get it. The object is not only to remove any moisture remaining, but also to remove as much as possible of the tiny dustlike particles which the sanding has left behind.

Allow the stock to dry until it has taken on a considerable white cast. This white cast will be due to the scratched surface of the remaining sanding sealer. While it is wet or damp it will have a dark, nearly transparent look to it, but when dry it will be light colored, or white. If in doubt it would be best to let the stock stand for an extra half-hour to make sure that it is dry. You will be in for some trouble if you put on some more sealer while water remains. Artificial heat could be used here but you must make sure that you do not char or burn the stock. The sealer will burn fairly easily and then you would have to start all over.

Now that the surface is completely dry you can apply another coat of the sealer in precisely the same manner. You will not have to be so careful about working it into the pores on this second coat. It will flow there readily of its own accord. When this coat is dry repeat the water sanding process.

Continue this sealing-sanding operation until the pores are well filled which will be indicated by the fact that they will not shine in the light after you have sanded the surface. Until you reach a point where the pores are filled you will not have finished the sealing, or filling. You will have to do that with the finish lacquer if you do not do it now, and it is much easier with this material.

After you have reached a point where you have completely filled the wood you must do one last sanding operation. This time go *all* the way down to the wood. If any of the sealer is left on the surface by oversight and you then apply the final gloss lacquer it will be a question of only a couple of weeks or less before you will see a myriad of tiny, hairline cracks or checks *under* the finish itself. These checks will come from the sealer which is notoriously easy to break down under temperature changes. The checks are made by the expansion and contraction of the surface of the wood and the sealer is not flexible enough to stand this stretching without cracking.

Because the sealer will be nearly clear, even after sanding it, it will be very difficult to determine just when you have removed it all without sanding so deep that you go below any stained surface present. You must get rid of all that remains on the surface and no mistake! Even a film one half of a thousandth inch thick will develop these cracks of which I have spoken. Probably the best way to spot any bad spots will be to sand the sealer first with a fine sandpaper of not less than 400 grit. Then take a rag and polish the stock as much as possible. This fine sanding and polishing will put a pretty good gloss on the sealer and it will show up rather glossy. Then, using a good, strong light on your wood go back after any of these shiny areas with 320 or 360 sandpaper. When the shine is gone polish again quickly with the rag. If any areas again take on a shine go after it again. In this manner you can effectively remove whatever sealer remains and be darned sure you have gotten it all. Inspect carefully under the strong light at a very nearly flat angle, and again at about 90 degrees, or straight down, and you will be able to see any remaining bad spots at one or the other of the angles.

After you are absolutely certain that your sealer has been removed down to the wood and that the only material of this sort left on the stock is that which now fills the pores you can proceed with the application of the gloss, finishing material.

Before you put anything else on the stock, and while we are giving the sealer a good chance to lose whatever solvents may be left in the film we better hash over the subject of thinners for the final coatings.

Undercoat "Lifting": It is true that you have used a lacquer type sealing material and that therefore a top coat, or coats, of the same base material should go on well and easily, but there is just one little thing. As mentioned before lacquers contain some of the most powerful organic solvents we know of. In fact, a lot of them are what make up most of the paint and varnish removers on the market today. Therefore, they will attack both lacquers and enamels. If you go ahead and throw on some lacquer over a still-fresh undercoat this undercoat will have a tendency to absorb some of those very powerful solvents. This is especially true if you are using a brush. The brush will more or less "scrub" the solvents into the undercoat and when this happens you will get considerable swelling. This effect will not be so apparent if you are using a spray gun and the undercoat is fairly old, say 24 hours. This is one of the big reasons why we should wait that long after using the sanding sealer.

In order to minimize this swelling or lifting we can use what is called a "non-lifting" thinner. This thinner is composed of solvents and diluents which will dissolve the lacquer to be applied, but which will not actively attack the undercoats. Such a thinner may be purchased, but you can make up one at home which will do the job just as well. The following formula for such a thinner *must* be followed carefully, as an error in making it up might cause it to go ahead and lift just as a regular thinner would do, or possibly cause a "throw out" of the lacquer in which it is used.

Non-lifting Thinner

Normal Butyl Acetate	30 parts by volume
Denatured Alcohol	10 " " "
LD (Lacquer Diluent) Naphtha	55 " " "
Butyl Alcohol	5 " " "

Reduce your lacquer with this thinner to the same viscosity you would any other lacquer. Then go ahead and use it. This thinner may be used for either brush or spray work. However, I would not reduce more than about 1 : 1.

You will find that this non-lifting thinner will evaporate rather quickly and therefore you must work fast with the brush. If it is too fast for you then put in a little of the slow brushing thinner, the formulae of which have already been given. You will have to regulate the amounts of each type of thinner by the satisfaction which each gives. Use as little of the slow brushing thinner as possible. This brushing thinner will cause swelling but there may be no help for it. A little experimenting will give you what you need to know as far as technique is concerned.

APPLICATION OF FINISH COATS

When you have decided upon using or not using the non-lifting type thinner you may proceed. With the non-lifting thinner reduce the finishing clear lacquer not more than 1 : 1. If you happen to choose a standard brushing material reduce that to whatever viscosity you find works best for you.

The actual application of the finishing clear is very similar to that of the sanding sealer. Only enough liquid should be picked up with the brush to fill the bristles. Do not allow the brush to leave the container dripping wet with lacquer. This sort of thing will result in a multitude of spots or drops on the finished surface which will only have to be removed later by sanding or rubbing.

Do as little actual work with the brush as possible. The role here is to carry the lacquer only, not to work it into the surface. Even with slow drying thinners the film will commence to dry rather quickly and the faster you can remove the brush from the surface the less chance there will be for brush marks to remain. Work over a small area at a time, making sure that the liquid is spread evenly, not too heavy in one spot and not too thin in another.

When going from one area to another make sure that the laps do not become more apparent than absolutely necessary. They will remain to some extent, but the quicker you can start another area the less the thinners on the first area will have evaporated and the more flow you will get. If the thinners are slow enough and you work quickly you will be able to blend one area into another with very little evidence in the dried film of the lapping effect. What little remains can be easily sanded or rubbed out when you smooth down the dried coat.

After the first finish coat is on and has hardened 24 hours then you may find that you can dispense with the non-lifting thinner altogether in following coats. If the first one is hard, little swelling will take place.

No matter what thinner you use you must work very fast with the brush. If you find that you cannot work with the clear because it sets up so quickly then the only thing left to do is to add more of the brushing thinner to slow down the rate of evaporation. You can go too far the other way, of course. You can get it so thin that it will run off the stock like water as soon as it is applied. In that case you will have to come back with some of the base clear material in order to thicken it up a little. This may be especially true on vertical surfaces and on edges, such as the corners of the inletting and the cheekpiece.

Each particular job will present particular problems. There are so many variables in the field of wood finishing (or any other field for that matter) that answering any specific question will call for a survey of the specific conditions present: atmospheric conditions, make of lacquer, method of application, and idiosyncrasies which may crop up. The greatest source of trouble, I have found, is errors made by the handler. Very often he has used the wrong thinners (for example, enamel thinner in lacquer), or has thinned the material too much or too little. As I say, it is strictly a matter of individual investigation of each individual problem. I have found very few cases, however, where a little intelligent thinking on the part of the person involved would not have cleared up the situation entirely.

Assuming you have had to employ a brush to apply the finish you will have gotten one finish coat on by now. The finish will not look so hot to you at this point, I will wager. In all probability there will be a certain amount of brush marks showing when that first coat has hardened. There may also be some dust and dirt in the film, though you sure will not get much if you had clean stuff to work with in the first place. This stuff dries so fast that there will not be time for any appreciable amount to settle on it from the air. That is figuring, of course, that somebody is not sweeping the floor or shaking out a rug next to the bench at the time you brush it on.

You may be tempted to go after this first coat with sandpaper when you find that the surface is fairly hard after an hour or so. Well, that would be a great, big, beautiful mistake. Even though the surface of the film is well set up there will be a great deal of the solvents left in the film which will gradually work their way out over a period of time. This trapped solvent will cause the film to remain relatively soft for at least 18 hours, during which time you could do a great deal of damage to it by using coarse sandpaper. Many lacquers are formulated especially for quick sanding and these will specify that sanding may be done after, say, two hours. In that case it would be okay to go to it. But in the case of the normal clear material you will be giving the film a fighting chance by waiting 24 hours or so before sanding.

Now is the time to consider the use of the drying cabinet and reciprocating type sander described in Chapter 5 and in the chapter on Equipment. They are very useful, not only for the varnishes, but also for these lacquers and for shellac as well.

The use of the drying cabinet will speed up the drying of a lacquer so that it may be sanded and/or recoated in a couple or three hours.

You may follow the same principles all the way down the line that you followed (or should have followed) in using varnish. Use the water type sandpaper of about 320 grit or finer, preferably 400. When the film is hard and dry enough to sand then use the sanding block cushioned with rubber or felt.

Sand the surface to smooth it only and to eliminate any flaws which may have sneaked up on you. If you find some faults that go all the way down to the wood surface then you, too, will have to go nearly that far to clear them up. You can touch-up such spots with a fine striping brush and let that spot dry. Then sand it so that the edges are feathered into the surrounding territory and the touch-up spot unnoticeable.

When you have the first coat to your satisfaction go ahead with the second one, following precisely the same procedures. Wait until each coat is hard and dry and then sand just enough to eliminate any surface imperfections. You may have to repeat the process as much as five times, depending upon how perfect each coat is, how much solid lacquer is left on the surface after each coat is dry, and how thick you want the final film. The average thickness of finished film will be the same or less than that for varnishes. For one thing, the thicker the lacquer film the greater will be the danger of its checking or cracking due to temperature changes. You will want the thinnest coating you can get which will still give adequate protection to the wood.

I would say, offhand, that five to six thousandths of an inch will be as thick as you will ever be safe to go. That is assuming that your coating is fairly uniform over the whole stock. It is highly probable that you may have spotty coatings in which the film over very thin sections, such as inletting edges, will be heavier than at other areas due to your reluctance to sand much there where the danger of cutting through corners into the stained wood would be relatively great.

Then again, you may have done considerable sanding over the areas where broad, flat surfaces present themselves. These areas, which nearly always will be on the cheekpiece face and the right-hand side of the butt, are very tempting when you have a sanding block in your itchy little palm and you think you spot a brush mark. I would not worry too much about these inequalities of the surface, though. As I said before, it is much better to have too thin a coat than a too heavy one.

THINNER COATING

Let us suppose you have gotten to what you consider will be your last coat. You can see as you put it on that you are going to have some brush marks and what to do about it? Well, there is always the old trick of using a coat of pure thinner on top of the final coat. The coat of pure lacquer thinner will tend to dissolve the uppermost layer of lacquer and make it flow out like nobody's business. The best time to use it is immediately after you have applied the lacquer itself and before it has had much of a chance to harden. And that means *immediately*. If you give the film a chance to lose much of its solvent content even this lacquer thinner will not allow much flow of the film.

It is a little tricky to work with, but here again a couple of minutes spent with a scrap board in practise will pay big dividends. The main danger is that you will flood too much on any one spot and thus dissolve so much of the lacquer that it actually starts to sag or run. You want to stop just short of that point.

I am darned sure you will not be able to use a spray gun for this trick, though that is just the ticket. If you had the gun you would not have used the brush in the first place! Inasmuch as the thinner by itself will have practically no body at all (or extremely low viscosity, if you want to put it that way) we have an easy way to get around that. Here we can use the Flit gun and do a good job! Even though this little gadget is frowned upon by Joe Schmoe down the road, he cannot do any better with his two hundred buck Binks outfit when it comes to spraying such thin liquids. As a matter of fact, sparks from the brushes on his motor may very well set off the fog of lacquer thinner which will form in the air and set the house on fire. Go ahead, laugh at him. I know just how you feel, Buddy.

The big point which I must stress here is to be sure and clean out that Flit gun well before you use it. Maybe the Flit or whatever it had in it will keep the bugs off next summer, but it sure will not do the finish one darned bit of good! When you are certain that it is good and dry then fill the liquid holder with the thinner and put it to one side where you can get at it as soon as you throw on that last finishing coat.

While brushing on that last coat you may finish one area and spray on some of the thinner coating. Then quick, like a Bunny, put it down and lacquer the adjacent area. Back again with the thinner, making sure that where the two coats joined, lap marks do not show. Up again, down again, Finnegan. This will call for a little quick work but the results will fully warrant the effort you put out. That coat of thinner will give you the finest, glossiest finish you ever saw, which you can then work on with the rubbing compound until the exact degree of lustre you want is brought out.

Of course, you can lacquer the entire stock before you work out with the thinner. That will be the more leisurely way, and in most cases will be perfectly satisfactory. This, like everything else in the gun game, will be a matter of perfecting by experiment and practise. Maybe you get tired of hearing it, but darned if it is not so!

RUBBING THE LACQUER FINISH

Now that you are finished with this phase of it let the thing harden up for 36 hours. That will be plenty long enough for the important amounts of thinners to have left the film and will give you a very hard, workable surface. Of course, there will be some trapped solvent left in the film for even as long as a month, but that will amount to so little that you can ignore it.

There is a chance that maybe you cannot wait for 36 hours before rubbing the stock. Maybe there is a good customer (is there any other kind?) on your neck about it. He wants to know when the dickens you are going to get that stock to him. He has a chance to go hunting tomorrow and he will not be worth a darn in deer country without a gun. So you heave a sigh and take the thing out of the rack. Probably it has only been a couple of hours since you put on the last coating but you will do the best you can. Let it wait another hour (about three hours will be the irreducible minimum) and start your rubbing. If the job has been a good one you will need no sanding here. The surface will be so smooth and perfect that only a pumice operation to cut down that glint will be required.

Once you have reached the finished stage the procedure is exactly the same as for varnish finishes. You may use the same type and grits of rubbing compounds you used for them. You can work out your own details for whatever limits of lustre you desire.

As with varnish you will probably best use some XXX or XXXX pumice and water or sweet oil. Using a felt cover on the sanding block you will cut down the surface until the high gloss is eliminated. Then you can take your rottenstone or prepared polishing compound on another piece of felt which will smooth off any edges left by the pumice and give you a good final satin finish.

TIME OF APPLICATION OF LACQUER FINISHES

The time it will take to procure a good finish using lacquer will depend upon the technique of the stocker and upon the equipment that he may have to work with. If he is careful and allows a full day between coats then he will stretch the time out, but he will also make sure he does not louse up the finish by sanding too soon after application.

Following is a typical schedule, though the times will vary.

Non-professional

Application and drying of sanding sealer	— 35 minutes (1 coat)
Sanding down to the wood	— 10 "
Application and drying of lacquer	— 15 to 18 hours
Sanding lacquer coat	— 10 minutes
Reapplication and drying of lacquer	— 15 to 18 hours
Sanding lacquer coat	— 10 minutes
Rubbing and polishing lacquer coat	— 30 "
Total	— 31½ hours

The above time schedule is based upon a two coat system and a minimum of drying time of the lacquer coats.

Professional

Application and drying of sanding sealer	— 20 minutes (1 coat)
Sanding down to the wood	— 3 "
Application and drying of lacquer	— 3 hours
Sanding lacquer coat	— 3 minutes
Application and drying of lacquer	— 3 hours
Sanding lacquer coat	— 3 minutes
Rubbing and polishing lacquer coat	— 10 "
Total	— 6 hours 39 minutes

This schedule is based upon the assumption that the shop or the professional will have equipment such as reciprocating sander (see Equipment chapter) and drying cabinet.

LACQUER OVER SHELLAC

There is one point which may be worth while discussing. That is the subject of applying lacquers of any sort over a shellac base coating. You will find in many articles the recommendation that this should not be done. That recommendation I question from the technical standpoint.

I question it because the adhesion of lacquers over shellac is very good. It is so good because the same solvents that go to make up the lacquer are also good solvents for shellac, in many cases. Lacquers contain ethyl alcohol which is the finest solvent we have for shellac. Therefore, when lacquer hits the shellac a portion of the surface of the shellac immediately dissolves, or at least softens considerably, under the influence of the solvent. The two coats will then bond together when dry in about the same degree that lacquer will bond to lacquer. And that, gentlemen, cannot be beat for adhesion!

As for using shellac *over* lacquer, though, that is another story. The solvent that is carried in a shellac solution is invariably a simple, single alcohol which will have very little effect in dissolving a hardened lacquer film. Therefore there will be no tendency for the two films to hold together when dry because there is no common bond between them. In this case the adhesion will be questionable, though I suspect it will be all right if very thin coats of the shellac are used and no especially rough handling is given the stock.

Actually I see very little reason for using shellac under a lacquer. If you intend to use a lacquer system you will find that the sanding sealers which I have discussed will be much easier to use than the shellac, and they will give you much better filling of the grain. If you insist on using shellac you may do so, but I would not use it myself when something as easy and efficient as the sanding sealers are available.

As an afterthought, and a matter of information only, there are in existence lacquers which are made from ethyl cellulose, rather than nitrocellulose. They differ chemically from the regular lacquers, but the use and application is about the same. For stock and wood finishing they offer nothing that the nitrocellulose based materials do not and have been used mostly for metal finishing. Occasionally they may be incorporated in a wood finishing lacquer to a certain extent to impart certain properties to the regular lacquers, but this practice is not common.

EFFECT OF TEMPERATURE CHANGES ON LACQUER FILMS

Lacquer based materials will crack much more easily than most good, resilient varnishes when exposed to *rapid* temperature changes. This is because the nitrocellulose base of which the lacquer is composed is a very hard, brittle material which cannot be stretched without breaking. Even though there are certain plasticizers (or softening agents) added to the lacquer the composite film is still rather sensitive to dimensional changes. Therefore, when the stock is subjected to rapid changes in temperature the surface of the wood will expand and contract to some extent and if this expansion and contraction is very great the lacquer will not be able to stretch this much and, as the adhesion to the wood will be good in most cases, the only thing left for the film is to rupture to relieve the strains. It is a condition where the film is not pliable enough to hang on at both ends and stretch in the middle.

For example, if you have been out in some of that good Maine weather where it gets down to zero without even trying, and you come into the shack with the red-hot stove a-bilin' away just pouring out the heat by the bucketful and you set your nice hand finished stock down any place near it do not be too surprised to find a network of hairline cracks running all over the finish when you pick it up again. In this case the extreme cold had first contracted the wood and the finish, and then the heat from the room had quickly warmed and expanded the stock. Rapid expansion such as this resulted in the rupture of the lacquer film and the rupture took the form of the very fine hairline cracks. A crack will have appeared wherever the film could not stand the strain imposed upon it.

Naturally I do not expect any hunter to do such a foolish thing as to bring a cold gun into a warm room. (I thought I better get this part in before some of you give me a hard time about know-from-nuthin' City Slickers.) The act of bringing the cold metal into the warm atmosphere would immediately leave the gun dripping wet in every part from condensation of atmospheric moisture on the cold metal. A dozen pairs of heavy, wet, wool socks hanging around the stove to dry plus the hot breath of even a couple of healthy boys would really raise the humidity of the place.

The example given was merely a hypothetical case which would show up the "cold checking" tendencies of a typical lacquer. Considerably less violent temperature changes over a longer period of time would have the same effect, but probably not to such a great extent.

Incidentally, this "cold checking" is precisely what made the old piano finishes go to pot. They were finished in varnishes usually made of brittle natural resins. These early natural resin films were even less pliable than are lacquers and the changes in temperature of a room from day to night eventually checked them badly.

The thinner the film on a stock the less chance there will be for "cold checking" to take place. Such a thin film will be more flexible than a heavier film.

Do not let the above scare you off, though. It was mentioned only as a matter of information. If you use a good lacquer you probably will not run into such checking at all, especially with thin films. You will like the way lacquer finishes up and handles and the fine results you can obtain will be well worth investigating. The danger of "cold checking" is practically nil on the average stock under normal conditions, so you can forget about it.

DESIRABILITY OF LACQUER FINISHES

Lacquers are not generally thought of as recommended stock finishes. They are used more than is realized, however, and definitely have their place under certain conditions.

These conditions are when a stock is wanted that need not face extremely rough handling or severe weather conditions. The lacquer will stand up well under average handling, and will give a beautiful finish. It will not take a great deal of moisture, though.

Therefore, you may use lacquer on a stock that is to be seen more than kicked around. It will do for the average stock and will stand up well. Do not use it when a maximum of protection is needed as the marine spar varnishes will answer the purpose better.

For beauty, lustre, clarity of film, and non-yellowing a lacquer will be better than any other finish you can apply. It will fall down when rapid temperature changes, high humidity and very rough handling are the rule, though.

FINISHING FAULTS WITH LACQUER

Brush Marks or Laps: Imperfections in the hardened film which show where the brush has touched the wet lacquer or where wet lacquer has flowed onto partially dried surfaces.

This is due to using the brush after the film has hardened to some extent and may indicate that the lacquer is drying too fast for this use.

In most cases this fault will be eliminated by using a slower evaporating thinner mixture to reduce the lacquer. This may also be partially eliminated by coating the surface with a coat of pure lacquer thinner after applying the lacquer and before it has had a chance to dry much.

Orange Peel Effect: This fault will appear as many minute bumps or ripples in the finish.

It is found only when a spray gun has been used to apply the lacquer. Usually it is caused by having the spray gun too far from the surface which is being sprayed. It may also be caused by using too high an air pressure at the gun.

The remedy is to either reduce the pressure or move the nozzle of the gun closer to the work. Experiment will show you which is the case.

Throw Out: This is found only when reducing the lacquer or when mixing two kinds of lacquers together in a container. It is caused by having some ingredient introduced into the lacquer in which the base nitrocellulose is insoluble. It is caused mostly by using enamel thinners by mistake to reduce lacquer. Some of the non-lifting lacquer thinners may cause throw out of the nitrocellulose if the lacquer is over-reduced.

The remedy lies in being sure that you have the correct thinners when thinning or reducing lacquer. In the case of the non-lifting thinners you should add some of the unthinned lacquer-base material to the thrown-out mass and stir thoroughly. This will nearly always bring the mixture back into the solution.

Lifting and Wrinkling: This fault appears through the surface of the lacquer and looks like wavy lines being forced up through the surface.

This will usually happen when a lacquer is used over a relatively soft varnish or enamel. The reason is that the strong solvents in the lacquer will be absorbed readily by the soft varnish and will swell it seriously. This swelling will loosen the varnish from the wood underneath and cause the varnish to pucker up enough to be seen through the lacquer top coat. This effect is noted immediately after the lacquer is applied. If it does not happen immediately it will not happen at all.

The remedy is to allow the varnish to dry at least 24 hours if it is a thinned varnish sealer, and at least four days if it is a thick top coat.

Bubbles and Bumps: Appears just as the name implies— minute lumps or bumps on the surface which do not seem to want to be polished out.

The cause is usually dust or dirt in the lacquer, the brush, or the surrounding air at the time of application. This dust or dirt will rise nearly to the surface of the lacquer, but will not break through. Consequently it will raise the surface at that point like a small hillock.

The remedy is to have absolutely clean lacquer (strain through cotton cloth if doubtful) and clean, dust-free brushes before application. Dust in the air may be minimized by dusting bench and rafters with a damp cloth.

Blushing: This will appear as white or opaque areas on the surface during and after drying.

It is caused by having too-fast thinners in the lacquer. These thinners will evaporate so quickly that they condense moisture from the air into the wet lacquer where it forms a type of emulsion.

It may be remedied in most cases by having a slower evaporating thinner to reduce the lacquer. In very humid atmospheres the slowest brushing-type thinners will not be too slow. Inasmuch as you will probably be using that type thinner anyway you will probably have very little trouble with blushing.

Poor Adhesion: This will be evident by having the lacquer top coat peel off the stock merely from rough handling. It will come off in sheets or large patches.

It is caused mainly by any of three conditions:

(1) Incompatible undercoat.

Some materials, such as completely hardened phenolics, will not allow the lacquer to grab onto it. This is especially true of smooth surfaces. The remedy in this case is to apply the lacquer after about 24 hours at which time the phenolic will still allow a certain amount of "grab" to take place. You must also make sure that the phenolic varnish is sanded to allow a rougher surface for the lacquer to adhere to.

(2) Grease or oil.

Grease or lubricating oils will never dry hard and therefore they will prevent the lacquer from having anything to hold onto. The lacquer will hold onto the grease, but the grease will not hold onto the wood. Therefore, even a trivial amount of handling will pull the whole finish away from the wood.

(3) Soft or wet drying oils.

While drying oils will harden over a period of time, if any finishing material is put over them before they have had a chance to dry completely the same condition will take place as though you had lubricating oil on the wood. There will be no bond between the lacquer and the wood.

Streaking: This is found mostly after a polishing or rubbing operation and will appear as dull streaks or areas on the lacquer.

It is caused by not having the lacquer completely dry. The polishing or rubbing compounds will dig into the soft surface easily and will imbed some of the abrasive in the lacquer.

The remedy is to allow the lacquer sufficient time to lose most of the solvents and thinners trapped in the film. This will require at least 18 hours with most lacquers to be sure of "through-drying."

Scratching: This fault will appear only upon close examination. The scratches will be very apparent under strong light and at a very flat angle.

It is caused by having a very harsh, coarse cloth used as the polishing backing, by having some relatively large grains of abrasive mixed with otherwise fine grains, or by a mixture of both causes.

Pitting: This is found only when a spray gun has been used. It will show up as minute, extensive pits or pinholes in the dried film. It is caused by having water or oil in the air line or compressor.

The remedy is to have either an air condenser in the line between the gun and the compressor or by making sure that the whole outfit is perfectly clean and dry before use. The condenser is the best bet.

CHAPTER SEVEN

Shellac

WE TOUCHED on the subject of shellac back in Chapter 5, but there is a great deal about that material which is both interesting and which is not generally known. Therefore, I think it is worthwhile to go deeper into the subject.

HISTORY OF SHELLAC

The first use of shellac is not definitely known, but it is very certain that it was far, far back in history. The early aboriginal tribes recognized the palas tree as the primary home of the lac insect which produces the resin and early Sanskrit mentions this tree and calls it Laksatary.

Jan Huyglen van Linschoten, sent to India in 1596 by the King of Portugal on a special mission, described the process the Indians used for producing the lac resin, and also for obtaining the red dye which is a by-product of the process.

The early Greeks and Romans knew it as an article of commerce and it was so described by Periplus in A.D. 80.

Europe, however, did not accept the products of the lac insect as commercially important until about the 17th Century. At that time a large trade was developed for the red dye obtained from the raw lac. The dye was brought in to supply demands for a cheaper red dye than the then standard cochineal.

Shellac, as we know it today, is a very romantic character. It takes a lot of work by a lot of fellows in places we never heard of to get you that little bottle of stuff you pay two bits for. Therefore, if you have never heard the story sit back and relax 'cause you are going to hear it now.

MANUFACTURE OF SHELLAC

It seems that at certain times of the year a whole flock of little bugs (politely called *Laccifer lacca*) gather for a family reunion in parts of Burma, India and Siam. They gather on the limbs of certain types of trees and secrete around themselves a red liquid, the same as silkworms weave a cocoon, and then retire for good. (They may not be aware it will be for good, but it usually is.) Now some of the local lads who have been watching for just this sort of thing call in the relatives and the relatives of the relatives and they all go to work.

They go into the woods and knock and scrape the crusted lac (as it is called) from the branches and take it home. There everybody sits down in the front yard and cleans as much dirt and twigs from the lac as possible. After the material is dried in the sun it is then ground in whatever kind of mill that is available. Usually it will be a sort of crude stone job with one stone being turned upon another.

The powdered lac is now soaked in special washing jars shaped like flower pots, only bigger. When it has been thoroughly soaked one of the local characters called a "Ghasander" goes to work. He stamps around in the pot to break open the cocoon-like seeds of lac and thus liberate the bodies of the now defunct insects. After this more water is poured into the jars so that as much dirt and foreign matter as possible is washed out. Then it is again dried in the sun. After drying the lac is sorted and sifted into three size grades— Seed Lac, Ghongi, and Gad.

Next the lac is stuffed into a long, round bag which may at times reach 30 feet in length. One end of the bag is held near a fire or hot stones to start the melt. While an assistant holds the far end of the bag a big wheel called a "Kariger" twists the hot end of the bag and the hot lac is forced out through the pores of the cloth onto a hot stone. The assistant at the far end continues to squeeze and twist and thus works the lac up toward the hot end in order to give the top man something to work with. During this time the "Kariger" uses a flat blade and works the lac into a flat mass.

After the bag is empty the "Kariger" turns the whole thing over to another expert they call a "Bhilwaya" and goes off to cool himself with a shot of bamboo wine.

The "Bhilwaya" now places some of the hot plastic lac on the outside of a jar containing hot water. As the stuff softens he takes a large palm leaf and places it over the mass which is gradually forming a sheet around the hot jar. When it gets to be about two feet square he takes a corner in his teeth, two other corners in his hands and also operates what is left with his toes. The sheet is stretched to about a four foot square in this manner and is about one-sixteenth inch thick. He makes it as large as he can after which it is cooled and broken into thin flakes which is the shellac of commerce.

The resulting commercial shellac may show big differences in quality depending upon the season in which it was gathered, the kind of tree from whence it came, and the locality in which it was harvested.

Different "crops" of shellac have different names depending upon the time of year.

The April and May lac crops are called "Baisakhi" from the month of Baisakh. A less important crop gathered in late May and June is called "Jethivi." The "Katiki" crop comes up in October and November and the most important crop of all is gathered in November and December and is called "Aghani." This latter crop may also be called "Kusmi" because it comes from the Kusum tree.

COMMERCIAL CLASSIFICATION

Shellac: Only the flaked form of purified lac is correctly called shellac. All other forms come under the name Lac.

Seed Lac: Raw lac, ground and washed.

Button Lac: Heat purified lac in the form of large buttons.

Garnet Lac: Used mostly in the field of plastics. It will have most of the wax removed and may or may not contain percentages of rosin.

PROPERTIES AND USES

Usually you will find on the dealer's shelf a straight solution of shellac in denatured alcohol. It will be called Orange Shellac from the noticeable color present unless it has been specially treated and bleached.

This bleached shellac, in addition to being heated, twisted, squeezed and strained in India like the orange shellac, will have been dissolved in sodium carbonate solution and treated with a hypochlorite to turn it colorless. After this it has been precipitated with sulphuric acid and dried, then dissolved in alcohol and bottled.

Both the orange shellac and the bleached or white shellac will react with the alcohol in which it is dissolved and over a period of time will change chemically (esterification) and the products of this reaction will make the shellac non-drying. White, bleached shellac will react much more quickly than the orange variety. When the shellac gets to this point it will have lost a great deal of its resistance to moisture and water as well as its properties of drying. In fact, most manufacturers of shellac will refuse to guarantee their solutions longer than about six months after manufacture. Therefore if you have some of the stuff that you have had in the workshop for a couple of years I recommend trying it out on a piece of scrap wood before putting it on a stock. It is probable that you will save yourself a lot of grief if it has gotten to a point where it will not dry no matter how long you let it set.

Orange shellac will give a stronger, more elastic film than will bleached shellac if methods of application are the same.

WATER RESISTANCE OF SHELLAC FILMS

Possibly the easiest way to get a good, hot argument started when discussing the subject of shellac films is to casually mention that you used some of the stuff as a waterproofing agent. Immediately you will have at least two, and possibly more, hot tempered gentlemen of the opposition climbing all over you.

They will state definitely and in no uncertain terms that any fool knows the stuff is no good for that purpose. That just about covers it, I guess. Any fool knows that. But it takes the ones who are not fools to know it *is* good for just that purpose.

Before I go any further and really stick my neck out let me say that there is a great difference between being waterproof and being weather durable. The difference lies in the fact that the attacks of the ultra-violet content of sunlight as well as temperature changes and the resulting stresses set up in a protective film will break such a film down more than water or moisture ever will. The stresses set up in such a protective film of shellac by temperature changes from hot to cold and vice versa will crack shellac quickly and then moisture will seep through those cracks. This cracking will loosen the film from the surface and it will start to peel off very shortly. This is the reason that I do not recommend the use of shellac on exterior surfaces.

For items which are to meet limited exterior weather conditions, or for those which will be used indoors only, it is a horse of a different color.

Shellac films, when whole and unruptured, will absorb a very small amount of atmospheric moisture, and this absorption tends to make the film impermeable to any further attempts of moisture to penetrate. Even liquid water left on a shellac surface will not penetrate to any extent. The film may turn white as it usually does, but it seems that this whitening is confined to the extreme top of the film and it does not indicate penetration *through* the film, but only *into* it a little way.

Shellac will be considerably more waterproof than any of the drying oils used by themselves. Thus it may be advisable to use thin solutions of shellac when a moisture resisting film is desired. It certainly will do the job a lot better than the linseed oil and turpentine priming solutions so often recommended.

BASE COATS OF SHELLAC

Shellac may be used successfully under lacquer top coats, and even under many of the varnish finishes, especially if they contain alcohol. If the shellac is used thin it will penetrate well into the wood and will thus insure adequate adhesion. The reason for specifying the use of a varnish topcoat which contains some sort of alcohol as a thinner is that shellac is soluble in very few of the commonly used thinners other than alcohol. As long as the two materials (topcoat and undercoat) have a common solvent then the adhesion of the two will be good. This is because the alcohol in the wet topcoat will partially dissolve, or at least soften, the shellac undercoating and the two will then blend together and become more or less fused into one coat.

The shellac by itself will resist moisture well and if the adhesion is good then there will be no danger of the topcoat peeling away from the lower. These two properties (water resistance and good adhesion) are the two most important things in finishing stocks (or any type of wood surface, for that matter) and if you have them you will have a good, durable finish.

PROPERTIES OF SHELLAC

There are a few do's and don'ts about shellac which you should know about if you intend to do any finishing work with it.

1. *Never* keep shellac solutions, either bleached or orange, in tin or iron containers. The solution will invariably attack the metal of the can and rust it badly. This will not only discolor the solution but at the same time the reaction will tend to decompose the shellac and destroy its properties of drying. *Always keep shellac in glass bottles for storage.*

2. Shellac should *not* be applied in atmospheres containing high percentages of moisture. This means a basement full of wet wash hanging out to dry or a warm, damp shop in the midst of a few days of heavy rains. The great amounts of moisture present in the air under such circumstances (or similar ones) will prevent the shellac coating drying well and will at the same time destroy the final moisture resistance of the dried film. If you must, hold up on that job for a few days until the weather clears and the humidity goes down.

3. Be very careful about applying varnish over shellac. There is an excellent chance that poor adhesion will result. If you must use varnish throw in some alcohol (even butyl alcohol will do) to help the bonding of the two coats together. Lacquers always contain a certain amount of pure alcohol and will have fair to good adhesion. Before applying anything over shellac make sure that the shellac coat has been well scuffed or sanded to roughen the surface. This roughening will increase the adhesion.

4. In applying shellac always do so in thin coats. A few heavy, thick coats will be more brittle, will take longer to dry, and will tend to flake away easily. Thin coats will lose their alcohol content much quicker and will tend to hang on better.

5. Do not wash or clean a shellacked surface with strong soap and water. Or with any soap and water, for that matter. The alkali in the soap (regardless of the claims of the radio announcer) will soften the film and partially dissolve it. If you must clean up a stock use one of the more gentle cleaning or polishing compounds recommended by a manufacturer of automotive finishes. If you wish you may successfully use any of the polishing formulae given in Chapter 10, especially formulae Numbers 10, 15, or 16.

STRENGTH OF SHELLAC SOLUTIONS

When you go into the dime store or the fancy paint emporium down the block and ask for a bottle of shellac you will usually get a more or less standardized material.

The commercial shellac solutions are generally what is known as a four pound cut. This means that for every gallon of alcohol used there will be dissolved therein four pounds of shellac resin.

You can procure solutions which contain more resin, however, by asking for (and making sure that you get) a five pound cut. This, of course, will be five pounds of shellac per gallon of alcohol.

It will seldom be desirable to use either the four pound cut or the five pound cut as is. For stock work both of these solutions should be cut or thinned with denatured alcohol to what amounts to about a two and one-half pound cut. The easiest way to remember that is to thin the shellac about 50% with alcohol before using. This is another way of saying for every gallon of shellac pour in about two quarts of alcohol. Such a thinned solution will dry more slowly than an unthinned one giving you more time to work with it and also giving better gloss because of increased flow. It will also keep you from applying too thick coatings with the resulting danger of having the film stay soft for a long time.

For those of you that wish to do any amount of finishing in this medium the following table will be handy:

Present Strength	Strength Wanted	Alcohol to add to 1 gallon shellac
5# cut	3# cut	3½ pints
5# cut	3# cut	1 gallon
5# cut	1# cut	2⅔ gallons
4# cut	3# cut	1 quart
4# cut	2# cut	¾ gallon
4# cut	1# cut	2⅛ gallon

APPLICATION OF SHELLAC

First of all, shellac films, no matter how thinly applied and no matter how carefully handled, will be brittle. They will tend to flake and crack easily under blows and temperature changes. Obviously, the ideal material would be a shellac which would retain its good properties and still be a bit softer and more resilient. This can be accomplished by the addition of a "plasticizer" or softening agent. The most efficient and probably the one most easy to obtain for the average man will be plain castor oil. Such oil will be non-drying and will soften the film just enough to take away the worst of the brittleness. Of course, you can easily overdo this. The addition of too much castor oil will give you a sticky, gooey mess which will never dry to a hard, usable film.

>   Shellac................96 cc (parts by volume)
>   Castor oil.............. 4 cc   "   "   "

The above formula will be about right for most uses. You could go a few points either way in adding the oil, but too much will soften the film too much and too little will show no softening effect at all. If you stay about in the range given above (4% oil) you should have no trouble.

I would use such a plasticizer in all my stock work when finishing in shellac. Even with French Polish I am not sure that the addition of this oil would not be beneficial.

Shellac may be applied in any way that other finishing materials can be applied. It can be brushed, sprayed, or rubbed on. Inasmuch as shellac is rather quick drying I would favor either the rubbing or the spraying methods. However, if you are quick and careful a very fine finish may be obtained by the use of the brush.

BRUSHING SHELLAC

Inasmuch as this will be the way most men will prefer to operate, being a little less messy than the rubbing and requiring less equipment than the spraying, I shall describe it first.

It makes very little difference what kind of a brush you use just so long as that brush is clean and free from dirt and dust. You may be familiar with the ruckus that one or two small pieces of dirt can raise with an otherwise excellent finish!

Place the shellac (thinned 50% with alcohol) in a convenient saucer or container. If you are really determined to have a good job you will strain the shellac through fine cotton (washed before use) or an old stocking your wife has discarded —wash this also before use. (This is not meant to cast any reflection on your wife but a piece of cloth which has been kicked around in the shop for even a few hours will gather tremendous quantities of dirt and dust.)

Place the stock in a checkering frame or other handy holder and make sure that it is securely fastened. I wonder how many times a lot of us have had a stock start to slip out of the holder and in desperately grabbing for it have ruined the still-wet finish? When everything is in order you can start.

Dip the brush in the shellac and allow only enough of the liquid to enter the bristles that they can comfortably carry without dripping all over the place. Transfer the brush to the stock and allow the shellac to flow out onto the wood with little or no help from you. If you try to stretch it out and press down much on the brush whatever air bubbles and dirt that may be in the bristles will be forced out onto the surface with that extra shellac and there they will remain forevermore. Or at least until you come along with some sandpaper and remove them.

You will find that you cannot go very far with this easy flowing before no more liquid naturally wets the wood. Stop and redip the brush and try again. This time be careful when approaching the already coated areas that you do not run the bristles headlong into the now drying shellac which you put on there a few seconds ago. Probably there will not have elapsed enough time for real drying to take place, but be careful anyway. If, for some reason, a considerable amount of the solvent has evaporated from the previously applied film then wherever you touch that film with the brush there will be left grooves or spots indicating where the bristles have touched, and these spots will not have enough solvent left to flow out and cover up the marks. When, and if, this takes place the only solution is to wait until the film is dry and then go after those bad spots with sandpaper. You can eradicate them but it means extra work which would not have been necessary if you had been careful in the first place.

If you work fast you will be able to cover the whole stock with one thin coat before any serious solvent evaporation takes place. Inasmuch as you should have thinned the original shellac with alcohol you can figure that it will take at least two to five minutes before a great deal of that alcohol has disappeared. This should be time and to spare for one coat over the average stock.

I have found that the most satisfactory system is to do one side of the butt, say, and then immediately turn the stock in the holder and work over the opposite side of the butt. Now you have the entire rear of the stock covered up to the grip. Now shellac the "up" side of the stock forward to the junction of the barrel with the receiver. Turn the stock and do the other side. Now finish the forearm right up to the tip and turn the stock once more. This time complete the other side from the barrel-and-receiver junction forward to the tip and you are finished.

Of course, during this turning and shellacking you will have covered edges and the top and bottom of the stock. It is a continuous process. If you can, shellac as you turn so that all areas are covered and you will not have to come back later and touch up some spot you meant to come back to but forgot about. The whole movement will resemble the curve and pitch on a giant corkscrew.

Now that you have one coat on leave the stock in the holder and let it dry for 24 hours. It will take this long for the great majority of solvent to leave a film, even a very thin one. Actually there will be some alcohol in that film for as long as six months, but for all practical purposes you can figure the film to be dry and hard if it sets from one evening to the next.

When the stock has dried for 24 hours (18 hours at least)

examine it for spots you have missed. If you find any such spots then touch them up for if you leave them to be covered by the next coat the chances are that they will be visible in the finished film.

When the first coat has dried to your satisfaction examine it for defects. A great deal will depend upon these inter-coat examinations. You will easily find areas which were gone over too lightly or skipped entirely. It is a simple matter to remedy such a fault when applying the next coat, but if you come across some foreign matter in the hardened film (such as loosened bristles or dirt) now is the time to sand that coat lightly to remove all traces of such matter. It is entirely possible that you may have to sand all the way down through the coat. If you find the fault to be of such magnitude that this is necessary then you had better do it now rather than wait till the stock is completed and hope that those bad spots will be covered. Inasmuch as any of the films we may put on wood will be transparent, any material which found its way into that film will remain visible for as long as there is any coating on the stock. Therefore remove it *now* or you will have to remove the whole darned finish eventually anyway.

The best way to remove such foreign bodies is to use sandpaper. The cutting action of the abrasive grains will remove the film layer by layer and you can stop where you want to. If the guilty particle is a small bit of dust which has fallen on the stock before the shellac has had a chance to become "tack-free" then in all probability it will be so minute as to be imperceptible. All the same it will probably have raised a tiny lump or bump in the film. In this case you need sand only enough to level off the bump. In going even this little ways down into the coat you will usually have removed the offending particle as well as the bump it caused.

If, however, you have encountered one of the loosened bristles that I mentioned before then there is little doubt that you will have to go all the way down to the wood in order to remove it. Do so if you must! These bristles will be a very unsightly "sore thumb" in an otherwise fine finish if allowed to remain.

When you have taken care of any bad spots or areas then lightly sand the stock all over with very fine grit paper. We do not particularly want to take off any of the shellac coat, but we do want to roughen the surface of the coat so that the following coats have as much adhesion or "grip" as possible. Then clean off any dust raised by the sanding.

Now you are ready to apply the second coat. Follow the same procedure that you did with the first coat. Make sure that you have enough thinner in this second coat so that maximum "flow" is given to the film. If you find that the shellac is a little hard to work with and is drying a bit too fast for you then add a little more denatured alcohol.

All brushing must be done smoothly and quickly in order to eliminate as many brush marks and laps as possible. While the first coat may have sunk into whatever filler you have used the second will tend to flow out on the surface and begin your actual finished film. From now on we will start to get the smooth unbroken coat and you must be very careful that you do not allow a little careless brushing or handling to ruin what otherwise would have been the finest finish you ever saw (you keep telling yourself).

When you have reached a point at which you consider the coating to be as good as you can make it, stop! The heavier or thicker you make the coat the more brittle it will be (even with the castor oil in it). We want just enough to give a good finish and a protective film and no more.

Now you are at a sort of crossroads. You can handle this finish in one of two ways—you can "spirit" it off and leave it that way; or you can smooth it down ever so slightly with polishing sandpaper and wax it. Let us look at both ways before we decide what to do.

The "spiriting off" is the classical way to handle a French Polish (which we will get to in a few minutes). It consists of applying alcohol to the film in such a way that it helps to increase the already high-gloss. While we do not have a French Polish here we do have precisely the same composition film (the only difference is in the method of application). Therefore we can approach the appearance of the French Polish by this method. The brushing on of the shellac has probably left a series of minute lines or depressions in the surface caused by the passage of the bristles. If these lines are so minute as to be practically invisible the spiriting off will eradicate them in most cases.

The polishing of the shellac by the second method (as opposed to spiriting off) will give a bit less of a gloss or high lustre to the surface. The lustre is cut down in this case by the addition of a wax film.

There you have it—high-gloss or velvet lustre. Take your choice. Personally, while the high-gloss finish has its place in furniture, I do not care for it on gun stocks. It smacks of a cheap, mass production object and most of us do not want our pet, handfinished stock to look like it came out of a production line. Therefore, if you will permit me to express my opinion, I personally prefer the second method. Anyway, the presence of the wax on the surface will add a bit of moisture resistance as well as personalized beauty.

SPIRITING OFF

This process is done by taking a bit of soft, absorbent cloth and making a small roll of it. Dip the roll in denatured alcohol and squeeze it out until it is only damp, *not wet*. If too much alcohol remains in the roll it will be forced out onto the finish, softening and totally ruining it. Now wrap the roll in another piece of very soft cotton which has been freshly washed. We do not want any dirt or dust at this point. The size of the roll and the covering cloth is not important, but they should be large enough so that the now enclosed roll is easily gripped by the fingers. Even a roll half the size of your fist will do, but if it gets much bigger than that it will be too unwieldly.

The cover, or second piece of cloth, should be only large enough to go around the cotton roll with enough left over to grasp it by.

When the dampened roll has been covered with the cloth grasp it firmly in the hand and *lightly* skim over the shellac film. There should be just enough alcohol in the roll to soften the film at the touch and allow it to be polished, as it were. As I said before, if too much alcohol is present it will be squeezed out onto the film and the presence of any appreciable amounts of the liquid will immediately soften the film to a point where the rubbing roll will roughen it rather than polish it.

This polishing is strictly a surface phenomenon. The very top of the film is softened and partially dissolved and then flows or spreads out under the smooth surface of the rubbing roll. Only that shellac in immediate contact with the roll is thus affected. The alcohol is in such small quantity that as soon as the cloth has left any given area the alcohol evaporates.

The effect of the rubbing roll is to smooth out any microscopic points or depressions and make a plane surface. This, in turn, will reflect most of the light faithfully, rather than scattering it, and this true reflection will give us what is termed a high-gloss.

SANDING AND WAXING

The method I prefer in finishing shellac films is this one wherein a softer, finer lustre is obtained.

When you have reached the end of the brushing operation and have allowed the stock 24 hours in which to harden well, take a piece of either 400 or 600 grit sanding paper. The 600 will be preferable for the final operation, though the 400 should be used first in order to clean up any visible imperfections in the film.

Sand lightly with the 400 grit paper until brush or dust marks are obliterated. Then take the 600 paper and polish out the marks left by the grains in the 400 paper.

Now take any good paste wax and give the stock a good coat.

Allow it to dry for a couple of hours and give it another coat. When this one has hardened polish the stock with a soft cloth, piece of felt, or a sheepskin buffing wheel. I have found that a good, limber shoe brush will be an excellent preliminary tool to shine up the finish, after which a soft cloth or piece of felt will give it that final touch.

If you wish you may use any of the paste or liquid wax formulae given in Chapter 10. They will be very similar to what you will buy at the store and will work very well. The paste or liquid wax formulae will be much easier to work with than a solid block of wax when applying this thin, protective coating as described above.

RUBBED FINISHES

If you do not like, or cannot make work, the brushing of shellac coats then the application of that material may be done more easily and just as effectively by one of the several methods of rubbing a finish on.

Inasmuch as French Polish is *the* finish (depending upon who you listen to) it shall be treated as a separate method, though it really is a rubbing finish and should go in here.

Place your shellac in a shallow dish or saucer. Make sure that it is thin enough to work with. Probably the 50% that you should have thinned the store boughten stuff will be okay in most cases. If you still think it is too sticky and heavy bodied to work with throw in some more alcohol. What the heck, the stuff will eventually evaporate anyway so you cannot lose anything, even if you go too far. It will take a little longer to build up a good film, though.

Now take some soft, clean cotton and fold it up into a sort of pad or wad, making sure that no folds are present on the rubbing surface. Now dip this wad or pad into a saucer of turpentine and rub it lightly across the edge of the saucer to get rid of any excess liquid which may be hanging on the face of the pad. Then dip the pad momentarily into the saucer of shellac and apply it to the surface of the wood. Rub in a circular movement and work quickly.

Continue this operation, making sure that you cover all spots well and that you do not miss any corners or edges. When you have gotten to the end of the stock come back and start again. You can go over the whole stock two or three times like this before any appreciable film is built up.

Now set the stock aside and let the turpentine and alcohol evaporate. This should take about 12 to 18 hours as the film will be very thin and will not hold solvent for very long. If you are in need of a quick finish you could even come back in a couple of hours and repeat the process, though I would recommend letting the shellac harden for the 18 hours I mentioned before.

Continue this rubbing and drying until you have built up a coat sufficient for your needs. As I have said before and will say again, the thinner the film you can get the better off you will be in the end.

When you have as much shellac on the stock as you desire then you can either leave it as it is or go ahead with the sanding and waxing described above. This is another place that you have a choice. I have always liked the appearance and durability that the wax film will give shellac and I shall continue to use it over shellac finishes until I find something better. If you like the looks of the stock as it is now, though, leave it that way. You are the master here and what suits you is best for you to do.

If, instead of the turpentine, you find that linseed oil meets your method of operation better use it. It has been mentioned many times in articles on stock work and is merely another twist to this rubbing method I have given. The only thing that I do not like about linseed oil is that once it is incorporated in a shellac film it will never dry completely. It will be surrounded by the shellac, and will not have a chance to absorb oxygen from the air. This lack of oxygen will keep it from hardening, though it will polymerize to a certain extent. Actually, in this method it will assume the properties of a plasticizer and we already have that in the presence of the castor oil. It may act as a sort of lubricant, but then so will the turpentine, and the turpentine will eventually evaporate from the film. This is another good chance for experimentation. If you find that the oil works better than the turps, by all means use it. But do not tell me about it if the film stays soft and refuses to polish up well.

SPRAYING SHELLAC

The use of the spray gun will be definitely acceptable here just as it was in using such a gun for varnishes and lacquers.

Shellac is a bit difficult to spray and still get a good, smooth film, but it can be done. You must make sure that the air pressure at the gun is not so high that it causes "Orange Peel" (wavy, bumpy finish). You must be sure that the shellac is well thinned with alcohol. If it is too heavy bodied it will dry too fast and will leave you with a very rough, flat finish.

If you have never sprayed shellac before I would say you had better try a couple pieces of wood that will not be hurt if you ruin them. These dummy pieces will allow you to become familiar with the handling of shellac and will permit adjustment of the gun air pressure, and the viscosity of the shellac so that you can handle it well before applying it to the stock.

When you have the combination so that you are getting good coats with satisfactory gloss then you may change over to the stock and have a go at it. As with any other method the ideal situation is to have the stock in a checkering frame for ease of handling.

Give the stock one good, wet coat of shellac and let it harden for the 24 hours I invariably recommend. Then give it another good wet coat and let that stand. By this time you should have a fairly heavy film built up. If you find that everything looks hunky-dory then take some of that 400 grit sandpaper I am always talking about and scuff the stock from stem to stern. This will smooth out any invisible imperfections which you may have without knowing it. It will also give the next (and last) coat a little better grip.

This time spray on a light coat well thinned with alcohol. The excess of alcohol will insure a maximum flow of the film. If it still does not look quite as good as you think it should take a little pure alcohol and spray on a light coat of it before the preceding shellac coat has had a chance to dry much. This should really flow it out and give you the gloss you are after.

With such a system you may get too much gloss, though. There is no doubt that you will have a much better lustre, or gloss, than either the brushing or the rubbing will have given you. In any case, it will be a little too much for the average man. Now you can take the 600 grit sandpaper alone and polish the coat followed by a good shot of paste wax.

Why bother about getting so much gloss in the handling of the gun if you are going to knock it out with the 600 paper, you say? The reason for my insistence upon maximum flow, even if we are not going to want the gloss it gives, is because that flow will insure that we have no hills or valleys in the surface of the film. This will guarantee that the final waxed coat will be as smooth and even as humanly possible, and that is what we are after, not the gloss alone.

FRENCH POLISHING

French Polish—what thoughts it conjures up. We see in our mind's eye a superb gunstock, beautifully figured, with an exquisite lustrous sheen to it. We think of a masterpiece of furniture, a desk with intricate carving upon it, perhaps.

All right, when you guys get through let me have a drag off that, will you?

The process of French Polishing is one which took the old masters many a moon to learn properly and adequately. It is a method by which shellac is applied to wood in such a manner that it is made smooth as glass and fully looks it! This is not a finish that you can master by reading a book (no matter which book you choose) but is one which takes considerable practise and great skill. I would not attempt to finish a stock with it until I had done a half dozen or so sample pieces and secured excellent results with the last four.

Do not let me discourage you, though. I definitely do not intend to do so, pessimistic as I may sound. It is just that it is so easy to make a botch of the job that you may very readily become discouraged and make no further attempts to master the system.

First of all, you must have clean shellac. The slightest bit of dust or dirt can ruin the best job, and for insurance I would say that you should (or must) strain the shellac through fine cotton or silk before using it.

Next you must have a "rubber" (rubbing pad). Such a tool is the base of the whole system and if it, too, is faulty it can ruin the whole job. This rubber may be made by rolling up a piece of clean cotton cloth into a roll about two inches long by about a half inch diameter.

For the first few coats you can use the shellac as it comes from the can if you wish. In all probability, though, it will be too thick for best results. Better still, thin the shellac with about 30% alcohol (100 ccs of shellac thinned with 30 ccs of alcohol).

Saturate the cotton roll with the shellac solution, and then squeeze out most of it. This will leave the roll well dampened with shellac but not too wet.

Now cover the dampened roll with a clean piece of cotton or muslin. You will find that the shellac will start to come through this outer covering when you squeeze the roll with your fingers.

To apply the shellac use enough gentle pressure with the fingers so that the shellac dampens the outer covering. Now put a drop of linseed oil on the covered roll face and start to massage the stock in a circular motion. The pressure of your hand forcing the roll over the surface will allow enough shellac to come through to slightly glaze the wood. This is all you are looking for. Do not attempt to build up a good film yet, but be content with this slight glazing appearance.

Occasionally add a drop or two of the linseed oil to the face of the rubber if it seems to be sticky. This oil acts as a lubricant and yet there will not be enough of it applied to the stock to constitute a non-drying portion of the film.

If you find that you are running out of shellac, and that further pressure by the fingers does not bring forth a glimmer of shellac, you can renew the shellac content, making sure at all times that you do not put too much in the cloth.

The rubbing of the roll over the surface is more of a sliding motion than anything else. Never lift the rubber from the stock and then set it straight down on another spot. If you must remove this rubber from the stock to add more oil or shellac skim or slide it off and back on at a very gentle angle. This will prevent you from making marks which a rubber set down abruptly upon the film will show.

Work from one end of the stock to the other and then set it aside. Even though the coat will be very thin it must be allowed to harden well before applying more shellac. If it is still soft then you will always tear it up to some extent when you apply a following coat.

If you do the job right it may take as many as ten to fifteen applications of the rubber to build up any kind of a coating. Even here you do not want the coating to be thick, but you do want it to be heavy enough so that it can be handled without danger of marring it.

When you have put on about four coats then thin the shellac with another 10% of alcohol. This will give you a little thinner solution to work with, but it will be easier to handle.

When you have applied another three or four coats throw in another 10 to 15% alcohol. By this time the shellac will be very thin indeed. But you will also be approaching the end of the job. You should have a good, smooth, glistening film by this time, and about all you want to do from here on in is to keep smoothing out that film rather than building it up much. The constant application of the shellac with a large alcohol content will tend to do that smoothing. Remember, though, the more of the solvent you have on the rubber the greater the chance will be of softening the film too much and thus digging into it.

Inasmuch as you will probably take from one to four weeks to do a good job of French Polishing you will have to take care of the rubber so that it does not become hard and thus increase the chance of digging into the film the next time you use that rubber. The easiest and safest way to store your rubber between applications is to have a jar with a little alcohol in it. Place the rubber in this jar and have just enough alcohol in it to keep the rubber dampened. Close the lid of the jar and the next time you take it out that rubber will still be soft and usable. If you allow the alcohol content of the shellac in the rubber to evaporate, though, it will harden up and your only resource will be to make another rubber.

When you have gotten to a point where the coat of shellac is smooth, glistening, and free from any rubbing marks or flat spots then you will have to think about the final operation—that of Spiriting Off. It is precisely the same as the one described earlier in this chapter, but you must be very careful. You are not going to be able to put any wax on the stock. You will lose all the advantage of the French Polish if you cover it up with a coating of that sort. Inasmuch as the surface is now about as smooth and shiny as you will ever be able to get it the slightest mishandling of the alcohol dampened cloth will disfigure it.

Handle the cloth carefully. Do not use too much of the alcohol and lightly touch it to the surface. You must use the same skimming or gliding motions that you used when applying the French Polish, and always leave and approach the surface of the wood at a very slight angle, never straight up and down.

If you feel that you have the stock as gleaming as you can possibly get it you may ignore the Spiriting Off. The idea behind this last little caress is to remove any oil (which you may have used as a lubricating film) which may be left on the shellac thereby dimming its lustre, and also to clean up any slightly rough or mishandled areas. If you have not used any oil (perhaps you used turpentine) or there are no bad spots then there is no point in using the alcohol. There will be nothing for it to do in that case.

The Spiriting Off is one of the traditional steps in this sort of finish, though, and many of those who can and do finish stocks in this manner adhere strictly to tradition. That part is up to you. If you think you need it, use it. If you think you do not need it, do not use it.

DESIRABILITY OF SHELLAC AS A FINISHING MEDIUM

The use of shellac as a finishing material is desirable under certain circumstances. These circumstances are those in which a finish is to receive little weathering and a minimum of handling.

Inasmuch as shellac, either alone or plasticized, is relatively brittle a great amount of handling or rough treatment will tend to chip or flake the finish. Also it will deteriorate rather easily under the influence of the ultra-violet light content of sunlight.

Therefore we may say that for stocks wherein beauty alone is desired the use of shellac is recommended. For stocks that will see quite a bit of field work it would be advisable to use one of the more stable materials, such as varnish.

FINISHING FAULTS

Brush Marks or Laps: These faults will appear as ridges or parallel depressions in the hardened film.

They are caused by allowing the shellac to stand too long or to lose too much of the solvent and then either going back over it with a brush or applying fresh shellac to an adjoining area as yet uncoated. In either case, the older shellac will be so near the dry point that there will not be enough solvent left in the film to allow the disturbed area to flow out and smooth itself. Therefore, the marks from the brush will remain until removed by sandpaper.

The remedy is to make sure that any brushing of the film is done while there is still enough alcohol in it to flow it out smoothly. In the case of lapping a fresh coat over partially dried ones this must also be done while the older film is still liquid. If that is impossible the shellac should be further thinned or reduced with alcohol until such a viscosity or body is reached that will allow the shellac to remain liquid for as long as required.

Dust Particles: These will appear as minute bumps or lumps in the film when it has dried. They are caused by dust or dirt from the air settling on the still tacky film.

The remedy is to be sure that all equipment, benches, walls and ceiling are cleaned with a damp rag before shellacking. This will prevent dust from being present to a great extent.

Gritty or Seedy Shellac: This will appear as grit, dirt, "seed," or pinpoints of foreign matter in the liquid shellac before use.

The cause is either dirt which has been allowed to fall into the liquid or, more usually with metal containers, the shellac has attacked the metal walls of the container and started them rusting. The rust then is dispersed in the liquid shellac.

The remedy lies in making sure that you strain the shellac before use and also in being sure that you keep it in glass bottles. Never keep it in metal containers.

Sticky, Non-drying Film: This fault is self explanatory. The film will remain soft and sticky for weeks or longer.

The cause is using shellac which has stood in solution for too long. In such a case a self-activated chemical reaction called "Esterification" has taken place. It may also be that, in using metal containers, the attack of the shellac on the metal walls has started a decomposition of the shellac itself.

The remedy lies in using glass containers and in making sure that the liquid is not older than about six to eight months.

If in doubt, brush out some on a board and see if it dries all right.

Poor Adhesion: This will appear as allowing the shellac film to peel or flake away from the wood or undercoat easily after drying.

The cause lies in having an undercoating material to which the shellac cannot adhere well. This may be old marine spar varnish or it may be unhardened drying oils of some sort.

The remedy lies in making sure that any oils which may have been previously applied are well oxidized or, in the case of an undercoat of varnish, that the surface is sanded with fine paper to allow a rough surface (and consequently greater surface area) for the shellac to adhere to.

Checking or Cracking: This will appear as minute checks, cracks or hairlines in the body of the coat.

The cause is usually temperatures which have rapidly expanded or contracted the wood underlying the shellac and the stresses thus set up have ruptured the brittle film which is not pliable enough to "give" without breaking.

The remedy lies in applying the shellac in films only thick or heavy enough to give the appearance desired. The heavier the film the more it will tend to check or crack easily. The use of castor oil as a plasticizer will help overcome this checking.

Flatting or Dulling: This will appear as very flat, dull, or streaked areas on the surface of a rubbed film.

It is caused by rubbing or sanding the film too soon after application. There will still be enough alcohol left in the film to keep it soft and the use of the sandpaper or rubbing compound will have roughened and dug up the surface rather than smoothed it down. It is possible that the surface will still be so soft as to allow some of the compound to embed itself in the surface.

The remedy lies in allowing the shellac to lose the great majority of its solvent content before working on it. This will be from five to 10 hours for very thin films and about 24 hours for heavy coats.

CHAPTER EIGHT

Plastic Finishes

THE word Plastic, as used to indicate a type of substance, has definitely been misused. People generally think of plastic as a new type of material which has only recently been perfected by science and which has wonderful properties and which is designated by a trade name or definite formula.

This is certainly not true. The word plastic refers to anything which may be worked or formed by chemical or physical treatment (such as heat) to shapes or forms in which they may be useful as an end product. Metals, such as steel and lead, are really plastics. Varnishes, lacquers, and shellac are plastics, therefore, in the fullest sense of the word.

The word has recently been applied to the whole field of chemical products which has been introduced as household items. Inasmuch as the substances of which the products are made are definitely plastic in nature the word has not been misapplied there, but it is certainly confusing to most of us.

Therefore when you find a stock or wood finishing product that bears the title of Plastic Finish do not immediately assume that here is something for which we have been searching for years and which will have properties completely overshadowing anything else you may possibly use. It may be only another varnish and oil mixture which is so commonly sold for stock work. Of course, there are always new products entering the field and it may also be possible that it is based upon the substances which we have been educated to think of as plastics. Therefore, unless you have the facilities to analyze such a product and determine precisely what it contains I would take it easy and run a few tests on a dummy stock or other piece of wood. This will allow you to determine for yourself just what the finish has to offer in the way of advantages in gloss, ease of handling, and adhesion. If you like the way it handles and the results it gives then I would say that this would be an excellent finish for you to use. But do not let the name plastic fool you—see for yourself!

POSSIBLE COMPOSITIONS

Vinyls: There are available today for use and experimentation substances which are based upon the vinyl derivatives.

This substance, vinyl, has been known for many years. It is only recently, however, that methods of use and improved materials have been developed to a point where they may be used by industry. It is very doubtful that gunstock work will see much use made of the vinyl substances for some time, but there is always the possibility that such a material will be offered.

The raw materials for manufacture are supplied by the chemicals vinyl chloride and vinyl acetate. Through an elaborate chemical treatment they are polymerized or acted upon in such a manner that the resulting clear substance will harden or dry when applied to a surface exposed to the air. The great disadvantage to these materials is that so far the only really satisfactory finishes have been obtained by subjecting the finished surface to considerable heat. These are comparable to the high-heat baking enamels with which household articles such as stoves and refrigerators are finished.

For the present, this sort of treatment is out of the question for any but the large scale arms factories, and even then it is doubtful that the cost of materials and labor would make its use practical. In some types of vinyl coatings the heat required to harden the coating is well above that which is permissible for wood.

It is possible to apply the vinyls to very porous surfaces and allow them to air dry with no heat whatsoever. Whether wood is porous enough to be used in this manner is not known, but there has been doubt cast on the subject by those who should be in a position to know. In cases where it would be possible to use it in this manner a drying time of at least a week must be allowed to permit evaporation of most of the volatile solvents which are in the film. Even though the film may appear to be hard after about 30 minutes there will still be a great deal of the solvents left and the coating will actually be very soft.

Vinyls would be an excellent finish for stocks if the air drying and hardening properties were improved.

Acrylics: Another type of finishing material is composed of the basic materials of which Lucite or Plexiglas is made. It is generally merely a solution of certain types of the plastic in volatile solvents.

This, too, has certain disadvantages that does not lend itself well to stock work.

As with the vinyls the acrylics are rare in this field, though they may soon be improved to a point at which they will be easily and efficiently handled.

There are a few solutions of this material already on the market. They are offered under different trade names, but the basic materials are the same in each.

These solutions may come in self-contained pressure cans, or they may be offered as bottled solutions just as are the other varnishes. In the latter case they are to be brushed or sprayed on with the regulation spray gun equipment.

While the drying time of such materials is fairly good, they show very poor water and moisture resistance. Laboratory tests run on methacrylate films show that the moisture resistance is not as good as that of raw linseed oil.

Chlorinated Rubber: One of the latest and probably least well known finishing materials is chlorinated rubber. This is either natural or synthetic rubber which has been chemically treated. Such a chemical treatment gives the substance certain properties that the original rubber does not have.

Chlorinated rubber is a white, hard, powdery material which dissolves readily in certain organic solvents such as toluol, xylol and high flash solvent naphtha.

The drying or hardening is done by simple solvent release. When the solvent evaporates, or leaves the surface of the applied film, it leaves behind the hard, smooth film. This is comparable to the shellac left behind when the alcohol evaporates, or the nitrocellulose and resin film deposited when a lacquer coating hardens. No oxidation or polymerization reaction takes place as in the case of certain varnishes.

This film will be very resistant to the passage of moisture. Tests show that it will have nearly the same resistance as a good marine spar varnish and as much or more than shellac. It is far and away better than any of the drying oils.

If available, chlorinated rubber is an excellent material to experiment with. It is simple to handle and apply and may prove to be at least a partial answer to the ideal stock finish.

For any of you that may be able to obtain small quantities of this material to work with the following formula will be a starting point toward developing a satisfactory finish:

Chlorinated Rubber Finish, #1

Natural Chlorinated Rubber—15 grams
Maleic Modified Resin   — 5 "
Toluol   —10 "
Xylol   —50 "
High Flash Solvent Naphtha—10 "
Raw Castor Oil   — 8 "

Place the rubber powder in a container, add the solvents slowly and stir well. When the powder has dissolved completely add the resin and dissolve that and then add the raw castor oil. Blown or processed castor oil will not dissolve in or be compatible with the rubber solution.

In this formula, the rosin resin is added to promote hardness and adhesion. The castor oil plasticizes or makes pliable the film. Too much castor oil, however, will make the film non-drying.

The above material may be brushed on the wood, but make sure that it is done quickly and in one or two strokes. It will start to set or harden in a few seconds.

This formula may be applied over other varnishes, but make sure that they are well hardened and dried before application. If they are not, the solvents will act as varnish removers and make a mess of the whole job.

When dry, the film may be rubbed and polished as with any other varnish film.

The greatest possible disadvantage of this material is the tendency to become yellow when exposed to very severe sunlight for long periods of time. For normal stock use this tendency may not be apparent, but for guns used month in and month out in the field it would be better to use one of the varnishes.

Phenoplast: This is the trade name for an entirely new type of phenolic finishing material which has only recently appeared on the market. Life magazine, sometime late in 1948, carried a rather glowing article concerning this material.

While Phenoplast is basically the same as other phenolic varnishes, the method of reaction (or hardening) is entirely new. Ordinary varnishes dry or harden by exposure to air at which time they commence a polymerization, but this material hardens only after the addition of a second liquid. This second liquid is necessary to induce the reaction.

The reason the material is described here rather than in the chapter on varnishes is that the makers claim it to be a plastic finish, and also because I think the new method of reaction is worthy of special note.

I have not had an opportunity to experiment with Phenoplast, but if the results obtained with it are as good as Life and the makers seem to think they are somebody's really got something here.

It is claimed to be impervious to all solvents except acetone (so are the other phenolics). It is supposed to be much harder and tougher than the others (I will not dispute their claims), and also impervious to heat and heated objects.

I am in no way connected with the Phenoplast people, but I am of the opinion that it would bear looking into. (I am not supposed to mention furniture in the book, but if I wanted to refinish a desk or table I would sure investigate this stuff.)

Probably there will be other similiar concoctions on the market before too long. This method of inducing polymerization is not new by any means, but it is new when it comes to a finishing material. Incidentally, this sort of polymerization is not limited to phenolic resins. There are a great many which will react in the same manner when correctly formulated and applied.

Phenoplast is distributed by L. Sonneborn Sons, Inc., 80 8th Ave., New York (11), N. Y.

Urea and Melamine: Any of you that happen to live in large communities may have noticed many of the billboard ads which implore you to have your car refinished with "genuine baked enamel" or some such thing. Maybe you have never given it a thought, or maybe you have, but the question should be brought up "If they do that with enamel, why cannot I do that with clear varnish?" Inasmuch as varnish and enamel are very similar in composition, except that the varnish does not carry any coloring matter, there is a definite possibility here.

The big advantage in using some sort of heat to dry or cure the varnish or enamel is that it will make that varnish or enamel set up or dry more quickly and harder than a plain air-dried finish would. The final hardness of the finish after about three months will be the same, but you will be able to turn out a finish that will not collect dust and fingermarks while waiting for it to harden on the surface.

First of all you must have what is called Baking Accelerator, Converter, or Low Bake Converter. This is merely a solution of urea-formaldehyde or melamine synthetic resins in thinner. This added to a clear varnish will cause the varnish to harden rapidly and smoothly when heat is applied. This sort of material may be purchased from any supplier of automobile refinishing paints and, while it specifies that it is to be used in enamels, it may be added to varnishes in the same amounts and under the same conditions.

The resins which these converters use will polymerize in the presence of heat, and at the same time will prevent the varnish film from wrinkling which it may do if applied alone and in heavy coats. The resin will have a terrible smell when fresh (reminding one of the down-wind side of the local fish market) but that odor will disappear upon hardening.

If you can beg, borrow, or otherwise appropriate the use of a bank of three or four infra-red heat lamps then you are all set. These lamps will furnish heat efficiently to a surface at which they are directed and the heat developed will be sufficient to set the wood afire if not carefully controlled.

In order to use this bank of lamps you must have a holder for the stock. The checkering frame which I so often mention will do the job very well, and will allow easy control of the heat source. Set the lights up so that they are about six inches apart (lamp center to lamp center) and about 18 to 24 inches from the surface of the stock. Such a distance will be optional, but if you get much closer to the wood with them you will run a fine chance of actually burning the wood before the finish is hardened.

The amounts of converter that should be added to the varnish depends upon the make of the converter; if your supplier carries it he will know how much should be used. If he does not carry it you can write to any of the manufacturers of automobile finishes and they can tell you where to obtain it.

When you have added the converter to your varnish in the amounts recommended upon the can then apply the varnish in the normal manner. Brushing will do if you have no other methods available, but a spray gun is the ideal method. Apply a good wet coat of the varnish (but make sure that it is not so heavy it starts to "run" or "sag").

Now place the bank of lights about 18 to 24 inches from the stock and turn them on. Turn the stock every minute or so in order to have all parts evenly heated. The wood should be heated to between 135° and 150° Fahrenheit for best results. If it goes much above this it will start to force out air and moisture and then you will have a lot of tiny bubbles and pinholes in the finish. Again, a practice piece of wood should be run first in order to determine just how close and for how long the lights may be used without running into this bubbling. Usually a period of about 15 to 20 minutes will suffice to harden the majority of the film.

When this hardening has taken place turn off the lights and allow the stock to remain undisturbed for 18 to 24 hours. When you come back to it you will have a "genuine baked varnish finish" the hardness of which will approach that of an automotive enamel. When that stock has stood for about a week it will not scratch any easier than the finish on a car. Of course, if you are going to give ole Betsy a barbed wire treatment then there is nothing in the world that will keep her from getting all beat up—unless, of course, it is a sheet steel shroud.

This type of heat treatment is applicable only to varnishes of the spar or marine spar type. Varnishes of the rubbing or general interior type will not take it well and lacquers will not even accept the addition of the converter, but instead will curdle into a stringy mess.

If you have the facilities, you could heat the stock in a convection (oven) type heating system. It will do the job just as well, but an oven which would be large enough to accept a stock is just not available to most of us.

Also, there is no increase in final durability or hardness over a plain air dried finish. The heat treatment will only set it up faster in order to do away with dust settling on the surface and thus marring it. After about a week the air dried finish will be just as hard as this heat treated one and the resistance to moisture and adhesion will be precisely the same.

For the individual working on his own stocks this method will probably not be very attractive, primarily because of the infra-red light equipment needed. For the commercial shop or for the gunsmith doing quite a few stocks a month it may be of interest and, if handled correctly, will be well worth the equipment and effort used in mastering it.

You should be warned of one thing, however. If you happen to put too heavy a coat of the varnish on the stock before subjecting it to the heat treatment you may find that any very heavily coated areas will have developed a series of minute wrinkles or waves in the film. This will be because the surface of that heavy coating has dried before the bottom and the stresses set up in the hardening film will tend to make the surface contract which will form the wrinkles or waves mentioned. The remedy here is to make sure that your films are not heavy or thick enough to act so, and to determine this while familiarizing yourself with the treatment, the best thing I know of is the practice or dummy stock.

CHAPTER NINE

Driers, Thinners and Solvents

THIS chapter is a short one, but because of all the misinformation which the layman is apt to run into the subject is important enough to be treated by itself.

WHAT IS DRYING?

The term "drying" as applied to the paint and varnish industry is a trifle ambiguous. It means the action of a wet or liquid film of protective material in changing from a liquid to a hard, solid state. This action does not take place by the simple evaporation of thinners as many of you may have been led to believe. While all of the spirit varnishes and common lacquers will harden by this action it is not called drying in the vernacular of the paint man.

Only those films which will harden by combining with the oxygen of the air or by reacting with themselves (as in polymerization) are termed drying materials. For a more complete picture of the drying (hardening) of such materials see Chapter 5 on Varnishes.

The agents which promote this drying action are many, and the end results are the same no matter which specific substance is used. While some will hasten the drying of the top of the liquid film first, others will start the film hardening from the bottom, and still others allow the film to harden more quickly by promoting this drying uniformly through the film from top to bottom.

For example, the use of cobalt derivatives as a drier will

tend to make the film dry faster at the surface. The use of lead derivatives will tend to make the bottom of the film dry as fast as the top; and so on. The particular action desired may be brought about by the proper selection and combination of drying agents, called Driers.

HISTORY OF DRIERS

The use of drying agents in paint and protective films is as old as the use of those films themselves. The early use of earth colors, such as umber and sienna, in paints was the first use of such articles, though the painters and would-be technicians of that day and age were not aware of their use as driers. They knew only that when these pigments were used their vehicles, or liquid base materials, would set up or dry much more quickly than if they were not present. They did not realize, of course, that there was a reaction of any kind involved.

It was not until about 1840 that the serious study of driers and drying agents was first attempted. At this time zinc oxide was substituted for white lead in some outside house paints and it was found that the newer zinc based paints would not dry nearly as fast as the old lead paints did. This failure to produce a satisfactory paint led to the study of drying action.

During the process of finding the whys and wherefores of the whole deal it was discovered that cooking metallic oxides with oils would give oil-soluble metallic compounds which would tend to increase the drying rate of paint materials with which they were mixed.

About 1885 the first liquid driers appeared as definite, useable materials. They were composed of lead and manganese resinates and linoleates and were termed soluble drying agents.

At the beginning of the present century these lead and manganese driers were the only ones available, but along about 1912 cobalt entered the picture with iron coming along a little later.

At the present time there are many metallic base substances in use, but the most important are the cobalt, manganese, lead and zinc naphthenates. Calcium has been used but is not particularly popular.

PROPERTIES OF SPECIFIC METAL DERIVATIVES

Lead: This is one of the oldest metals used for promoting drying. It is not a very powerful agent, but is used in the great majority of paints seen today. This metal will tend to make the film dry through from top to bottom evenly.

Cobalt: This metal produces the most powerful drying action known today. It is about forty times as effective as lead when used with drying oils.

Cobalt will tend to produce drying mostly at the top surface of the film, that is, at the surface nearest to the air. An excessive addition of cobalt drier to a material will tend to produce wrinkling of the surface and surface stresses which may cause early breakdown of the hardened film. This metal is used in many of the so-called Wrinkle Finishes which are used for novelty effects.

Manganese: This is the third principal drier used in the industry. It is very much more effective than lead but not as much so as cobalt.

Manganese will cause drying at the surface of the film in the same manner as cobalt, but also helps to promote drying of the film toward the bottom. The finished film may be apt to be hard and brittle if manganese is used alone. This drier will not cause wrinkling as readily as cobalt.

Iron: Driers of this base metal are not particularly effective at normal temperatures. They are used mostly in baking finishes of a dark color due to the dark color of the drier itself.

Zinc: This is not a particularly good drying agent, but it has the desirable property of eliminating wrinkling of a film upon drying.

JAPAN DRIERS

Japan driers as offered by paint suppliers consist of solutions of mineral spirits containing from 1 to 5% lead metal and from .2 to 1% straight cobalt or cobalt and manganese combined.

Such driers have their place and do a fine job, but the big objection to their use is that the average man has no idea how much of them to use and he usually uses a great deal too much. A little bit of this stuff goes a long way and may do considerable damage to the finished film if used in excess. The manufacturer of whatever item you intend using has incorporated drying agents in that item in the correct amount and in the proper manner. These drying agents will hasten the drying of the material as much as possible without harming the film and any extra that you may throw in for good measure will almost always have a deleterious effect, if not immediately then sometime in the future.

Unless you happen to have a can of paint or varnish which has stood around for several years and has thereby lost some of the drying qualities it originally had I would definitely recommend avoiding the use of Japan driers in all cases.

EFFECTS ON DURABILITY

The amounts of drying agents that a manufacturer will add to any given product will have been determined in the laboratory and, as such, will give optimum drying aid with no harmful effects on the hardened film. He will have been able to determine just what point may be reached in addition of drier to give the best effect. He also will be able to determine how far he can go before any specific drying agent will begin to harm the material.

It is possible, by adding too much drier, to decrease the effective life of the film produced by the product and thereby cause early breakdown of the protective film. He will never have gone this far. Durability of a product is more important than quick drying and in nearly every case the manufacturer will seek to protect his name by producing quality goods. This, of course, is not necessarily the case with the fly-by-night joker who wants to have a quick turnover and get out of there. Nationally or even locally recognized trade names are your best protection against a quick worker such as this.

Excessive drier in a paint or varnish will cause it to check or crack early, or even to peel off whatever it was put on. This may not be important in the case of many of the cheaper materials which are meant to be used indoors only, but when you have something that must take a lot of weathering then it is the most important thing. Spar varnishes which protect wooden objects, whether they be gun stocks or boats, must hang on for the life of the varnish and this life must be lengthened as much as possible.

It is very probable that the average gunstock will take very little weathering and will have excellent care. In such a case the life of a protective film will be nearly as long as the life of the stock itself. But in the case of the gun that is out in all kinds of weather for weeks or months then such protective material will be hard put to retain its "protective integrity."

Inasmuch as lacquer, shellac and spirit varnishes harden only by the evaporation of the thinners or solvents, driers have no place in these materials. They will have no action whatsoever in hastening the hardening of the film and may even do damage if added. These materials never contain driers.

Drying oils used by themselves may be helped by small amounts of driers but even here I would not recommend additions of such agents. Raw oils such as linseed contain non-drying materials which will tend to mask the action of the drier and will not dry a great deal faster. Raw oils such as tung and oiticica must not have driers added. These oils will produce wrinkled films in a raw state and the addition of driers will only accentuate the wrinkled condition. Tung and oiticica oils will dry hard in about 24 hours anyway so there is no need to hasten the drying.

THINNERS AND SOLVENTS

In every paint, varnish, or lacquer used today there is a material which is used to dissolve and thin the solid constituents which make up the mixture. While innumerable substances can be used, there are a few which are the mainstays of the paint and varnish industry and which will be used in the majority of protective film forming agents available today.

These thinners are used because of their properties of dissolving oils and resins and because they will evaporate rather quickly (depending upon the properties of the individual thinner) and thus leave the solid matter behind in a thin, smooth film.

Turpentine: This was perhaps the first material used as a solvent or thinner for the early paints and varnishes.

According to Herodotus, the early Egyptians knew it as Cedar Oil and used it considerably. The Persian designation Termentin or Turmentin was later applied and changed gradually into the name as we know it today.

Turpentine as it is used at the present time is the by-product of the production of pine-tar and charcoal. It is produced by distillation of pine wood, or pine wood sap.

This substance is an excellent solvent, better than many of the petroleum solvents but not so good as most of the so-called aromatic solvents. It will dissolve most of the varnish resins (synthetic) but not many of the natural, fossil resins in their raw state. After these natural, fossil resins have been heat treated they will be readily dissolved by turpentine, however.

Turpentine may be used in lacquers, but only to a limited degree. It will not dissolve the basic nitrocellulose.

The study of turpentine in both the fresh state and when oxidized has given rise to the theory that possibly the oxidized turpentine may aid the durability of paints and varnishes when exposed to weathering.

Pine Oil: Pine oil is produced from the same source as turpentine; that is, from the distillation of pine wood sap.

It is an excellent solvent, dissolving even natural, untreated fossil resins which turpentine will not do. It may be used to dissolve many of the phenolic resins which turpentine will also fail to do.

While pine oil is not a solvent for lacquers (nitrocellulose) it will act as a latent solvent, giving the true solvents in the mixture the power of dissolving more of the nitrocellulose than if the pine oil were not present.

Pine oil is of low volatility and therefore will not leave a film before good flow of the surface has taken place.

Petroleum Solvents and Thinners: There is a definite class of thinners and solvents which are obtained from crude petroleum oil. All of the materials in this class are obtained in one of two ways: (1) distillation; (2) selective solvent action.

(1) Distillation of crude oil consists of heating the oil to a certain point at which a particular portion of that crude oil will pass off in vapor. Then that vapor is cooled, or condensed, and purified.

(2) Selective solvent action is brought about by the fact that liquid sulfur dioxide will dissolve only these particular portions of the crude oil. Then the solvents and thinners dissolved in the liquid sulfur dioxide are separated into their particular component portions. The sulfur dioxide is used over and over again for more extraction treatments.

The ordinary thinners obtained from petroleum follow:

Mineral Spirits: This was first introduced as a turpentine substitute. It has since come into its own as a first class thinner and solvent for the synthetic type resin materials. It is probably used more than any other of the petroleum based thinners. It is much more volatile than kerosene.

Kerosene: This material has been used for many years to make brushing of paint easier, and to eliminate brush marks from the finished film. Because it evaporates very, very slowly it allows the film to flow out and smooth off before hardening. It will increase the dangers of the film sagging or running because it will allow that film to remain liquid for so long.

Generally it is used in very small amounts, and never as the sole thinner present.

VM & P Naphtha: This is the trade name or designation for Varnish Makers and Painters Naphtha.

It is generally used to shorten the setting and drying time of a film because of its rapid evaporation rate. This fast evaporation will increase the danger of brush marks and will make the brushing of the paint or varnish more difficult.

It is more volatile than mineral spirits, due to its rate of evaporation. It is a definite fire hazard if used around an open flame.

LD Naphtha: Trade name or designation for Lacquer Diluent Naphtha.

It is used in lacquers to thin the mixture, though it is not a true solvent in the sense that it will dissolve the nitrocellulose. It will merely be tolerated by the nitrocellulose, rather than actively dissolve it.

Because of its rapid evaporation rate it may increase the tendency of a lacquer film to "blush," or show moisture condensed upon the surface of the film due to this rapid evaporation rate.

It may be used with varnish, but is more expensive than regular varnish thinners and will leave the film too quickly for best results.

Lighter Lacquer Diluent: This is used in the same materials as LD Naphtha. It is very volatile and is never used alone as a thinner.

High Solvency Naphtha: This is a special class of petroleum thinner that will show more solvent power than VM & P Naphtha. It will have nearly twice the solvent power that other naphthas have, though it may not be compatible (will not mix) with some of the synthetic resins that the ordinary naphthas will dissolve with ease.

COKE OVEN DISTILLATES

These are of the hydrocarbon type and are obtained during the process of making coke from coal. This is done by heating the coal in a closed container or oven. The gases given off are dissolved in high-boiling petroleum oils, and the volatile content of the coke gases are then distilled off at certain points in the distillation process and caught. They are then purified.

The more common coke oven distillates are as follows:

Benzol (sometimes called Benzine): This may be used in paint and varnish removers and in coatings where a fast evaporating solvent is required.

90% Benzol: A special grade of Benzol more widely used than the above thinner.

It is used where accelerated drying time is required, such as in traffic paints. It may also be used as a nitrocellulose thinner or diluent.

Toluol (sometimes called Toluene): The most generally used diluent today for lacquers. It has remarkably little tendency to cause blushing of lacquers.

It may be used in varnishes with excellent results, but is relatively more expensive than other commonly used varnish thinners.

Xylol: Industrial xylol is sometimes known as solvent naphtha. It is used as a lacquer diluent, and is slower evaporating than toluol.

For use in varnishes and enamels it has great solvent power. Usually it is used in these materials together with a balanced blend of petroleum thinners so that desirable properties may be obtained and the cost held down.

High Flash Solvent: This thinner is used especially in the production of the phenolic type varnishes. It will reduce the tendencies of this varnish to gel or become solid in the can.

Generally speaking, high flash solvent is one of the most desirable thinners for use in the varnish makers field.

It has a flash point of above 100° Fahrenheit so that the fire hazard is not great.

LACQUER THINNERS

The following materials are used almost exclusively for lacquers. They are generally produced from raw materials in special chemical reactions and are never secured from either petroleum or coal tar sources.

Ethyl Acetate: A very fast evaporating solvent. It will dissolve the nitrocellulose base of the lacquer and carry it in solution.

It may possibly increase the blushing tendencies of a lacquer film if other solvents are not included to balance the mixture.

Isopropyl Acetate: This is used as a substitute for ethyl acetate and is slower evaporating.

Methyl Ethyl Ketone: A very volatile solvent. Will cause blushing more than ethyl acetate. It is a true solvent for nitrocellulose.

Acetone (dimethyl ketone): This solvent is a true solvent for nitrocellulose and was one of the major components of the first lacquers. It evaporates very quickly and thus promotes blushing if used in large amounts.

Ethyl Alcohol: This is not a true solvent for nitrocellulose. It is what is termed a latent solvent (see the chapter on lacquers). It may cause bad blushing.

This substance will give excellent flow to a lacquer and thus produces good gloss.

Butyl Acetate: A true solvent for nitrocellulose. It is rather slow evaporating and thus gives resistance to blushing.

It is considered the standard slow lacquer solvent.

Secondary Amyl Acetate: This is used as a substitute for the above, but is very poor.

Fusel Oil Amyl Acetate: This was the standard slow lacquer solvent before the introduction of butyl acetate, but has now been superseded by that most excellent material.

Butyl Alcohol (butanol): This is not a true solvent for nitrocellulose, but is rather a latent solvent.

It has a slow evaporation rate and is used as the solvent for the natural or synthetic resins which are invariably incorporated in modern lacquers.

High Boiling Point Solvent: As the class name implies, these materials evaporate very slowly. They are used to some extent in most lacquers, but the greatest use is in specialty items.

This class includes: Butyl Cellosolve, Cellosolve Acetate, Butyl Lactate, Ethyl Lactate, Methyl Lactate, and Diacetone Alcohol.

VARNISH AND PAINT REMOVERS

Whenever a surface is to be repainted or revarnished for some reason, the old coating, if any, must first be removed. This is usually because that old finish has deteriorated to some extent and the new coating is needed to protect that surface. If any appreciable deterioration of the old coating has taken place then that coating will not offer a good base upon which to lay any further coats. Thus the removal is indicated.

There are a great many substances which may be used as varnish removers, but not all of them will be satisfactory in all respects, and many of them will be definitely harmful.

Lye: Sodium hydroxide, or lye as it is popularly called, is a first class paint and varnish remover. It will act upon the film, attacking it chemically, and thus destroying it and its adhesion to the wood. While lye will do a first class job it should never be used upon wood surfaces.

This seemingly contradictory statement is based upon the fact that lye is a solid substance. When dissolved in water it is liquid, true enough, but when that water evaporates it then changes back into the solid form. If any of the lye solution is left on the surface because of incomplete rinsing of the surface then, upon the evaporation of the water, crystals of the lye will be deposited down deep in the pores and crevices of the wood. Even though they are very tiny and few in number any subsequent organic coating which is laid down on top of those crystals will be immediately attacked by the lye and will eventually be destroyed. This will result in the film becoming soft and under handling will peel completely away from the wood at those spots. Then you have a job of refinishing the stock all over again. If you do not remove all the lye this second time whatever is left will again attack the finish and the whole process will be repeated.

DRIERS, THINNERS AND SOLVENTS

Rather than take a chance that you may not have completely flushed the lye from the wood, pores and all, it would be much better to use one of the solvent type removers which are so easy to make or obtain.

Solvent Type Removers: This type varnish remover will destroy an organic film by softening and dissolving the film. Then it can easily be peeled away from the wood. In some cases it will dissolve completely, and in others it will swell, pucker up, and crumble into powder.

There are a great many solvents available to do this job. The commercial mixtures will contain many different solvents, depending upon the particular formula that the maker used.

Following are some representative formulae which you may follow if you so desire:

Varnish Remover Formula #1

Benzol	—3 parts
Butyl alcohol	—2 parts
Ethylene dichloride	—2 parts

Varnish Remover Formula #2

Benzol	—4 parts
Fusel oil	—3 parts
Denatured alcohol	—1 part

Varnish Remover Formula #3

Benzol	—4 parts
Acetone	—2 parts
Toluol	—3 parts

Varnish Remover Formula #4

Toluol	—2 parts
Denatured alcohol	—2 parts

Varnish Remover Formula #5

Benzol	—2 parts
Fusel oil	—2 parts
Acetone	—3 parts

Varnish Remover Formula #6

Methyl acetone	—10 parts
Benzol	—25 parts
Denatured alcohol	—18 parts
Ethylene dichloride	— 8 parts

Remover for Shellac (French Polish) Formula #7

Denatured alcohol	—10 parts
Butyl acetate	— 5 parts
Acetone	— 5 parts

All of the formulae listed above are to be used in the same manner, and the remarks that fit one fit all of them.

Application of Varnish Removers: Inasmuch as these removers attack a film by softening and partially dissolving it obviously they must be placed in direct contact with the film. The easiest way to do this is to place the stock or other object to be cleaned on a pad of folded newspapers. Then brush the remover liberally over the surface, taking care to apply as heavy a coat of the remover as possible without having it all run down onto the newspapers and be soaked up.

The substances of which all these removers are made are very volatile and will quickly evaporate from the surface upon which they have been brushed. Continue bathing the surface of the wood with repeated applications. When the coating seems to be drying out in one spot splash some more on that area. As the solvents attack the film it will become soft and soggy and may even pucker up and fall off the wood. When this point is reached all that is necessary is to take a scraper of some kind and scrape off the loose portions. Continue this process until all or the very great majority of the film has been removed.

At times you will find that certain types of varnishes will resist the attacks of the solvents more than other kinds. If this happens you will get very little of the puckering of the film. Instead, occasionally scratch at the film with a putty knife or the scraper, and when it softens sufficiently to be scraped off do so without waiting for the puckering effect.

Lacquers probably will not pucker so. Instead, they will merely soften and actually dissolve under the influence of the solvents.

As you continue the softening and scraping operations you may notice that the varnish or lacquer which you are removing may tend to harden up again and resist all attempts to remove it. This will be because you have allowed that area to lose all solvents by evaporation and as soon as the solvents leave, the film will no longer be in a liquid form. Reapply the remover until this stubborn area is again soft and pliable.

Nearly all of the solvents used in these varnish removers listed are active ingredients of lacquers. This will give you an idea of why lacquers applied (especially by brushing) over fresh varnish films will cause a lifting or puckering. The same action is taking place. The solvents will be able to dissolve that fresh varnish easily and actually start to remove it from its base. The older a varnish is the harder it is for these solvents to dissolve it.

Many varnish removers and their formulae available to the public will contain wax. The purpose of the wax is to form a thin film over the remover once it has been spread out on a surface, and this wax film will prevent the solvents from evaporating very quickly. Thus a varnish remover containing wax will last longer and will remove more varnish per unit volume.

But, and this is a big point, that same wax will get down into the pores in the wood upon evaporation of some of the solvents and that wax will be very difficult to remove. If an extremely thorough job of removing the wax is not done before refinishing then it could cause following coats of varnishes, lacquers, or drying oils from drying properly or at all. Most important, however, the wax will not allow the following protective coating to grip the wood well and thus very poor adhesion will result. In fact, the presence of such a wax under varnish could make the varnish actually peel off in large sheets under normal handling. Use removers containing wax if you must when refinishing your automobile, but Heavens to Betsy, Gertrude, never use it on wood surfaces.

It is only fair to say that many wood finishers and stockers have and do use wax-containing removers with good results. This is only because they are extremely careful to remove every trace of the wax from the wood before applying a finish coat of any sort. I also suspect that it is due to very good luck rather than to an acceptable practice which should be followed at all times.

CHAPTER TEN

Waxes, Polishes and Rubbing Compounds

VARIOUS kinds of wax and combinations of wax with other materials have long been used for finishing gunstocks and furniture. Wax based finishes were probably the first durable items that wood workers used for this purpose. Certainly the use and properties of waxes of a sort were known to craftsmen back in early Oriental history and until they developed the well known varnishes and lacquers for which they are famous this sort of thing was all they had to work with.

There are many kinds and types of wax, any of which may do under certain circumstances, but only a few of which have properties which lend themselves well to wood finishing. The use of such materials will impart a certain beauty and lustre that no other finishing substance can match. While the durability of such wax finishes has its limitations, for interior work they will be highly satisfactory.

KINDS OF WAX

Beeswax: Beeswax is probably the most well known of the so-called natural waxes. It is obtained from the hives of the honey bee *Apis mellifica*. After the store of honey is removed from the combs they are melted down to recover the wax of which they are formed. This wax is light yellow in color but may turn dark yellow or brown with age. Wax from wild bees has the same properties as that from the hives of domesticated bees.

Beeswax is used for polishes and candles. The melting point is about 145° Fahrenheit.

Carnauba Wax (Brazil wax): Carnauba wax is obtained from the leaves of the palm tree *Copernica cerifera*. The leaves are pounded or bruised to remove the incrustation of wax which forms upon them.

There are two forms of carnauba wax—*olho* and *palha*. The olho wax is a light gray and comes from the young leaves. Palha wax comes from older leaves and is a darker color. The best known yellow carnauba wax is of the olho variety.

This wax is used in polishes, furniture waxes and for increasing the hardness of other waxes. The melting point is about 185°.

Japan Wax (sumac wax, Japan tallow): This wax comes from the berries of the plants of the genus *Rhus*. It is really a vegetable fat and is obtained by steaming the berries.

The crude wax is a greenish color but is usually treated to obtain the yellow product.

This wax is used in candles and polishes. The melting point is about 124°.

Ouricury Wax: Obtained from the leaves of the palm tree *Syagrus coronata* or *Cocos coronata* of Brazil.

It is darker in color than carnauba wax but is used for the same purposes. The melting point is about 185°.

Ozokerite (mineral wax, earth wax): This material is a natural paraffin obtained from the ground. The rocks in which it occurs are crushed and heated to extract it.

The color of this material may range from yellow to black depending upon the locality in which it is found.

It is used in polishes and candles and by the electrotyping trade. The melting point will range from about 131° to 230°.

Ceresine Wax: This is merely a refined form of ozokerite. The raw material is alkali treated and then filtered. This refined form will be light yellow and has a melting point of about 142° or less. The main uses for this refined form are in waxed paper, polishes and candles.

Montan Wax (lignite wax): This material is very similar to ceresine. It is produced in Europe from lignite and is used for leather finishes and candles.

The melting point is about 185°.

Spermaceti: This material is a true wax and is obtained from the head cavity of the sperm whale *Physeter breviceps* and the bottlenose whale *Physeter macrocephalus*. When the sperm oil is boiled the white flakes which precipitate are gathered and this is the spermaceti.

It is used mostly for ointments and compounds at the present time. The melting point is about 109°.

Candelilla Wax: Obtained from the stems of the shrub *Pedilanthus pavonis* and *Euphorbia antisyphilitica*.

It is light colored and is used in polishes and as an adulterant for beeswax and carnauba wax. The melting point is about 153°.

Paraffin Wax: Obtained from the refining of petroleum. The color is whitish gray.

It is used in waterproofing and sealing compounds. The melting point is from 105° to 135°.

Esparto Wax: This is obtained from the dried Esparto grass in Great Britain.

It has properties similar to those of carnauba and is replacing it to a great extent at the present time.

Waxes differ from fats and oils in chemical composition and the mineral waxes differ from the true waxes also in the same manner.

Inasmuch as the newer synthetic waxes have so many different properties they are used extensively as replacements for the natural waxes.

These synthetic waxes are offered under a rather confusing array of trade names and unless you are familiar with the specific properties of each of them it would be better to stick to the use of the natural waxes in making up any of the formulae given in this book. If you are able to obtain samples of such waxes and can run tests to determine specific properties as compared to the natural wax you wish to replace then there is no reason why you should not use the synthetic materials.

The following lists the various common natural waxes in their correct categories:

Vegetable Waxes

Wax	Melting Point
Carnauba	181–183
Candelilla	147–154
Ouricury	177–179
Esparto	167
Japan	122–129

Mineral Waxes

Wax	Melting Point
Montan	185
Paraffin	105–135
Ozokerite	131–230
Ceresine	142

Insect and Animal Waxes

Beeswax	145
Spermaceti	109

FINISHES AND POLISHES

There is almost no limit to the uses of wax in finishes and polishes. It may be and usually is combined with other substances depending upon the properties desired in that particular compound.

The use of ethyl cellulose in waxes is increasing. The presence of the ethyl cellulose will raise the melting point and increase the toughness of the wax and the wax will increase the water resistance of the cellulose. This sort of combination may readily be applied in the melted form or in a solution or suspension of some sort.

Polishes are an important use for waxes. They may be combined with some sort of a gentle abrasive, they may be used only to build up the thickness of an already existing film, or they may contain agents which will remove dirt and grit on the surface of whatever it is desired to polish. Along with the wax and possible abrasive there are incorporated resins of some sort (shellac, for instance) and volatile solvents to produce a solution or suspension for easy handling. These solvents are usually petroleum or mineral spirits, turpentine or possibly an oil such as linseed or mineral oil.

Wax finishes may be applied to nearly any surface in any condition, but the smoother and finer the surface the finer the resultant finish will be.

WAX FINISH FOR GUNSTOCKS

A wax finish is placed on a stock for two reasons. First, the application of wax is a relatively simple matter and may be done quickly and easily. Second, wax will give a beautiful finish and one which will be both durable and easy to keep in good condition. Both of these reasons will appeal to the average amateur and professional I have found. Unless such a stock is to receive harsh treatment and be in the rain and snow for very long periods I see no reason why wax cannot be used.

Wax is very waterproof. Such a finish on a stock, if kept in good shape, will be much more waterproof than most of the drying oils you may use and will approach if not exceed the moisture resistance of many of the varnishes. This is another excellent reason for using wax. The only thing about it is that the use of very soft waxes will allow a considerable amount to be worn off the wood through repeated handling, and when the bare wood pops up through the coating of wax then you have a fine chance that moisture will creep in. With some of the harder waxes this chance is lessened and for all general purposes such a hard finish will be among the best available.

APPLICATION OF WAX FINISHES

To apply wax on a new piece of wood you must have finished all staining, grain raising, and sealing. The treatment with wax will be the last step and the surface must be smooth as possible. The use of a filler will be optional as, with proper treatment, the body of the finish will assume filling properties. Possibly the use of a filler will add somewhat to the appearance of the finish as it may be colored or tinted to the shade you wish the pores of the wood to take. However, a perfectly satisfactory finish may be obtained by the use of the wax alone without the filler. This, of course, assuming that you use a wax combination which does not contain a great deal of solvents or thinner.

If you figure on using a liquid wax then it probably would be advisable to use a filler because of the many applications or coats which would be required for the liquid material to do much filling. These liquid waxes have a great deal of thinner or solvent in them and when a coat of it dries it shrinks considerably as the bulk of it was the thinner which has now left the film.

Let us take a look at the application of liquid waxes first. These will either be true solutions or they may be suspensions of insoluble materials in a liquid medium.

When you have made sure that the basic operations of sanding, staining, grain raising and sealing have been completed decide whether or not you intend to use a filler. If you want one put it on now. If you do not want to use one forget it.

When all these basic operations are completed take a little liquid wax and spread it out on the surface of the stock. Rub it in well with a wad of some kind of cloth so that it gets down as far as possible into any pores or cracks. If you wish you may thin that liquid with a little mineral spirits or turpentine so that this first coat will have maximum penetration. Set the stock aside until all the volatile thinners in the wax have evaporated and then repeat the process as many times as you wish until the surface takes on a uniform lustre. This lustre will appear only after all porous spots in the wood and all pores or cracks have absorbed as much wax as they are going to after which the wax builds up on the surface rather than sinks down into it. Until this uniform lustre is obtained there will be dull or flat spots and areas dotting the surface of the stock. These are the points at which a good coat has not been built up but rather sinks down in and therefore will not have a smooth surface to reflect light in the same manner as other well coated spots.

When you have the stock in such a condition that no more coats will increase the lustre then you may take a good soft piece of cotton or felt and rub until all marks left by the applicator pad are removed. If you wish you may apply the stock to a sheepskin buffing wheel. This will do the rubbing in record time and will really polish the surface as nothing else can shine it up.

Paste waxes (purchased already prepared) will give you the same results as will the liquid waxes. They will contain less solvents so that they will build up an appreciable film much more quickly. The methods of application are precisely the same as with the liquid wax compounds. When you have reached the final coat polish or rub it in the same manner.

Paste waxes will contain enough solvent to allow easy application with a rag or pad but if you still do not like the way they work they may be further reduced or thinned with turpentine. This will make them more liquid and will spread out easier. They will take longer to dry than the normal, unthinned wax, though.

FORMULAE FOR WAX-FINISHING ITEMS

If you do not care to use an already prepared paste wax or are not in a position to purchase them you may very easily make such compounds yourself. In working with the following formulae you may alter them at your pleasure if you find that some particular property does not suit you. If you find that any given formula results in a mixture too thin for your liking then add a bit more of the solid substances. If it turns out too thick or heavy then add a bit more of the liquid until you have just what you want.

Paste Wax Formula (#1)

Carnauba Wax	2
Beeswax	2½
Japan Wax	3
Paraffin Wax	6
Turpentine	30

The waxes should be melted together and the heat turned off. Then the turpentine should be added a little at a time, stirring well all the time. If the waxes start to solidify before all of the turpentine has been added reheat until just above the melting point and continue stirring in the turpentine until all has been added.

This formula will produce a lustrous, waterproof finish which should wear well.

Paste Wax Formula (#2)

Beeswax	6
Carnauba wax	28
Montan wax	8
Ceresine wax	16
Naphtha	89
Turpentine	10
Pine oil	4

Melt the waxes together, turn off the heat and add the solvents by rapid stirring. Continue the stirring until the mixture has solidified. Be careful about heating this mixture over a flame. The naphtha is very inflammable.

This formula will produce a wax which, with rubbing and polishing, will give excellent durability with great lustre. Use it in the same manner as any paste wax.

Paste Wax Formula (#3)

Carnauba wax	10
Ceresine wax	10
Montan wax	15
Turpentine	40

Melt the waxes and add turpentine in the same manner as the other formulae. This mixture will be hard and durable and will polish to a fine lustre.

Paste Wax Formula (#4)

Carnauba wax.................... 5
Beeswax........................ 3
Turpentine.....................10
Burnt umber.................... 2

Melt the waxes and add the turpentine, stirring well. When all the solid materials have been well dispersed add the burnt umber powder. This should be well mixed to eliminate any possible lumps remaining.

This formula is used where the wax is intended as a filler as well as a finish. Do not allow much of the film to build up over the wood as the umber content will tend to hide the surface. Just enough of this should be applied to bring out an even lustre over the whole stock with no remaining flat spots.

Liquid Wax Formula (#5)

(a)   Beeswax........................ 5
       Carnauba wax...................15
(b)   Turpentine.....................85
       Pine oil....................... 2

Melt the waxes together (a) and while still hot stir in the thinners (b).

This is a liquid finishing material that will give a good lustre but which would be easiest to use as a finishing item only. The thinner content is so great as to preclude use as a filling material.

Liquid Wax Formula (#6)

(a)   Carnauba wax...................20
       Ceresine....................... 5
(b)   Turpentine.....................15
       Naphtha or white gasoline...........60
       Pine oil....................... 2

Melt the waxes together (a) in the same manner as formula #5. Then add the thinners (b), stirring well.

This formula will dry more quickly than #5 and will give about the same lustre upon polishing. It will not build up a heavy film quickly.

POLISHES

Polishes differ from wax finishing materials in that they will clean a surface of dirt and dust and will increase the lustre by leaving a very thin film of wax or oil on the surface. They are not designed to nor will they ever give a heavy protective film. They merely add to the surface appearance.

They are invariably applied by means of a soft cloth pad which is wet by the liquid. The cloth is then rubbed well over the wood.

Liquid Polishing Formula (#7)

Carnauba wax	15
Paraffin wax	25
Ceresine	30
Benzine	170

The waxes are melted together and then the benzine stirred in. This formula will work best over an already waxed or finished surface. The wax will be distributed in a very thin layer and will not build up a heavy film.

Apply by means of a pad. Pour some of the liquid into the pad and vigorously rub over the surface. Allow to dry for 15 minutes and then polish with a cloth or sheepskin wheel.

Liquid Polish Formula (#8)

Carnauba wax	30
Beeswax	60
Pine oil	5
Turpentine	220
Soap flakes	1
Water	10

Dissolve the soap in water. Dissolve the waxes in the pine oil and the turpentine. The two solutions are then mixed together with vigorous shaking. An emulsion will have been formed which must be well shaken each time before use.

This polish is to be used on any finished wood surface, either waxed or varnished. It will be especially good over a French Polish.

It is applied by means of a soft cloth. The bottle is well shaken to mix any settled portions of the wax and then a little poured out into the cloth. Vigorous rubbing will distribute a thin lustrous film of wax over the surface.

Liquid Polish Formula (#9)

(a)
Carnauba wax.................... 30
Rosin........................... 5

(b)
Soap flakes...................... 10
Turpentine...................... 2
Water...........................250

Melt the wax and the rosin together (a). Dissolve the soap, water and turpentine together (b), heat to boiling and add to (a) with vigorous stirring.

This polish must be applied with a soft cloth and rubbing.

Liquid Polish Formula (#10)

Mineral oil......................1 gallon
Powdered carnauba wax............3 oz.

Heat the oil and wax together until the wax is completely dissolved in the oil. Let cool and use with a soft cloth and rub in well. The mineral oil will never completely evaporate, but such a thin film of it will remain on the surface that, together with the wax, a good lustre will be gained.

This formula should be used on objects which are never used outdoors.

Liquid Cleaning and Polishing Formula (#11)

Stearic acid	2
Boiled linseed oil	1
Turpentine	5
Pine oil	1
Soap flakes	1
Water	10

Melt the acid and dissolve in it the linseed oil, turpentine and pine oil. Dissolve the soap flakes in the water and heat to boiling. Quickly pour the boiling water into the first mixture and stir vigorously until cool.

This polish will be more of a cleaner than anything else. A small amount of the linseed oil will be left on the surface after rubbing.

30 MINUTE STOCK FINISH

I suppose nearly every woodworker, gunsmith, and technical writer has been asked time and again by the various and sundry interested persons to give him a system whereby a stock could be completely finished in a half hour's time. This question usually revolves about a stock they wish *refinished* and as such will have had any staining done that was necessary at the time the gunstock was first finished and also will probably have had the grain raised.

I mention the staining and the grain raising (whiskering) because these two operations themselves will take at least an hour and the finishing of the stock therefore will not include those operations.

If you wish a system of stock finishing which involves going from the bare shaped, inletted stock then I am afraid I can offer no help. The preparation of the stock to take the final finish will take at least an hour. If you think of stock finishing in the sense that a customer brings in a stock which he wants refinished with a protective coat, though, that is something else again. This placing of a final protective film on the wood can be done in a half an hour or less.

This system goes about as follows:

At four-thirty Friday afternoon the door of the shop bangs open and here comes a jerk with a sporterized Springfield or Enfield. He has put a stock on the thing and has done a pretty good job, too. The only thing is that he has got some sort of a concoction on it that looked good when he threw the formula together but now it is either starting to peel away from the wood or it did not take at all.

Maybe, instead, he has a rifle or shotgun that he bought from the local second-hand store down the street and there is not much to offer in the way of any kind of a finish. The guy that owned it before had doused it well with linseed oil (raw) three times a week and had half heartedly rubbed it now and then to get the Dull London Oil effect. His oil had not dried between coats (it usually will not the way many of the boys pile it on) and now six months later the stock is still sticky and gooey when the heat of the hand gets to it.

Anyway, no matter what the situation, this eager beaver is going hunting in the morning and has gotta' have that stock tonight. You, being a gunsmith, naturally are the local wizard to whom he turns. He wants a smooth, lustrous, water resistant coat on the stock, the grain must be filled (it never is when you get it), and the whole job must be done in about half an hour because he must pick up his wife at the local grocery then. And he wants the stock before supper.

You know that if you put varnish or oil on the blamed thing it will take at least a week before any kind of a decent finish is brought out. If you put even quick drying materials on it (such as lacquer or even shellac) you will never have it done tonight.

So you grab the gun, tell the guy to sit down on the box in the corner, and to peruse the Stoeger's catalog on the counter and you go back into your inner sanctum to see what you can do with the problem.

First you dismount the gun; take the barrel and action and trigger guard assembly off the stock and remove the buttplate, gripcap and sling swivels (if there are any present). Now you have the stock in the nude, so to speak.

Take a bottle of half and half toluol and denatured alcohol (which you have on hand as a varnish remover) and liberally douse the stock with it. Using a rag (clean and free from oil and grease) work that thinner bath around and into the wood in order to remove as much as possible of the old, still wet oil with which the wood had originally been treated. Soak the rag in the thinner again and rub it around some more. As long as there is much of the old finish on the wood you will continue to get dirtying of the rag from the oil and/or varnish which is being softened and removed. When you are reasonably sure that there is no more appreciable amount of any old finish present lay the rag and thinner bottle aside.

Now the problem is to heat the stock until it is fairly hot on the surface and for this a bank of about two or three infra-red heat lamps will be best. These lamps will throw off a great deal of heat and when placed about a foot away from the surface of the wood will heat that surface up to about 150° in a minute or so. Practice will show you just how far away from the wood you can place the lamps and for how long you can heat it without causing damage. Even a series of 200 watt light bulbs will give you the same effect, though with less efficiency. The light bulbs will give off more light and less heat for the same current than the infra-red bulbs which were designed for heat emission only.

The ideal setup would be to place the stock in a checkering frame or some other type of holder so that it could be turned freely and still not be touched or held by the hand any more than necessary.

With the stock in such a holder turn the lamps on and turn the stock occasionally so that the whole surface is heated evenly and within a few minutes will be so hot that you can hardly touch it. It should not be allowed to get so hot that it burns or darkens, though.

While the stock is being heated uniformly in this manner you have melted your special, hotsy-totsy formula over a hot plate. Bring this wax mixture to a point just under which it starts to smoke. The hotter it is now the more penetration it will have.

When both the stock and the finishing material are heated to a point where you have found they will work well turn off the hot plate and the heat lamps, but leave the stock in the checkering frame. This frame will make an easy job of the finishing.

Take an old spoon or dipper of some sort and pour a dipperful of the melted wax mixture over the stock. Immediately take another dipperful and treat another section of the stock until the whole works has had a bath of the mixture. You will find that seemingly most of the wax will run down and drip off the stock onto the sheet metal plate which you have previously placed there for the purpose of catching just such overflow. Papers would work as well but would absorb a lot of the hot wax and make its recovery impossible. Whatever drips on the metal will harden and can be used again the next time by scraping it off and putting back in the heating pot.

Turn the stock a quarter turn and repeat the wax bath. Do this turning and soaking until the stock and the wax grow cool enough to start the wax solidifying on the wood instead of immediately running off. Then stop.

At this point take a knife blade of some sort and scrape off whatever wax has built up on the end where the buttplate will go, on the grip where the cap will be placed, and in the inletting and barrel channel where the action and barrel will rest. It will be to your advantage to do it now while still warm and very soft rather than to wait until it is cold and will have to be chipped off.

At this same point in the waxing process clean out all checkering or carving which may be on the stock. This may best be accomplished by using a stiff bristled brush, such as a toothbrush, while the wax is soft enough to work out of the minute cavities made by the checkering or carving. If an appreciable amount of wax is left on those surface areas it will solidify into an unsightly mess. Obviously we do want a protective coating over such surfaces, but only to a minute extent. Clean them out by brushing vigorously and reheating the stock at that point if necessary. It does not matter if you seem to remove all the wax. There will be some that will have penetrated into the wood and you can come back later with a touch of liquid or paste wax to blend that portion in with the appearance of the rest of the coated stock.

When using the buffing wheels later to give a final polish to the wood be careful that you do not burn or rip out any fine edges or points which may be present. It may even be wise to keep away from such decorated areas entirely with the wheel and do your polishing there with a soft cloth and elbow grease. In a pinch medium to fine grade steel wool dipped in a little naphtha or mineral spirits can be scrubbed lightly over the area to remove any excess wax which the brush may fail to get.

As soon as the wax has been removed from these prohibited areas take a soft cloth pad and rub over the stock vigorously. This is to pack the still soft wax down into the pores and to even up the now-bumpy coating. It will be bumpy because the wax has started to solidify on the surface and will do so in "runs" or "sags." It should be still soft enough to remove easily with the pad.

The wax will build up on the pad so that further rubbing will redistribute the wax "runs" over the surface in a built up coat. This is just what we want.

If you find at any time that the wax is too hard to work with turn on the heat lamps for a few seconds. The heat will warm the wax and the surface of the stock enough to make easy spreading of the wax.

When you have the coating fairly evenly spread out take a clean, coarse rag and rub the surface. This will remove most of the excess wax on the surface. If this rag tends to pick up wax to a point where removal of excess wax no longer takes place take another coarse rag and continue the cleaning up process until the stock is well rid of most of the heavy built up coat.

Now let the stock get cold. Inasmuch as only the outer skin of the stock was heated by the infra-red lamps this will not take long. It may even have cooled off during the waxing process so much that an additional heat treatment was necessary to make the wax warm enough to be workable.

When cold take the stock out of the holding frame and examine it. Is the coating uniform all over? Have you removed all very heavy spots or lumps? If so then put a soft, loose-sown buffing wheel on the polishing head and give the stock a good polishing. The heat generated by the buffing wheel will be sufficient to partially melt the surface wax and even up the film. When the stock shows a uniform, even, lustrous coat overall then change to a very soft polishing wheel such as a sheepskin buff. Give the stock a final polishing with the sheepskin buff to eliminate any marks left by the first wheel and to bring the lustre up. Then you may place the metal parts back in the stock and the job is finished. If you have not lost much time and have worked efficiently you should be able to do a rifle stock in at least 20 to 25 minutes.

The wax will have gone right down to the bottom of the pores (if any were open) and done its own filling. Then it will have built up a good film on the surface of at least one to two thousandths. You must have a little practice behind you in order to estimate just how much of a film can be built up with any given method of operation.

Such a wax coating will be extremely waterproof, will be very durable if the owner throws on a coat of paste wax occasionally after he has used it, and will give a fine finish. As a matter of fact, for the average gun, whether it be a knockabout utility piece or a gun cabinet baby, this finish will leave little to be desired even when the question of time of application is not involved.

I do not recommend this finish above all others, however. The spar varnish or lacquer finish will definitely have its place, one which even this excellent finish cannot take. For extreme conditions of handling and long periods between protective maintenance the spar varnish with a good varnish sealer will be much more efficient. For stocks that deserve and call for fine, transparent finishes with high standards of lustre and sheen the lacquers will be more suitable.

Now as to the materials that you may use for the basic wax coating there are many which will be satisfactory. You should use waxes which are as hard as possible because of the resistance to handling abrasion and because of the beauty and lustre which such hard waxes will give upon polishing.

The following general formulae will be a guide, but any of these may be combined or changed as suits the taste and experience of the user. You will find at times that any formula given, no matter how it works for the original user, may require a slight modification to work best for your methods of application or because the raw materials that you have been able to procure have slightly different properties than those that the original formulator had to work with.

Hard Finish Formula (#12)

Beeswax..........................10
Carnauba wax....................25

Melt together and allow to solidify. Remelt for use.

Hard Finish Formula (#13)

Carnauba wax....................10
Beeswax..........................10
Paraffin wax..................... 5

Melt together and allow to solidify. Remelt for use.

Hard Finish Formula (#14)

Carnauba wax....................10
Ozokerite........................ 8
Paraffin wax..................... 5

Melt together and allow to solidify. Remelt for use.

SUITABILITY OF WAX FINISHES

The use of wax, either alone or in conjunction with oil, is desirable under most conditions of use. Wax will give a goodly degree of protection against moisture, and will also stand up well under considerable handling.

Wax should not be used for a field or knock-about stock when time between protective maintenance periods is extreme. For instance, if the gun is never given additional coats of wax or maybe if wax is placed on the stock once a year (when the owner happens to think about it) then that stock would be better off with one of the marine spar varnishes.

For nearly all other stocks, however, wax will be very suitable and will give beauty and protection.

VARNISHES AND LACQUERS LATER USED OVER WAX

If at any time in the future you desire to refinish the now waxed stock with any of the other conventional finishes such as varnish, lacquer, shellac, or drying oils you are going to have quite a bit of trouble. Unless every trace of wax is removed from the wood the adhesion and drying of those materials will leave much to be desired.

Therefore I would suggest that if you think you are going to want one of these finishes on your stock put it on now. Do not wax the stock! You will have a devil of a job getting every last bit of it off the wood, and in many cases you cannot do it. That wax is usually there to stay and once you thoroughly wax a stock you had better figure on keeping it waxed until you take it off and throw it away.

This, of course, does not mean that if you happened to put a coat of Johnson's Wax or some that you made up on the stock at some time or other that you cannot get it off. I am referring to the type of wax job typified by the thirty minute stock finish I described above. This wood will have wax down into it as far as an eighth-inch in some cases and whenever you put a solvent on the wood to dissolve and remove the finish some of that wax deep down in the wood will be dissolved and drawn up to the surface where it will stay in the pores. In this case unless you have access to a vapor degreaser you have had it, Brother.

RUBBING COMPOUNDS

Many times throughout this book I have mentioned rubbing compounds, mostly in connection with rubbing and smoothing the final coats of finishing items. These compounds are readily purchased already prepared, but it is possible to manufacture your own if you so desire.

Rubbing compounds are mixtures of substances that will produce abrasion of whatever surface they are used on. They will vary as to degree of abrasion which to all practical purposes means the depth to which they will cut readily and the degree of lustre which they will give. The lustre or gloss of the rubbed surface will depend upon the size of the abrasive particles in the compound because the larger the particles or grit the larger and rougher the scratches will be and the less light will be reflected from any given area. If the particles are small they will leave what amounts to a plane surface and this surface will reflect a great deal of light without scattering it. The less the reflected light is scattered the truer the light reflection will be and therefore the greater the gloss or lustre.

Most rubbing compounds are made in the form of a semi-solid or a paste. They may include mineral oil, drying oils (such as linseed), solvents (such as turpentine and pine oil), waxes, drying oil fatty acids, stearates, alkalies (to produce emulsions), water, and/or abrasives. All of these substances are not found in every rubbing compound and many proprietary compounds will have only a few of them.

The abrasive substances that are most generally used are as follows:

    Tripoli   —a form of silica
    Pumice   —powdered volcanic glass
    China clay—powdered aluminum silicate
    Whiting   —pulverized limestone

These are only a few of the more common abrasives used, though the possible materials would run into the hundreds.

Most of the better compounds offered today contain tripoli to some degree. It may be used alone, but generally for sake of economy it is combined with others listed. The more the tripoli is diluted the lower will be the efficiency of the compound but also the lower the cost of manufacture.

Fine rubbing compound formula (#15)

Stearic acid	5
Mineral oil	3
Turpentine	5
Soap flakes	2
Rose tripoli	10
Water	12

Melt the acid and dissolve the turpentine and mineral oil. Heat the water to boiling and dissolve the soap flakes.

Add the tripoli to the oil mixture with stirring. Pour in the hot water solution and stir vigorously.

This mixture must be well stirred and shaken before use each time. It will be a gentle polish rather than a highly abrasive cutting compound.

Pour some on a felt pad and rub well for use.

Fine rubbing compound formula (#16)

Stearic acid	3
Mineral oil	4
Petrolatum	2
Soap flakes	2
Denatured alcohol	1
Water	10
Powdered silica	10

Melt the stearic acid and dissolve therein the petrolatum, mineral oil, and denatured alcohol.

Heat the water to boiling and dissolve the soap.

Add the two solutions with vigorous shaking or stirring.

Then add the silica a little at a time with vigorous stirring. This mixture will give about the same results as formula #15. It should also be shaken vigorously each time before use.

Pour some on a felt or cotton pad and rub well for use.

Coarse rubbing compound formula (#17)

Stearic acid	3
Mineral oil	3
Paraffin wax	4
Soap flakes	2
Rose tripoli	8
XXXX pumice (or finer)	5
Water	8

Melt the acid and the wax and add the mineral oil.

Heat the water to boiling and dissolve the soap.

Pour the two solutions together with vigorous stirring.

Then slowly add the tripoli and the powdered pumice with vigorous stirring.

This mixture should be well stirred or whipped before use.

The presence of the pumice will give a faster and deeper cutting action than the compounds in formulae (#15) and (#16).

Place some of this compound on a felt rubbing pad and keep the surface well supplied while rubbing. The presence of a liberal supply of the cutting compound will cut down a finish very quickly so be sure that you do not go too far before you know it. Every so often clean off the surface with a clean cloth to see how far the cutting has progressed.

CHAPTER ELEVEN

Forearm Tips and Grip Caps

Possibly you will have noticed on the photograph of the finished stock (Chapter 5) the forend tip and grip cap. There are a few of these tips and caps floating around, but they are mostly seen on privately finished stocks. Such things are not procurable through the normal channels of supply and are strictly items for home manufacture, as far as I can determine.

The general run-of-the-mill forend tips and accessories found on the various makes of semi-finished stocks offered to the trade are usually composed of Tenite (cellulose acetate or acetate-butyrate) or something very similar. In my experience these Tenite materials, while very tough and easy to work with, will not take and hold as high a polish as some of the other plastic materials available. In addition to this, they are rather soft and will scratch and pick up dirt and grit which adds to the dulling of the polished surface.

In looking around for something a little harder which would take a much better polish and keep it I discovered that Plexiglas (lucite) could be had in various colors. This Plexiglas, or lucite, is one of the family of acrylics and is very hard, takes an extremely high polish, and is easy to work with. It may be worked with ordinary sandpaper, edge tools, and files. It polishes well with crocus cloth or polishing compound on a buffing wheel.

The most useful colors in which Plexiglas may be procured are jet black and white. This stuff comes in sheets anywhere from one sixteenth of an inch thick up to one quarter inch.

As shown in the photograph a thin (one eighth inch) spacer of white is placed somewhere in the bulk of the otherwise black forend tip. This adds a touch of something that you will never find in the ordinary completely black tip, at least I think so. Also, a strip or spacer placed between the stock and the grip cap also adds a little something. Of course, these spacers may be placed anywhere in the tip and cap, or left out entirely, depending upon the personal choice of the maker.

The question will now arise—how the dickens do you get the spacer in the otherwise solid block of black?

That is a sixty-four dollar question, but the answer lies in the method used to make that block. We build up the block from ¼" sheets and therefore the spacer may be placed anywhere we wish in the building-up process. Just stick the spacer wherever you want it. You could make the whole thing out of ¼" white plastic and stick a black spacer in. Or you can make the whole thing out of either color with no spacer, or you can—but with all the combinations available I could go on all day like this. You can fool around with the stuff and decide what you like, whether it be alternate strips of different colors or plain solid colors.

If you have a good sense of color balance you could use some of the other colors available—dark green, red, maroon, or blue though I would use them sparingly. Jet black and pure white seems to be the best for most stocks. You will have to finagle around with the color of the wood and the stain you want to use before you come to a final decision, probably. However, once you have mastered the trick of using the plastic then these are all minor matters.

Now to get down to the important matter of the source of plastic. I usually buy my plastic from one of the stores around town that deals in the different kinds of plastic, mostly for the benefit of hobbyists and model makers. You will find them listed in the telephone directory under the classified heading of Plastics. For those of you that live in small towns a letter to the Plastics Division, duPont Company, Arlington, New Jersey, or to Rohm & Haas Company, Washington Square, Philadelphia, Pennsylvania, will bring you an answer as to where you can buy it in your area.

Having secured my supply of one-eighth inch and one-quarter inch sheets in whatever colors I have chosen I decide upon the external dimensions of the finished tip or cap.

The best way to determine these dimensions is to measure the outside of the particular stock on which the tip is to be placed. If it is a stock which has been finished before and on which I wish to place a new tip then take the side to side and top to bottom dimensions of the stock as it is now and allow at least one eighth inch over for tolerance. If it is a blank which has not yet been cut down to size then figure about what the outside (side to side and top to bottom) dimensions will be. Here, too, it would be best to allow at least a quarter of an inch over in case you do not cut the wood down quite as far as you thought you were going to.

It is much better to have the rough block larger than you need and to have to cut down to size than to find that you have not figured large enough, in which case you will probably have to tear that tip off and start all over. Once this tip is on there is no patching possible. You either do it right the first time or you do it over again.

For example, let us say that the stock you are putting the tip on measures 1½" x 1½" at the very end of the forearm. So you figure on being economical and cut out square plates exactly 1½" x 1½" square. This should fit just right with a minimum of cutting. So you go ahead and place the tip securely on the stock and what happens? You find out too late that in using a coping saw to cut out the plastic you cut a crooked line and now the tip is too small. It has a definite concave curve to it and the only way to fix it up is either to sand the forearm down another quarter inch or to take it off and start over. If you had allowed a quarter inch extra in cutting this would not have happened.

FORMING THE PLASTIC TIP

Draw a rough diagram (full size) of how you want the tip to look. From this drawing you can figure just how long the finished tip will be and also how wide and high. Let us say you want it to extend out from the forend 2″ and it will be 1½″ wide and 1½″ high.

Cut out eight (8) plates from the ¼″ thick sheet. They should be about 1¾″ square. This will give about ⅛″ over on all sides for working errors. Eight ¼″ plates, when placed one on top of another, will make a stack 2″ high.

Now the problem is to bond the plates together in order to make a solid block of them. In order to understand how such a bonding can take place it is necessary to first understand that the plastic is readily soluble in certain organic solvents. Different plastics are soluble in different substances, but in the case of Plexiglas, acetone, ethylene and methylene dichloride will do an excellent job.

It is possible to buy "cement" or bonding solutions from the same source of supply that furnishes your plastic. In fact, they will be more than happy to sell you what you want. The only thing is that the price of the stuff is outrageous. It is a lot cheaper to make it up yourself and it works just as good.

Plastic Cement Formula #1

Ethylene dichloride—10 cc. (parts by volume)
Acetone   —10 cc.   "   "   "

Plastic Cement Formula #2

Ethylene dichloride —20 cc.

Plastic Cement Formula #3

Methylene dichloride—10 cc.
Acetone   —10 cc.

Any of the above formulae will do a good job and the volumes given will be sufficient for about five complete forend tips and grip caps.

Incidentally, these formulae are highly inflammable. Do not have any open flames around while working with them.

When the formula that you choose has been made up drop a small piece of clear Plexiglas into the bottle and let it dissolve completely before using. The piece need only be the size of a pencil eraser.

When you have the squares of plastic cut to the size you wish then strip off the protective paper which adheres to the sheets. Do not remove this paper even when cutting the squares to size. The paper will protect the plastic surface from dirt and scratches and will keep oily fingers from contaminating the faces. If oil of any kind gets on them they will not take the cement well.

Now place some of the solvent in a saucer or dish and drop the plates into it. Allow them to soak in this bath for a minute or so in order to soften the faces. Then remove them from the bath and place them face to face until the block has been built up and place the whole thing in a press or vise and tighten. Allow them to remain in this press or vise for a couple of hours, though in a pinch fifteen minutes will do. The longer they are held together under pressure the better will be the bond between the plates.

There is just one thing I have neglected to mention. Leave one plate out of the operation. That is, if you are going to use eight plates for the whole tip then soak and press seven of them now. Leave the eighth one as you cut it out of the sheet. This is because this last plate will be fastened to the stock securely and then the other seven bonded to this last one.

After the section of seven plates has been allowed to set for a couple of hours in the press it is ready for attaching to the stock.

While you are forming this block in the vise you can be working on the end of the forearm getting that ready to take the tip.

This will involve cutting off that forend to as plane a surface as you can possibly make it. The flatter this surface to which the tip will be attached the less chance there will be that it will tend to "rock" or wobble. If there is any doubt in your mind as to the planeness of this surface it will be better to make it slightly concave (about one thirty-second of an inch at the deepest part). Then the concavity can be filled in with plastic wood which will help secure the tip in place. The solvents in plastic wood will soften and partially dissolve the tip surface against which it rests. Then when the wood hardens it will give that extra grip which will keep the tip from rocking when in place.

As you can see in the illustration the actual securing of the tip to the forend is done by means of a large coarse wood screw together with two small dowels. The screw will securely fasten and hold the first plate against the face of the wood and the dowels and the plastic wood will keep it from twisting.

The fit of the barrel as it passes through and over this tip should be as close as possible and still have a hairline crack all around. While the very top edge of the tip should appear to be extremely tight to the barrel the rest of the tip should be relieved slightly to keep the barrel from resting upon the tip at any point. The dark blue steel against the black forend tip will allow you to have a satisfactory gap which will not be seen. If the barrel ever rests directly upon the tip at any point, when the guard screws are tightened up the pressure of the barrel may very well force it downward and completely loosen it. If this happens you will have the job to do over again.

Before fastening the block to the forend it might be well to cut a rough groove in it as a starter toward the barrel channel. You will find that once you have the tip on the stock it will be a long, tedious process to make that groove without spoiling it. I find that the easiest way out of this problem is to take my rough cut block and lay out the approximate dimensions of the barrel at the point at which the barrel will lay. Then, with a coping saw, cut this groove to nearly finished size. Now you can place the block in the vise and file the groove to as nearly accurate size as possible. It does not make too much difference if you open it too much on the bottom of the groove, but for Pete's sake do not overcut on the upper lips. It will be better to leave it too small here and afterwards spot in the barrel with Prussian blue, just as ordinary inletting is done. Incidentally, even though the plastic is jet black the cutting and filing of the surface will leave it in such a condition that Prussian blue is easily seen. Then after it is polished it assumes that really jet appearance which is so desirable.

Also, be careful at the extreme forward plate that you do not get the groove too large. Here the fit can be seen all the way around and you want that fit to be as close as the two top lips should be.

FITTING THE TIP

Now that we are ready to assemble the tip to the wood (we have cut the rough barrel groove) take the one plate that we have not touched yet, which will be the eighth plate we did not dip in the solvent bath. Cut that with a barrel groove also.

Drill a hole through what will be the center of the plate after it is worked down to shape. This is to make sure that you do not get the screw too far down toward the bottom of the stock in which case it will tend to split the wood. Countersink it for the head of the screw. Both the size of the hole and the depth of the countersink will depend upon the size of the wood screw you have chosen to do the job. The larger the screw the better hold it will take on the wood, but the more chance there will be for it to split the stock. You will have to use your judgment on this, but if you have a screw in the junk box that came off the buttplate of an issue Springfield then you will have about the right size.

Now drill two small holes, one on each side of this large hole. These small holes should be about one eighth inch diameter. They will be for the two small dowels that you will put into the stock to keep the tip from twisting under any sort of pressure which may later be applied.

Place the tip in about the correct position and using the

first, large screw hole (in the tip plate) for a guide drill into the stock. The drill you use should be smaller than the first one so as to give the screw a chance to dig in and grip the wood. If you have used a $\frac{1}{4}''$ drill to make the hole in the tip plate then you should not drill a larger hole than about $\frac{3}{16}''$. Much smaller than this will give the screw too much chance to split the forend, especially if it is thin.

Now soap the screw you intend using, to eliminate splitting as much as possible. Place the tip plate in position and screw it up tight. Now you can go ahead and drill the holes in the stock for the dowel pins. Use the same size drill here that you did for the small holes in the tip plate. Inasmuch as the dowel will be the same size in its entire length you should use the same size hole. It is permissible to drill the holes just a few thousandths smaller than the dowel pins so that they will be a drive fit and thus prevent later loosening.

The dowel may be made of metal, but I find that a good, tough hardwood dowel will be better. This may be glued in place and will never break under the smaller strains which are placed upon it. Ash, oak, birch or maple—any of them will be acceptable.

Turn or whittle the dowel to size. Now place a good glue coat (preferably waterproof, though this is not too important) on the lower end of the dowel and just a touch of it in the hole. If you get too much in the dowel hole and the fit is airtight you will not be able to get the dowel all the way down to the bottom of the hole and it will not be as good a job. This dowel, incidentally, should be about an inch or an inch and a quarter long. Drill the holes deep enough so that about three quarters of the dowel is below the surface of the wood. The other quarter above the surface will fit into the holes in the tip plate.

Before the tip plate is finally fastened into place you should smear a thin coat of plastic wood on the flat face of the wood against which the tip is to rest. Use just enough so that all hollows are filled, but not enough so that it will prevent the tip from resting against the wood at the periphery of the forend at that point.

Now place the tip plate in position over the dowels, forcing it down as far as possible on them. Then insert the screw again, this time drawing it up as tightly as you can possibly get it. A screwdriver bit in a brace will really tighten it up, but be sure that you do not exert enough force to turn the screw after it reaches the bottom of its seat. If this is done you will make the "lands" of the screw cut through the wood which is gripping it and it will then continue turning "round and round." If this happens then you will have to remove the screw and use a larger size. In screwing into this end grain (which it will no doubt be) it is fairly easy to destroy the hold of the wood on the screw threads in this manner. Turn it up only as far as it is definitely tight and then stop.

It is permissible to use a mallet of some kind at this point. Give the tip plate a couple of good whacks to make sure that it is driven down as far as possible. If you happened to make the dowels a trifle too large the screw itself will not be able to pull the tip all the way down. A couple of blows of the mallet will insure that these dowels are not giving us a hard time.

Now we have the first plate securely fastened to the stock. The rest of the tip will be in the form of the block that we pressed in the vise a little while ago.

Take an eyedropper full of the cement that we used to bond the small squares into a block and place a thin coating of it on the exposed face of the tip plate now fastened to the stock. Of course, the stock should be placed in a vertical position for this as the cement is very thin in body and will run down onto the stock if the tip is inclined very much. Allow this cement to remain on the tip for a minute or so. If you see that the cement is evaporating then add a drop or two more. The idea is to see that the tip plate surface is kept well wet with the cement. This will soften the surface and allow a good bond to take place.

At the same time place either the one end or the other of the block in a saucer in which is placed some of the cement.

This bath will soften that face also.

After a minute or so remove the block from the bath and place the softened or wet face against the face of the tip plate. Then press together as much as possible.

CLAMPING THE TIP

There are several ways in which pressure may be brought to bear on the union. First, you could use some sort of a press. Most of you will not have anything of this sort available. However, it is possible to buy some simple clamps consisting of cast iron stops threaded for a screw. They are made to fit around ¾" gas or water pipe and a piece of pipe four feet long with this type of clamp upon it could be used to good effect. Most hardware stores have this sort of thing in one form or another and they sell for a couple of bucks. For anyone contemplating doing tips for others it would probably be a darned good investment.

For those of you that do not see the utility of putting out even a couple bucks because you are only working on your own stock, then you can use a weight. The weight consists of anything that is small and heavy. I use pigs of lead, about eight or ten pounds weight. These pigs are balanced or secured in some manner on the upturned tip. Inasmuch as the tip will yet be square or flat on the end (we have not done any shaping of it yet) this could best be done by placing the stock in a vertical position in the angle formed by two walls meeting, or by placing in the corner of the gun cabinet. The two walls meeting at right angles will prevent the stock and the weights from falling.

It is very, very important that the two plastic faces which are being bonded together be in an absolutely horizontal plane. The faces, when first placed together will be very slippery and if any angle is present at all the weight of the lead on the tip will make the one face slide over the other. This will move the barrel channel out of line, and if the discrepancy is not noticed at once you will have to cut the tip off. When it has once hardened there is no way in the world of loosening the bond and starting over again with the same block.

If at all possible I would recommend some sort of a clamp rather than the weight idea. There is too much chance for error and slipping. Even a slight pressure will do. The only requirement is that the two wet faces be placed together and held there, though the more the pressure the better the bond will be.

Allow the tip to remain under whatever degree of pressure you are able to generate for five hours at the least—24 hours would be much better. Now remove the weight or the clamp and you are ready to finish inletting the barrel.

INLETTING THE TIP CHANNEL

Using Prussian blue complete the shaping of the barrel channel to as small tolerance as you can manage. As mentioned before, the most important place is the top of the tip where the lips and the barrel meet. This should show as little opening as possible, and the tighter the apparent fit the neater will the job appear. The same holds true for the very forward end of the tip. Here it is also possible to see where the tip contacts the barrel all around its circumference.

The rest of the fit which will be unseen can be as large as you choose to make it. The less chance there will be for the barrel to bear upon the tip *at any point* the less chance there will be for that tip being forced completely off the gun when the guard screws are tightened. The only real holding is done by just one wood screw and the doubtful value of the plastic wood and that is not a great deal, though it will stand up to all the recoil and bumps you can give it if it does not have to also hold up the barrel and action.

One of the handiest tools that I know of for enlarging that barrel channel little by little is a cutoff section of a rifle barrel. Take an old barrel that has been cast aside as useless and cut off about a foot of it, preferably someplace in the middle. Then file and grind the two ends as flat as you can get them. If they happen to run a little under a square right angle in the grinding that is okay. By turning the barrel hither and yon as you use it you can get the different obtuse and acute angles to work, whichever works the best for you. Occasionally file the end when it shows signs of rounded corners from too much scraping.

Obviously, this tool is to be used as a scraper. By nibbling on the wood or plastic you can get an extremely smooth cut, and that cut will be a lot deeper than you think would be possible. If one end of the barrel scraper is too large for the opening you are working in, then turn it end for end and the chances are that the other end will do the job.

This barrel scraper is not my idea. The late Alvin Linden mentioned it in his booklets on inletting, and when I tried it I was sold! It really does not matter whose ideas these things are—if they work they should be passed on to others for their benefit, and Linden was no one to hoard any so-called secrets, more thanks to him.

SHAPING AND POLISHING

When you have finished cutting, filing, and nibbling at the barrel channel then you need only shape and polish the tip to your individual taste. A sanding disc with coarse grit will take this stuff off in no time and when you have gotten the basic shape you can shift over to a finer grit disc. When you have removed the marks left by the coarse abrasive then take a strip of sandpaper, back it with a narrow strip of rubber or composition wall board and remove those sanding marks. By this time you can use paper as fine as 240 grit or 360 grit. Next go on to papers of 400 and 600 grit. By this time, having removed the marks left by the preceding coarser paper, you should have a very smooth, semi-polished surface. Even in using 600 grit or crocus cloth you will find a myriad of tiny hairline scratches.

Now take some of the cement that you used to bond the

plastic sheets together and soak a soft cloth with it. Squeeze out any excess and rub that cloth over the tip. Do this very quickly because the solvents in the cement will evaporate fast and if you still have the cloth in contact with the tip when it starts to dry the impression of the weave will be left in the surface. Go over the tip with this wetted cloth a couple of times and then let it dry for a minute.

Put a soft, loose-sewn buffing wheel on the polishing head and use just a touch of the finest polishing compound you have around. This will remove all of the sanding marks and you will then have a surface the gloss of which will appeal.

While we do not want the finish of the wood itself to have this much gloss, or lustre, the presence of that glistening bit at the very end of the forend will dress the stock up like nobody's business.

Incidentally, while you are using the sandpaper and the polishing buff on the tip it would be an excellent idea to secure a one-inch strip of adhesive or masking tape to the stock immediately adjoining the tip. This precaution will prevent any accidental marking of the finish on the wood. Of course, if you have not yet applied a finish to the wood you can shape, sand, and polish the tip during the shaping, sanding and polishing operation on the finish itself.

Formation or manufacture of pistol grip caps and butt plates is done in precisely the same manner as that of the forend tip. The number of sheets desired (depending upon the thickness of the plate or cap) are cut to rough dimensions and then bonded together with the cement formula given.

Securing the plate or cap to the stock will be a bit simpler than the operations necessary to fasten on the forend tip. There we did not want any sign of screw or other means of fastening. It must appear as though it were grown on the stock. Here, though, the standard appearance will be that of the plate or cap fastened through the material itself into the wood with a screwhead obviously doing the holding. That, at least, is the normal method.

If you want to be a bit unorthodox then you can use the same system that you used at the forward end of the stock. Secure one plate to the stock with screws and plastic wood, and then bond on the rest of the material to hide the presence of the screwheads. I have never seen it done this way, but it is not only practical, but seems to me to be very desirable. I am going to use it on my next stock and I rather imagine I shall get some favorable comment from the owner, whoever he may be.

TIME OF APPLICATION OF TIPS

The time it will take you to apply a tip as described above will vary, but will be fairly close to the schedule listed below:

Cutting plates to rough size	— 7	minutes
Bonding to make block	— 1	"
Bonded block in vise	—30	" (minimum)
Roughing barrel channel in block	—15	"
Fastening block to stock	—10	"
"Curing" bond to stock	—30	" (minimum)
Finishing barrel channel fit	—15	"
Shaping and polishing	—10	"
Total—	118	minutes

If you have a supply of rough tips on hand this will cut out an hour's time and all you will have to do is allow the half hour minimum for the block to be bonded to the tip. That, together with the finishing of the barrel channel to fit the individual barrel and the shaping will leave you about an hour's work to attach a tip.

Thirty minutes of this is waiting for the bond to cure or harden properly so actually a half hour's work (if you charge by the hour) will see the job done.

FAULT IN BONDING

There is just one thing that will crop up in using plastic in this manner. You may find at times that after having bonded together several plates, or portions of sheets, there will be tiny hairlines between each plate after the bonding cement dries. They may look as though they were caused by poor bonding, but do not cut down too deeply to try to sand them out. That hairline depression will remain all the way through the block and you can go from one side of the block all the way through to the other side without eradicating them. They are not cracks, as they may seem to be, but are something else, just what I do not know.

Just what causes this condition I do not know either. Sometimes you will get it and sometimes you will not. Usually if you get it in one union, you will get it in all unions of that particular block. They are not displeasing to the eye; rather they will add something to the appearance. Therefore, if you run across them do not worry about it. They will not affect the strength of the bond at all and are to be considered a sort of beauty mark rather than anything else.

Even the large factories in some of their work will get this sort of fault. They have not worked out a successful system to rid themselves of this condition so I do not feel too bad about getting it now and then myself.

Just as long as you are sure that the line is not caused by dry spots where the solvent evaporated before the bond was made you can safely ignore them entirely.

FOREND TIPS OF RARE WOODS

It is rather easy to obtain pieces of rare and beautiful woods (see Suppliers' List at the end of the book) which may be easily made into and attached as forend tips and grip caps.

Nearly any contrasting wood may be used, depending upon the color of the stock, as no particular strength is needed. No strains will be imposed upon such tips and caps and the beauty that they add will certainly be worth the trouble that it takes to locate such woods.

Samworth tells me that in a recent trip of his out through Arizona and California a great many of the better guns had just such tips attached. Not only were they sometimes made of foreign woods, but also some of our domestic woods such as mesquite. They added a certain something to the gun, especially if chosen with an eye to either harmonizing or contrasting with the rest of the stock.

Such tips may be placed with the grain running at right angles to the stock line. They could also be placed with the grain running in the same direction, but I would prefer the other way myself.

There are several ways in which such a tip could be attached to the stock, but probably gluing with a good, waterproof glue would be best. Any attempts to screw or bolt such a tip on would be visible and look like the devil. In gluing you must make certain that both surfaces are as clean and flat as possible to insure a satisfactory bond.

CHAPTER TWELVE

Refinishing Operations

I SUPPOSE that the great majority of home gunsmiths and stock finishers have stocks which were at one time or another finished and which the owner now intends to refinish. In fact, it is probable that the majority of stocks which will be worked on are those which are at the present time on a rifle and which are in need (real or imaginary) of a bit of primping.

I know just how you feel, fellows. I have an old Mossberg .22 in the cabinet which has gone through at least five refinishings, not because it really needed it, but because I had an idea that something I had just heard about would give me a better job than what was on the gun at that time. The poor little popgun has gone all the way from a genuine Dull London rubbed oil finish to the latest in lacquers, and I am still contemplating tossing that out for something else I have in mind. I do not suppose it will ever get any rest as it is sort of a guinea pig for experimentation only. Well, I guess things are rough all over.

No matter what sort of a finish your stock has on it at the present time you should figure on doing any work necessary to give the contemplated future finish a good base upon which to adhere and one which will allow that new finish to work to its best advantage.

For example, let us suppose that you now have a rubbed oil finish on the wood (and do not tell me that 80% of you do not). Now you get the bug about lacquer and nothing will do but that you must have a hand rubbed lacquer finish. Inasmuch as the stock you have in mind is on that super accurate Springfield that you prize so highly you want it to be at its best in appearance.

Okay, so we will put lacquer on it. But first of all how long ago was it that you rubbed in a coat of linseed oil (raw)? You and I both know that at least twice a month you wander down in the basement and gloat over the collection of charcoal burners you have managed to scrape together and every time you do you pull each one out and lovingly caress it. In doing so you figure that another coat of oil is about due and so you rub it in.

No matter how long ago it has been since you rubbed some oil on it you can be sure that down in the basement it has not had a chance to dry well between coats. Even if a full month has gone by since the last time, raw linseed oil will still contain enough non-drying foots to remain in a semi-liquid state. With all the coats you have probably put on there is not a chance in the world that you have a solid, well-hardened film on that wood.

It will probably consist of many coats of more or less gelled oil and its oxidation products. Even though it may seem hard and dry to your hand, down under the top coats you will have this incompletely reacted semi-liquid. This sort of coating *must* be removed completely before you put on anything else, especially if that anything else is a lacquer or a varnish.

The reason for all this worry about such an an insignificant thing (it may seem so to you at the present time) is that any strong solvents, such as those that lacquers and some varnishes carry, will swell and lift the incompletely hardened oil films and extremely poor adhesion will result. This will manifest itself in the coating pulling away from the stock in sheets or strips the first time that stock encounters any rough handling. Also, the oil films may be wet enough yet to actually prevent varnish (if that by chance happens to be your choice) drying. The solvents in such a varnish will have dissolved enough of the oil to make it seep up into the varnish film and this non-drying material will also keep the varnish from drying well, or at all. In such a case the surface of the varnish may be wrinkled, flat, or dull in appearance, and very soft.

It is for all these reasons that you must remove any and all of the previously applied finish. The example given above was for materials over drying oil films.

It is also very probable that you will run into similar trouble if applying lacquer or varnish over certain types of natural resin or spirit varnishes. If these spirit varnishes are of the type that remain soluble in certain solvents no matter how old they are then the solvents in the lacquer or varnish will certainly dissolve and soften this old coat and the same situation will be had. You will run into poor adhesion and possibly wrinkling of the surface.

To prepare a stock correctly for taking another finish is even more important than applying that finish correctly. It makes no difference how fine a workman you are or how excellent the materials you have to work with, if the base upon which the finish is to be laid is faulty then nothing in the world can give you a good job. On the other hand, if you are sloppy and have used second rate materials it is still possible to produce a tolerable finish by touching up and sanding down.

REMOVAL OF THE OLD FINISH

There are only two things that you will be able to use in removing that old finish. One is sandpaper and the other is a paint and varnish remover of some sort.

In Chapter 10 specific directions are given for both the manufacture and the application of varnish removers. Incidentally, the term varnish remover is a misnomer. While it may have been formulated with the thought in mind that it was to be used for removing varnish only, it will be suitable for removing almost any organic finish, no matter what the composition.

Here I would like to qualify that statement. Some organic

finishes (such as baked enamel and completely polymerized phenolics) are tough babies to work with. You will never run into the baked enamel, but the completely polymerized phenolic is another thing altogether. The marine spar varnish type of material will be completely polymerized after a period of several weeks, and it is here that you will have the most difficulty. In fact, for very old films of 100% phenolic nature varnish removers will be practically worthless. In case you run across such a finish (you will not recognize it as such until you have put about a gallon of remover on it and it refuses to budge) then your only recourse is sandpaper.

Incidentally, I doubt very much that you will run across such a finish twice in a Blue Moon. The boys just have not gotten around to using this sort of material for some reason and I have never seen one myself, other than what I have applied.

Place the stock that you are working on in the ever-present checkering frame. This is a must for any kind of stock work and is easily thrown together out of odds and ends, if necessary.

When the stock is in position try and remember what it is that you used last time. If you got the stock factory-finished then you will not be able to figure it out, perhaps. But if you did a job before on it you will make things that much easier for yourself.

If you used a shellac finish before (or you know the stock is finished in that material) then the remover for you is alcohol, either denatured or grain. Most of us have a little trouble securing grain alcohol so the denatured will have to do, I suppose. I would not use anti-freeze grade if I were you. It will contain substances which will not dissolve the alcohol, and also will contain a goodly percentage of water, usually.

In case you find that plain alcohol does not do the job fast or well enough you could throw in a little acetone or butyl acetate corresponding to Varnish Remover Formula #7 given in Chapter 10. The presence of these solvents along with the alcohol will do the job very well.

For any of the ordinary finishes, whether they be lacquer, varnish or drying oils the ordinary varnish removers will be sufficient. They will soften and dissolve the hardened films and allow easy removal by scraping.

When employing any solvents of this type the easiest way to work with them is to saturate a rag with the remover and rub over the stock. Be sure that the rag is nearly saturated with the solvents in which case there will be enough of them present to act upon the film. As you rub with the wetted rag bear down fairly hard so as to work the solvent into the surface rather than just allowing it to lay there. This working into the surface will shorten the job considerably.

As long as there is some finish left on the surface you should continue to employ the wetted rag. When you remove all of the film, or nearly all of it you can then concentrate on the areas where there is still a bit left. Once you have removed the coating from the wood there is no point in going back over it time and again just because one small area is a little tougher to remove. Work only on the areas that have coating left on them.

In the case of the drying oils there is always some of that oil soft enough to pick up dirt and retain it. This dirt will be apparent on the rubbing face of the cloth as dark brown spots or stains. Continue the rubbing until the rag shows no more of this darkening. At that time you can figure that you have removed nearly all of the coating which will come off.

Now set the stock aside for a couple of hours. You want to allow all of the solvents which penetrated the wood to evaporate before you put on any finish. If you still have some solvents in the wood they will work their way out to the surface and then will soften and loosen whatever film you may have applied.

If you figure on doing any sanding or cutting of the surface before applying a new finish then you may go ahead and do that work. During the process of sanding, or whatever it is you are going to do, the solvents will have time enough to work out and disappear. That is, if the time is more than a few hours. If you figure on smoothing down a spot which will take only a few minutes then wait the recommended period. You do not want to take a chance on ruining that new finish just because you were a little too eager.

At all times when working with any of these solvents recommended as varnish removers it would be an excellent idea to wear rubber gloves and have a little ventilation. The solvents are very strong and some of them may even be toxic over a long period of time. While you will not pass out or anything like that they can make you feel darned uncomfortable, and the amounts that you may absorb through the skin of the hands, if rubber gloves are not worn, may be serious if much work is done.

The amount that you will absorb or inhale when working on one stock is negligible, but if you have several stocks to do then it is very wise to observe these elementary precautions. Just an open window someplace near the bench will help a great deal.

That is about all there is to varnish removers. They are simple to use and to make and will work very well with 98% of the finishes with which you may come in contact.

Let us suppose that you have run across one of the really hard phenolic varnishes which some wise guy threw on the stock just before selling it. He was really on the beam if he wanted to get a first class finish, but it does not make it any easier on you. You have taken quite a few swipes at the stock with your pet remover and nothing has happened. You have gone so far as to experiment with a solution of lye in the hopes that by being very careful you could remove the finish without letting the wood absorb too much water. Nein, even dot iss no goot, Hans.

So you sigh, pick up a sheet of #2 or #1½ sandpaper and prepare to work it out the hard way. Using the sanding block to avoid digging in and making a lot of valleys and ridges you use the paper and a couple pints of sweat. The paper will probably clog up rather easily and you will have to renew the sandpaper facing on the block often. Too bad, but there is no way out of it here. The only thing that will tear that finish off is abrasion and plenty of it.

Once you get down to the base of the film you can take it a little easier. Work one area down and then go on to another until the entire stock is in about the same shape. When the wood starts to peek through the varnish then you can shift over to some #0 or #2/0 paper. This will smooth up the grooves left by the coarse abrasives in the first sheet.

You do not usually have to go all the way down to the roots of this varnish finish. If you do not figure on doing any extensive staining work then removal of the surface only will be enough. The varnish which is left in the pores will be the best filler in the world and there is no use destroying that if you can help it.

Of course, if you figure on restaining the wood then you must remove the greater portion of the varnish in the pores. This will prevent any appreciable penetration of the stain and the resulting color will be only skin deep and the first scratch that you put in the wood will really stand out.

Now that your finish has been removed you must stop and consider what you intend to do with the wood at this point.

Once the old finish has been removed from the stock you should raise the grain of the wood, especially if you intend to use a drying oil finish. No matter what the finish is to be, however, the big advantage to raising the grain (whiskering) is that the grain will then not be able to raise by itself sometime in the future with the possible loosening of the film.

Whiskering a stock which is being refinished is precisely the same as whiskering a new surface. The water and heat operations mentioned in Chapter 2 are followed exactly.

There is a good chance that the wood has been whiskered some time in the past and that you will not get very much grist for your steel wool mill but that is okay. So much the better. But if it has never been whiskered before then you will find it out immediately. The first coat of water and flame you give the wood will raise those needle points up to where you can feel them with your hand, even if they have been buried under a thousandth of an inch of linseed oil for two years.

SEALING AND STAINING IN REFINISHING

Inasmuch as there is only one chance in two or three hundred that you will have had a phenolic varnish on the stock before, your attempts with the varnish remover will nearly always do the job in good shape. Now that you have that finish removed you want to seal the stock, as mentioned above.

There is always the possibility that the stock had been sealed correctly some time in the past, but the chances are that it has not. As mentioned in Chapter 2 the very great majority of stock finishers (amateur and professional) do not even know of the existence of such a sealing material or the advantages which result from using it. A liberal dose of raw linseed oil is about as close as they come to it, and that is a long way away, believe me.

Follow the instructions as set forth in Chapter 2 on sealers. Make sure that your sealer is very thin in body and that the stock is liberally soaked with it for as long as that wood will take any more. When it refuses to absorb more of the sealer then wipe the stock off with a rag and let it harden.

When the sealer coat has apparently dried on the surface (this will take only a few minutes) you are free to go ahead with whatever you wish.

Right here I had better back up a bit and talk over the staining situation with you. Some stains should be applied before and others after the sealer coat. It is up to you to decide what kind you wish to use, and that will determine how and when the staining is to take place.

Chapter 3 has a rather more complete discussion of the staining operation and it will pay you to go back and look that information over before you make up your mind.

If you intend to use some of the extremely durable water stains or some of the chemical stains then you should attend to this matter before you seal the wood. The presence of the varnish sealer will prevent the stains from penetrating and the surface color will be too thin to be of much use.

If, however, you intend to use one of the oil soluble stains then you had better wait until after the sealing has been done. The solvents in the sealer will dissolve the staining agent and will partially wash it away and you will then have to go after it again to darken the stock to a point that you thought you had the first time. If you apply the oil stain when the sealer is still minutes or seconds fresh you will get some penetration because the varnish in the pores will not have hardened completely and will still be able to absorb and dissolve some of the stain which works its way down into the wood.

If you intend to use one of these new stains which are actually soluble in alcohol but which the makers claim are light fast then you will do better to use them before the sealing. The solvents in the sealer will not dissolve them and the penetration will be better.

In most cases, however, the stock will be of the color which you wish and no staining will be necessary. While the action of the varnish remover will have removed some of the color the chances are it will not have removed all of the color and what remains may be okay.

The finishing of the stock will follow exactly the same operations as those which were given for finishing a new stock. This is primarily because you are right back where you would have been with a new stock after you have sealed, whiskered, and stained it.

Even with average handling the average stock will lose some of its finish over a long period of time. This is more true in areas around the grip and the magazine well than elsewhere. Here the hand naturally grips the gun whether in just taking it out of the rack to look at it or in the periodic cleaning operations.

When such areas have become slightly worn or lose their gloss then you should figure that enough of that original film has been worn away to bring about this effect. Therefore, the logical thing is to replenish the film at that point.

If the original finish has been made of linseed, tung, walnut, or any of the drying oils then all that is necessary is to rub into the surface a good coat of whatever oil you wish. This must not be heavy, but should be very thin to allow proper drying and oxidation to take place.

Usually when such an oil finish is placed on a stock the owner will have rubbed in a coat ever so often so that this wearing down of the film is counteracted automatically. Thus he will hardly ever need to practice any protective maintenance.

Other than in the case of the drying oils where the film will no doubt be replenished occasionally every other type of finish will show the signs of wear.

In attempting to build up an already existing film very little material will be needed. The same processes should be followed as were used in building the original finish, but this time you are only replacing that material which has been worn away rather than building from the ground up.

When such a situation is encountered remove the metal parts from the stock. Place the stock back in the faithful checkering frame and go over the worn areas with very fine sandpaper. The finer grade you use the less scratches you will create, though some abrasion is necessary in order to give the following coat a relatively coarse surface to grab on to.

Once the "scuffing" on worn areas is completed you are ready for the finishing.

Now take whatever material you have originally finished the stock in and thin it down well. In the case of the lacquers, lacquer thinner will be necessary. In the case of the varnishes VM & P Naphtha or turpentine will usually do. If you have one of the phenolic (marine spar) varnishes then I would recommend either the thinner sold by the paint supplier or possibly high solvent naphtha. Even xylol would do well.

When the finishing material is thinned well take a clean, narrow brush and flow on some of it. Make sure that it does not run or sag down onto the parts of the stock you are not going to refinish.

When that thin coat has hardened for 24 hours then come back with a little very fine sanding or polishing paper to remove the brush marks, if any are present. With such thin material you probably will not have to worry much about them as there will be excellent flow to the material.

If you have succeeded in building up the film enough to suit you then stop, but if not lay on another coat.

Two coats will nearly always be sufficient to rebuild the film to where it originally was or even heavier. When the last coat has set 24 hours use some coarse rubbing compound and then fine compound and blend the edges of the new film into the body of the old film. This is termed "feather edging" and is self-explanatory. The idea behind this process is to make the edge of the new film so thin that it is impossible to see where the touched up area and the old area join. This can be done very easily and satisfactorily by the use of these rubbing compounds.

REFINISHING FACTORY GUNS

Now suppose you had bought the gun new and the finish is the one which had been applied by the factory. You will not know what material had been used and in this case (the most usual one, incidentally) you will have to do a bit of constructive thinking.

First, what is the appearance of the stock? Is it dull, soft looking or is it a smooth, homogeneous film? What the original finish was really does not matter a great deal. The important thing is what you can put on it that will appear the same.

If the finish filled the pores well so that they are not noticeable under light reflected from the surface of the film then you will be able to use almost any of the varnishes or lacquers to rebuild that worn surface. This is assuming that you handle the material and subsequent rubbing or polishing operations correctly.

Of course, if the film appears soft and spongy then you can figure that probably the only thing you will be able to use that will blend in with the existing finish will be a rubbed oil. This is easily done and will be satisfactory in many cases.

To use varnishes or lacquers to build up an existing film the operations are the same as when refinishing the gun from the bare wood up.

Clean off the wood with a solvent such as cleaning fluid or naphtha. Make sure that all lubricating oil has been completely removed.

Now scuff off the surface slightly, not enough to scratch the finish much but enough to roughen it slightly. Take your thinned-down finishing material and apply thin coats of it, allowing drying between each coat, until the finish is what you want. This will be one or two coats only in the majority of cases, unless the finish has been worn enough to expose large areas of completely bare wood. In this case three and even four coats will be required.

When the film has hardened take fine paper and remove brush marks and dust marks and then go at it with your coarse and fine rubbing compounds. The amount and degree of blending that you will have to do will be dependent upon the condition of the rest of the finish. The finer and more lustrous the stock the more lustrous the spotted areas must be.

Occasionally wipe off the spot and polish it with a piece of felt. This will allow you to see just how close the appearance is to the untouched stock finish.

When you have come as close as possible to the appearance of the rest of the stock then stop rubbing. Polish the touched up areas with felt and there you have it! Even if you have not blended the surface in so that it cannot be told from the rest of the stock a little wear by the hand will quickly place it in that condition.

For general stock retouching I would recommend the use of a spar or marine spar varnish. This will prevent perspiration from the hand attacking and penetrating the finish and thus ruining it.

CARVED AND CHECKERED SURFACES

Carving and checkering will not offer too much difficulty if care is taken to clean out the surfaces.

Checkering is composed of a series of lines cut into the surface in such a manner that the untouched lands or areas between the lines take the form of minute pyramids. In applying a finish the previous owner (or you yourself) may have filled in the lines or cuts to a certain extent, depending upon what the finish was.

The use of the varnish remover should have removed the material which had gathered in these cuts, but if it has not, then it has at least softened it so that a good, stiff bristle brush (such as a new toothbrush) would take it out easily. Make sure that this area had special attention paid to it and that all the finish was removed. The brush will not be stiff enough to have damaged any of the pyramids so you need not worry about that.

When the finish has been removed completely and the solvents have been allowed to evaporate then you may proceed with the whiskering of the stock.

Checkering may also be whiskered, but here you must be careful that in using the steel wool you do not loop some of the tangled fibers over the pyramids and pull them off. The best way to approach this is to take a bit of the wool and grasp it between the fingers. By compressing it you can make a small, rather fine-edged bundle of it. Then using it carefully (as you would erase a smudge from a piece of delicate paper) clean out the lines. The finer the edge you can get the less chance there will be for you to tear off some of the protruding points or pyramids.

You do not need to polish the bottom of the lines by any

means. The chances are that there will not be enough grain raised to be perceptible to the eye, and you certainly will not be able to feel down in those lines with your hand.

Therefore, a cleaning of the surface and of the upper portions of the pyramids will be sufficient.

If you are really going to be sanitary about the whole thing you could go down in those cuts with a bent three-square file. This is very similar to what was used to make the lines in the first place, but you will not do much cleaning with it. True, you may clean it up, but you will not remove any raised grain ends this way. You will probably cut so deep that you will expose a new surface and it will go ahead and raise the first time water hits it anyway.

Choose your own poison. The steel wool will not do a complete job, but for my money it will be as complete as the use of a bent file or the re-use of a checkering tool.

Carved surfaces may be treated in the same basic way as was the checkering. It will probably be very delicate and here, too, you must watch out that you do not pull off any protruding corners, edges or points with the steel wool.

The use of as fine a grade of wool that you can procure will be the best guarantee of safety. The finer the wool the smaller and finer the loops will be.

Take a little wool between the fingers and using it cautiously clean up any large curves or planes. Then turn to the smaller ones and use the same process. Care and care alone will insure a good job. Take your time and change the steel wool frequently. When it is new it will reach down into very small lines and spots, but once it has become matted it will only polish the surface and leave the recesses untouched.

The use of varnish sealers will be the same over these areas. They should be soaked with the sealer when applying it to the stock. However, as soon as absorption has ceased then they should be cleaned out with a toothbrush again. If you allow the sealer to harden in the lines and cuts then Heaven help you. If it hardens for more than about 24 hours there will be no getting it out. Varnish remover will not touch it, and the only way open will be to recut the carving or the checkering.

This can be eliminated by the timely use of the toothbrush before the sealer material has hardened at all.

Staining such areas will present little change in operations. If you intend using the stain after you seal the stock then you need not worry about darkening the checkering too much. The varnish sealer which you have previously applied will seal the surface, even the tremendous end grain areas which the cutting of the wood has produced, enough so that great penetration will not take place. In such a case you need not worry about darkening that end grain by this penetration.

However, if you are going to use a stain which must be used *before* the sealing takes place then you have a little problem. The wood will be very absorbent because you have removed from it every vestige of coating. If you then apply stains, no matter how dilute, to the checkering or carving the very great percentage of end grain that will now present itself will drink up that stain solution like a sponge, and when it dries it will be nearly black.

In order to avoid such a situation you should use what is called a wash coat. This consists of something which will limit that penetration. The usual wash coat is a very thin coating of shellac. (Usual for furniture work, that is.) Such a wash coat is brushed into the wood and allowed to dry. Then the normal staining operations are completed.

You can use this shellac material if you wish. It will be a fairly good waterproofing agent and, inasmuch as it will be applied very, very thin it will have excellent adhesion. In case you do not care to use it you can use a coating of the varnish sealer which you will afterwards use to seal the rest of the stock. In this case thin that sealer down even more than normal and let it soak in well. Allow it to dry about two hours and you can then go ahead with the staining.

The big thing to watch here will be that you do not get any of the wash coat (whatever material it may be) on the adjoining surfaces of the stock. If this happens then that adjoining surface will not absorb the stain like the rest of the stock and it will appear as a light, spotty area.

Probably the best thing to use to prevent this flowing of the wash coat onto adjacent surfaces will be either scotch tape or adhesive tape. Place the tape around the carved or checkered areas, carefully molding the tape edges to conform to the shape of the carved area. When this has been completed you may take a brush and apply the wash coat. When you approach the edges of the carving or checkering take a thin striping brush. This will prevent you from becoming sloppy and accidentally splashing the verboten surfaces.

When the wash coat has soaked in, dry those areas with a porous cotton rag and remove the protective tape. Then allow the stock to dry for an hour or so before applying the stain.

The actual application of the stain should be done on these touchy areas before the rest of the stock is touched. In doing this you will be able to devote all your attention to these areas rather than having a whole stock to watch all at once with the attending danger that things might get out of control while you are watching elsewhere.

Go lightly on the staining of the checkering and carving. Apply a rather thin coating first in order to see just how much protection the wash coat is going to give you. If it seems to be doing a good job of preventing much penetration then you can come along with a little heavier solution until you reach the desired color. Then you can do the rest of the stock, matching the coloring in the carved areas so as not to have a patchy appearance when finished.

When the subject of what I call Maintenance Refinishing comes up and checkering is mentioned there is no need for one to assume a blank look. The touching up of worn spots which contains this checkering or carving is precisely the same in principle as the finishing of smooth areas of the wood. The only thing that need change is a detail or two of application. Even here the basic principles remain unchanged.

Let us suppose that you were figuring on touching up a few worn spots on the stock and they included the forearm on which you had grown an elk head, antlers and all. It is a cinch that we cannot just put on a coat of varnish and let it go at that. When the varnish hardened it would cover up quite a bit of the fine line work over which you labored so long and diligently.

Also, we do not want to go and rub a drying oil in because the rest of the stock had a varnish or lacquer finish on it and it would not look the same for one thing, though most important of all is the fact that that oil would allow most or all of the perspiration from the hand to penetrate and get down into the wood. That we do not want!

The answer lies in the use of varnish, but applied in such a way that it neither covers up fine lines nor does it appear shiny when it dries.

First of all, finish all adjoining areas in a normal manner, using whatever varnish you have chosen. Then mask off these adjoining areas with masking or adhesive tape. Scotch tape will do but it is usually too narrow to provide much masking.

When everything but the checkering or carving is masked then apply a thin coat of the varnish to the checkering or carving. Allow it to soak in and set for a half an hour. Then wipe over it with an absorbent cloth and also use a toothbrush. With the brush clean out all of the crevices and let the coat dry overnight.

Now apply another coat in the same manner as the first. Make sure at all times that varnish does not run down and congregate in the bottom of lines. When dry such a gathering will shine and reflect light and look like a very poor job. The judicious use of the toothbrush will keep this from happening.

When you have two coats in the checkering it is time to stop. You will not find any wear taking place down there and the very thin coat that you have applied will be more than sufficient to protect the wood. As a matter of fact, the use of the absorbent cloth and the toothbrush will have removed most of what you put on the wood. That is all right. All you really want to adhere is that which may have soaked into the wood. Any that will have built up on the surface will be strictly excess and will reflect light. This we do not want!

When applying this varnish to the checkering it would be advisable to use one of the mixtures of varnish and oil as given in Chapter 2 under Checkering and Carving. Formulae numbers 1, 2, 3, or 4 will do the job very well and eliminate much of the light reflection.

CARE OF THE FINISHED STOCK

No matter whether the gun nut has an old, beat up job that he treasures for sentimental reasons or a snappy, first rate museum piece, the care of the stock and the metal portions are the same.

Dirt, dust, lubricating oil, water, cleaning preparations, and alcohol are all ever present and each of these will have a deleterious effect on a finished wood surface, the degree of which will depend upon the kind of material with which the stock is finished.

Alcohol will probably be the least of the damaging elements. The average gun owner will be very careful that it does not come in contact with nor remain on the surface of the wood. If it is accidentally spilled on a spirit varnish or a shellac finish it can quickly soften and spot that surface. The main remedy is, of course, to allow no compounds containing alcohol to get close to such a finish. Inasmuch as the spirit varnishes and shellac are readily soluble in the alcohol it will not take very much to actually remove the finish entirely at that spot.

If this happens the only way out is to spot in that finish with a fine striping brush or air gun as best you can. This may be done satisfactorily, but usually is noticeable for the rest of the life of the finish.

Cleaning preparations, such as "powder solvents" contain amyl acetate or something very similar to it. Inasmuch as this liquid is a fair solvent for nitrocellulose, lacquer finishes and also shellac finishes may be easily spotted. It will take quite a while for the solvent to dissolve any of the lacquer or shellac film, but it can quickly soften it enough so that if it is not noticed immediately, when you rub your hands over the finish it will be badly marred. This should be watched for especially when cleaning the gun. It is rather easy to spill some of the solvent on the stock when passing a dripping patch over it on the way to the muzzle.

Cleaning preparations will not harm drying oil films or the majority of synthetic (spar type) varnishes if removed shortly after the accident happens. It will damage the drying oil (linseed type) films somewhat more than the varnishes, however.

Lubricating oil will not bother most of the organic finishes much. In fact, the amounts that usually get on the stock in oiling the gun will be harmless. Even so, that small amount should be wiped off when discovered. The presence of even a thin film of it will collect dirt and dust. If allowed to gather in the crevices of checkered or carved surfaces it may build up a gummy mass from the dirt and particles of skin which will be brought to it by the hand. This will not hurt the finish any, but will be very unsightly. Also, when the gun is being refinished it may be difficult to remove such traces from the end grain of which the checkering is composed and this may prevent any following coats of finishing materials from hardening and adhering properly.

Dirt and dust may seem to be very small factors in commencing deterioration of a finish, but they are probably the biggest items on the average stock.

Particles of this dirt and dust act as abrasives and under handling will actually "sand" or remove the outer layer of finish. True, this removal of the film will be very, very slow and very, very minute but over a period of some months or years will wear that film down considerably. Also, if you have a brittle material on the wood such as unplasticized shellac, spirit varnish, or rosin-ester gum then the scratches which the abrasive particles will make in the surface will serve as starting places for the checking and cracking of the film. This may be likened to the scratching of a piece of glass by a glass cutter. The scratch will be very tiny, but it can start a fracture which will extend the length of the glass under pressure.

Therefore, to avoid both early breakdown of the film and to keep the lustre as fine as possible it is a wise precaution to wipe the stock frequently with a soft, clean cloth, especially before handling it.

Naturally, a stock which is to be taken out into the field is going to gather dirt and dust but there is nothing you can do about this. The number of times that the shellac or spirit varnished finished stock is used as a utility or constant hunting gun are very few. Even if this is the case with your stock a wiping by the clean, soft cloth when it is returned to the rack or cabinet will prolong the life of that finish considerably.

SHELLAC FILLING OF CRACKS

There comes a time in the life of every gunsmith, would-be gunsmith and plain, ordinary gun owning citizen when he is confronted with the presence of a cut, gash, or crack in that fine hand finished stock adorning the beloved smokepole.

He may possibly try to repair such a disaster by the same processes that he used to raise a dent. With a shallow dent, of course, it is a simple process to swell those crushed fibers by placing a hot iron over a wet cloth laid upon that dent, and the steam formed then swells the fibers back to normal, or nearly normal, condition. But with a crack or cut he is facing something entirely different.

Here the fibers are actually severed and there is nothing on earth that can mend them.

If the cut is indeed serious or very extensive then the only way out is to place an inlay at that point, but the average mishap will leave only a small, unsightly scratch or cut in the surface which usually will extend downwards only a fraction of an inch. In such a case the most satisfactory and easiest method of repair is to use gunsmith's shellac.

Gunsmith's shellac is carried in stock by most of the gunsmith suppliers such as Stoeger, Brownell, or Mittermeier. Your local gunsmith may even be so completely stocked as to carry these sticks.

Such sticks are composed of shellac, rosin, and some coloring matter, usually umber or sienna. The whole mess is melted together and allowed to cool in stick form.

There are many colors available for you to choose from. These sticks are made in shades ranging from transparent to dark brown with walnut, mahogany, and maple shades in there someplace. There is no set rule for matching of such sticks with any given kind of wood. The color of the stock will depend not only upon the individual specimen of wood you have, but also upon the method you have used to finish that stock, and the stain or lack of stain which you have. If in doubt the best thing would be to describe the general color with your order and hope the lads at the other end do a good job of matching their idea of reddish-brown to yours. If possible color a piece of paper with crayon or find an advertisement in a magazine which carries something in the color you want. Send that colored paper or cut out advertisement to the supply house with the request that they send you the stick which most nearly matches the shade of the paper you enclose.

The most efficient way to do things would be to have a full selection of shellac sticks on hand, but that would not do for you who would not use a stick again in ten years.

For those of you that like to roll your own here is a general formula that may be worked over and changed if you do not like the way it handles.

Patching Shellac

Shellac flakes— 10 parts by weight
Rosin —2½ " " "

Melt the shellac in a double boiler affair. You can use the lid of a coffee can over an open flame, but make sure that you do not get the heat so great that the shellac catches fire or smokes.

Now stir in the rosin which should be powdered as finely as possible.

Allow the mixture to brew for a few seconds and shut off the heat. When the melt has cooled enough to become semi-solid then work it around with the end of a blunt knife so that it forms an elongated cake.

When it has become cold break it away from the can cover and place in a closed container for future use. This shellac-rosin mix will be the base patching material that you will use for all such jobs.

When you have a patching job to do take a portion of the lump and melt it in a can cover again, still being careful that you do not get it so hot that it catches fire. Now stir in some coloring matter until the color is about the same as that of the wood you are repairing.

The coloring matter will consist of burnt umber, raw umber, burnt sienna, raw sienna, red oxide, or whatever is available to you. By varying the amounts of coloring matter you add you will vary the color and shade and if you are careful you can get a doggoned close color match.

If you find you have hit upon a color that pretty well matches most of the stocks which you may be called upon to repair you can make up a pretty good supply of the colored patching shellac for the times when you will be in a hurry and do not want to have to stop and make some up.

To use these sticks for repairing minor cuts and injuries the process is as follows: Clean out the cut or injury as much as possible. Be sure that you remove all traces of flakes, dirt or dust that may have accumulated in the injury. If you must, scrape them out with the point of a knife or the end of a pin. Be sure that you do not enlarge the opening any more then you can possibly help.

Now take a cloth pad composed of two or three layers of

cotton. An old rag will do, but make sure that the thread making up the rag is fine, not coarse like burlap. Lay this pad over the injured spot and thereupon lay a very warm soldering iron, electric iron or just plain piece of steel. The metal must be large enough to hold its heat for quite a few seconds. The presence of the cloth will insure that you do not burn or char the wood which is near and under that hot metal. (The ideal material for this pad would be asbestos.)

Obviously, the idea behind this heating of the wood is to allow it to approach more closely to the temperature of the shellac which is to be applied in a melted condition. The hotter the wood the longer it will take for the melted shellac to harden and the better adhesion that patch will have.

While this pad and hot iron are heating the wood (keep an eye on it so that if the iron accidentally gets too hot you can remove it before any damage takes place) place the blade of a knife or long slender piece of iron over a flame and heat it to a point where it will melt the shellac when the end of the stick is pressed against it. If you get the iron too hot it will start the shellac burning and this will destroy its properties of adhesion and the color will also be a sort of burned-roast black.

When the iron is hot enough to melt the shellac easily, melt just enough on the tip of that iron that you figure will fill the crack with only a tiny bit left over.

Now remove the pad and hot soldering iron from the stock and immediately place the melted shellac on the cut and work it in and around with the end of the iron or knife blade. You must work fast because, even with the preheating of the stock, the whole thing will cool off very quickly.

The melted shellac will flow down into the cut and will harden there. If you have used not too much and not too little there will be a bit left over on the surface in a sort of hump or bump. That is okay. Let it cool for five minutes.

Now you can come along with a small piece of sandpaper on the end of your finger and erase that hump down to where it will be level with the rest of the stock surface. If you are careful you can use a file on this operation, but there is really too much chance that you will dig into the adjacent wood and cut that up also. I think that the sandpaper is the best idea.

When that hump has been leveled off and the area is once again smooth and unbroken take a cloth dampened with denatured alcohol and whisk it quickly and lightly over the surface of the shellac patch. This will smooth out the scratches left by the sandpaper and help to blend the surface in with the rest of the stock. Now you can go over that area with a touch of whatever the stock was originally finished in and if you have been careful that spot will be invisible.

A word of warning is advisable here. In heating the applicator rod over a flame make sure that that flame is not a smoky yellow. This will leave a beautiful layer of soot on the blade of that rod and when the shellac is touched to the rod and melted the soot will mix with it and be carried to the stock. Even a small amount of soot left on the iron will discolor the shellac so that it will have to be removed if applied to the wood. A candle or kerosene lamp will give off this soot and smoke and the best burner that I know of is a Bunsen type which consumes natural or artificial gas. In this burner the gas is mixed with air in the correct proportions to completely burn the gas and no smoke will be had. In a pinch the next best thing will be to heat the applicator rod over the burners in the kitchen stove. Even the burner in the hot water heater will do a good job. Assuming, of course, that you burn some sort of gas. If you have a completely electrically powered house then you will have to do the best you can. Come to think of it, an electric stove coil will heat a rod laid upon it almost as quickly as will a Bunsen burner.

CHAPTER THIRTEEN

Refinishing of Military Rifle Stocks

IT IS probable that the great majority of members of the National Rifle Association have at least one of the guns issued by the government through the Director Civilian Marksmanship. A great many have two or more.

Besides the various models of the M-1903 Springfield they will include the M-1917 Enfield and very probably also at least one M-98 Mauser rifle. The Mausers are a little easier to come by and make fine guns and because of the great numbers of them which were brought back from Europe, either at the end of this scrap or after the first one, a considerable number have turned up in the channels of commerce.

However, no matter which gun or guns you happen to have there will probably have arisen the desire to turn them into "sporters" without much outlay of ready cash.

You can only get out of anything what you put into it, and this goes for the issue rifle, too. You will not be able to make a high grade sporting arm out of the issue guns without throwing a little cash to the winds, but you can make a fine, practical rifle out of it—one of which you need not be ashamed. Needless to say new sights, blueing, stock and accessories will tear quite a hole in a fifty dollar bill, but by working over the old stock and leaving the original sights as they were you can get by with a small supply of oil or varnish and a few hours work.

This book is not intended to be a guide to metal working.

It is concerned only with the wood working angle, and of that it limits itself to the finishing of the shaped and inletted wood portions. However, inasmuch as there seems to be such a demand for information on the conversation of the issue stock it is not out of place to go through the whole process, from the reception of the gun from the arsenal to the finished product, with the production of a finished "sporter" stock from the rough, issued wood.

MODEL 1898, 7.9 MM MAUSER

All of the military rifles are stocked in the same manner. They have a full length stock running all the way to the muzzle of the gun, and on top of the barrel is another piece of wood which is called a "handguard." In military circles rapid fire is not out of the ordinary, especially in combat. The heat generated by the burning of the powder and by the friction of the projectile as it forces its way through the barrel is very great and it takes only a few rounds of ammunition fired in rapid succession to heat the barrel to a point where you cannot lay your hand on it without burning it. The handguard protects the hand from touching the barrel.

In civilian or sporting circles, however, this sort of thing is frowned upon. Not only is there no necessity for firing more than two or three (at the very most) shots quickly but such a practice is very hard on the bore. A barrel used in rapid fire will wear out much more quickly than a barrel which has the same number of rounds fired through it more slowly in order to prevent the barrel from heating up. Therefore this handguard is not necessary on the sporter and only adds weight where it is not wanted.

The gun is dismantled by taking out the screws that hold the triggerguard assembly in place and by loosening and removing whatever bands are around the stock. These bands usually are attached to sling or stacking swivels. The band closest to the bolt has a sling swivel attached to it and the one at the extreme forward end of the gun has a stacking swivel and bayonet stud. Both must be removed to dismantle the rifle.

With the bands removed the handguard should come off easily. Then by removing the guard screws the barrel and action should come away from the rest of the stock. It may be a bit reluctant to separate, but it will come if you worry and pull this way and that.

Set the barrel and action aside and turn to the base portion of the stock. We will not need the handguard any more either so you can put that away under the bench where you can find it again as we will need it to test the staining and finishing material preparatory to actually finishing the stock proper.

Incidentally, most all of the military Mausers made after about 1939 were stocked with laminated wood. This lamination helped prevent the warping of the stock, and it also allowed the production of stocks out of undersized and poor grade wood. The models made prior to 1939 were of one piece construction, and the farther back in the history of the Mauser you go the better the wood of which the stock was made.

Now remove the buttplate and sling swivels from the rear of the stock. The forward end of the stock will be cut off so do not bother about that part now.

Here we pause and try to figure out how the dickens to get rid of the round steel plate which is on either side of the butt halfway between the triggerguard and the buttplate. It can not be pushed or driven out as it is merely sunken down into the wood and the hole does not go all the way through the stock.

These plates are held together and in the stock by a rivet-like tube of steel which extends all the way through the stock. It is peened over on each side so take a vixen file or abrasive wheel and grind off the top half of one of these plates. It does not make any difference which one it is—they are both alike. When you have cut down into the surface of the plate for about one eighth inch then take some sort of a driving rod a little larger than the central hole and give it what-for with a heavy hammer. Even though you have filed or ground off the lips which were holding the central tube in place it will be a dog-goned close fit.

Inasmuch as the central tube, or rivet, has walls about $\frac{1}{16}''$ thick you can not use too large a rod. If you do you will be pounding on the plate itself instead of just on the rivet and you will not do any removing that way.

Continue the pounding until the rivet starts to go through. Then change over to a rod as close to the diameter of the rivet as possible. In this way you can continue to force the rod down through the hole in the plate and out the other side. When this has been done then merely pry out the two plates which will be easily removed in this manner. Be careful that you do not split or splinter the edges of the recesses in prying, though. The plates are a close fit and if not watched carefully will break out splinters.

Now you have the stock in the nude, so to speak. Before we go any further let us figure out what we are going to do and in what manner.

You say you want a sporter, eh? Well, what is a sporter? To the majority of us a sporter is a gun which has a stock reaching only part way out the barrel. In addition, the stock is as light as possible and usually has a cheekpiece and pistol grip. At least, that is the general description I have gathered.

To make a sporter the first thing that must be done is to shorten the forward end of the wood. This will be a matter of personal choice. The length of the stock from the recoil shoulder to the tip of the wood is about 18″, therefore, a good length to remain about halfway along the barrel would be 10″. So measure off 8″ from the very forward end of the wood and cut the forend off square. We can come back later and shape it or add a tip if we wish.

The length of the stock from the very rear edge of the receiver to the buttplate is 12″. Cut the stock off at the buttplate to remove all of the recess which was cut into the wood for the top lip of the plate to fit in to. This will leave you with

11½" of butt, measured from the rear of the receiver.

For myself, being rather long and lanky, 13" is the minimum length here, though such dimensions will have to be fitted to your build.

The angle at which the cut should be taken will determine the "pitch" of the stock, but to avoid any complicated calculations and measuring if you make the cut along the line that the issue buttplate took (as near as you can figure it) then that should be okay for our purpose.

Now that we have the forend shortened and butt cut off let us consider the openings in the stock that were placed there for the sling and racking rod. These recesses and openings will be very unsightly and they should be covered in some way.

There are two ways to attack the problem. First of all, we can use a piece of plastic and back it up with wood so that there will be no chance of pushing the inlays in after they are in place. The second way would be to use wood itself and allow that to show.

You can take your choice. In the first instance, the plastic will show up like nobody's business, no matter what color you use. The idea behind the use of a contrasting plastic patch is not only to admit the use of a patch at that spot, but also to give a touch of the bizarre. Personally I do not care for this method. Plastic inlays are fine in their place, but here I do not like them. There is just too much area to be covered.

The method of using wood appeals to me. Choose a piece of wood nearly the same color as the stock wood and let it into the surface of the stock. Smooth off the inlay level with the rest of the stock face and carry on the staining and finishing from there just as though no inlay were ever on this stock.

You may run into a bit of difficulty in working in wood so that it shows a minimum amount. The stocks that you will probably have to work with are laminated and are very light in color. A piece of ash or pecan wood flooring will have about the same color as most of the stocks. They will be hardwoods, but not very close grained; still, they will work.

Choose the system you wish to follow and go to it. Cut out as much of the stock as you need in order to get a good, close fit of the inlaying block and have sufficient strength to back it up. Fasten the inlay there with good waterproof glue and clamp it in place for a couple of days. If the wood was free from oil and grease and the fit was close all the way around then you need not worry about that piece ever coming out or breaking away.

Besides the sling recesses there will be a hole in the end of the forend into which the cleaning rod of the gun was originally placed. This, too, must be closed up with a light colored piece of hardwood. Glue a dowel there and when dry cut it off flush with the end of the stock.

You will find that when you have removed the handguard from the lower stock that there will be a certain gap or opening between the barrel and the barrel channel walls. Here you will have to glue in strips of wood to cover such openings. The strips may easily be cut from the discarded forestock.

Make sure that you make the fit of the barrel in this new channel snug but that the strips do not bind the barrel and prevent proper seating in its place.

You will also find that, when you reassemble the barrel and action to the main stock, there is a lip on the forward end of the rear sight base. The rear edge of the handguard normally fits under this overhanging lip.

In order to make a smooth job of the conversion this lip should be cut, filed, or ground away so that the sight base has an even curve from the barrel to the top of the base. A file will do for this job very well. Remove the lip and round the place where it was originally attached to the base. In this manner all trace of it may be completely removed. Obviously, a touchup blueing job will be necessary on the filed area.

Now we have the major repairs completed. Using a rasp or sanding disc cut whatever portions of the inlays that may protrude above the surface of the stock. They should be smoothed down to the general contour of the stock surface.

You may lighten and thin the stock considerably in this process. The stock will be bulky and very thick, to gain strength. Take a rasp or spokeshave and thin down the stock to your individual taste. Work it over from buttplate to forend but make sure that you leave enough wood around the grip and action so that sufficient strength is left to withstand the shocks of recoil and just plain handling.

Before you go too far with the thinning down of the butt decide what kind of buttplate you want or need on the gun. Inasmuch as we have cut off some of the length of the stock it will no doubt be advisable to use one of the rubber cushion-type plates. These are most often seen on shotguns and will allow you an extra inch or more, which will be generally needed.

Fit the plate to the stock now, rather than waiting until the stock is lightened and finish sanded. If you place it on then you will have to be very careful that you do not dig into the finished wood at the point where the plate and the stock join. This is especially true if you are going to use some sort of an abrasive disc on a polishing head or flexible shaft. It is very easy to slip and allow the edge of the disc to cut into the wood badly at the adjoining points.

Place the plate on the stock and do all your cutting and smoothing after. It is easy to finish the stock with this plate on, though you should be careful that you do not smear the rubber with stain and varnish or oil, whichever you intend using for the final finish.

The grip consists of a sort of modified pistol grip. It is better suited for a sporting rifle than some of the other military stocks but still leaves something to be desired. However, unless you want to do a risky job of cutting the grip nearly through and then placing thereon a new block of wood to be made into a genuine pistol grip I would suggest you work with what you have.

Leave the curve in the present grip just as it is. You can deepen it a bit by rasping and sanding some in the center of the curve, but this will depend upon the individual hand and how long the fingers are.

If your hand is large and fingers are long you can profitably deepen this curve, but if you have small hands and short fingers you will not be able to do much along these lines.

You can very well cut down the diameter of the grip, though. It is very thick through and taking $\frac{1}{8}''$ off each side will make it seem much more comfortable.

The butt itself can be thinned down this much. A plane or spokeshave will be good here as the use of a rasp over such large flat areas will be a lot of useless work which could be done as well with a cutting tool.

Before you go too far with thinning down the buttstock, stop a moment and wonder if maybe you would like to have a cheekpiece on the gun. If so then before you touch the stock at all lay out the outline of the cheekrest where you want it and as large as you desire. There will be enough wood on the stock for you to make one, but it will not be any thicker than a quarter of an inch or so. It will be strictly a matter of looks as it will not be thick enough for any practical use.

If you do decide to work out this accessory then do most of your thinning of the stock from the left side (all around the cheekpiece). Leave the wood as is where this is to be and the wood around the penciled outline will soon cut down enough to leave the quarter inch cheekrest. Then you can carve and curve the face of it to suit yourself and even it up around the edges.

When such a cheekrest is being added to the issue stock be sure that you move the general centerline of the stock over to the right a quarter inch. This will allow the buttplate to be placed in the proper position in relation to the cheekpiece. Be sure and figure on this shift before you fasten the plate permanently to the wood.

Inasmuch as there will not be enough wood to build a good, practical cheekrest you will do just as well to omit it entirely. This, however, is a matter of personal choice.

You must have done all the thinning from the left side because if you cut from the right side, too, you will thin the stock so much that there will not be anything left from which to build the hump.

When the cutting and whittling has taken the stock down to decent proportions then go after it with the sanding block and coarse paper. You are now removing any and all tool marks and rough spots which have appeared before or during the thinning process.

While you are doing the rough sanding of the stock make sure that the buttplate is also cut and sanded at the same time. If you do it as you go along you will not run into the difficulty so many amateurs experience. This is the trouble of waiting until the stock is shaped and sanded and then trying to cut and fit the plate to fit the exact shape of the stock. When it is done in this manner either they tear up the surface of the wood in the cutting or they do not get a smooth, snug fit. Fastening the plate on the stock before the final sanding will eliminate this trouble.

When the stock is shaped to your wishes then go at it with 2/0 or 3/0 sandpaper. This will remove the final scratches left by the coarse #2 or #1 paper.

Now whisker the stock with the traditional water-and-heat treatments until the grain is no longer raised. Then you are ready for staining.

Inasmuch as the most common Mauser stock is the laminated fruit wood affair (common after 1939 manufacture) the wood will be very light and have little grain. Some grain may be apparent on the side of the stock where the only large areas of one of the pieces of wood is seen, but the rest will be composed of ends or edges of thin pieces of the lamination.

About the only thing you can do is to make sure that the overall color of the wood is pleasing. This is done by using a dark reddish-brown stain of the penetrating type. This, of course, will mean the use of a water or penetrating oil type material.

If you wish you may take some of the basic stain shades given in the chapter on Stains, or you can start with the following and see what your particular wood color requires.

Oak Wood Stain Formula #1 (water stain)

duPont Tartrazine Conc. —$3/64$ oz.
duPont Resorcin Brown 5G —$1/2$ oz.
duPont Nigrosine WSB Conc.—$1/4$ oz.
Water —3 qts.

This formula will give the wood a light brown cast and resembles a light oak.

Oak Wood Stain Formula #2 (water stain)

duPont Resorcin Brown 5G —$7/8$ oz.
duPont Nigrosine WSB Conc.—$1/2$ oz.
Water —3 qts.

This formula will give a deeper, darker brown than Formula #1.

Walnut Wood Stain Formula #3 (water stain)

duPont Orange II Conc. —$1/10$ oz.
duPont Nigrosine WSB Conc.—$1 1/16$ oz.
duPont Resorcin Brown 5G —$1/2$ oz.
Water —3 qts.

This will give a dark walnut effect to most woods.

Mahogany Wood Stain Formula #4 (alcohol stain)

Luxol Fast Orange GS —$1/16$ oz.
Luxol Fast Brown K —$3/8$ oz.
Luxol Fast Red B —$5/32$ oz.
Luxol Fast Black L —$1/8$ oz.
Alcohol —1 gallon

This stain will be relatively light fast and easy to use. Apply in thin coats as it may be too dark for use on some of the darker woods.

Apply the stain in the prescribed manner, but here do not use the stain (if it be a water type) as a combination stain and grain raising agent. You want as much penetration as you can get, and the laminated stock will not warp from any of the small amounts of water you may get into it by staining. If you use it as a grain raising agent also you will cut down the penetration a great deal and that we do not want here where the wood will need as much help as it can get to look halfway presentable.

When the wood has been stained then you may proceed with the rest of the finishing operation exactly as described for any particular material. Incidentally, if you use a filler probably the only place you will need it will be on the side "panels." There are the only spots where real grain structure and pores will show. The ends or edges of the laminations will be taken care of by whatever finishing material you intend to use. Two or three coats of the finish will then be sufficient to give you a smooth, uninterrupted film.

Drying oils, of course, will do no filling whatsoever, and in this case you had better plan to use either some sort of a filler all over the stock or a coat of shellac to fill the pinholes in the lamination edges.

MODEL M-1917, ENFIELD, .30–06

This gun is one of the most popular issue rifles. Primarily this is because the gun can be bought for as little as $5.00 (for one classed as unserviceable, though it very often is as good as the new $17.50 one). Therefore, there are thousands upon thousands of them kicking around the basements and attics all over the country.

When first viewed the Enfield looks like a lost cause. It is a very ungainly, ugly weapon. Some say that this is because its father was English, but I do not think so. I am English, too, and I think it is a fine little gun.

Anyway, no matter how it looks when first pulled out of grease and goo it can be made into a practical rival of the

Mauser, Springfield, and the various civilian guns if properly handled.

As mentioned before, the working of the metal portions of the gun is not included here and only the finishing of the wood and a bit of the primary woodworking concerns us.

Assuming you have done whatever brand of murder you fancy on the sight ears, barrel and other steel parts, now the problem is to make the stock look like something.

First of all, let us assume that you have left the triggerguard alone and have not straightened out the "frog leg" in it. This will make the gun still seem a yard high from top to bottom if you have to carry it very far, but will simplify the woodworking angle.

The barrel, action, triggerguard assembly, barrel bands, buttplate, and sling swivel will have been removed from the gun by this time. This is accomplished by the removal of the guard screws and the loosening of the screws holding the barrel bands tightly against the stock. Then the whole thing will simply fall apart; or words to that effect. Occasionally you run across a rifle which has not been dismounted since the day it left the arsenal and it may stick a little. This is especially true if you have thrown a few good, wet coats of linseed oil on the thing in the mistaken notion you were waterproofing it.

The stock, as issued, runs all the way out to the muzzle of the gun. This should be cut down quite a bit if you intend to make a conventional sporter out of it. The place to cut the stock off (forend) to get the best effect is about 13" back from the very nose of the stock. This will leave you a forend 10" long measuring from the extreme forward tip of the triggerguard.

Cut the stock off square and leave it alone for the moment.

Now turn your attention to the buttend. This will be all right for length for most of us, but the buttplate leaves a lot to be desired. Here you may follow the same operation that you used in working over the Mauser. If you do not like the issue plate cut the butt off just enough to eliminate the lip or heel of the plate which extends over the top edge of the butt. In cutting follow the same general angle which the present plate seems to follow.

Then apply a buttplate of your choice. If the stock is now a trifle short for you, use one of the shotgun plates which is built up of rubber and which will add at least an inch to that end of the stock.

If you have short arms and a chubby build (excuse it, please) then the stock may be long enough for you without such an extension. In this case place a thin composition or steel plate on the stock. If it follows the general pattern it will be flat on the stock side so you will not have any trouble in fitting it snugly to the wood. If, however, it is of the deeply curved type then you will have to work out with lampblack or Prussian blue in spotting the plate in for a close fit.

Now turn your attention to the grip and the sides of the stock. It will probably be too thick through for your tastes. It is for mine and most of the fellows I know. The side-to-side dimensions of the grip are 1½" and this can be reduced to at least 1¼" without sacrificing any strength. This means you can whittle and rasp ⅛" off each side of the grip which will look much better for it.

The top to bottom dimensions of the grip should be left alone. It is none too thick as it is and any taken off here will give the effect of a goose-neck lamp rather than something to grab the rifle by.

Inasmuch as the grip is too wide the rest of the stock is also too wide. This can be taken care of partially by planing and sanding the entire stock from nose to tail. Be careful in reducing the thickness of the wood over and around the magazine and action. The thinner you get the wood here the more flexible the stock becomes and it is easy to take off so much that necessary strength is lost. It would be better to round the top and bottom of the stock at this action-and-magazine area to give the illusion of thinness and to leave most of the wood where it is. The forend and the buttstock, however, may be worked on profitably.

The buttstock may be reduced in thickness at least one-eighth and even three-sixteenths of an inch without losing anything but the bulky appearance.

Blend the grip into the butt with long, gentle swells and never place quick curves or angles any place where long lines are the rule.

The forend is just crying to be cut down and once you have the length reduced it will be easier to see just how heavy the stock should be at that point for proper aesthetic value. Plane it down, starting at the forward end of the triggerguard and gradually reduce the diameter until, at the nose, the stock is about 1 1/8" from top to bottom. This will mean that the original stock which measured 1 5/8" will have had a half-inch hacked off it.

Perhaps this will be too thin for you. As you are working the wood down, constantly check it with your eye. When it looks harmonious and well shaped then stop.

The same goes for the width of the stock at this point. It may be planed down so that it measures about 1 1/4" here, too. This is about as thin as you can go and still keep any wall thickness at all.

While planing or cutting down the width of the forestock (if you so desire) you will run into the "grasping grooves." These may be filled in with an inlay of walnut, or even of wood with a contrasting color. Personally, I like to use walnut as even if the color and grain do not match too well it looks less like a make-shift job.

The easiest way to go about filling these grasping grooves is to cut the bottom of the grooves square cornered, and then to glue in place a rectangular block of walnut which was cut and shaped to fit the depression. Leave the top of the block protruding a bit above the surface of the stock, and when the glue is dry then cut or plane it down to blend in with the rest of the stock surface.

When you have the basic dimensions as you wish them then take the plane and round the edges of the "block" thus formed. The shape should be circular and your eye will tell when you have reached a pleasing shape.

There is nothing in the world that can be done about the abrupt drop that the stock takes at the forward end of the triggerguard. At least not without cutting off and working down the triggerguard itself.

In the case of the ambitious lad who has cut off the triggerguard at the "drop" and had it welded back again straight and cut down the magazine about $\frac{1}{2}''$, then the stock may be cut off straight and the "drop" eliminated. This is done by virtue of the fact that the triggerguard now no longer sticks up in the air the way it did and the lines may be made to harmonize.

The general run-of-the-mill stocks on the M-17 (and the M-1903, for that matter) are of open grained walnut. The wood will be a very dirty brown color due to the oil it has absorbed and also because of the dirt and sweat it has picked up in its travels. While the stock may be left the way it is a considerable inprovement may be made in the appearance, not only by a good finish, but also by improvement of the color.

Before you go much farther in the finishing of the wood you should apply heat in such a manner as to drive out most or all of the liquids which may have been spilled on the stock at some time in the past and which were absorbed.

This is done by subjecting the stock to the heat of a Bunsen burner or a gas plate. The flames of the burner or plate should be used in the same manner as when whiskering the wood. They should be played quickly and evenly over the wood, just far enough away so that the wood is not burned or charred. This heat will force the liquids in the wood near the surface to come to the top where they should be quickly removed with a rag. If you allow the stock to cool off before removing the oil or bore cleaner (which it will probably be) it will again sink into the wood and disappear. Then when you heat the stock to whisker it it will again pop up.

Do this over the whole stock and at least twice, or until no more of the liquid appears upon heating.

You will find, when you have cut or planed down into the wood of such an issue stock, that the deeper you go the lighter the wood becomes to a certain extent. Once you have gotten below the line of oil and dirt absorption the color will be a sickly yellow or yellow-brown. This is the natural color of the wood, and if you have done much planing or cutting of the wood those spots will appear much lighter than the untouched areas of the surface.

You must now make sure that the wood is as much the same color or shade overall as you can make it. This can be done to a certain extent by sanding the stock with varnish remover. The varnish remover will help to soften and dissolve whatever oil has been absorbed into the wood and will tend to loosen it enough for the sandpaper to remove it easily.

If the stock has a great deal of oil in it no matter how far down you go with the sandpaper and varnish remover the color does not seem to change. In this case all you can do is to remove as much as possible of the absorbed oil and let it go at that for the time being. The varnish remover will evaporate quickly, but keep the surface at least dampened. It would be a good idea to wrap the stock with rags and to saturate the rags with varnish remover for a half hour or so before doing any sanding. This will soften the oil near the surface and make the removal that much easier. Before actually sanding pour some of the remover on a cloth and scrub the wood vigorously. This will remove a great deal of the oil and dirt which will show up on the rag as a dirty brown stain. Then take the sandpaper and pour a little of the remover on the wood.

Now, using coarse paper (#1 or #½) sand over this wetted area and run a rag over it. You will be surprised at the amount of additional oil and dirt that will adhere to the rag. Continue this process over the whole stock where it has not been cut into. The cut-into areas will not have the oil in them any more and the operation would be unnecessary.

When you have cleaned the wood as much as you can you may still have quite a bit of color left in those uncut areas. Well, we will have to do the best we can. Remember, you have a stock which is more or less of a makeshift as far as choice is concerned. If you wanted a beautiful job in the first place you would not have fooled around with the cutdown issue job.

Before we go any further let us whisker the wood. This is done in the usual manner (see Chapter 2) and for the usual reasons.

Now bring out your selection of staining agents and prepare to do a little art work. This will involve touching up the light sections of the wood to match the old, oil stained areas. Choose the stain which will be nearest the color of the old wood. This, in nearly all cases, will be a decided brown. There is no red or yellow in linseed oil soaked wood but only brown. In this case a thin naphtha solution of asphaltum is good.

When you have played around with the stains and have gotten what resembles the uncut areas then you should allow the stained wood to dry thoroughly. When that has been done you can come back with an overall stain job which will give you the overall color you want.

A light brown with a touch of red and yellow in it will give a rich, mellow tone to the wood, even to poor grade walnut.

You may use any of the stains given in Chapter 3, especially those which are listed as adding red and yellow to the wood. For stocks which are too dark to suit your taste, even after cleaning and sanding, use any of the formulae which are recommended for use over dark woods to lighten them. Then you may come in with a touch of red, yellow, or brown as you think the stained wood needs.

When the staining is completed continue the finishing operations as described in the various chapters for each material.

Incidentally, the use of a sealer will not often be necessary in working over issue stocks because I understand the government uses just such a sealer on the stocks when first made. This will explain why it is so difficult to remove all of the oil color from the stock before staining it.

M-1903 SPRINGFIELD, .30–06

This grand old doll is the favorite of thousands of hunters and shooters, and with darned good reason! The action, when properly worked over and smoothed up can not be beat any place even by one of these fancy civilian guns which costs more than a used car used to.

The operations for conversion of the Springfield are precisely the same as for the Enfield. The only big difference is that here we have a gun that looks like a gun, and the stock can be worked over to produce something a little closer to what most of us have been brought up to think of as a gunstock.

There are two ways in which the M-1903 issue stock can be worked over. The first is a sort of semi-military look, and the second is the new or the civilian look. Let us take them one at a time.

The first way is to leave the rear of the upper handguard on the stock and to cut off everything (on the stock) forward of this point.

The way to attack this problem is to dismount the barrel and action from the stock and reassemble the stock, handguard and all. This is done by replacing the handguard on the lower stock in the position it would normally occupy if the barrel and action were in position. Then fasten the sling swivel as tightly as the binding screw will allow. This will hold the handguard firmly, though it would also be wise to tape the two pieces of wood together with adhesive tape.

Scribe a line around both the handguard and the lower stock with a pencil. This is done about an inch and a quarter in front of where the sling swivel is holding the wood. Now take a hack or other fine toothed saw and cut through both the handguard and the stock on this line. This will leave you with a shortened stock, and also a shortened handguard. The fine teeth will prevent your tearing out splinters.

Take the sling swivel and the tape off the wood and separate the two pieces. With a plane cut down the forward end of the guard and the stock so that they take on a more pleasing approach angle to the now new end of the stock. If you wish you may cut the top of the handguard off so that the bump or hill which is immediately in front of the rear sight will be removed and the entire top of the handguard will be more or less flat. This will remove some of the clumsy appearance of the stock and will make the gun appear slimmer and lighter than it really is.

The edges of the lower stock and the handguard should be planed so that they meet flush with one another. The very forward end or tip of the stock(s) should be rounded to suit your taste but they should not be thinned very much. An abrupt curve from the straight line of the stock into the tip gives the best appearance.

You will find that, when you have cut off the stock and handguard and replaced them around the barrel that there will be a considerable gap or opening appear around the barrel. This is because the barrel channel is considerably larger than the barrel all the way up to the muzzle where it is constricted.

The neatest way to fill in such an opening is by piecing or inlaying walnut wood and then cutting it out for the passage of the barrel. This will take a little fine work, but the barrel channel may be cut into a square edged groove and then a rectangular block of walnut glued into that groove. If the fit of the block in the groove was done carefully the join will be practically unnoticeable. This same procedure may be carried out in fitting the cut-down handguard, but inasmuch as the wood of this guard is much thinner than that of the stock you must be careful that you do not split it in making an insert.

Another way to do this is to place a heavy coating of walnut or dark brown plastic wood in the stock. Then either place a good coat of grease on the barrel or wrap it in waxed paper. One thickness of waxed paper will be sufficient. Then the guard screws are tightened up and the plastic wood will set or mold itself around the barrel. When this is hard remove any excess wood which may have squeezed out around the barrel and onto the surface of the stock. The grease or waxed paper will prevent the plastic wood from gripping the barrel so that its removal from the stock without splitting it or tearing out the hardened wood is impossible.

Follow the same system in filling the opening under the handguard. Plastic wood should be placed at the very forward end of the guard in a layer heavy enough to squeeze out the forward end of the opening when sling swivel is put in place and tightened.

Be careful that any wood upon which plastic wood is to be placed is free from oil or grease as this would prevent any adhesion of the hardened material to the wood and it would merely fall off in a lump at some later day.

When you finish this operation then turn your attention to the possible grasping grooves in the forestock. Some models have them and some do not. If you do not then do not worry about them. However, if you have a stock that has these grooves you should figure on filling them in in the same manner as was suggested for the Enfield stock.

The bottom of the grooves should be cut or routed out square and then shaped rectangles of walnut glued in place.

There are quite a few of the boys who rather like the appearance of the grasping grooves, particularly if they have left the forestock long enough to allow the full length of the grooves to remain. In that case they should be left alone with no attempt to work them over. I rather like them, myself, but that is a matter of choice. It is a bit like planting a garden. You put in radishes and I will put in carrots. Personally I hate radishes, but for the guy that likes them they are just as good a choice as carrots were for me.

The edges of the stock proper where it meets the action and receiver should be rounded to eliminate the sharp corners which are on it at the present time. This may be done by sandpaper or a rasp, but be certain that you do not tear out splinters or pieces of the wood by using a very coarse rasp in a vigorous manner. Be very careful here. If you do happen to split some of the edges out badly the only recourse will be to patch or inlay the stock at that point with wood cut from the discarded part of the stock.

The butt need be thinned very little, if at all. The standard stock is of pleasing dimensions from the grip on back, and thinning the wood much here will only make the finished gun look like it is stocked with a toothpick. The grip itself will usually be of the straight variety, though there are also many M-1903-AI stocks that have a semi-pistol grip formed on them. These may be thinned some, but for Pete's sake leave enough wood there to furnish sufficient strength against the shocks of recoil and field handling. If the grip fits your hand well as issued then I would not advise doing much work on it. If it does not fit your hand then thin it down only enough to give you a pleasant handful.

When the handguard and stock has been cut and thinned down to what you think is a good shape you are ready for finishing.

The second method mentioned at the beginning of the article results in the new look. This approaches more closely what we are accustomed to think of as a sporter type stock. In this operation the handguard is discarded entirely and only the lower or main stock wood is used.

Before dismounting the barrel and action from the stock try to figure out where the stock should be cut off to look best. Usually this will be about at the same place the lower stock was cut off in the process described above. This will be about one or one and a half inches in front of where the sling swivel fastens. Incidentally, it is much better to cut the stock too long than too short. If it is too long you can cut more off, but if you have made a mistake and whittled off two inches too much wood then it is a deuce of a job to put it back on without showing.

When you have marked the approximate place to cut remove the metal from the wood. Then scribe a line around the stock at that point and cut it off.

When the fore part of the stock has been removed place the barrel and action loosely in the stock and see if it gives you the effect you thought it was going to. If it still looks too long then lop off another inch or so and try it again. When the effect is what you want then remove the barrel and action.

Here we run into a little difficulty. When you removed the handguard from the stock entirely it left not only an ugly gap between the barrel and the sides of the barrel groove, but it also left the forward part of the rear sight base sticking out like a sore thumb. This must be taken care of in some way. As with everything else there are two ways to tackle this problem.

First, you may remove the rear sight and base entirely and mount a receiver sight on the rear of the action. This is by far the best and most costly way. The other way is to place a band of metal around the barrel in front of the base so that it hides the abrupt drop from the leaf sight down to the surface of the barrel on which it is placed. This band may be cut from an old Springfield sight base in the same manner that a band is cut to place over the spline cuts in the barrel when the sight base is removed and a receiver sight substituted.

In either case, there will be a large gap between the barrel and the walls of the barrel channel. These gaps must be filled in some manner. Probably the best method is to use strips of walnut cut from the discarded portion of the stock. These strips should be securely glued to the inside of the barrel channel and when dry should be inletted or cut to allow the barrel to fit snugly without binding.

Now the outside of the stock may be worked over in the same manner as when making the semi-military sporter described above. The forend and the grip are thinned to your taste and build and if desired a new buttplate may be placed on the stock.

In finishing the wood the same operations are followed as were recommended for the Enfield. The wood used in the Enfield is precisely the same as that used in the M-1903 and the operation will be the same.

These operations, of course, will include heating to drive out liquids such as lubricating oils and bore cleaners which may have been spilled on the stock and which the wood absorbed. Then the grain raising and staining (or vice versa) and the finishing follow in that order.

JAPANESE ARISAKA '38 AND '99, CAL. 6.5 AND 7.7 MM

These rifles are seen mostly in the second hand stores and in the closets of returned servicemen who served in the Far East. They are ungainly looking things, and to all intents and purposes are strictly souvenirs and nothing else. Inasmuch as the issue cartridges are relatively unavailable the issue guns do not cross the counters of the gunsmith very often.

The two models indicated by the heading are both available to the amateur, depending upon how careful he is in answering ads offering Jap rifles for sale.

The Model '38 (M-1905) was issued in 1905 and in 6.5 mm. This rifle was well made, is very strong and is an excellent basic action for reworking (either in metal or wood). It is generally confused with the second rifle, described below, and for that reason the two different models are spoken of as one.

This rifle has the reputation of being the best the Japs ever put out and one which is relatively available, if you specify that this is the one you want. There are no safety strings attached to this gun.

The second rifle is the one which is most commonly offered for sale. It is the Model '99 in 7.7 mm and was issued in 1939. This gun was definitely a war baby and is neither strong nor well made. Incidentally, it is this gun which gunsmith's ads so often offer to remodel to .300 Savage caliber for a nominal sum.

For remodeling in wood this gun is okay (if you can find issue cartridges for it) but I would not want to be behind one of the rechambered guns when it goes off. You might get by with the .300 Savage and it seems that many of us do, but under no circumstances have some joker rechamber it to .30–06. This is strictly a "life in your own hands" set-up and I do not want to be around when it is fired. It is too easy for the fragments of the receiver to strike one, unless he happens to be lying down behind a stump at the time.

For a rifle which has been converted to this .300 Savage cartridge there are certain limited steps which may be taken to make it a little more presentable. As with the other conversions described the metal work is not touched upon, but the working over of the stock (such as it is) may be done with a fair amount of success.

The wood of which the stock is made is usually found to be a poor grade of very open grained wood. Not only is the wood poor, but the rifle was originally designed to fit a man considerably smaller than most of us. Therefore, the buttstock will be quite a bit too short for the average man.

First of all, this gun, in common with the arms of other governments, has an upper handguard. It runs only part way out along the barrel instead of up to the muzzle as the rest of the issue guns do. This may be either removed entirely or left on and a semi-military look achieved, just as in the case of the Springfield.

You should figure where you want the forestock to end. This will be a matter of choice, but if you want to retain the handguard feature on the rifle then it should be cut off at the same spot that the handguard ends, or perhaps an inch and a half forward of that spot. The reason for allowing the lower or main stock to extend out farther than the handguard is that it will give you enough room to curve or taper the lower line of the stock up to the cut-off nose in a graceful curve. If it is cut off too short then you will have to retain a nearly square tip in order to keep the sling swivel secure around the stock.

If desired, the stock may be cut so that the sling swivel can be moved back towards the butt an inch or so. In this case the handguard and the lower stock may come to an end together and do away with the protruding lower lip appearance that will be present if the lower stock extends out farther from the breech then the guard.

When the length of the forend suits you then turn your attention to the buttend. Here you will find that the lower half of the buttstock is composed of two pieces of wood. One piece is fastened with a tongue-and-groove to the other. Evidently the reason for this is that they did not have enough wood to make the stock one piece, so they used narrow boards and built up the lower half of the butt with other small pieces.

Anyway, the line where the two pieces join will be very noticeable. About the only thing you can do here is to cut out the wood along this line about an eighth or a sixteenth of an inch deep and inlay that groove with wood strips cut from the discarded forend section that you cut off. Unless this inlaying is done carefully there will still be gaps between the inlay and the adjoining wood and you will not be any better off than you were before. The whole idea is to hide or cover the crack or line in the butt as much as possible, and if you go and leave another line or crack or two with a poor inlaying job there is no point in inlaying in the first place.

The butt will be very short for most of us. This can be taken care of by building up the length of the stock with a piece of walnut glued and fastened to the end of the butt. Inasmuch as the original issue stock is of poor grade wood, similar to pine, you are going to have a tough job trying to add wood and still make it unnoticeable. In fact, I do not think you can do it successfully. However, do the best you can. Match the added wood section as nearly as possible to the wood on the stock at the present time. Incidentally, this added section will probably have to be from one to two inches in added length for most of us.

When adding this length figure on the thickness of the buttplate to be added. If you are going to use a simple steel or plastic plate then no figuring is necessary, but if you are going to use the rubber cushion type shotgun plate then there will be an inch or so that you will not have to put on in the form of wood.

When all inlays, additions, and such have been placed and secured then go back to the forend and round off all edges to pleasing curves. Round the forend tip at a pleasing angle and see that the curve blends in with the general shape of the finished stock.

If the semi-military look is not wanted then the handguard may be left off the stock entirely. If this is done any gaps between the barrel and barrel channel should be filled in with strips cut from the discarded forend or handguard.

The finishing of the wood presents a little more of a problem. Inasmuch as the wood is very poor and very open grained considerable care must be taken for any kind of a decent finish.

First of all, however, go over the stock with varnish remover and sandpaper. Remove as much as possible of the old finish. Now see how different is the color between the old wood and any new inlays you may have had to make. This as much as anything will be your cross. You will find that the two different kinds of wood will take stain differently and it will be a problem to match the colors. There is little outstanding grain structure to this old wood so you do not have to worry about hiding the grain. Any grain structure present is so coarse that it is easy to work over it and still have it show up well.

The basic color of the wood is a washed-out yellow brown, usually. This should be improved with the use of a penetrating red-brown stain. If you wish wash the stock with a thin solution of asphaltum in naphtha and then go over that staining with a slightly red-yellow stain. This combination will not only darken the stock toward the walnut or mahogany shade but will also add a little richness.

The wood should be whiskered with the usual steps and then a finish applied. For finishing this type of wood it would be better to stay away from the use of a filler. The grain and pores are so coarse that a dark colored filler would show up too much. My recommendation would be to use a varnish or lacquer coating and let that finishing material do the filling. When the stock has been thus filled an additional one or two coats to improve lustre will do the job.

Of all the guns which are to be converted to sporter type weapons the Jap Arisaka is the least suitable. Not only is the cartridge unobtainable, but the stock is the poorest of any of the issue guns. Unless you intend to spend a bit of dough in a new stock, though, this converting of the old stock will be about the best you can do.

CHAPTER FOURTEEN

Antique and Early Gunstock Finishes

Way back before Hector's grandpappy was a pup they had rifles. These rifles were fired by means of a piece of flint which was struck against steel to make a spark, which, in turn ignited a train of powder which led to the actual chamber of the weapon and initiated the explosion. Or maybe they even had one of the new-fangled cap rifles which was looked upon with so much suspicion at first. There warn't nuthin' could beat the old tried and true flintlock and they did not care who knew it.

Some of these rifles are still in excellent condition and the few really good specimens you may run across have fine finishes.

It also seems that there are a certain class of gun nuts for whom the old guns have a deadly fascination. But there are not enough of the old babies in good enough condition to go around. So they are making a flock of duplicates of the old Pennsylvanias and are having themselves one heck of a good time shooting them.

Now the question arises, "I have a gun that is a dead ringer for one of the Lancaster masterpieces so what can I use on the stock that will also duplicate the original finish?" That is a good question, boys, but maybe we can beat the rap once more.

There were quite a few different materials in common usage

way back in those days, but most of them were of the same general type. Generally speaking, the stock was finished in a drying oil of some kind, a wax or wax and oil combination, or a spirit varnish.

These three material types were all they had to work with, though they turned out some fine works of art. The best way to cover the whole thing is to take the materials type by type and look them over.

Drying Oils: No matter how far back into history you go (if you stay this side of 1500 A.D.) you will find that linseed oil, either raw or treated, is mentioned in formulating protective coatings for wood. This oil was used precisely the same way as it is used today and for the same purpose. It has always been a standard finishing oil.

Walnut oil is another finishing material that was used to a certain extent up until about 1800. It is the product of the nut of the walnut tree, *Juglans regia*. By crushing these nuts the oil was released and collected.

To a lesser extent cottonseed oil and sunflower seed oil were also used, but they were neither as good nor as plentiful as the linseed and walnut oils.

The application of such drying oils was done by the old tried and true hand rubbing operation. The oil was applied thinly, rubbed in well, and allowed to harden. This will apply to any of the above oils, though even in those days of extremely limited technology they were fond of the linseed oil which had been heat treated with copperas (to act as a drier).

Waxes, Waxes and Oils: Probably the most common wax substance which was then available to the clan was beeswax.

Other waxes were known, but they were impossible for the average man to buy because they had to be shipped from other portions of the globe and by the time they got inland the cost was prohibitive.

The wax was applied to the stock with a hot iron and in a melted condition, usually. As can be easily seen the wax acted as both a filling and a finishing agent.

Many times this beeswax was incorporated with linseed or walnut oil to make it work easier.

Spirit Varnishes: The subject of the spirit varnishes is rather extensive if taken up in great detail. This will be gone into further along in the chapter but for the present we will briefly scan the materials in use.

Shellac was a great favorite. It was, and is, a true spirit varnish, and is easy to use.

Various of the natural resins or gums were used. These included sandarac, benzoin, copal (manila), rosin, elemi, and mastic. They were invariably dissolved in alcohol with the possible addition of a little turpentine. Sometimes a little linseed or castor oil was added to make the varnish more flexible. (This corresponds to our modern practice of using a Plasticizer.)

Filling Agents: The crudest materials were used as fillers, primarily because they had very little with which to work. Other than the waxes they used Spanish whiting rubbed into the pores and then covered with one or the other of the finishing compounds. This was the most common method if filling was to be done.

Solvents: At this time the only solvents or thinners in use were turpentine or alcohol.

The spirit varnishes all required alcohol but the oils and waxes needed nothing. Therefore, inasmuch as oil-resin varnishes were very rare, no need was felt for any other thinners.

Coloring Wood: For a long time artificial coloring was not applied to wood because there was enough good wood available from which they could choose their stocks. Maple, walnut, birch, and cherry were used to a considerable extent and there was plenty to choose from, and not only was it well colored but it was also properly seasoned.

When the finely colored and grained specimens became more scarce the practice was followed of using natural dyes (such as herbs and root stains), and acids for giving the wood the desired color.

BONE POLISHED FINISH

The subject of bone polishing is rather old and is referred to at long intervals in articles on wood finishing.

Basically it refers to the smoothing of the surface by the action of rubbing a piece of smooth bone vigorously over the wood. This type of finishing action was no doubt popular when there was no such thing available as abrasive paper. It goes rather farther then sandpaper will, obviously, as the action of the bone over the wood compresses the topmost layers of fibers and eliminates any and all surface imperfections. No scratching of the surface is present (which even the finest paper will do) and therefore for a superlatively fine finish this would work.

It is very probable that any such bone rubbed finish will meet disaster if moisture or water is allowed thereon. If a previous whiskering operation has been done then the raising of the grain would be considerably less noticeable, but for the systems and materials which the old boys used this would be out of the question for any but a strictly cabinet show gun.

It is probable that, together with the boning of the wood, a coat of wax (such as beeswax) was applied. The action of the bone would impregnate the wood well.

Incidentally, this bone should be a fairly large bone such as a beef rib. There must be enough of it to allow a good grip with the hands and considerable pressure should be applied while rubbing.

I had hoped to be able to give accurate, authentic information concerning the burning in of tiger-tail patterns on stocks with a piece of tarred rope, but have been unable to get reliable, definite data on this subject. Rather than resort to imagination or guesswork I have deleted the subject entirely for such stock figuring.

DUPLICATING ANTIQUE STOCK FINISHES

The production of a finish on modern wood which will duplicate in all properties the appearance of an old finish is rather difficult. A piece of wood which has been mellowed by time and countless rubbings of unknown hands will have something about it, perhaps that which is termed a patina, that only the passage of time and those many operations of rubbing and handling will produce.

Perhaps it would be most accurate to say that the production of a finish which will duplicate the *original* finish is easily possible. Further than that I hesitate to go.

Preparation of the Surface: First of all the preparation of the wood to take a finish is a very important point.

It makes no difference whether you are going to finish off one of the most modern of guns or one of these old timers. The methods are and were basically the same, though the tools and appliances with which that preparation was accomplished have changed.

Sandpaper is a relatively new tool. The cutting of wood has always been done by means of edged tools of some sort, but when it came to smoothing down the surface then sharp, water washed sand was the best that was available in those early days.

When the fully inletted and shaped stock is ready for finishing you will use the same principles that you would use on any stock. The surface must be as smooth and free from cuts and splinters as it is possible to achieve. This, of course, is done by the use of #½ or o paper followed by 2/o or finer paper. All rough spots are to be removed.

As in all stock work you must be very careful that you do not round off sharp edges and corners. This applies especially at the points into which locks and ornamentation are to be fitted. Even with the very limited selection of tools that they had the better gunsmiths turned out some very fine jobs—a great deal better than many stocks seen today, let me add.

Of course, even in those days poor workmanship was prevalent but the stocks which had lasted down through the years were the better pieces, usually, which were treasured and kept in good condition.

Once you have made the surface smooth and the points where wood joins metal as snug as possible then you will be ready for the other operations.

Whiskering: I have been unable to find any authentic data concerning this phase of wood finishing, but I would be inclined to think it was lacking, at least in the very early guns. Inasmuch as the removal of the raised grain sections cannot be accomplished to any extent by the use of sand alone this would preclude the application of this operation.

Even if it were true that this phase was never done it would be an excellent idea for you to raise the grain on your stock. As in any other piece of wood which is exposed to moisture, whether it be atmospheric or perspiration from the hand and cheek, the grain ends will be raised by the first sign of moisture and any accompanying heat. The heat will evaporate the moisture which has been absorbed by the wood and this passage of the moisture out of the wood will pop the grain ends up where they can be easily felt by the hand. (See Chapter 2.)

The whiskering is most easily done by dampening the wood well with water and immediately thereafter applying a flame evenly and quickly over the surface of the wood. This will force the grain ends to raise artificially, so to speak, and they may then be removed by fine steel wool.

Coloring or Staining: This operation may be done if necessary (and it will nearly always be necessary in the woods available today) by the use of many different substances.

Let us take up the use of the old methods first. This will most nearly approach the methods actually used by the ancients, though I doubt very much that there will be any great advantage in so doing. The use of modern stains and dyes will give you as fine and finer results and will not be detectable on the finished stock as having been brought about by different materials than those that the old timers used.

Red Stain, #1

Alkanet root — 4 oz.
Linseed oil — ½ pint

Heat the oil and put therein the root. Allow the color to steep out until the oil is a bright red.

For application heat the colored oil and wipe or rub over the stock until enough oil has been absorbed by the wood to give the stock the color you wish.

If desired, the oil may be thinned a bit with turpentine to achieve greater penetration.

Red-brown Stain, #2

Dragon's blood — 4 oz.
Common soda — 1 oz.
Alcohol — 2 pints

Paint the surface of the stock with nitric acid. As far as I can find out the old timers used acid of about S.G. 1.42.

When the wood has been brushed and dried apply the soda-alcohol-Dragon's blood mixture with a brush. The soda will neutralize whatever acid is left in the wood.

When dry brush off whatever may remain on the surface.

Mahogany Stain, #3

Water — 2 quarts
Madder — 4 ounces
Fustic — 2 ounces

The water should be boiled, and then put into it the madder and the fustic. Allow the color to become as deep as it will and then brush on while still hot.

When penetration has taken place and the stock is still damp remove any excess with a rag.

When dry apply a second coat until the color is deep enough.

Allow to dry and remove all loose matter which may remain on the surface.

Cherry Red Stain, #4

Annato — 2 ounces
Water — 1½ quarts
Potash — ½ ounce

Boil the dye in the water until dissolved. Then add ½ ounce potash (potassium carbonate).

Brush or rub this liquid over the wood and allow to dry.

Dark Walnut Stain, #5

Asphaltum — ½ pound
Turpentine — 2 quarts

Dissolve the asphaltum in the turpentine.

Rub or brush over the wood until the color is deep enough to suit you. Probably one coat will do in most cases.

This stain may be used in conjunction with any of the red stains to overcome the yellow-brown tinge that asphaltum will give the wood.

Black Stain, #6

Logwood — ½ pound
Water — 3 pints
Cream of tartar — ½ ounce

Steep the logwood in the water (boiling) until the water is a dark red color. Then add the cream of tartar.

Apply the hot solution to the wood and let dry. Repeat. Then set the stock aside to dry.

Now boil 1 pound of logwood in a gallon of water and add a pint of vinegar.

Apply hot to the already stained wood with a brush. When dry rub off all loose matter.

Brown Stain, #7

Potassium permanganate — 2 grams
Water — 2 pints

Heat the water until the permanganate is dissolved. While hot brush the solution over the stock and allow to dry.

If the color is not yet deep enough apply another coat.

This stain is well suited for coloring maple brown.

Brown Stain, #8

Nitric acid (S.G. 1.42) — 1½ oz.
Iron filings — 1½ oz.

Heat the acid until the filings are dissolved.

Rub this solution on the wood with a rag (taking care that you do not get any on your hands). Allow to dry. If not deep enough, repeat.

The above formulae are those which have been used for many years. If you prefer to use one of the more modern stains, then Chapter 3 should be consulted, not only for materials to be used but also for methods of application.

It is very difficult to take a piece of modern wood and use even the old stains and come out with a wood that is the same color that the old stocks are. The effects of age, handling, and rubbed-in dirt will have darkened these old stocks and they will probably not be very close to the color they were when first finished.

Most of the old guns which are available for inspection have a rather dirty brown color to them. This is due to the darkening of the finish and the rubbed in dirt, grime and oil of which I just spoke.

To duplicate them it will be necessary to darken the wood to a greater extent then you might like. This, however, is necessary if you wish to attain the appearance of antiquity which seems to be so desirable in some quarters.

For my money I prefer to place stocks in the best possible condition with the appearance that is the most pleasing to the eye. This will not result in the aged appearance but will give you a fine stock on a gun that deserves the best.

For the staining of stocks in the modern media refer to the chapter on stains.

Filling the Wood: There are two methods which may be used here.

One is the filling of the pores in the same manner in which the old stocks were filled, and the other is to use the newer, better materials.

The first method used to fill the pores of the wood, especially of walnut, was to use common whiting. This was done in the following manner:

Antique Wood Filler, #9

Whiting — 5 parts by weight
Coloring matter — 1½ parts by weight

The coloring matter was composed of any of the earth pigments such as umber, sienna, red oxide and the like. The color which the mixture will assume is governed by the amounts of coloring matter which is used.

Old formulae call for the whiting to be colored until the color was the same as that of the wood which was to be filled.

Apply a coat of linseed oil to the stock and rub in well. Then sprinkle the stock with the filler mixture and rub that into the pores until they are filled. Allow the coat to dry.

Personally I do not think this system is worth the powder to blow it up. The whiting is not a good filler as it is too liable to crumble out of the pores. Then there is nothing to hold the mixture in the pores except what little linseed oil the whiting has absorbed.

The formula is given as a matter of interest rather than that of a material to be used. It is no good in my opinion, but has been often used by finishers.

Antique Wood Filler, #10

Whiting — 5 parts
Linseed oil — 2 "
Umber — 1½ "

The umber and the whiting are mixed together well. Then the linseed oil is poured slowly into the powdery mass stirring well all the while.

When the three ingredients are well mixed they are spread out over the wood and rubbed in well.

Remove the excess from the wood and allow to dry.

This formula is in about the same category as the preceding one. The linseed oil will have a better hold on the whiting, but it will still be very poor.

Antique Wood Filler, #11

White lead — 5 parts
Linseed oil — 1½ "
Umber — 2 "
Turpentine — ½ "

The white lead is ground in the oil and the umber is then worked in.

The whole mixture is then thinned with the turpentine, increasing the amount if desired to make a workable mixture.

The filler is then rubbed into the pores and the excess removed from the surface of the wood. The stock is then set aside to dry.

This formula may be slightly better than any of the foregoing, but is still very poor. The white lead will crumble away easier, and is a definite health hazard.

I would not recommend the use of this formula under any conditions because of the danger of lead poisoning present each time the skin is brought into contact with the white lead.

After reading this section on fillers you may come to the conclusion that the author had better make up his mind one way or the other. First he lists and details formulae, but then he turns around and says that they are no good and not to use them.

You are absolutely right, laddy. The only thing is that I have made up my mind. I am either in favor of using a present day filler formulation or of using the finish itself as a filler as described a little farther on.

These formulae are given for your information but, just as with anything else, materials and methods have changed and improved. Use them if you wish, but you have a whole flock of other things which will give a better appearance to the stock and which will have much greater durability. Incidentally, it is the final finish that will determine how good or bad a stock looks. You can use an antique type finish over a modern filler and get the antique look without anyone being the wiser about what you have used underneath.

FINISH MATERIALS AND METHODS

Here we come to the largest field of all. There were three basic types of finish materials listed back aways, but those types may be broken down into a host of individual items. We shall take them one at a time and list the applications with each formula.

Drying Oils Finishes: Drying oils and their application have not changed a bit from the earliest times. Of course, you can get boiled oils which are made in the most modern factories and which are treated with new, modern substances but the final end properties of that oil are not too much different from the boiled oils that were used quite a while ago.

Inasmuch as those boys used what boiled oil they could lay their hands on or make, we may use boiled oil available to us today. The appearance of the final finish will not be changed, though the drying time may be decreased considerably from what they knew.

Antique Finish Formula #12

Raw linseed oil — 2 parts
Turpentine — 1 "

Mix the two ingredients together.

In applying this formula precisely the same steps are taken as for modern (?) rubbed oil finishes.

A few drops of the mixture is placed in the palm of the hand. It is then rubbed briskly over the surface of the wood which has been stained and/or filled in whatever system you desire. When the entire stock has had a bath set it aside to dry. Allow at least two weeks between coats.

When the finish has been built up to your liking do not apply any more. Occasionally a thin coat may be rubbed in, but this should be done only every two or three months.

This formula has long been an old standby. The old timers as well as a great many of the modern stock finishers swear by it. There are many others that swear *at* it, but they are in the minority. Inasmuch as raw linseed oil is used the film which is built up will *never* dry completely though it may appear to be hard on the surface.

This finish is one which was used on a great many stocks in the past and with which a fine appearance may be procured *if enough coats are applied and the drying time between each coat is sufficient.* The average man will never apply enough coats and will never allow sufficient drying time between coats to achieve a satisfactory surface coating.

Ideally this finish should have between 20 and 30 coats with from two to three weeks between each coat.

Antique Finish Formula #13
Boiled linseed oil — 2 parts
Turpentine — 1 "

This formula is intended to be handled in precisely the same manner as the preceding formula.

The presence of the boiled oil will cut down the drying time necessary between coats, but it should still be at least a week.

At least 20 coats should be applied for a satisfactory finish.

Antique Finish Formula #14
Walnut oil (*Juglans regia* tree) — 2 parts
Turpentine — 1 "

This formula is handled the same as the preceding two.

The walnut oil will have about the same properties as the linseed (raw) and will give no finer finish or no faster drying time. It was used, however, and for that reason is listed here.

Waxes, Waxes and Oil: These materials were probably used more than the drying oils because of the very short time that it took to bring out a good finish and because they actually are more waterproof than the drying oils.

Antique Finish Formula #15
Beeswax — 5 parts
Raw linseed oil — 3 "
Turpentine — 3 "
Umber — color as desired

The beeswax was melted and the linseed oil and the turpentine added. Then the umber was stirred into the melted mixture. Only enough was used to approximate the color of the wood to be finished.

This mixture was then allowed to cool and was rubbed into the wood with cloth as a polishing pad.

Rub in one thin coat and allow to harden for at least five hours. Then another thin coat may be applied in the same manner. Repeat this process until the pores of the wood are filled and the surface is shiny.

The wax acts as a filling agent and quickly fills the pores of the wood so that the surface is level and smooth. The turpentine and the linseed oil act as lubricants and reduce the viscosity of the wax so that it may easily be spread with the rag.

The turpentine evaporates within a few hours if the coat of wax is thin, but the linseed oil never does so. The oil will probably reach a state of incomplete polymerization and stay that way inasmuch as no oxygen from the air will be able to get at it and oxidize it completely.

This finish was one of the most common ones used, and is a fairly good one. Aside from the fact that the linseed oil constituent will never dry I see no reason why such a finish cannot be used with success.

Antique Finish Formula #16

Beeswax — 5 parts
Turpentine — 4 "
Umber (burnt) — 1 "

This formula is used in the same manner as the preceding one.

It should be soft enough to work easily with a rag. The turpentine will evaporate leaving a hard film of pure wax behind it.

You will note that no linseed oil is mentioned. The absence of this ingredient will give a harder film and one which will polish better.

After rubbing in enough of the wax so that a good finish is had it may be polished with a piece of felt or soft cloth. This will give a good lustre and will be excellent on nearly any of the antique or antique duplicates you may have in your possession.

Antique Finish Formula #17

Beeswax — 5 parts
Shellac solution — 5 "

Melt the wax and then add the shellac with vigorous stirring. Continue the stirring until the mixture has cooled at which time you will have the shellac well incorporated into the wax body.

This mixture should be thin and soft enough to work with a rag. If not then remelt the mass and add enough turpentine to make it soft when cold.

Apply this material with a rag by rubbing it into the wood until the pores are filled and the finish smooth and lustrous. It may then be polished with felt or cloth.

Antique Finish Formula #18

In this finish beeswax alone is used. A clean, soft cloth is wadded up into a sort of pad. Then melted beeswax impregnates the face of the cloth.

Use the cloth in a vigorous rubbing motion over the whole face of the wood. Use plenty of pressure against the wood and make sure that the whole stock is well worked over.

The pressure and speed with which the wax filled cloth is passed over the wood will partially melt the wax and it will pass on and adhere to the wood, glazing it. After several coats of this sort have been applied the stock is polished with a felt pad. The harder the felt the better the polish will be and the more lustrous the finish.

Such a finish will not build up a very heavy coat, nor will it do a great deal of filling. Obviously it should be used on very close grained woods for optimum effect. If used on open grained woods it may bridge across the pores but will not penetrate to the very bottom of them and do a good job of the filling.

Such a finish is recommended for maple and birch.

Spirit Varnishes: Here we come to the most diversified field of all. There are literally hundreds of different materials and formulae which have been used with splendid success. Inasmuch as most of the materials used will resemble one another except in the matter of hardness and gloss only a few representative preparations will be listed.

The base of the spirit varnish is alcohol and some sort of natural resin which is soluble in that alcohol. The method of preparing the varnish is a simple dissolving of the resin in the solvent.

These spirit varnishes were used for centuries and did their job well, but had many shortcomings. The durability of such varnishes is very poor when exposed to any weathering or when used in moist or water soaked conditions. They will give an excellent gloss, usually, and are rather hard. As matter of fact, such resins are still used today as a base for the rubbing varnishes found on the market, though even these are being replaced by certain synthetic (manmade) resins.

Spirit Varnish Formula #19

 Mastic   — ½ pound
 Sandarac — 2 pounds
 Elemi   — 4 oz.
 Alcohol   — 1 gallon

This formula will give a hard, white varnish which will be excellent for rubbing purposes.

The resins are dissolved in the alcohol and filtered through a piece of fine cloth. Bottle in glass and set aside for use as desired.

This varnish is brushed on with a clean brush making sure that brush marks are eliminated as much as possible. If it hardens too fast then add a little more alcohol until such a viscosity is reached that allows good flow of the varnish and resulting elimination of most of the marks.

The varnish will dry very quickly, but if any kind of a heavy coat has been applied it would be best to wait at least 18 hours before any rubbing or recoating is done. This is to make sure that the great majority of alcohol has evaporated and the film is hard enough to work with.

Such a finish may be placed on either open or close grained woods. If placed on open grained woods it may also be used as a filler. In this case apply several coats of varnish, allowing good drying between each coat (18 hours or so) and sand the finish off down to the wood. When the pores are filled or built up enough to be level with the surface of the wood place one more good, heavy coat of varnish thereon and when dry the film may be rubbed with pumice and rottenstone to smooth up whatever imperfections may be there.

Spirit Varnish Formula #20

Mastic	—	½ pound
Sandarac	—	1 pound
Turpentine	—	2 ounces
Alcohol	—	1 gallon

The mastic and the sandarac are to be dissolved in the alcohol. When that has taken place then the turpentine is added slowly with stirring.

This is another hard, white varnish which may be used for rubbing finishes. It also may be used over either open or close grained woods and on the open grained woods may be used as a filler as well as a finish.

The same instructions should be followed for filling and finishing as were given for Formula #19.

Spirit Varnish Formula #21

Sandarac	—	1 pound
Alcohol	—	1 gallon

This varnish is primarily the same as the preceding two.

Instructions for making and handling are the same as for #19. It may be used for a filler as well as a finishing agent.

Spirit Varnish Formula #22

Shellac flakes	— 1¾ pounds
Sandarac	— 4 ounces
Mastic	— 4 ounces
Alcohol	— 1 gallon

This varnish was very popular as a furniture varnish and was also used considerably as a stock finish.

The shellac is dissolved in the alcohol and then the other resins added.

Use in the same manner as Formula #19. May be used as a filler as well as a finish. This one will rub up a fine lustre.

Spirit Varnish Formula #23

Manila copal	— 24 parts
Rosin	— 12 "
Venice turpentine	— 4 "
Alcohol	— 50 "

Dissolve the rosin and the manila copal in the alcohol, add the venice turpentine with vigorous stirring.

This formula is handled in the same manner as #19. It will be a very hard varnish and rather brittle, though it will rub and polish well.

Spirit Varnish Formula #24

Bleached shellac flakes	— 3 parts
Alcohol	— 12 "

This is a straight shellac solution and was used more than any other type of spirit varnish for stock work.

The shellac should be placed in a glass container and allowed to stand in the alcohol until thoroughly dissolved. This may take a couple of days' time. When dissolved strain or filter the solution through a fine cloth.

Inasmuch as bleached shellac was used this solution will be

clear and nearly water white. It may be used without fear of changing the color on light stocks.

Brush the solution on the wood with a flat brush, making sure that as many brush marks as possible are eliminated. This may be done by thinning the varnish with more alcohol if necessary.

Allow each coat to dry for 18 hours before recoating. After each coat is hard sand it lightly with fine sandpaper to roughen the surface slightly. Then brush on another coat until you have reached the desired thickness of film. This will be in about two or three coats on filled wood.

Such a varnish will be rather brittle and thus the thinner the coat the less chance there will be for the varnish coat to flake and chip away from the wood under handling.

When the last coat has been applied and has hardened take some fine pumice powder on a wet cloth pad and rub the stock well. This will cut the film down and will take off any dust particles or brush marks which may be there in the dried film. Then clean the film off with a clean cloth and sprinkle rottenstone on the finish. Using another wet or damp cloth work that powder around and rub well. This will polish the surface and will bring out the beauty possible in the film.

Such a varnish may be used as a filling agent, the same as with the other spirit varnishes. Inasmuch as the shellac will be brittle this finish will not take the rough knocks of field use very well, but with care will stand up satisfactorily.

An alternate method of use of this or similar shellac varnishes is to fill the pores of the wood. This is done by brushing on coats of the varnish, letting them dry, and sanding the film off down to the wood. When the pores have been filled completely sand the surface once more.

Now make up the following formula:

Finish Formula #24 (a)

Beeswax — 2 parts
Turpentine — 1½ "

Melt the beeswax and add the turpentine, stirring well.

When the wax mixture has cooled take some on a rag and spread out a good coat over the shellac filled surface. Allow it to dry and then polish with a soft cloth or with a piece of felt.

The use of a shellac filler and a wax finish as described above was one of the favorite methods for a great many years as it could be applied rather quickly and gave a fine, waterproof finish.

Spirit Varnish Formula #25

Shellac flakes — 1½ pounds
Alcohol — 1 gallon
Linseed or castor oil — 4 ounces

The shellac flakes are dissolved in the alcohol, and then the castor or linseed oil is slowly added with stirring. The presence of the oil was to make the film more pliable and less likely to crack or chip in use. This corresponds to a plasticizer in a modern lacquer.

This varnish will be darker and more yellow or red than the varnish made up from Formula #24. Ordinary shellac has been used which will have considerable color to it. Therefore, this formula should be used only over dark colored woods.

Use this material in the same way, with the same handling methods, and for the same results as the varnish in Formula #24.

It may be used not only for a finish, but also as a filler and under wax if so desired.

Spirit Varnish Formula #26

Sandarac — 14 oz.
Mastic drops — 7 oz.
Shellac flakes — 14 oz.
Alcohol — 3½ qts.

Dissolve the shellac in the alcohol, and then add the mastic and sandarac and allow them to dissolve. Strain or filter through clean, fine cloth.

This formula you are gazing at was the first and original French Polish formula which was used successfully. It has since been outmoded by the use of shellac alone, but it is listed here as a matter of interest and possible experimentation.

In order to use this formula as a French Polish follow the instructions given under Chapter 7.

If desired, this material may be used as a straight spirit varnish which is brushed on, allowed to dry, and then polished with pumice powder and rottenstone. It may also be used as a filler and under wax.

Spirit Varnish Formula #27

Shellac flakes — 8 parts
Gum benzoin — 1 "
Alcohol — 33 "

Place the resins in a container, add the alcohol, and dissolve.

This is another of the first French Polish formulae. It, too, has been superseded by straight shellac solutions but may also be used for experimentation.

Handle in the same way as other spirit varnishes, or for French Polish in the manner described in Chapter 7.

The use of any of the spirit varnishes or other finishes given above will be the closest approach you can make to the original finish on the flint and percussion guns. The methods of handling given above are precisely the same as were used way back then and only your individual development or lack of development of technique and care will determine how successful you will be.

No book in the world can make an expert workman of you. We can only point the way and give you as much help as possible. From there you are on your own.

If the preceding information is used carefully and with regard to the dignity of the age which the gun represents then you should have no trouble in turning out an excellent bit of work, one which anyone would be proud of.

CHAPTER FIFTEEN

Auxiliary Equipment

WHILE the great majority of amateurs have little in the way of equipment to help them in their work there are available many pieces of such equipment which should be investigated by anyone considering doing much work in this field.

The best way to obtain information concerning the various products on the market is to pay close attention to advertisements in technical and popular magazines. Very often you will find notices of a new product which is on the market and which may be precisely what you are looking for.

In this chapter, I have tried to include general types of equipment as well as individual makes. There is no doubt that there are makes available other than what is specifically described in the text and when these are known to me they shall be listed, unless they embody special characteristics which make them worthy of special mention.

Some of the equipment described is available only through your own efforts and manufacture, though it is none the less desirable.

DRYING CABINET

This is strictly an item of home manufacture. It may be made from plywood, sheet metal, or odds and ends of lumber which are lying around the basement or shop.

It is suitable for both the amateur and professional, but the occasional stock that the amateur may work over probably will not justify the effort expended in its making. It is a must for the large shop or the individual gunsmith if any work other than straight rubbed oil finishes is to be done.

As shown in the illustration, the cabinet is nothing more than a box into which may be placed the varnished or lacquered stock. The box keeps dirt and dust from settling on the

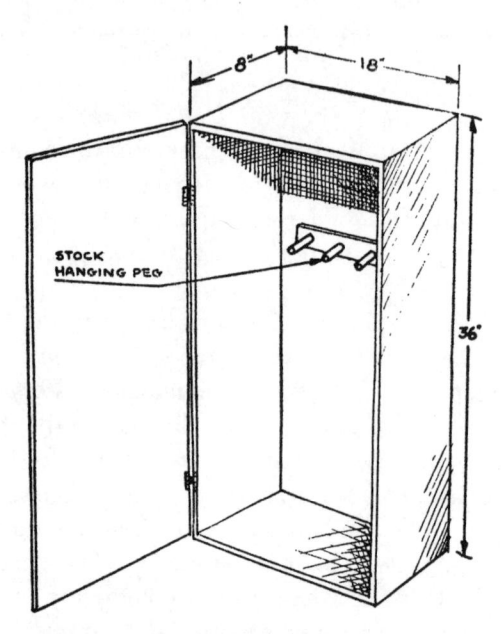

Stock drying cabinet
If any volume of work is done, a heating coil or hot plate element should be placed in the bottom of the box.

wet film, and a heating coil in the bottom of the box may be used to keep the air temperature up around 130° to 140°.

The heat makes the varnish or lacquer dry and harden in a very short time.

The control of the heat source may be as simple or as complicated as desired. A simple off and on switch together with a resistance or rheostat will enable the heat to be turned up or down as a thermometer placed in the box indicates more or

AUXILIARY EQUIPMENT

less heat is needed. A few practice runs will show you about what is needed in the way of time and resistance setting to keep the heat where you want it (which will be about 135°.)

For the very busy shop there are on the market heat control gadgets which will automatically keep the air at a certain temperature. These are very desirable, but rather expensive. They can be made at home, but you had better get someone who knows what he is doing to make them for you.

The stocks may be suspended in the box by simple pegs or hooks or elaborate suspending arangements may be made. Vary the design to suit yourself.

Under no circumstances should the air temperature in the box be allowed to exceed 145°. Above that point air and moisture in the wood will be driven out and trapped in the finish. This will result in a bubbled finish and you will have to do over the whole job.

Incidentally, the box should be insulated in some manner for the sake of economy and efficiency. A simple double wall with dead air space will be very effective, especially if the inside of the outer wall is painted with aluminum paint.

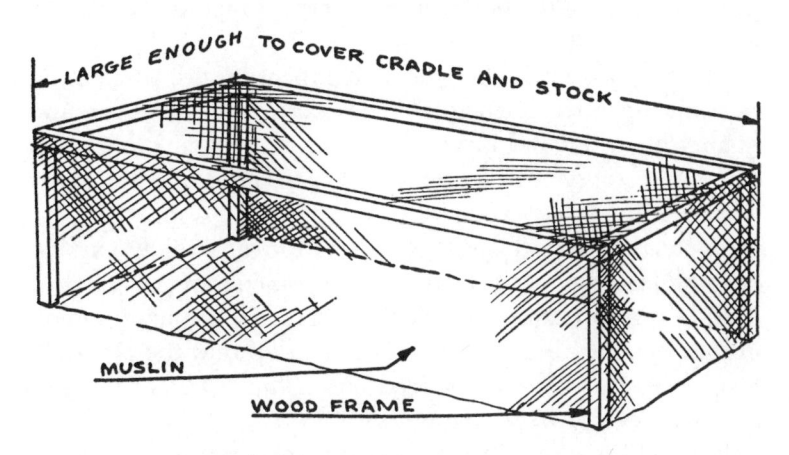

Muslin cover for freshly varnished gunstocks

Cotton or muslin cover: If you do not want to go to the

trouble of making a drying cabinet as described above or have not enough stock finishing to do to warrant the making of it then you can make up a dustproof cover which, while it will not cause the varnish or lacquer to dry any faster, will give comparative freedom from dust settling.

The cover should be made by fastening cotton or muslin over a light wooden or metal frame as shown in the drawing. The dimensions should be such that the cover will fit freely and completely over and around the checkering frame and stock held therein.

As soon as a stock is coated it should be covered with this frame to keep off accidental dust and possible handling by inquisitive customers or friends.

This cover works very well, but for more than one or two stocks I find it worth while to make up the drying cabinet with heat source.

SPRAY GUN AND EQUIPMENT

While it is possible that you may be familiar with this sort of thing the majority of amateurs (and professionals) are entirely ignorant of the possibilities inherent in this sort of equipment.

All spray guns, whether cheap or expensive, are based upon the same operating principles. The details of construction and quality of workmanship will differ, of course, but that is all. The two basic systems by which all spray guns operate are as follows:

Siphon or suction; this system allows the air to flow past an opening leading into the paint or varnish container. The flow of air at high pressure and velocity creates a vacuum or suction in that opening and the paint is drawn up into the air blast. From here it is blown or forced out of the nozzle of the gun onto whatever is being painted.

Pressure; this system introduces air pressure into the closed paint container. This pressure forces the paint up into the gun proper where it is carried out the nozzle by the air and thence onto the object being painted.

Preference of gun types: While either system will operate well I recommend the use of the suction or siphon type gun. This siphon gun will allow thinner coats of material to be applied. Or, in other words, the gun may be adjusted so that less varnish may be thrown in any given time than from the pressure type gun.

The siphon type costs more than the pressure gun in the lower price ranges, but when you get up into the $20.00 and $30.00 guns then you may have either type for the same price.

SPRAY GUN MAKES

Binks: The Binks Company is one of the two big manufacturers of spray guns and accessories. It is a very reliable firm and produces a very high grade product.

DeVilbiss: The other of the big two. It also produces a high grade product and for quality there is nothing to choose from between these makes.

Electric Sprayit: This gun is produced by a company of the same name. From what I have learned the quality of the gun and accessories they sell is very good and may be seriously considered by even the larger shops. A photograph of one of their guns is shown. This equipment is in the low price range.

Airmite, Model AB: This air brush is produced by the Edmonds Engineering and Manufacturing Company, 315 N. Francisco Avenue, Chicago 12, Illinois.

It is a small tool, but does a good job if sufficient air pressure and volume are used. The specifications state that from 25 to 150 pounds should be used and that it will then cover at about three square feet of surface per minute.

The gun (or brush) is cleverly made of metal and can be used either with the standard half-pint glass jar which is furnished with the gun or has an adapter which may be fastened quickly and directly on a half-pint metal paint or varnish can.

It has an adjustable air valve which will allow large or

small air volume to be used and thus is able to handle not only heavy finishing jobs, but also can be turned down to allow delicate touchup work.

The air connection is threaded for a standard tire pump thread and has an adapter which is threaded for standard air lines.

My homemade compressor was set up to about 30 pounds pressure and handled a clear lacquer well. Obviously, in such a case the compressor rather than the gun is a determining factor. If you can get higher pressure the material will handle easier. Especially with lacquers. But for all miscellaneous and stock work this tool seems to do a fine job.

The price is $5.75 and among others Montgomery-Ward carries it in stock.

For a low-priced tool I would recommend this one wholeheartedly.

Burgess Vibro-Sprayer: Recently there has appeared on the market a small home-type spray gun which has a self contained power unit. All that is necessary to use it is to plug the cord into an electric outlet. This gun has been widely advertised and it should be mentioned here as a finishing tool.

I attempted to get a sample gun for test, but the manufacturers seemed reluctant to let me test it out. Despite this I did latch onto one and tried it out on a sample stock.

This gun does not have much power and it is definitely deficient in atomizing properties. That is, the film is formed in droplets rather than a mist or fine spray. This gun did not function well enough to give what I consider satisfactory performance.

Miscellaneous guns: The above specifically named spray guns are those about which I have been able to gather information. There are no doubt others on the market which are well made and which will do a satisfactory job. They will be made and operated in exactly the same manner as any of these guns.

If you run across some piece of equipment which is not

widely advertised or which has not had much publicity do not discard it as being worthless. It just may not have been discovered yet by the brethren. Investigate it and if it works out okay then use it.

This is especially true of small organizations or manufacturers who do not have the money or means to advertise, but all the same may have a first-rate product.

Among the other possibilities are the tank type vacuum cleaner with the spray gun attachment. These arrangements are fairly common now and have definite possibilities.

The big difficulty in using this sort of thing is that there is no means of control of either the air supply or the liquid. You place the liquid in the glass jar, turn on the vacuum cleaner and go to it! The spray will be very heavy and you must work very quickly with fast sweeping motions or you will throw on so much that it will sag all over the place.

When you become familiar with this you can do a fair job, but I would not recommend it except in cases of emergency.

Compressor Equipment: Equipment to furnish air pressure for the operation of most of the spray guns available varies in price and quality. You can buy portable compressors which operate by electric motors, gasoline engines or even little ones operated by the foot. Obviously, the better and more complete the apparatus the more it is going to cost.

Incidentally, compressors operate on two basic systems. They are the piston type and the diaphragm type.

The piston type works in precisely the same manner as a gasoline engine. As the flywheel is turned by outside power a piston or series of pistons are actuated in cylinders. As they make a downward stroke they draw air into the cylinder proper. Then when they start upwards again they squeeze or compress the air ahead of them and this is forced out into a tank, storage chamber, or the air lines themselves leading to the gun.

Diaphragm type compressors do not have pistons. They contain a flexible diaphragm or membrane which is fluttered or moved in and out by a cam arrangement. When the diaphragm is moved in it throws or compresses the air ahead of it and this is forced into the tank or air lines. When it flutters back the other way it allows air to be drawn in behind it. Then the cam flutters it back the other way and this air is pushed or compressed into the lines and so on.

Actually the principle in the two types is the same. The only difference is that the diaphragm type uses the flexible membrane instead of the piston. Obviously the piston type will give greater volume or capacity and pressure than the diaphragm type.

The diaphragm compressor is satisfactory for small guns under small or light pressure, while the piston type will give large volume and as high a pressure as the motor operating it will allow.

For home or small shop work a refrigerator compressor recovered from a discarded box will give sufficient volume and pressure for small guns. These compressors may be picked up for just a few dollars and fitted with a quarter-horsepower motor.

Air Transformers or Condensers: This sort of equipment consists of certain valve and diaphragm arrangements which will allow a high pressure in the air storage tanks or lines, and when placed between those tanks and the gun will allow only a definite, regulated pressure to reach the gun. For large, powerful compressors and production work they are necessary.

The transformer will also condense and catch any moisture, oil or dirt which may find its way into the air lines. This will prevent the contamination from reaching the gun and thus being thrown onto the surface of the work.

For very small, occasional work the transformer and condenser is not necessary, though it is desirable. For any extensive work it is a virtual necessity.

Material Pressure Tank: This is merely a large five or ten gallon container which holds a large volume of the material which is being sprayed. It is used mostly for pressure type guns (as opposed to siphon guns) and the material in the pressure tank is constantly under air pressure.

This sort of tank is used on production work where large volumes of paint or varnish are being used constantly. For small work it is not necessary or even desirable.

SANDING MACHINES

There are increasingly greater numbers of small, home type electric sanders being placed on the market. The great majority of them consist of hand-held circular discs which are fitted with sanding discs or buffing wheels. Most of them run about $15.00 to $20.00.

They are very fine little machines and for miscellaneous work about the house and shop they work very well. But for stock work they are unsatisfactory, other than for buffing and polishing.

The circular motion of the wheel or disc will be seen readily in the numerous cross-grain marks which they leave. Inasmuch as they work in a circle they will cross the grain at some point, no matter how careful the worker is. When these cross-grain marks are placed in the wood then you must come along later by hand and remove them with sandpaper. In that case you are just as well off by not using them at all.

For buffing and polishing, though, they do a fine job. They have sufficient surface speed to polish out well and will give good service.

Dremel Moto-Sander: This is the only tool in the low price range which will operate in a reciprocal manner. That is, it will sand or polish in a back and forward manner. Sure, there are other fine machines which will do this also, but those others are strictly production, heavy duty items which cost well over a hundred bucks to buy.

The big advantage to this reciprocating action is that it duplicates exactly the movements of the hand in sanding and leaves no cross-grain markings either in sanding or polishing. While the machine is not large or heavy enough to do extremely coarse sanding, it will use 2/0 or finer paper. It sands at about 7200 strokes per minute and this is sufficient to do most anything called for in stock work.

Felt and sheepskin pads may be used for buffing and polishing and it will work well as a rubbing machine. For the next to last operation with the rubbing compounds this should do a fine job.

This Dremel Moto-Sander costs about $15.00 and looks like the answer to the gunsmith's prayer.

Porter-Cable Sander: This machine is in the medium price range, costing about $58.00 the last time I looked.

It is a belt sander. That is, it has a revolving abrasive belt which gives the same effect as the reciprocating, back and forth movement of the Dremel Moto-Sander.

This machine is no toy, but instead is a well made, sturdy outfit which will do heavy work and stand up to it.

The price is above what most amateurs and small shops will want to spend, but for the large shop or individual doing a great deal of stock or wood work it is just the ticket.

It is carried by Porter-Cable dealers, or can be procured from Albert Constantine & Son, Inc., 797 E. 135th St., New York, N. Y.

MISCELLANEOUS EQUIPMENT

Infra-Red Light Banks: As described in the chapter on Plastic Finishes a bank of infra-red lights may be used to harden and dry finishes in a fraction of the time that it would normally take.

The infra-red bulb (heat bulb) will furnish energy to whatever surface it is directed at and when the energy reaches the surface it is changed into heat. Thus no appreciable heat or energy is wasted or lost in the intervening air space. A small amount will be taken up by dust, but in a fairly clean atmosphere it will be negligible.

The amount of heat that such a bulb will give to any surface is dependent upon the distance from and the condition of the surface. A clean, polished piece of white or light metal will reflect or turn away a great deal of the energy directed at it. A rough piece of dark metal or other material will absorb and use most of it. This is true of wood, and very little energy will be reflected from the surface.

To use such a bulb it is placed in some sort of a holder or bracket so that it may be held securely while heating the wood. The distance at which such a bulb should be placed for best results will have to be determined by your own tests, but I would say that such bulbs should not be closer than 15" from any wood surface nor farther than two feet.

The closer the bulb the more heat the wood will take on and if the temperature of the wood reaches above about 145° there is danger of not only burning the wood, but also of forcing air and moisture out of it where it will be trapped in the finishing material and be seen as bubbles.

A general rule may be set up as follows: use heat lamps at about 20" from the wood for not longer than 20 minutes. If you use them at 15" distances then turn them off after 10 minutes. Above 20" you probably will not get enough heat to bother the finish though it will still work on the varnish or the lacquer.

For quick stock work it would be best to use at least three and probably four lamps in a bank, spaced out to cover the whole length of the stock. The more lamps you use the more heat you will get and the quicker the finish will set up. If you use only one or two lamps you will have to move them about so as to cover the whole surface of the stock evenly. While this will be a saving in original investment the constant attention necessarily paid to the stock will cost quite a bit not only in time consumed but also in irritation.

For the large shop it would be advisable to have one person in charge of the heat treating of the stock after application of a finishing coat. This one person will be able to learn quickly and easily the efficient use of the lamps and for how long and at what distances they should be used on any given kinds of woods and finishes.

While the use of such equipment is an unknown thing in most gun shops it is extremely valuable and should be investigated thoroughly before deciding it will not work for you.

Incidentally, these heat lamps may be used for a great many miscellaneous things around a shop. They may be used in the production of plastic forend tips to hasten the setting of the bond between plates by turning the lamps on for a few minutes so that the whole block is well heated. They may be used to thaw out frozen pipes without danger of overheating and bursting. In a pinch they could be used to heat a container of varnish for the Hot Application of a finish (see Varnish chapter) with no danger of fire (a hot plate would be more efficient). They may be used to dry hands and clothing quickly if water or solvent is spilled upon them. They may be used anyplace that a flameless heat is needed.

One such heat lamp will draw about 250 watts on a 110 volt circuit. With the average line this will mean about 2½ amps per lamp. Therefore, you should make sure that with more than two lamps going you have a line just for this purpose.

The individual in a small shop or working in the home could use four lamps on a line fused for 15 amps, but he must make sure that nothing else connected to that line is in use at the time. It is awful easy to blow out a flock of fuses in a hurry if you do not watch yourself!

For small work such as stocks there are no reflectors necessary in such a bank of lights. The ideal thing is to use a reflector coated with an extremely thin gold film, but that is for extreme efficiency. For small or occasional work this would cost more than it would be worth.

It has been suggested that such a bank of lights would be useful for whiskering work, but I doubt it. It is a possibility, of course, but it would take a minute or so for the heat to reach a point where good results are seen, and in nearly every case you will find that a Bunsen or other gas burner will do the job faster and at less cost.

These bulbs cost about $3.50 each, or possibly less, depending upon where you buy them. Many chain drug stores carry them under the name Heat Lamps.

Do not confuse them with ultra-violet health or sun lamps.

SELECTION OF PAINT AND VARNISH BRUSHES

In any of the operations mentioned we have given a choice between spray guns and brushes. The spray gun is the best and most satisfactory method of applying any of the finishes, but it can be done with a good brush.

There is more than one type and quality of brush available, though, depending upon where you buy your supplies. If you patronize the dime store exclusively then you may be able to get a nice little one-inch sash brush for 39 cents. It looks fine and does a good job the first time, but after it has been washed out in thinner a couple of times and beat against the bench leg to rid the bristles of thinner and paint it looks sort of seedy. In fact, it starts to lose its bristles darned quick, and when that happens you must stop every couple of strokes to pick out a bristle which has come loose at a very critical point.

First of all, let us discuss the question of brush sizes and types. This is rather important as there is no point in using a quarter-inch wide striping brush for varnishing a wide buttstock.

Brush types include the straight flat brush with which we are all familiar. This is the kind that is so commonly used for painting around the house. Such a flat brush may come in widths from a quarter-inch all the way up to four inches or wider. This is used for large, flat surfaces.

Next is the oval or semi-round brush. This is just as the name implies. Looking at the bristles from the bottom they will take the shape of an oval. This sort of brush is useful in varnishing as it carries a large load of varnish. The more bristles in a brush and the finer they are the more liquid they will carry.

The last brush with which we shall have anything to do is

the striping brush. This is really a small, round brush. Usually they will be a quarter of an inch in diameter or less. This sort of brush is best around thin edges and corners as it allows delicate touching up of such surfaces without spreading varnish all over the adjoining areas.

All of the brushes, no matter what the size or shape, will be made from one of two basic materials. Either the bristles will be of natural animal hair or they will be of synthetic material such as nylon.

The best brushes are those which carry Chinese hog bristles. They are more expensive than the other kinds and are a little harder to get, but they should be obtained as in the long run they will last longer and give much better service.

Besides the Chinese bristle, horsehair, goathair and vegetable fibers are used. They all have their fields of use, but for fine varnishing or lacquering the Chinese bristle or goathair will do the best job.

In the synthetic field the various bristles will be satisfactory for varnishing, but for lacquering they are usually poor. This is because the solvents in the normal lacquer may tend to soften or dissolve the bristles and this really gums up the works. Never use a nylon or other synthetic brush for lacquering. Varnish will not usually have this effect so that it would be all right to use it.

No matter what type of bristle is used, the method of fastening them into the handle of the brush is the same. For the flat or oval brush they are usually vulcanized in rubber and then fastened with a metal band to the handle.

For the small striping brushes or cheap flat sash brushes they may have only the retaining metal band. They are not usually secured in rubber. This accounts for the ease with which such a brush will lose its bristles in use. Once some of them come loose then the rest are also loosened and they start to come out with ease.

When using a brush, if you find that you are starting to lose strands of the bristle into the work discard that brush. You are only making it harder on yourself, and that brush can be kept for use around the shop on jobs such as painting the woodwork or the walls where a bristle or two will not usually excite any comment. Leave a bristle in the finish on a fine Winchester M-70 restocking job, though, and you will get enough comment to last you the rest of your life.

In buying brushes, as in anything else, get the best you can afford at the time. The results will fully warrant the additional expense and if cared for they will stand up for a long time.

This caring for, incidentally, covers the cleaning of the brush thoroughly after you have used it and storing it away clean and dry in a paper cover till the next time. Every bit of dust that gets on the bristles will eventually end up in the finish of some stock as the flow of the varnish down off the ends will carry the dust with it.

I have nothing against the dime stores or the local War Surplus Center, but the brushes they usually carry will not be of a quality line. You will do much better to consult either the local paint dealer or a Sears Roebuck catalog. Get the best quality they offer, even though it may seem to be a bit expensive to you at the time. By that I do not mean to go out and buy the most expensive brush they have, but look around and see what they have in Chinese bristle or goathair. The one that is well made and seems to be bound well with rubber and a *secure* metal band will be good. Some of them may be advertised as bristle, but will have a stingy band with only one rivet or brad through it. You can be pretty sure that it will not stand up too long.

Incidentally, secure the brush with the *longest* bristles in it. A short brush will be okay, but the longer the bristles the more load it will carry and the better job it will do. Even if you have to pay quite a bit more for an extra inch of bristles do so if you can afford it. It will pay in the long run.

For the average varnish or lacquer job on a stock a good general size to choose will be a flat brush about $1\frac{1}{2}''$ wide.

This will allow you to work both the wide areas and the forend.

For delicate touchup work or finishing around cheekpieces and inletting edges a striping brush of goathair would be desirable. This will let you get at tiny spots without slopping.

If you are disposed to spend a bit more money an oval brush of about 1½" width would be a good investment. This one will allow you to go over a large area without stopping to redip the brush in the varnish or lacquer and thus will do away with the most of the dangers of showing laps where the brush was picked up and laid down again. This is especially true when using a lacquer or shellac.

Use a brush for only one type of material. Do not use a brush in lacquer and then clean it out and transfer to varnish, or vice versa. The chances are that you will have enough of the original material left in the bristles to cause "throw-out" and the resulting dirt or particles will be carried on down into the finish the next time you use that brush in anything at all. *Use a brush for one material only.*

CARE OF EQUIPMENT

The first and foremost rule of any finishing shop should be to be clean. I say should be because there are many, many furniture and stock finishers who work under conditions which are deplorable.

How they turn out any kind of a decent job is beyond me, but they have dust over the whole shop, the bench may be littered with shavings and rasp cuttings, and they would not know a filter or strainer if they saw it lying dead in the street.

These conditions are unnecessary and completely undesirable. If a man is going to try and do a good job of work he should make it easy on himself rather than stacking the deck to his disadvantage.

He should always see that all dust has been removed and tools and benches cleaned off with a damp rag before even opening the can of varnish. It does not do any good to sweep the floor dry because the dust that he stirs up will be left floating in the air for a long time and it will invariably head toward the freshly varnished wood where it and all its thousands of brothers immediately settle—at least it seems that way.

The biggest item which causes the most disappointments, though, is unclean equipment. It does not matter if you have a three hundred buck Binks spraying outfit or a dime store brush. The same conditions will plague a man until he becomes careful and alert enough to remove the causes of the many failures he usually cannot explain, even to himself. These causes will range from hardened particles of lacquer in the spray gun material tube to dirt and varnish particles in the brush.

Care of the Spray Gun: The spray gun is a rather simple piece of equipment to keep clean. The easiest way to keep such equipment clean is to take care of it immediately after you are through with it. If you allow it to sit around for several hours or days then anything you may have used will be hard and dry and the job of removing such material will be extremely difficult.

First of all, when you are through with spraying clean out the cup or container which you have used to hold the bulk of your finishing liquid. In most cases this cup is a part of the equipment and it should be cleaned along with the rest of the gun. This cup should be wiped out with a clean cloth or paper towels which can then be thrown away. Then rinse it out with a little thinner. Use just enough to do a thorough job. There is no use being wasteful if you can help it—this stuff costs money!

Now place a little thinner in the cup, place the cup on the gun in a normal position and press the trigger of the gun (this should be done with the air pressure on). The air will force the thinner through the gun just as though it were paint.

While this thinner is being forced through the gun place a cloth over the nozzle so as to stop the passage of thinner completely. Quickly pull the cloth away from the nozzle and put it back again. By doing this several times in rapid succession you will create a "surge" in the passages through which the paint or varnish normally travels. This "surge" will wash those passages clean after a few seconds, *providing the paint or varnish coating the passages is still fresh.*

Now wipe off the nozzle of the gun with a rag soaked with thinner. Remove the cup and wipe off the material tube (the tube which extends down into the paint and through which it reaches the gun proper).

Wipe out the cup again with a dry rag and you are through.

If the method outlined above is followed carefully and consistently you should have no trouble with foreign matter being blown out onto the finish the next time you use the gun.

Care of Brushes: Brushes are very easy to take care of if you catch them while they are still freshly wet. It is easy to remove liquid matter, but next to impossible to remove hardened particles of varnish and shellac.

When you have completed part of a stock and you have to lay off until the next evening there is no point in completely cleaning and drying a brush. You know you are going to be using it again very soon, and the easiest way to care for it is to use what is called a "keeper." This keeper is merely some sort of a can or container in which the brush is suspended. Inside the keeper is a quantity of whatever liquid you are using to finish the stock, or even plain varnish thinner.

If you are varnishing then varnish will be used. If you are using shellac then put shellac in the keeper. The same thing goes for any other material in use.

The reason for using such a liquid is that if the keeper is covered to prevent evaporation of the solvents then the brush will be kept soft and whatever is left in the bristles will stay that way. It will not dry up and harden on you.

Pour in just enough of the liquid so that it covers the bristles of the suspended brush. You can put in enough so that it comes up the metal retaining band (which holds the bristles in place) about a quarter of an inch. Do not let it come halfway up the handle. This will only necessitate cleaning off the handle and the metal band again when you return.

The brush should never be allowed to rest on the bottom of the keeper. If it does so the bristles which will be holding the brush up will become bent and damaged. Drill a hole

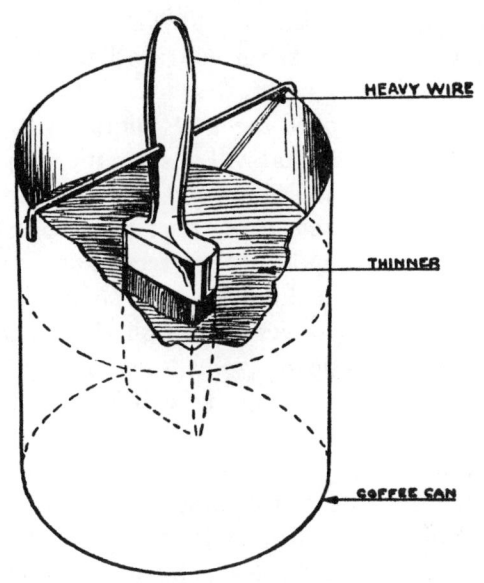

"Keeper" for used brushes

through the handle of the brush in such a place that when a piece of stiff wire is run through that hole and placed over the rim of the keeper the brush will then be hanging, held up by the wire, with the lower end of the bristles about one-half inch above the bottom of the can.

Now place some sort of a cover over the can to keep the solvents from evaporating and dust from entering. In such a setup a brush may be left for weeks at a time, renewing the liquid when the level falls below the lower edge of the metal retaining band of the brush.

If you contemplate leaving a brush out of use for several

weeks then it would be better to clean and dry it and store it away. However, such a keeper can would do if necessary.

To clean a brush for such dry storage first squeeze out the bristles as completely as possible with a paper towel or clean rag. Do not draw the bristles over the rim of the can to free them from excess varnish. This will not hurt the brush if done in moderation and only occasionally when actually brushing, but if done to clean the brush you are liable to scrape too vigorously and damage the bristles.

When you have removed the excess liquid with a rag take some thinner (of the kind that will dissolve the varnish you are using) and work the bristles around in the bath. Use your fingers and make sure that every part of the brush gets this bath. This will remove most of the varnish.

Now take more clean thinner and repeat the bath. This should remove the last traces of varnish if done thoroughly. Do not push the brush down against the bottom of the can to work the thinner in and out. This will help to damage the bristles also.

When you are sure that the brush is well cleaned grasp it by the handle and with a swift downward motion swing the brush several times. This will create enough centrifugal force to free the bristles of most of the entrapped thinner. (Be sure that you lay down a few newspapers, though. Such a motion will force a considerable amount of liquid out onto the floor and you may leave spotted areas on the floor when the thinner evaporates, especially if there is much varnish dissolved in that thinner.)

Now take some water (warm) and dissolve therein some good, mild soap such as Ivory, Dreft, or the like. This solution will remove whatever varnish may be left. By working the bristles around in the soap bath with your fingers and continuing this process until the bristles stay wet when lifted out of the bath you will be sure that all oil and varnish have been removed.

Now rinse the brush in clean, warm, running water until

all trace of the soap is gone. Again swing the brush to rid it of the majority of water and place it in a warm spot to dry.

When the brush is completely dry wrap it in paper and put it away until ready to use it the next time.

Instead of the soap and water you can use some of the commercial brush cleaners which are available at all paint suppliers. They are formulated especially for this purpose and will not harm the bristles. In all cases, though, I would free the brush from as much varnish as possible by the use of the thinner bath first.

Now, let us take the case of the lad who has used one brush for everything including varnish, house paint, and the like. He has left the brush sitting in a can of turpentine or linseed oil between each period of use and he assumes that, inasmuch as linseed oil and turpentine are the universal bases for paints and varnish he is doing all right.

First of all, he is wrong in assuming that these two liquids are the universal base for protective coatings—they are not! There are many varnishes on the market that will not tolerate linseed oil and in the presence of that oil will precipitate resinous substances.

Second, he has some badly bent bristles from allowing the brush to rest upon them for so long. There will be no way he can straighten them up without ruining them because they are already ruined.

His solution to the problem is very simple, though he seldom applies it. He had better toss that brush out and get a couple of new ones. And he certainly had better take better care of these.

The paint, varnish, and shellac he has been using will not dissolve in one another and the chances are a million to one that he has his bristles loaded with insoluble, thrown-out particles of pigment and resin. If he uses this brush again for clear varnish most of those particles will be carried out of the bristles by the passage of the varnish and they will appear in the finish as myriad pinpoints or bumps. He will then wonder what is the matter with the confounded varnish he is using and will switch to another make hoping to get better stuff this time. Needless to say, this switch to another make will produce no improvement. Eventually he will get disgusted and will go back to hand rubbing with oil and figure that these guys who use varnish are off their rockers. If a careful worker like him can not do a good job he does not see how the rest of them can.

CHAPTER SIXTEEN

Laboratory Tests and Notes

WHEN I first started out to do stock finishing I searched all the available literature for information concerning durability and moisture resistance of the various materials which I had heard were recommended for stock work. I wanted something that I could depend upon to keep my stocks in good condition and, having not had enough experience in the field to judge from that, I felt sure that someone should be able to tell me what I wanted to know.

Alas and alack, nobody seemed to really have any dope other than what they had heard others say about this or that material. None of these sources seemed to be accurate or sufficient. Therefore, when I had an opportunity to do some accurate, systematic testing I jumped at it. The following information may be of interest to most of you, and it probably will be just what some of you are looking for.

Hardwood (ash) panels, 3″ x 6″ x ¾″ were treated with certain finishing materials in precisely the same manner that a stock would be finished. These panels were chosen to have the same type of grain running in identical patterns.

None of the panels had the grain raised artificially because this was to be my determining factor in checking relative permeability of the applied film to water. When the grain was raised to a certain point it was assumed to be the point at which the film had allowed enough moisture to penetrate to do that raising. In other words, if one panel had the grain raised in half the time that it took another panel to raise the grain to the same degree, the material on the first panel could be assumed to have about half the resistance to moisture that the material coating the second panel had.

Also, when the materials coating the panels disintegrated or decomposed to such an extent that the film actually appeared to be disappearing from the face of the wood then that point was taken as the point at which the protection to the wood ceased and was assumed to be the end of "durability" of that particular material.

The test panels were broken down into two sections. The first group or section was composed of panels treated with a good wood sealer (see Chapter 2) of the phenolic type over which were placed the items to be tested. The second group was composed of panels left bare, except for the finishing of the surface by the materials which were to be tested.

Therefore, the first group versus the second group would not only tell me how good the materials were in relation to each other, but also would tell me how much more efficient would be that item if applied over a sealed surface.

The details of the testing process are unimportant and extremely lengthy and therefore will not be included in this report. The general method, however, was to subject the coated panels to a laboratory test in which weather conditions were reproduced exactly. The life of the panels were measured in hours and ten hours in the test would be equivalent to about two months' exposure to normal weather conditions.

The following materials were tested as being exemplary of all stock materials available:

        Raw linseed oil — rubbed (Dull London Oil) finish
        Oiticica oil   "
        Clear lacquer — polished
        Marine Spar (phenolic varnish) — polished

The following list gives the time required to achieve equal grain raising and also the final durability of the film.

Material	Grain Raising	Durability
Linseed oil (bare panel)	20 hours	200 hours
" " (sealed ")	75 "	200 "
Oiticica oil (bare panel)	300 "	500 "
" " (sealed ")	590 "	500 "
Clear Lacquer (bare panel)	150 "	150 "
" " (sealed ")	600 "	600 "
Marine spar varnish (bare panel)	1200 "	2400 "
" " " (sealed ")	1830 "	2400 plus "

It can be seen from the above results that raw linseed oil is the poorest of any of the materials tested. Not only did the grain raise through the oil very quickly, but it started to disappear entirely from the panel at a very early time.

The clear lacquer (representative of all lacquers) allowed moisture to penetrate early and failed quickly. When a good varnish sealer was used the durability of the film was greatly increased. This sealer prevented the moisture from damaging the adhesion of the lacquer.

The oiticica oil (very similar to tung oil) was much better in all respects than was the linseed oil and was about as good as the lacquer.

The marine spar varnish (phenolic type) was the best of all and exhibited extreme durability and moisture resistance.

Evaluating Test Results: From the above tests (since verified by other similar tests) I would place desirability of the different items as follows:

Raw Linseed Oil: Entirely unsuited for stock work if the stock is to meet any adverse weather conditions at all. If a rubbed oil finish is wanted use boiled linseed oil with a 50% tung or oiticica content.

Oiticica Oil: Inasmuch as this oil is very similar to tung oil the same remarks will apply to either oil. These oils should be incorporated to at least 50% content in any rubbed oil finish. They may not be desirable alone due to the wrinkling of the film upon drying. The presence of 50% of either oil will increase the moisture resistance and durability of any other oil used in conjunction with them.

Lacquer: Strictly a glamour girl. This material is excellent when used on a show gun or on a gun which is taken out only a few times a year. For the average gun it may be okay as the average gun in these times does not see very much use. Do not use for a knock about or utility stock, however.

Marine Spar Varnish (phenolic): This is the stuff to use if you do much hunting or shooting, especially in bad weather. It will take everything you can give it and come up smiling. The finish will not be as pleasing to the eye as would a lacquer finish, but even so a fine lustre may be applied by correct rubbing. If a customer wants the best (durable) stock finish you can put on, use this material.

Inasmuch as no stock will ever be out in weather continually the results of this test as given in hours may be slightly misleading. I would say, from my observations during the test, that 100 hours in the above test would be equivalent to about four years of actual, average use. This is figuring that even if the gun were used twice a week for six hours at a time it would not always meet conditions even approaching the severity of those encountered in the test.

The amount of handling that the gun will get will determine just how long any finish will remain in good condition. Handling will wear down a finish rather quickly, and even if it never meets any weathering at all it is possible that a finish will go to pot from being worn away rather than being decomposed.

The results quoted are only relative, as I have said, and should not be taken as actual life of any certain substance. If you know that any one type of material will last so long (from experience, perhaps) then the list could be used to determine approximately how long any other general type of finish will last under the same conditions.

This test shows very clearly just how effective is the presence of a wood sealer (varnish type) in preserving a film. Not only does it prevent moisture from entering the stock, but it increases the adhesion of a following coat and also the durability.

I had been searching for some time for information on permeability of finishing films to moisture. As far as I can find there has been only one published article concerning such tests. That was made back in 1911. So I figured I may as well run some of my own. However, this is a little tougher than it sounds.

First of all I ran a series of tests on small wooden blocks, dipping each for a given length of time in the material to be tested. This did not prove to be satisfactory. There were too many variables which I could not control and the results varied from test to test. So this was out.

I then worked out a method whereby I got excellent results and these results checked as they should. Briefly the method is as follows for those of you who may be interested in running similar tests.

A series of wide mouth glass vials was chosen and the edges of the mouth were ground with water and aluminum oxide abrasive to give a perfectly flat contact area. These vials were about an inch in diameter and four inches long.

Then 15 cc.s of water was placed in each vial. The amount of water is not important, but it must be uniform from vial to vial.

Over the mouth of the vial the film of material to be tested was placed and secured in position by a thin cement made of shellac with about 5% clear lacquer added. Such a cement will be impervious to moisture and will not allow any to escape and result in false readings.

These vials were then placed in a dessicator containing calcium chloride and readings taken every 24 hours. The vials were weighed to determine the amount of water lost.

Inasmuch as the water which was lost could escape only by penetrating through the film of varnish or whatever the test material was, the greater the amount of moisture which penetrated the greater the permeability of that film.

The vials were weighed down to a tenth of a milligram, but this was unnecessary as even a milligram would be plenty close enough.

The most important feature of the whole test is the method by which a film of the protective material could be made. This was done in the following manner: a piece of #3 filter paper, 1¼" x 4" long was dipped for three seconds into the test material. It was then pulled out and suspended free in the air. This strip was allowed to dry for ten days after which it was again dipped and allowed to dry for ten days more. Then a circular portion of the paper one inch from the lower end of the strip was fastened to the mouth of the vial and any excess was trimmed away with a razor blade.

The reason for choosing an area one inch from the end of the paper was to eliminate any very heavy coatings which might have formed in the form of a "bead" but which did not drip away. Inasmuch as all strips were chosen at the same point the coatings would be about the same thickness, in relation to the viscosity of the liquid, of course.

This test I consider to be very accurate and will give trustworthy readings.

The following lists the results obtained in my first series of tests. Other tests are being conducted at the present time, but will not be ready for interpretation by the time this book goes to press.

Test Material	Moisture Loss	Relative Efficiency
Raw tung oil	.1677	91%
Raw linseed oil	.2973	84%
Boiled linseed oil	.2651	86%
Soybean oil	.4055	78%
Spar varnish	.0624	97%
Uncoated filter paper	1.8492	0%

The above results were based upon the fact that a plain uncoated sheet of the base filter paper passed 1.8492 grams of moisture and this was taken as being 100% permeability (or 0% protection).

The tests are showing more and more that our theories are correct. Thus, raw linseed oil containing foots and non-drying materials passes more moisture than the boiled oil which we calculated would be more effective as a protective film. Also, tung oil contains substances which theory says should be much better than linseed oil. The tests bear this out.

The figures shown above indicate that linseed oil will pass more than two and a half times as much moisture by weight than will one coat of spar varnish and that tung oil will pass only about half as much moisture as the raw linseed oil.

A second, additional test performed sometime later verified the results on linseed oils (both raw and refined), tung oil, and spar varnish (phenolic type), but also gave valuable information on permeabilities of the listed materials:

Film	Moisture Loss	Relative Efficiency
Alkyd varnish	.3935	72%
Methacrylate clear	1.2264	13%
Chlorinated Rubber	.1803	87%
Clear lacquer	.6072	54%
Shellac	.1680	88%

This second test shows the relative resistance of a shellac film to moisture penetration, and that an alkyd film *by itself* is not a particularly good protective agent against moisture.

Any of the materials listed in either of the two tests give entirely different results when used over or in conjunction with another, less permeable material.

For example, the alkyd clear tested will impart excellent weather resistance to a phenolic varnish, while the phenolic varnish will add moisture resistance to the alkyd.

The percent figures for relative efficiency are based upon

my own calculations and represent no standardized system. Inasmuch as all tests are relative, or comparative, this should make no difference in evaluating results obtained.

VISCOSITY

This little word is very important to anyone who does much finishing of wood. For the average man who finishes maybe a chair and the storm windows every three years it will have little meaning. However, for those who have a great deal of woodworking to do it should mean more than it usually does.

Viscosity, stated simply, means the properties of a liquid which cause it to flow, or to resist flow, readily. Heavy or thin body is another way to put it.

For example, if you open a can of any liquid, dip a stick in it, and lift the stick out of the liquid the viscosity will be very apparent. If the liquid runs off the end of the stick like water then the viscosity is low. But if the liquid drips slowly and laboriously from the stick then the viscosity will be termed very high.

The reason that this subject of viscosity is so important is that only within certain limits will any given finishing material perform efficiently. If the viscosity is above or below those limits that material may be wasted and the stock will look like it was brushed with a dirty sock.

Let us just take the situation in which a varnish is being used. It is to be applied by means of a spray gun, but the finisher does not know and does not care anything about viscosity. He opens the can of varnish and finds that it is fairly heavy bodied (high viscosity). So he tosses some of it in the material container on the gun and starts to spray. Because the varnish was so heavy bodied it will not atomize properly when it leaves the gun. As a result the finished film will be wavy and bumpy because the varnish was unevenly distributed by the gun nozzle. Also the film may be very thin because the gun may not have had enough pressure used to pull that heavy liquid up to the nozzle.

On the other hand, suppose the finisher knew that the varnish should be thinned before spraying, but he did not know how much of the thinner to use. Therefore he threw in what he thought was the right amount of thinner, but actually it was quite a bit too much.

Now he sprays again. This time the stock gets a lot of varnish thrown at it because the gun could easily draw up the very thin liquid to the nozzle. Consequently, there is so much liquid thrown on the stock that it builds up too fast, and the large thinner content of the varnish makes that heavy coating run and sag.

For efficient results the body of any finishing material, whether it be varnish, lacquer or shellac must be within the limits mentioned above.

Now by listening carefully, I can hear a lot of you telling me in no uncertain terms that you do not own a spray gun and that you do all your finishing with a brush. So what have I got to say about that?

For those of you that use a brush habitually either from force of habit or because you can't afford a spray setup the subject of viscosity will also be important. Not as important as to the spray man, that I grant you, but nevertheless important.

You can run into the same kind of trouble that the other fellow did. If you overthin your varnish or brushing lacquer then you, too, will get a lot of runs and sags. This is especially true where portions of the surface will be in a vertical position. On gunstocks you always have some part of that stock which is vertical.

If you get the varnish too heavy you will not notice it so much now, but when that coating dries then you may find that you have a lot of brush marks. This will be because there was not enough thinner in the varnish to allow it to flow out well before it hardened. Proper regulation of the viscosity will prevent this.

Determination of Viscosity: In order to determine how

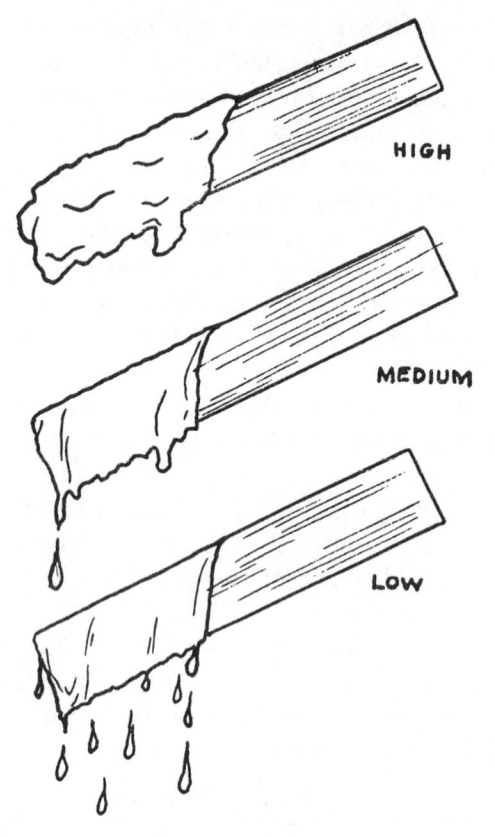

Viscosity "drip" test

heavy bodied your varnish is there are two main methods.

The first is known as the Drip Test. It consists of dipping a stick or knife blade into the varnish and lifting it out. The rate at which the varnish runs or flows off the end of the stick or blade will indicate the viscosity of the varnish.

This test is only relative. By that I mean that you can dip test a varnish that you know will give you good flow and no sags and then dip test another varnish, the viscosity of which is unknown. If the two tests show drip or running of the two to be at about the same rate then you can figure that the second, unknown, varnish will act in about the same manner as the first.

If you find that the unknown varnish flows off the blade much more slowly than does the known varnish add thinner until subsequent tests show the dripping rates to be about the same.

However, if the unknown varnish drips off the blade more quickly than the known varnish you may be in for trouble. This could mean that with your personal method of application you could easily get sagging of the film on vertical areas. About the only answer to this situation is to change your method of application and use less varnish per coat. This will keep you from running into this sagging trouble and will make each coat harden faster. Here you will have to work out the details for yourself—just how much you can apply without it running all over the place.

The second method of determining viscosity is much more accurate and will be highly satisfactory if you do much spray work, though the brush man can also use it to good advantage in getting uniform results on every stock.

It consists of using a Viscosity Cup. Such a cup will be a container of any size with a hole in the bottom. The rate at which the cup empties itself will be a measure of the body or viscosity of the varnish or liquid which is being tested.

The commercial cup used in paint laboratories is called the #4 Ford Cup. It is a well built brass affair and costs about eighty or ninety bucks. Obviously such an instrument is completely out of the question for even the largest shops. Therefore you should make one of your own which may set you back about three cents plus labor.

The drawing accompanying this chapter shows all the details. Take a quarter pint tin can and slightly punch out the bottom with a rod or hammer handle. This will make the bottom of the can curve out and will facilitate drainage. Now take a #35 or #40 drill and drill a hole in the center of this curved-out bottom. There you are, all set to go.

The method of using such a cup (as it will be called from here on) is to hold one finger over the hole in the bottom (from the outside, of course) and fill the cup to the brim. If you wish you may scratch a line around the inside of the cup someplace up near the rim as a "Full" mark. Now, using either a stop

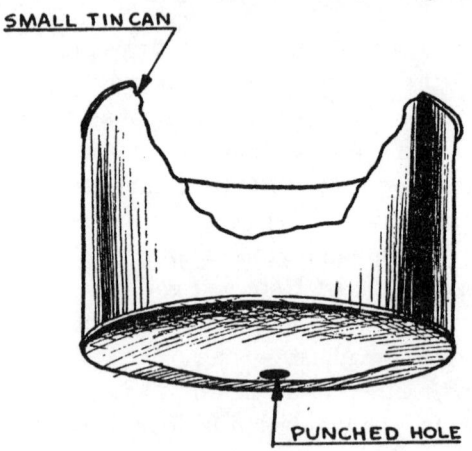

Improvised viscosity cup

watch or the second hand on an ordinary watch release your finger which is stopping the hole and let the varnish run out. When the solid stream of varnish stops and turns into a series of drops consider that as the end point and note how many seconds it has taken for the varnish to go from the full mark to the point where the stream becomes drops. This will be the viscosity of that liquid in seconds.

The best way to use such a cup is to take the viscosity reading of a material that works well for you. Then any other varnish that you may have to use may be tested and thinned (if necessary) until the number of seconds it takes to run through the cup is the same as the time it takes your regular, known varnish. In this manner you will always have known conditions under which to work.

This viscosity cup is especially important to the man who is going to use a spray gun. Viscosity in this case must be within certain limits for best results and the Stick or Dip test will not be accurate enough.

For proper use of the viscosity cup the temperature of any liquid to be tested should be about 60° to 70°. The higher the temperature the lower the viscosity will be, and vice versa. However, if you always run a test of the known varnish against an unknown varnish this temperature difference will not be important. As long as the unknown material is the same as the known stuff they will work in the same manner. It might even be advisable to keep a half pint jar of this "standard" viscosity material on the shelf to be used solely for calibrating other varnishes.

NATURAL RESIN LIST

Resin	Tree	Country of Origin
Accroides	Xanthorrhea	Australia, Tasmanis
Batavia dammar	Hopea, Shorea	Sumatra, Borneo, Java, East Indies
Batu	Shorea	Malaya, East Indies
Black East India	Burseraceae	Malaya, East Indies
Boea	Agathis Alba	Netherlands East Indies
Congo	Copaifera	Belgian Congo, Africa
East India Macasser	Dipterocarpacae	Celebes, East Indies
East India Singapore	Balanocarpus	Sumatra, Borneo, Malaya
Elemi	Canarium communis	Philippine Islands
Kauri	Agathis australis	New Zealand
Manila	Agathis alba	Netherlands East Indies, Philippine Islands
Mastic	Pistacia lentiscus	Chios, India, North Africa
Pontianak	Agathis alba	Borneo
Sandarac	Coniferae	North and South Africa, Australia
Singapore dammar	Dipterocarpacae	Malay States
Shellac	Insect type	India, Burma, Siam
Rosin	Coniferae	United States

HARDNESS LIST

#1—hardest		#15—softest
#1—Congo	Pale East India	Batavia dammar
Kauri	Black East India	Mastic
Boea	Batu	Sandarac
Pontianak	Manilas	Accroides
Loba	Singapore dammar	#15—Elemi

SOLVENT EVAPORATION LIST

The following table gives the approximate time required for a given sample of the liquid to evaporate naturally:

Acetone	5	minutes
Pure benzol	12	"
90% benzol	15	"
Pure toluol	36	"
High flash solvent naphtha	310 to 360	minutes
Gasoline	10	minutes
Ethyl acetate	10½	"
Butyl acetate	65	"
Amyl acetate	90	"
VM & P naphtha	175	"
Turpentine	450	"
Kerosene	4000	"

DRYING TIME OF FINISHING MATERIALS

Following are the hardening or "tack free" times required by the listed materials as determined on glass slides:

Raw linseed oil	80	hours
Boiled linseed oil	24	"
Raw tung oil	15	"
Soya (soybean) oil	120	"
Spar varnish	8	"
Oiticica oil	15	"
Shellac (4 lb. cut)	¼	"
Lacquer (clear)	¼	"
Methacrylate solution	½	"
Chlorinated rubber	¼	"
Spirit varnish	¼	"

STANDARD LIQUID MEASURE AND EQUIVALENTS

Units of measure of volume differ depending upon the field of use. Chemical formulae are usually given in cubic centimeters (cc), one cubic centimeter (cc) of water weighing 1 gram; paint and varnish formulators usually use liquid ounces (oz.) measure; and pharmacists use still another unit of measure. Following are given equivalent measure listings:

    1 cc of water weighs 1 gram
    1 cc of anything equals .03382 liquid ounces volume.
29.573 cc " " " 1.0 " " "
    1 cc " " " .2705 apothecaries' dram
3.697 cc " " " 1.0 " "
    1 cc " " " .8116 " scruples
1.232 cc " " " 1.0 " "

Miscellaneous Measures

1 pint equals ⅛ gallon equals 16 liquid ounces
1 quart " ¼ " " 32 " "
1 gallon " 128 " "
1 " " 3.78 liters
1 " " 3785.4 cc.

Weight Measures

   1 grain equals 0.0023 ounces (avoir.)
437.5 " " 1.00 " "
   1 " " 0.0647 grams
15.43 " " 1.00 "
   1 gram " 0.035 ounces (avoir.)
28.35 " " 1.000 " "

Use of Measures Tables

To use the tables given above let us say that you have the following formula given (this happens to be Stain formula #12):

Luxol Fast Orange GS	⅒ oz. by weight
Luxol Fast Brown K	1 oz.
Luxol Fast Red B	1/12 oz.
Luxol Fast Black L	⅜ oz.
Alcohol	3 quarts

This formula will give you about three quarts of stain, but suppose you do not want that much. How do you convert the formula easily for a smaller amount? The tables will give you the answer, especially if you have a reloader's balance reading in grains weight.

First, you observe from the table that one quart is 32 liquid ounces and that therefore three quarts would be three times 32 or 96 liquid ounces. For one stock you should be able to get by with 100 cc of stain easily. So let us convert this formula into one giving approximately 100 cc.

Next, convert 96 liquid ounces into cc. This will be done by taking the number of cc in one liquid ounce and multiplying it by 96.

29.6 (cc) times 96 (liq. oz.) equals 2842 cc.

Now that we know the formula as given will make 2842 cc, in order to get about 100 cc we would have to divide it by 28. By dividing everything by 28 we cut down the total volume, but the proportions remain the same.

Now change all dry weights into grains. Inasmuch as the table shows that 437.5 grains equals one ounce weight this will be easy.

The formula now looks like this:

Luxol Fast Orange GS	1/10	oz. times 437.5 or		43.75	grains
Luxol Fast Brown K	1	oz. "	" "	437.5	"
Luxol Fast Red B	1/12	oz. "	" "	36.5	"
Luxol Fast Black L	3/8	oz. "	" "	164.0	"
Alcohol	2842 cc.				

Now, to cut down the volume we divide everything by 28 to give us the resulting approximately 100 cc of solution. The final formula now looks as follows:

Luxol Fast Orange GS	1.6	grains
Luxol Fast Brown K	15.6	"
Luxol Fast Red B	1.3	"
Luxol Fast Black L	5.9	"
Alcohol	101.0	cc

If working with any of the formulae given it is usually not necessary to go any farther than one decimal place. Anything below 5/10 is read as the lower figure, and 5/10 or higher is read as the higher number.

For example, 65.733 would be rounded off to 65.7 because the second and third decimal place are below the $5/10$ figure. But 65.753 would be rounded off to 65.8 because the second and third decimal places equal more than $5/10$.

The stain formulae are usually open to some tinting to allow the stocker to get exactly the color he wants, anyway, so you do not have to be too doggoned accurate in your measuring.

Glossary of Terms

ABRASIVE: A substance which wears away a surface by friction. It may be coarse, as pumice, or gentle, as rottenstone.

ACID REFINED OIL: An oil which has been treated or purified by means of an acid. This usually refers to a drying oil, such as linseed.

ADHESION: The property which allows or causes one material to stick or adhere to another.

AIR DRY: The process of aging or allowing a film to harden by subjecting it to room temperature—as opposed to baking in an oven.

ALKYD: A substance (termed resin) chemically obtained from phthalic anhydride and glycerol used in varnishes and enamels.

AMBER: A natural resin or gum which was formerly used in making varnish. It is scarce at the present time.

ANILINE: An oily substance obtained from coal tar. It is the base of most of the modern stains or dyes.

ANTI-SKINNING AGENT: A material which is sometimes added to paints and varnishes to inhibit the formation of a skin over the liquid in a partially filled can.

ASBESTINE: The trade name of a natural magnesium silicate. It is used in paints.

ASPHALTUM: Same as asphalt. A complex mixture of natural bitumens and asphalts.

BATAVIA: A special grade of dammar gum which is obtained from Batavia, Java, and Sumatra.

BATU GUM: A semi-fossil dammar gum or resin.

BEESWAX: A wax secreted by bees.

BLACK, EAST INDIA GUM: A semi-fossil dammar resin.

GLOSSARY OF TERMS

BLEACHED LAC: White shellac, or shellac which has been treated to remove coloring matter and wax.
BLUSHING: See Finishing Faults List.
BODY: Synonym for viscosity.
BOEA GUM: A fossil manila copal.
BOILED OIL: Usually linseed oil which has been heat treated and had drier added. This oil is never actually boiled.
BRAZIL WAX: Same as carnauba wax.
BUNG HOLE OIL: Raw or refined linseed oil which has had drier added, but without proper heat treatment.
BURNT SIENNA: Sienna pigment which has been heated and thus darkened.
BURNT UMBER: Umber pigment which has been heated and thus darkened.
BUTANOL: Butyl alcohol.
BUTTON LAC: Refined lac in the form of large buttons or globules.
CARNAUBA: Name for a wax obtained from Brazil. It is yellow or green in color and comes from the young leaves of a tree.
CASTOR OIL: Oil which has been pressed from the Castor Bean.
CERESIN: Synonym for earth wax. It is a refined form of mineral wax.
CHECKING: See Finishing Faults List
CHINAWOOD OIL: Tung oil. A drying oil imported from China.
CHINESE BEAN OIL: Same as chinawood or tung oil.
CHLORINATED RUBBER: A resin made by treating natural or synthetic rubber to a special chemical process.
CICOIL: A trade name for oiticica oil.
COMPATIBILITY: The ability of two or more liquids to mix together.
CONGO GUM: A fossil copal resin.
COPAL: A type of hard resin obtained from trees.
CRUDE: Means raw or untreated.
CUT: The amount of resin added to each gallon of solvent. It is used mostly in conjunction with shellac-alcohol solutions. Also means dissolved.
DAMMAR: Same as damar. A type of resin obtained from trees.
DIATOMACEOUS EARTH: Also called Kieselguhr. An earth which is used in filtering, and gentle abrasives.

DILUENT: A liquid which is blended with active solvents to decrease the cost and to thin the liquid. It may not actually dissolve the base resin or substance, but only thins it. Too great an amount may go beyond the permissible limit and cause the resin to be thrown out of solution or precipitated.

DILUTION RATIO: A method for determining the permissible amount of diluent to be used in a solution.

DRIER: A substance or mixture of substances which will increase the rate of oxidation of a substance (as drying oils) and cause it to dry or harden more quickly.

DRYING OILS: Liquid oils which will react with themselves or with the oxygen of the air to form a hard film.

DRYING TIME: The measure of time required for a drying oil to become hard or non-tacky.

DURABILITY: The ability of a film to withstand the destructive effects of its environment. This may include sunlight, water, abrasion or solvents.

EARTH PIGMENTS: Coloring agents or materials which are obtained from mining operations in the earth. They include sienna, umber and red oxide.

ELEMI: A gum derived from certain trees.

ESTER GUM: A resin made from rosin by chemical treatment.

ESTERIFICATION: The formation of an ester by chemical means.

FLOW: A property of a varnish film which is shown by the degree to which the film will level itself or smooth out after brushing. The greater the flow the smoother will be the film.

FOOTS: Non-drying matter which is present in unrefined drying oils.

FRENCH POLISH: A special application of shellac by rubbing.

GARNET LAC: A refined form of lac or shellac from which most of the wax has been removed. It will usually be dark red in color.

GLAZE COAT: A very thin coat or film of any material. Usually applied over wood to prevent penetration of stains.

GLOSS: The ability of a surface to reflect light.

KAURI GUM: A fossil copal resin.

LAC: Same as shellac.

LACQUER: Usually a nitrocellulose base liquid which dries by evaporation of the solvents contained therein. May instead be based upon ethyl cellulose or a natural resin.

LAC WAX: A wax obtained from the refining of shellac.
LENGTH: The amount of oil per 100 pounds of resin contained in a varnish.
LINSEED OIL: Oil pressed from the seeds of the flax plant.
MANILA GUM: A type of copal resin.
MOISTURE RESISTANCE: The ability of a film to resist the passage of moisture through it.
NATURAL RESIN: A resin obtained from trees.
NITROCELLULOSE: A form of nitrated cotton or cellulose which is used in lacquers.
OITICICA OIL: A drying oil obtained from Brazil.
OZOKERITE WAX: A mineral wax obtained from the earth.
PERMEABILITY: The ability of moisture to pass through a film.
PLASTICIZER: A non-drying oil or liquid chemical which is used in lacquers to add pliability to the hardened film.
POLYMERIZATION: A reaction in which molecules of a liquid combine together to form longer molecules with different overall properties.
PONTIANAK GUM: A semi-fossil copal.
REFINED SHELLAC: Shellac with the wax removed.
RESIN: An amorphous material, usually of natural origin, which may be dissolved in solvents to make varnish. Manmade or synthetic resins are being used more and more at the present time.
ROSIN: The resinous substance which is obtained from the manufacture of turpentine. It occurs mostly in pine trees.
ROTTENSTONE: A natural abrasive which is used for polishing.
SANDARAC: A resin from the pine trees of Africa.
SHELLAC: Resin obtained from insects.
SIENNA: An earth pigment of brownish-yellow color. May be heated or burnt to a darker brown.
SPAR VARNISH: A varnish which was originally formulated for use on the spars of ships. Is usually weather resistant.
SPIRIT VARNISH: A varnish which is composed of natural resins dissolved in solvent, usually alcohol.
TUNG OIL: See chinawood oil.
UMBER: A dark brown earth pigment.
VARNISH: A liquid which, applied to a surface, will dry to a hard film. It is usually transparent.
WOOD ALCOHOL: Methyl alcohol.

FINISHING FAULTS LIST

ALLIGATORING: A form of Checking or Cracking. It appears as wide, deep crevices and may appear in fresh films applied over a checked undercoating.

BLUSHING: This will appear only when using a lacquer with fast drying solvents. The cause is the rapid evaporation of the solvent from the surface which will condense moisture from the air. The condensed moisture will form an emulsion with the lacquer but will not dissolve. It will appear in the dried film as white, opaque spots.

BUBBLES: Minute bubbles or pinpoints appearing in a dried film. The cause may be dust or dirt which settled before it hardened. It may also be due to having used dirty material.

BUMPY SURFACE: See Orange Peel.

CHECKING: A form of disintegration of a film. It appears as many minute lines or cracks in the surface and indicates the breakdown of the film surface.

CRACKING: A more serious form of Checking.

CURTAINS: See Sagging.

FLATTING OR DULLING: This appears as dull or flat spots on the surface of a hardened film. It may be due to having applied the film over undried oils, or having neglected to clean the surface of wax and grease before applying.

GRIT: See seed.

LIFTING: Appears when using lacquer over fresh varnish coats. The powerful solvents in the lacquer act as a varnish remover and swell the varnish film. This appears through the surface of the still-wet lacquer as wavy lines or large wrinkles.

ORANGE PEEL: Found only when using a spray gun. It appears as minute waves or bumps on the surface of the film. The cause may be having the nozzle of the gun too far from the surface being sprayed or by using too high an air pressure at the gun.

POOR ADHESION: This appears when a protective coating is easily loosened from the surface to which it was applied. Normal handling sometimes removes such films in sheet or strips. It is caused by having oil, grease or wax on the wood before application of the film.

PITTING AND PINHOLING: This is seen most often when using a spray gun. It is caused by having water or oil in the air lines.

SAGGING: Sometimes called Curtains or Running. It is caused by applying too much liquid to any given area, or by using a normal amount of liquid which was thinned too much before use. This is especially apparent on vertical surfaces. The name Curtains is very descriptive.

SEED: This appears as tiny pinpoints all over the surface. The cause may be that the material was allowed to freeze and then was thawed out, or it may be due to tiny particles of dirt which have fallen into the liquid.

SWEATING: Appears as flat, dull areas upon polishing. It is caused by having the film too soft. This soft film allows particles of the rubbing compound to embed itself in the film. The remedy is to make sure that all films have dried at least 24 hours before rubbing or polishing.

STICKY, NON-DRYING FILM: This appears when grease, wax or non-drying oils have not been properly cleaned from the surface before finishing. The varnish or lacquer will absorb part of the grease or oil and become non-drying itself.

In the case of shellac such a condition would mean that the solution was allowed to stand in storage too long before use. Be sure that shellac solutions are tested before use to insure proper drying.

THROW-OUT: This appears only when using lacquer. The cause is using enamel or varnish thinners to thin or reduce the lacquer. The nitrocellulose base of the lacquer is not soluble in the enamel thinner and will be precipitated to the bottom of the can in a stringy, gummy mass. *Never use enamel thinners or turpentine to reduce lacquer.*

Sources of Supply

ABRASIVES (bentonite, diatomaceous earth, talc, tripoli, pumice):
  Eimer & Amend, Greenwich & Morton Sts., New York, N. Y.
  Hammill & Gillespie, Inc., 225 Broadway, New York, N. Y.
  Monsanto Chemical Co., 1700 S. 2nd St., St. Louis, Mo.
  H. N. Richards Co., 1203 E. State St., Trenton, N. J.
  Whittaker, Clark & Daniels, Inc., 260 W. Broadway, New York

ANNATTO:
  Eimer & Amend, Greenwich & Morton Sts., New York, N. Y.

DRAGON'S BLOOD (*sanguis draconia*):
  Philip A. Hunt Co., 253 Russell St., Brooklyn, N. Y.
  Meer Corporation, 318 W. 46th St., New York, N. Y.

EARTH COLORS (umber, sienna, oxide):
  Harshaw Chemical Co., 1945 E. 97th St., Cleveland, Ohio
  Mineral Pigments Corp., Muirkirk, Md.
  Charles B. Chrystal Co., Inc., 57 Park Place, New York, N. Y.

LACQUERS (clear, pigmented):
  Ditzler Color Div., 8000 W. Chicago Blvd., Detroit, Michigan
  duPont de Nemours & Co. Inc., Finishes Division, Wilmington, Del.
  Monsanto Chemical Co., 1700 S. 2nd St., St. Louis, Mo.
  Howe & French, Inc., 99 Broad St., Boston, Mass.
  Bell Chemical Co., 19 W. 44th St., New York, N. Y.
  Grand Rapids Wood Finishing Co., Grand Rapids, Michigan
  Craftsman Wood Service Co., 2727 S. Mary St., Chicago (8), Ill.
  Albert Constantine & Son, Inc., 797 E. 135th St., New York, N.Y.

NATURAL RESINS:
Accroides:
Wm. M. Allison & Co., 162 Water St., New York, N. Y.
Colony Import & Export Corp., 11 E. 44th St., New York, N. Y.
Asphaltum:
Howe & French, Inc., 99 Broad St., Boston, Mass.
Velsicol Corp., 120 E. Pearson St., Chicago, Ill.
Benzoin:
Bendix Chemical Corp., 420 Lexington Ave., New York, N. Y.
Congo:
Dalton-Cooper Inc., 200 W. 34th St., New York, N. Y.
Paul & Stein Bros., 100 Gold St., New York, N. Y.
Copal:
Adlud Trading Corporation, 565 5th Ave., New York, N. Y.
Elemi:
Barclay Chemical Co., 75 Varick St., New York, N. Y.
Howe & French, Inc., 99 Broad St., Boston, Mass.
Macasser:
Wm. Diehl, 334 W. 42nd St., New York, N. Y.
Lincks, Inc., 155 John St., New York, N. Y.
Mastic:
City Chemical Corporation, 132 W. 22nd St., New York, N. Y.
Zophar Mills, Inc., 116 26th St., Brooklyn, N. Y.
Rosin:
Amsco Products Co., 4619 Reading Rd., Cincinnati, Ohio
Sandarac:
Dodwell & Co., Ltd., 79 Wall St., New York, N. Y.
S. B. Penick & Co., 50 Church St., New York, N. Y.
Ester Gum (chemically treated rosin):
Scher Brothers, 519 Getty Ave., Clifton, N. J.
Chemical Service Corp., 92A Beaver St., New York, N. Y.
OILS:
Castor, raw:
Baker Castor Oil Co., 120 Broadway, New York, N. Y.
Baker Chemical Co., Phillipsburg, N. J.
Brown Oil & Chemical Corp., 72 Pine St., New York, N. Y.
Howe & French, Inc., 99 Broad St., Boston, Mass.

Chinawood (tung), raw:
  Grace & Co., 7 Hanover Square, New York, N. Y.
  Kingston Chemical Inc., 15 William St., New York, N. Y.
Cottonseed:
  Elbert & Co. Inc, 2 Broadway, New York, N. Y.
  Herbert H. Parker, 2 Broadway, New York, N. Y.
  Swift & Co., Union Stock Yards, Chicago, Ill.
Linseed, raw and boiled:
  Archer-Daniels-Midland Co., 600 Roanoke Bldg., Minneapolis, Minn.
  E. F. Drew & Co. Inc., 15 E. 26th St., New York, N. Y.
  Pittsburgh Plate Glass Co., Linseed Oil Div., Red Wing, Minn.
  Sherwin-Williams Co., Pigment, Chemical & Color Div., 295 Madison Ave., New York, N. Y.
  Thompson-Hayward Chemical Co., 2915 Southwest Blvd., Kansas City, Mo.
Oiticica:
  Barclay Chemical Co., 75 Varick St., New York, N. Y.
  Concord Chemical Co., Ledger Bldg., Philadelphia, Pa.
Perilla:
  Wah Chang Trading Corp., 233 Broadway, New York, N. Y.
  G. A. Wharry & Co., Inc., 95 Broad St., New York, N. Y.
Sunflower Seed:
  Export Finders Bureau, 8 Bridge St., New York, N. Y.
Walnut:
  Brown Oil & Chemical Corp., 72 Pine St., New York, N. Y.
  W. R. Grace & Co., 7 Hanover Square, New York, N. Y.
POLISHING FELT:
  Brownell Industries, Montezuma, Iowa
  Frank Mittermeier, 3577 Tremont Ave., New York (61), N. Y.
QUALITY BRUSHES:
  Grand Rapids Wood Finishing Co., Grand Rapids, Michigan
  Craftsman Wood Service Co., 2727 S. Mary St., Chicago (8)
  Albert Constantine & Son, Inc., 797 E. 135th St., New York
SHELLAC (flakes, solutions):
  Adlud Trading Corporation, 565 5th Ave., New York, N. Y.
  Export Finders Bureau, 8 Bridge St., New York, N. Y.
  O. J. Weeks Co., Inc., 16 Hudson St., New York, N. Y.
  Colony Import & Export Corp., 11 E. 44th St., New York, N. Y.

SOURCES OF SUPPLY 435

SIENNA (raw and burnt):
  Mineral Pigments Corp., Muirkirk, Md.
  Smith Chemical & Color Co., Inc., 55 John St., Brooklyn, N. Y.
  Whittaker, Clark & Daniels, Inc., 260 W. Broadway, New York, N. Y.

SOLVENTS:
  Acetone (dimethyl ketone):
    Baker Chemical Co., Phillipsburg, N. J.
    Central Solvents & Chemicals Co., 2545 W. Congress St., Chicago, Ill.
    Commercial Solvents Corp., 17 E. 42nd St., New York, N. Y.
    Griffin Chemical Co., 1000 16th St., San Francisco, Cal.
  Butyl Alcohol (butanol):
    Advance Solvence & Chemical Corp., 245 5th Ave., New York
    Eaton Chemical & Dyestuff Corp., 1490 Franklin St., Detroit, Mich.
  Denatured Alcohol:
    Harshaw Chemical Co., 1945 E. 97th St., Cleveland, Ohio
    Superior Chemical Sales, 1210 W. 9th St., Kansas City, Mo.
  Mineral Spirits:
    Bergstrom Trading Co., 233 Broadway, New York, N. Y.
    Phillips Petroleum Co., Chem. Prod. Div., Bartlesville, Okla.
    Sunnyside Oil Co., 2212 Sunnyside Ave., Chicago, Ill.
  Solvent Naphtha:
    Amsco Products Co., 4619 Reading Road, Cincinnati, Ohio
    The Neville Co., 190 Neville Island P. O., Pittsburgh, Pa.
    Ohio Mineral Spirits Co., 3520 W. 140th St., Cleveland, Ohio
  VM & P Naphtha:
    CP Chemical Solvents, Inc., 60 Park Pl., Newark, N. J.
    Standard Oil Co., 910 S. Michigan Ave., Chicago, Ill.
    Ohio Mineral Spirits Co., 3520 W. 140th St., Cleveland, Ohio

TOOLS (hand and power):
  Brownell Industries, Montezuma, Iowa
  Frank Mittermeier, 3577 Tremont Ave., New York, N. Y.

WAX:
  Beeswax:
    Allied Asphalt & Mineral Corp., 217 Broadway, New York, N. Y.
    Barclay Chemical Co., 75 Varick St., New York, N. Y.

Concord Chemical Co., Ledger Bldg., Philadelphia, Pa.
Will & Baumer Candle Co., Inc., Syracuse (1), N. Y.

Candelilla:
Barclay Chemical Co., 75 Varick St., New York, N. Y.
Koster Keunen, Sayville, N. Y.

Carnauba:
W. R. Grace & Co., 7 Hanover Square, New York, N. Y
Concord Chemical Co., Ledger Bldg., Philadelphia, Pa.
Eaton Chemical & Dyestuff Co., 1490 Franklin St., Detroit, Mich.

Ceresin:
Frank B. Ross Co., Inc., 6-10 Ash St., Jersey City (4), N. J.
Baker Chemical Co., Phillipsburg, N. J.
Koster Keunen, Sayville, N. Y.

Japan:
Allied Asphalt & Mineral Corp., 217 Broadway, New York.
Denver Fire Clay Co., 2301 Blake St., Denver, Col.

Montan:
Fallek Products Co., Inc., 163 Broadway, New York, N. Y.
Frank B. Ross Co., Inc., 6-10 Ash St., Jersey City, N. J.

Ozokerite:
Cornelius Products Co., 386 4th Ave., New York, N. Y.
Robinson-Wagner Co., Inc., 110 E. 42nd St., New York, N. Y.
Ziegler & Co., 233 Broadway, New York, N. Y.

Paraffin:
Boler Petroleum Co., 1330 Widener Bldg., Philadelphia, Pa.
Harwick Standard Chemical Co., 600 Akron Savings & Loan Bldg., Akron, Ohio
Socony-Vacuum Oil Co., 42 Broadway, New York, N. Y.

RARE WOODS:
Craftsman Wood Service Co., 2727 S. Mary St., Chicago, Ill.
Albert Constantine & Son, Inc., 797 E. 135th St., New York.

Artificial Graining of Gunstocks

The original material in this section appeared in *The American Rifleman Magazine* of various dates. In order to supplement the information in the original printing of this book I have used the photographs as they appeared, but have expanded considerably on the copy since Tom Samworth has more space to spare than the *Rifleman* did at the time.

The various methods of treating or altering stocks to give them additional eye appeal has been pretty well covered in the first part of this book, particularly chapter three. For the average stock a simple overall staining will generally be sufficient, but for some of the lads who are always playing with something new this additional data may be interesting. In a few isolated cases it may even prove instructive.

When you sink five bucks into a semi-inletted blank the manufacturer has furnished not only the wood, but also roughed it out on both the inside and the outside. In this case you shouldn't feel too disappointed when you tear open the package and find something considerably different from the flame circassian you envisioned when filling out the handy order blank.

Maybe you're a heavy spender; you sent a money order for ten bucks. Chances are you'll get something with a bit closer grain and maybe even a fair color pattern in wood. You might even be lucky and receive what can be passed off to the dope next door as Domestic French Walnut, providing he doesn't read the same gun writers you do.

At any rate, the lower priced stocks (blank or finished) will do a nice job of keeping the metal parts where they belong, but seldom will be beautiful enough to brag about to shooting pals. Fortunately for us poor-type people there is more to life than the run-of-the-mill if we use a little imagination. To keep away from the philosophical, however, let's get right into it.

It is usually much easier to work with a new, raw stock than with an old, previously finished one since any finish or coating which was on the wood must first be completely removed before any serious attempts are made to change the appearance of the wood. Generally a good varnish remover will take off most anything which might have been put on, but be sure it doesn't contain any wax. Wax-free removers are quite common now.

The first method to be covered here is that of introducing a new grain pattern right into the wood. When properly done it is almost impossible to tell that artificial methods were employed, and even one familiar with the system will often be in doubt as to whether the resulting pattern was applied, or grew there naturally.

One point should be brought out here. In chapter three I talked about a method of flame treating wood to give what the late Alvin Linden called the Suigi Finish. That method is most useful on maple or birch to bring out patterns which are in the wood naturally, but which normally cannot be seen.

The flame graining I wish to cover now is entirely different in theory, but is based on the same element—heat. Here we actually impart a grain pattern where none existed before. While we may at times use some existing pattern as a guide line, or place to start, there is a definite distinction between the Suigi Finish and this method.

The photograph shows the general setup, though I am using a panel for sake of simplicity and clarity where ordinarily a stock would be used. The hand torch you see there is a neat little item for sweat-soldering, paint burning, flame graining, and what-have-you. It has interchangeable tips (both coarse and fine) and costs about ten bucks at a chemical supply house. It burns any kind of compressed gas and compressed air. I get my air from a converted re-

frigerator compressor, and the gas comes out of the city mains under sufficient pressure to operate the torch.

Almost any kind of flame will work, from a plumbers blowtorch (the kind you put gasoline in, pump up, and stand back to light hoping the blamed thing won't blow up) on down to a tiny job which burns gelled alcohol. One of the neatest things today is a self-contained torch with replaceable fuel containers. The fuel builds up its own pressure and requires no pumping, yet puts out enough heat to melt a penny in just a few seconds. There are several now on the market, any of which will be perfectly satisfactory for the job.

Regardless of the type, however, a flame about three-quarters of an inch in diameter is best. A larger flame is too hard to handle and increases the chance of actually burning deeply into the surface. A plumber's blow-torch is really too big and clumsy, though it can be used in emergencies.

The planed section of stock (the panel) in this shot had little obvious grain pattern, nor was it dark enough to look like anything. Instead of trying to bring out the pattern (a la Suigi) it was disregarded entirely and the torch was merely swept along the wood, darkening it here and there to give a psuedo pattern. It doesn't look like much, but that's because we've only started.

To make the picture the torch was turned off so the time shot could be taken without burning the whole business up. The flame *must* be kept moving every second since we are after a deep brown, not a charred black. When you have your pattern browned into the wood take a bit of fine sandpaper and work over the entire surface. The sanding helps blend out the edges of the browned areas and adds considerably to the natural appearance. When you think it looks right then finish your stock with whatever you like, whether it be oil, varnish, or wax.

This next is a nice block of walnut W. R. Hutchings of Los Angeles, sent me. As you can see, the wood has a well marked pattern but is of no special beauty. As a matter of fact, the overall color is light with little or no contrast so that the pattern is barely distinguishable with the naked eye. This is the perfect example of a good place to use flame graining. No other treatment would yield quite such spectacular results in such a case. The left section was obviously left untouched while the remaining portion was gone over lightly with the torch. A fairly broad flame can be used for this sort of thing. This case is a typical example of the Suigi treatment results on walnut. The existing pattern is brought up only.

Since only a darkening, or browning, is needed the big trick is to learn to handle the flame without over-doing it. I have found that I get what I want in the way of color by

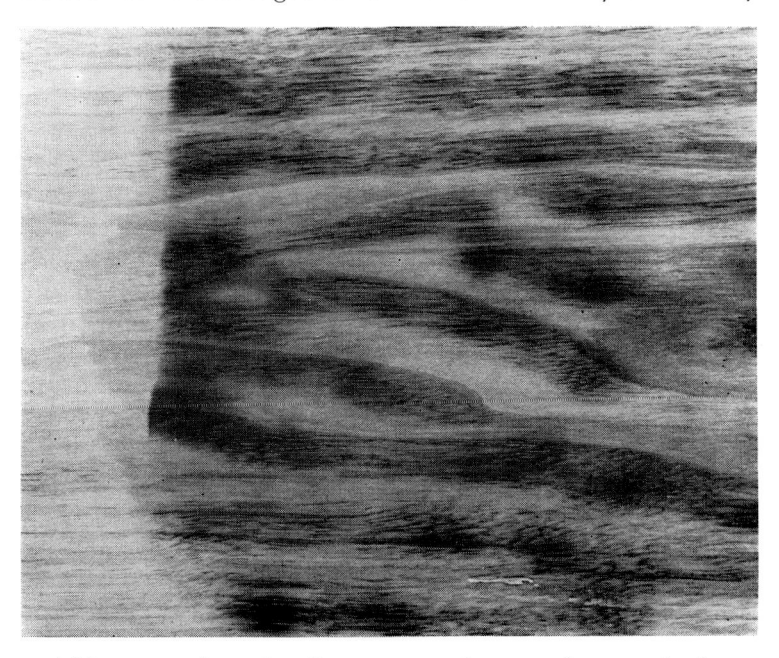

quickly sweeping the flame over the wood several times. Each pass adds a bit of color and you can control the degree of darkening easily. With a small or narrow flame you must follow the path of the previous pass very closely, but a broad flame covers a wide swath and you needn't worry too much about missing spots. If you try to slow the speed of the torch to make just one pass bring out enough color you run a real danger of burning the surface.

One big disadvantage of flame-graining is that the only way to eliminate an overdone area is by sanding. When you get a black spot it is because you have charred the wood. Nothing in the world but complete removal will help then. If you do linger a bit too long somewhere and find sanding is called for be sure you use a sanding pad or block. Those charred areas cut down very fast and you will positively end up with hills and valleys in the surface unless the pad is used.

I put a thin coat of boiled oil on this section prior to taking the picture so that the grain pattern (both before and after) would be brought out as vividly as possible. I used oil since it was handy and does a good job for grain contrast. I sure wouldn't use it on a real stock for my own use, though.

Next is a combination of the two previous effects. While the wood has considerable natural grain pattern present, it is light in color and shows very little contrast in its natural state.

The two effects were used to give as much life as possible to the wood. First, the long stretches of straight grain were darkened by running the torch lengthwise wherever a straight run was possible. Not all the existing pattern was darkened, but only strips a quarter inch or so wide. The most noticeable ones in the picture are running transversely across the lower left-hand corner of the panel.

When all the long, straight stuff was taken care of the torch was lightly brushed across the grain at random. This gave a semi-tigertail effect which isn't at all unpleasant if done with restraint, but looks like the devil if you burn it in too deeply.

When you figure you've gone far enough you might come along with a little ordinary stain to bring up the background color. Just a touch of reddish-brown will do wonders for the average wood.

Now a typical "before-and-after" shot. This forend is of very nice walnut with considerable potential, but little color or contrast in its natural state.

We could use flame graining to good advantage here, but let's see what we can do with a standard staining solution. It doesn't have to be any special kind, but just any old thing you happen to have on hand for changing a light colored wood to something a bit more somber. Even dime store stuff in walnut or mahogany shades will do, though usually what they call mahogany is a little too red to do the nicest kind of a job.

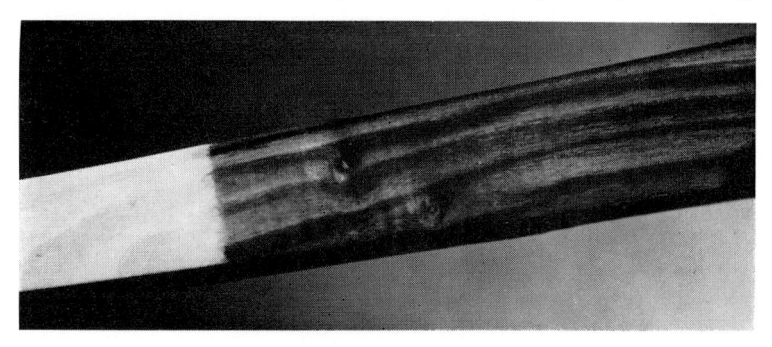

Probably the best bet is to get a couple cans (of the smallest sizes) of different shades and play around with them.

You might even want to get something like Golden Oak for odd effects or blends. Mix some of 'em together and see what they do to a piece of scrap stuff you have around. Might be you'll find something which looks pretty nice. Of course, you won't remember what quantities you used to make it up but it's all right. By the time you get through adding this and that you will have enough to stain a dozen stocks.

I am assuming, of course, that your stock has been whiskered and is all ready for the stain and finish coats. Oh sure, I'm only fooling, but you'd be surprised how many stocks I stained and finished before I realized that I'd forgotten to whisker 'em.

A good many low cost stocks (in the under-fifteen-buck range) will have graining similar to that on this stock. If properly handled the existing grain can be brought out very nicely.

Find the streaks and lines you think should be emphasized. If they are very faint wipe a little alcohol or paint thinner over the wood (never use water). Any pattern in the wood will pop right out at you, but will disappear when the liquid evaporates.

Now take your stain and thin it down as per the directions on the can. If none is mentioned, try a little paint thinner. It may work, or it may not. If it doesn't work try a little denatured alcohol which should be okay. Incidentally, this test should not be made in the can of stuff you intend using for the stock. A couple drops on a piece of glass should be enough to give you an idea, without running the risk of lousing up the whole batch.

Next, make a small swab out of cotton batting, or even a piece of clean cotton cloth. Dip the tip of the swab into the stain, press it against the side of the can to get rid of most of the excess, and lightly run it along the places you want to stand out. You needn't be too precise about where you run the swab, but keep it within the borders of your streak. Obviously, the stain will darken whatever wood it touches and bring that area up in sharp contrast to the adjoining areas.

It is better to use the swab too dry than too wet since dry wood will absorb the stain like a blotter, and if too much stain is present it will spread over into places you don't want it to go. Make two or three trips with the slightly-more-than-damp swab. Each trip will darken just a bit more than the previous pass and will help blend in the edges.

Even great care will not keep a certain amount of artificiality from being obvious. You are bound to have places where it looks exactly like you wiped a rag along the grain: which is exactly what you did, of course. Therefore it helps a lot to take a larger swab, dip it in thinned-down stain and vigorously scrub the whole surface of the stock. This helps to even out any bad spots you might have accidentally made and also gives just enough background color to the wood to make the artificial graining appear extremely natural.

With this operation it is obvious that only existing grain can profitably be worked on. It is very difficult, and usually impossible, to try to make a naturally-appearing pattern where none existed. But it's the cat's meow for bringing out stuff that's really there, but to which nature didn't give much pigmentation.

Here is a good example of what not to do as mentioned in the previous shot. Another "before-and-after" shot, it shows an attempt at cross graining or striping with stain.

The same type of cotton swab was used, but since existing pattern was not followed, the results I wouldn't write home about. The biggest source of trouble in this case is that the wood has a very open grain with large pores, almost like an oak. The stain gathered in these pores, regardless of how much wiping was done, and tended to emphasize the pores instead of darkening evenly a long, narrow area.

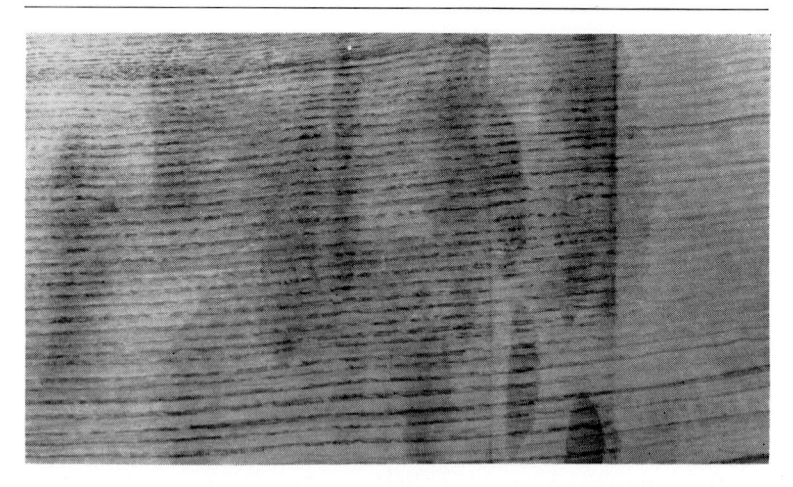

Birch and maple will take this sort of treatment alright, because they have practically no pores to catch and hold the staining solution, but I wouldn't advise trying it on walnut or mahogany.

An example of a chemical type stain. These stains may be made of almost any liquid that we think of as chemical ordinarily. They may be one of the many acids, alkalies, or even something like potassium permanganate which is available at the local drug store in purple crystals. In this case I used the permanganate which I dissolved in just a little water.

Permanganate solution is purple when dissolved in water, but after drying on wood turns to colors varying from light brown to almost black. A lot will depend upon the concentration (strength) of the solution and also the nature of the wood on which it is used. In this shot the solution was fairly weak and the color was a walnut-brown, though a little light in shade.

You can see how the solution collected in the pores of the wood rather than remaining spread evenly over the whole surface. When this happens (and it always will with coarse grained hardwoods) the overall color isn't changed a great deal, but the grain is accentuated.

At the left of the panel is a slightly darker section of wood. This is where a light coat of linseed oil was rubbed in. It will invariably help to bring out grain structure, regardless of the type of staining medium used.

Of course, the biggest (and very serious) disadvantage of chemical type stains is that they usually are dissolved in and carry great amounts of water. They can be successfully used without getting too much moisture down into the wood, but it's tricky. The best bet is to use them with infra-red heat bulbs that boil off the water the minute it hits the wood. (See the next section, on Heat Finishing.)

This one shows how the permanganate was handled, if you really want to take a crack at it. The method is not limited to permanganate, however. Acids, alkalies, and all the others get the same treatment.

The rubber gloves are very important. While many of the chemicals useable are in dilute form (mixed with water) and are not highly dangerous as such, they will always stain the fingers and dry the skin. Most of the time the fingers turn brown, yellow, or black and the color is permanent. You either use some sandpaper or let it wear off by itself. Won't take more than a couple months.

In this shot the permanganate crystals were put into the cup (beaker, if you're a chemist) and some water added. How much depends on how deep you want the color. A little bit goes a long way. Scrub it into the wood with the cloth swab and let 'er dry. Nothing else to it.

This next is similar to one some place back in the book, but here a little something's been added to show the difference in final effect when apparently similar substances are used to stain with.

The "before" section to the left is obvious without any labels on it. The wood is a very nice piece of birds-eye maple but the eyes don't show up very well. What is lacking, of course, is some sort of contrast to make them stand out from the background. OK, so let's add something to bring it out as well as anything else the wood may have for us to see.

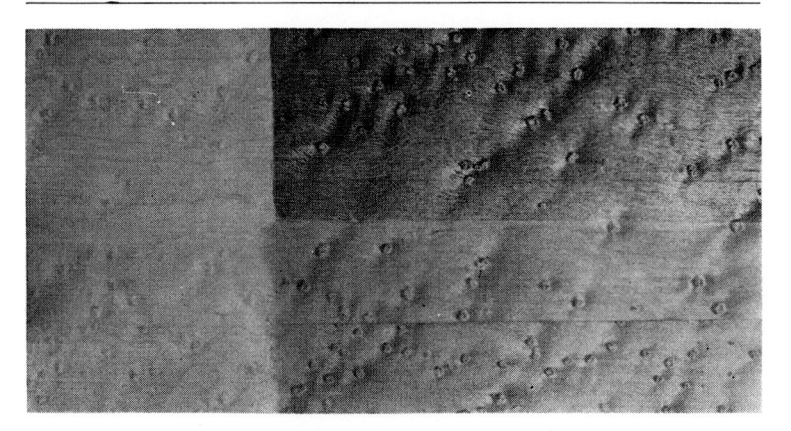

The lower half of the treated portion has had a coat of fairly dark aniline stain rubbed into it. The overall color of the wood is darkened somewhat, but the most noticeable effect is the way the eyes stand out. Also, what appear to be ridges or valleys are now apparent. While you don't usually want to darken maple or birch much, a little color, properly applied as we've done here, serves to give a lot of life to the wood. You can't do this with oil.

This is typical of most of the stains you will be able to get. Whether they are aniline, alcohol, or the popular NGR stains the action will be about as you see it here.

Now look at the top half of the treated section. This is the way it should look. You now have the same thing as in the lower half, but to a much greater extent. It is true that the color is somewhat darker, but a touch with very fine sandpaper will take out most of the surface color. This section actually is as close as you can get to being 3-D in a gunstock. As you turn or rotate the stock the grain structure seems to move and dance right in the wood.

The material used here to get this effect is nothing but plain old asphalt dissolved in gasoline or naptha. The color is a washed-out brown black, but a regular stain may be used over this wash coat to add color if desired. The function of the asphalt is solely to bring out the effect seen in the photo.

It's a good idea, incidentally, to lightly scrub the stained surface with a rag dipped in paint thinner. This removes any asphalt which may be *on* the surface instead of *in* it, which is where it should be. If much is left on the surface it will interfere with the drying and hardening of whatever you put on top of it, whether it be linseed oil, varnish, lacquer, or shellac.

Und now giffs der chenooyne t'ing on the opposite page.

The real artificial graining is practically a lost art, though it was widely known and practiced not too many years ago. In fact, I tried for a long time to get some first-hand information on the subject and hunted for several months before I could locate one old-timer who had done it years ago. Even he was a little vague since it had been years ago in "de olt countree" that he last practised it.

There are two ways to go about this. First (based on the system as used many years ago) the extreme end of the panel shows the bare wood which we are going to try to alter to look like something. This wood has been whiskered and sanded.

The next section has had a coat of primer paint applied, and then was sanded down to the bare wood after it had dried hard. If the pores of the wood are still not completely filled it may take another operation of painting, drying, and sanding. A good filler can be used in place of the paint if the grain structure is particularly open, such as with oak, but the average walnut or mahogany grain will do quite as well with one hardened coat of unthinned paint. Any kind will do except white house paint. The main thing is to have a perfectly smooth, even surface upon which to lay the following materials.

The third strip (and step) is to completely paint the surface with a Buff or Light Brown enamel. After drying thoroughly it was sanded smooth to take out any lint or dirt particles which might have dried on the surface. Finish the sanding with very fine grit paper, preferably of 360 grit or finer.

The last strip has been given the start of a straight grain design. The application of the graining material will be enlarged upon in the next shot, but this shows the basic steps.

Now comes a good example of how to go about real graining. It doesn't look too promising at this stage. As shown in the preceding shot, the wood has been well filled and smoothed off, with a coat of Light Brown enamel of some sort to give a background color.

Now take some good varnish (Ward's or Sear's make a good grade of stuff) and mix in a little burnt umber or black tinting colors from the local paint emporium. It usually comes in little tubes and sometimes doesn't mix very well with your varnish, but in most cases it will be okay. Don't mix in too much. It's a matter of cut and try, but a few drops will probably be enough for a half pint or so of varnish, which is all you'll need.

You want your mix (which we'll call ink from now on) to be good and strong in color so, as you are mixing it together, smear out a couple drops on a piece of glass or a coffee can cover. When it appears to be fairly opaque, stop. You don't want the mix to be mostly tinting color since it won't dry worth a darn, yet you need enough paste to give you color. It won't take long to get the idea once you've smeared some out on wood.

Now use a little turps or paint thinner and thin this ink out so it is fairly runny, though not so thin as water. Now take an old sweat shirt or other piece of coarsely woven cloth and cut out a piece about four inches square. Make sure this cloth has been well washed and dried since any threads, dirt, or lint which is loose on the surface of the cloth will be left in the dried ink before you get through. An old woolen sweater is ideal because of its texture, but wool often leaves lint no matter how often you launder it. Burlap is another good material to use, but you run into lint problems here, too. The coarser the texture the better the final graining job will be.

Fold your cloth into a little bundle, or wad, and dip it partially into the ink. Dab it on the surface of the painted wood here and there, each spot an inch or so from the next one. Squeeze the wad as dry as possible against the side of the ink can (the inside, if you please). Now, using the wad like a scrub brush (but without any pressure) blend one inked spot into the next, using long strokes.

The most important thing here is practise. You'll quickly get the hang of it and eventually you'll find your ink streaks looking somewhat like natural grain. To give the design a little life make a few swirls or quarter-turns here and there as you travel along. Now gently stroke the wad from the center of the swirls outward to blend them into the long strokes, but leave enough of the swirls to make them stand out.

These swirls are more than a little tricky to handle and still remain (or become) natural appearing. If you foul up the detail, though, a little paint thinner on a rag will clean off the ink and you can start over on that spot.

Straight grain, however, is what we're concerned about in this shot. Since they tell us that properly behaved forends should contain as much straight grain as possible to prevent warping and twisting of barrels, let's keep them straight. Who knows? You might want to sell the old smoke pole to a purist some day.

Now turn the page and see where we have a little trickier design being worked on.

Putting a fairly heavy coat of smears or spots down the middle of the area gives you a control or central area from which all strokes are made outwards.

Fold the cloth wad into several folds as you see in the picture, put it down on the center streak and draw outward, giving a half twist as you go. The folds will leave a multiple path and give a fair rendition of crotch grain.

Leave the center section very dark, adding ink if you have to. Play with the cloth, giving some pattern there in the center, but make it as dense and dark as possible. In natural wood such structure as crotch figuring will be dense and dark with little apparent figure, though it's there if you take the trouble to look for it. That's what we're after here. A nice effect can be had by dabbing at the ink with the wad, working it straight up and down. This is especially good in dense, dark areas, though on lighter colored areas it does not look so natural.

Since you will want a crotch effect in only one area, probably somewhere on the butt, make much of the remainder of the stock with a fairly straight grain and blend in the crotch effect to meet the straight strokes.

Below is a closeup of a finished crotch effect. This one was made by the operation shown in the preceding illustration.

You can see the fairly dark, dense area from which the folded cloth was worked. No definite line of demarcation is apparent since the dark section was blended evenly into the

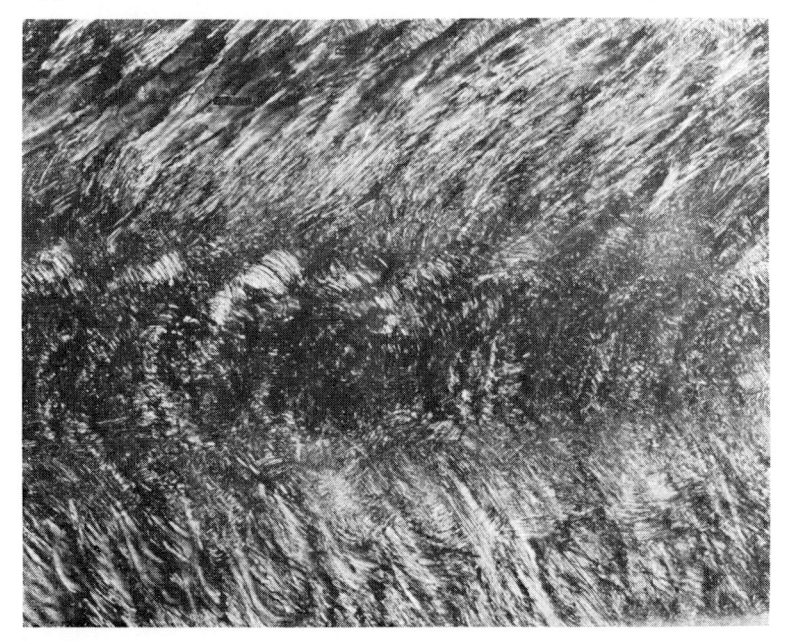

lighter ones. However, the crotch center itself is almost black and the other sections are considerably lighter.

This shot is strictly a closeup and the farther way you get from it the better it looks. Within reason, of course, and no wise guys need apply. If done properly, this sort of figure is the cat's meow.

The biggest trouble encountered is with lint from the wad which we use to make the figuring. Every little hair or fiber which stays in the ink is very apparent when coated with a clear varnish. This clear topcoat, incidentally, is extremely important. The ink, even when dry, is relatively thin and fragile and requires a protective topcoat of good varnish.

Let the pattern dry overnight, or longer if necessary, and then examine it at arms length. If there is any repairing or touching up to do now is the time! Don't go at it with a magnifying glass since the design will then look like (which is what it really is) a meaningless, random pattern of lines and blotches. A couple of feet away, though, suddenly transforms it into a coherent, naturally appearing grain structure.

Now take a good grade of varnish and thin it down with turps. It is best not to use commercial paint thinner since that kind of concoction sometimes contains solvents which would dissolve the ink you've so carefully laid down. Using a *clean* brush, one which has been washed with soap and water and allowed to dry thoroughly, brush on a *thin* coat of varnish. Let it dry overnight.

When dry examine carefully, this time closely, by eye. Now you aren't looking for imperfections in the pattern, but are looking for lint or dirt in the clear varnish coating. If you find rough spots try to smooth them out with *fine* grade sandpaper, but don't sand enough to get down into the ink pattern.

Now add another coat of varnish and your job should be done. Usually, however, the varnish topcoats will have a high gloss, or shine, which cheapens the job. Take some rottenstone, or automobile cleaner-polish and rub vigorously. This should give you a nice luster, without annoying glare.

The next system is essentially the same as the previous one, except for the preparation of the wood to take the ink.

Here we do not use paint, or primer, but instead put the

graining directly on the wood itself. Of course, the wood must be non-porous and fairly smooth so that the ink will spread and handle properly without sinking in or blotting. In order to accomplish this we use a neutral colored filler to smooth out the pores and then cover it (after it dries) with thinned-out shellac or varnish. It must be thin so that it does not actually build up a surface coating, but instead seals the wood so that the ink isn't absorbed like a blotter.

This non-primer system is the more useful of the two since it requires much less surface preparation and a much

thinner total film thickness. Heavy or thick films chip easily when cut or scratched.

When the wood has been filled, sealed, and sanded smooth it is ready for graining.

The panel in the photograph has some figure but it is so faint that it does not even appear on the negative. In this case you can consider it the same as a painted surface (a la system No. 1) and work as you wish, putting grain wherever it suits your fancy.

If, however, your stock should be plain and lifeless but with enough pattern to be seen (and the majority of even poor stocks fall into this category) you can still build your crotch figure where you want it and follow the existing, natural grain structure everywhere else. This is another case of "when you can't beat 'em, join 'em."

Just as before, when you have finished put on two thin coats of varnish and polish out the shine.

This poor fella below has taken a beating all along the line for the last twenty years or so since it was full of dents, gouges, cuts, dirt, sweat, cosmoline, and probably a few tears.

A good scrubbing with cleaning fluid and a brush removed the worst of the litter, but it was still badly oil stained and nothing cleaned it up completely.

Since the wood was still pretty dark I used an almost black ink. Fortunately there were no porous spots on the stock, those having drunk their fill of oil in years past. In

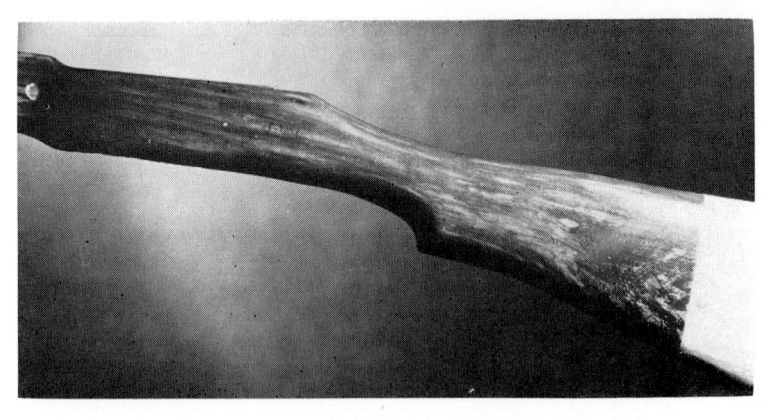

fact, on some spots the varnish wouldn't even dry too well because of the oil in the wood. Eventually it hardened up, but not without a fight.

You may sometimes find this situation when you attempt to refinish a stock which has been liberally and repeatedly doused with raw linseed oil. So much oil has soaked in without drying that a varnish or shellac coating will not dry.

You can see part of a burl pattern which shows up well

even on this dark wood. The grip and forend took straight graining well, though there was considerable natural pattern present to help out.

The unfinished strip at the butt end is not really white, but shows up that way because of photoflood lights on the varnish topcoat.

The next was a much better subject than the previous stock. It is of new mesquite wood with very little figuring. The color was of a uniform yellow so a reddish brown ink was used.

After the normal varnish-sealing coat following by sanding, the ink was applied and rubbed out as you can see. By dabbing on a few spots here and there and blending them

together you can sometimes get very nice effects indeed. This was a pretty decent stock when I got through with it.

Normally, stocks with poor coloring, so-called, will have plenty of color, but it will be sort of a light brown or brown-straw. The reason it doesn't look like much is that there is nothing to relieve the monotony of the over-all color. Adding a touch of color in the right places (as in making artificial grain) relieves the monotony and dresses the stock up surprisingly.

Actually, it is easier to get good results in graining if your wood is a light over-all color. Then you can vary the color of the graining ink and do a bang-up job. With dark woods the ink must be nearly black to be seen and then you have little or no contrast to work with. Never, never use a light ink on dark wood. It looks like the devil. Always go darker than the background. If you should happen to miscalculate (as I did on this one the first try) and get everything too dark, dip a rag in gasoline or cleaning fluid, squeeze it out, and remove the ink altogether. Then try it again.

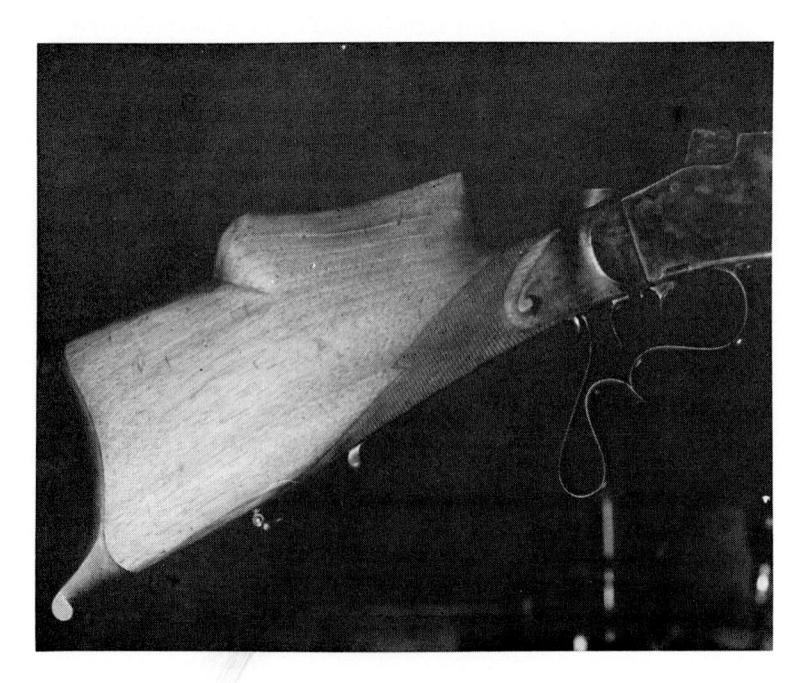

Sometimes you can achieve a very nice effect by darkening the whole stock and then using a thinner-dampened rag to remove some of the ink in streaks. Let the whole thing dry overnight and the next day lighten the streaks even more with a touch of sandpaper. What you are doing is adding light-colored streaks to a darker background. Sounds complicated, but if you fool around a bit with it you'll catch the hang of the thing. Makes a nice job, though only for straight grain work.

You just saw what was once someone's pride and joy. It was laying on a pile of grenades and other toys outside Cologne when I found it in the spring of 1945. No, I didn't swipe it and I didn't win it in mortal combat. Our infantry company rounded up everything that could be fired or thrown in this little village and this was among the lot.

It was raining for fair, like you can find only in Germany on a cold, wet spring day with snow still on the ground. Anyhow, what do I find but this Scheutzen. There was another one, but it was pretty beat up. This one, though, was fresh since the bore wasn't a bit rusted. Being the lucky one I tossed it aboard the half-track among the half-ton or so of other junk. Eventually everything went by the board but this baby.

By the time I got it home the stock wasn't in the best of condition. This shot is the "Before" part of a "Before-and-After" duo.

What now follows is the "After" part.

Before discarding the stock prior to building a new one I worked it over a bit to see what could be done. It was dismounted from the barrel and action and given a good scrubbing with cleaning fluid. Incidentally, whatever you use for this kind of a job, whether it's gasoline, cleaning fluid, carbon tet, or what-have-you, should be used where there is plenty of ventilation and no open fires. These solvents are all highly poisonous, and many of them dangerously explosive.

Most of the grease and dirt were removed by the cleaning, but a light sanding helped even more, especially in cuts and gouges where dirt had collected. Now the wood was very light in color, sort of a greenish-yellow.

First, a little color was added to the wood by using a

normal stain. I picked a brown mahogany which was available ready-mixed at the local paint store, but almost anything from a golden oak to a rich walnut shade would have done as well. Personally, I'm prejudiced towards a certain amount of reddish-brown in my stocks, though not very much.

Now with a bit of life in the old girl we figured to bring out a bit more of the natural grain pattern. There wasn't much natural pattern to follow so flame graining was a good bet. The top after portion of the cheekpiece hollow was darkened considerably, and a little longitudinal straight graining was done on the lower area of the butt. Of course,

a bit of judicious sanding was done to blend out the edges of the browned areas to meet the lighter, untouched sections adjoining them.

The forend was a small piece and separated entirely from the butt, so there was no problem of keeping patterns continuous. Running the torch first lengthwise and then across the forend brought out a surprisingly nice tigertail effect.

The coloring was now just as I wanted it, and the added touches of the flame graining pepped it up 100 percent. It looked so good, in fact, that I abandoned plans to restock the relic.

The last operation was to give it two separate coats of very thin varnish and polish out with rubbing compound. The varnish coating was thin enough to avoid having much of a film built up, and yet was definite protection against ground-in sweat and dirt. With such a base coat, it is perfectly all right to rub on a light film of *boiled* linseed oil once in a while and really rub it hot. This helps to counteract wear of handling, yet there is little danger of it staying gummy since it is held out of the wood where the air can get at it and dry it up hard.

Heat Finishing

The average time required for finishing a stock with ordinary materials (varnish, shellac or oil) runs somewhere in the neighborhood of a week or so.

Of course, in setting that time limit I'm figuring that the average Joe has only a couple of hours an evening to work. However, even the professional stocker has to allow nearly that much time for his finishing materials to dry. There is one way to beat this rap, though, and still come out with a good stock finish, both for beauty and for durability.

The next time you're in the local hardware store look at their Infra-Red heat lamps. They come in different wattages, but the usual household size is 200 or 300 watts. They run about a buck and a quarter each.

Add a goose-neck lamp or clamp—on holder and you're in business. Two or three of the lamps in movable holders will add up to a lot of heat, and the holders let you put it where it will do you the most good.

A word, first, about Infra-Red light. It differs from ordinary light in that it is almost pure heat energy. As a matter of fact, what you feel as heat from any luminous source came to you mostly as Infra-Red light. So this electric bulb is simply an efficient generator for Infra-Red light which is converted into pure heat as soon as it strikes any surface.

The bulb will not appear to be extremely bright, but that's because the normal human eye cannot perceive Infra-Red light. But put your hand in front of the bulb and you'll pull it away right now! The heat's there, but you just can't see it.

Also, don't confuse these heat lamps with Ultra-Violet health lamps which may even be in the same bin at the store. Be sure the bulbs you buy are marked INFRA-RED right on the glass face. The Ultra-Violet gives off little heat and are used mostly by us poor people to get a nice tan in the winter months.

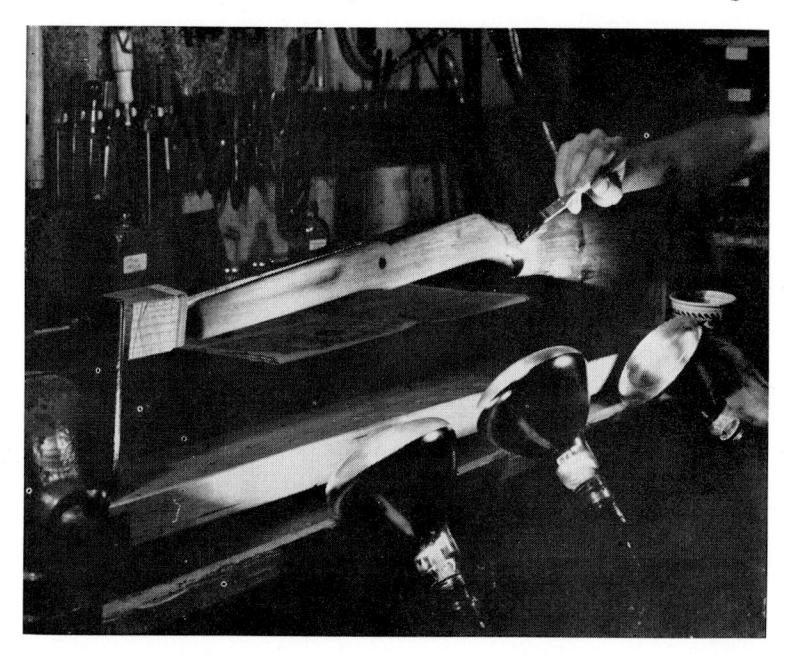

Above I've set up the bulbs in movable holders. It helps a lot if you can clamp the stock in a cradle of some sort so that it can be rotated. In this way you move the work, and not the bulbs.

466 *GUNSTOCK FINISHING AND CARE*

Anyhow, the sanded stock is ready to be stained. Brush or pad on the staining agent and turn the stock so that a fresh area is constantly under the brush. As the stock turns in the cradle the lamps heat the stained surface and evaporate the water or other volatile liquid in the stain. The stain is "set" right now and you don't have to worry too much about the liquid soaking down into the wood. This is about the only way I would trust water-based stains to be used.

Once around the whole stock and you should be pretty well ready for the next operation.

One important point is that the stain sets up very quickly under the heat and you must watch out for lap marks. If you find them, blend them into the adjacent areas by lightly scrubbing with a rag dipped in whatever liquid the stain will dissolve in.

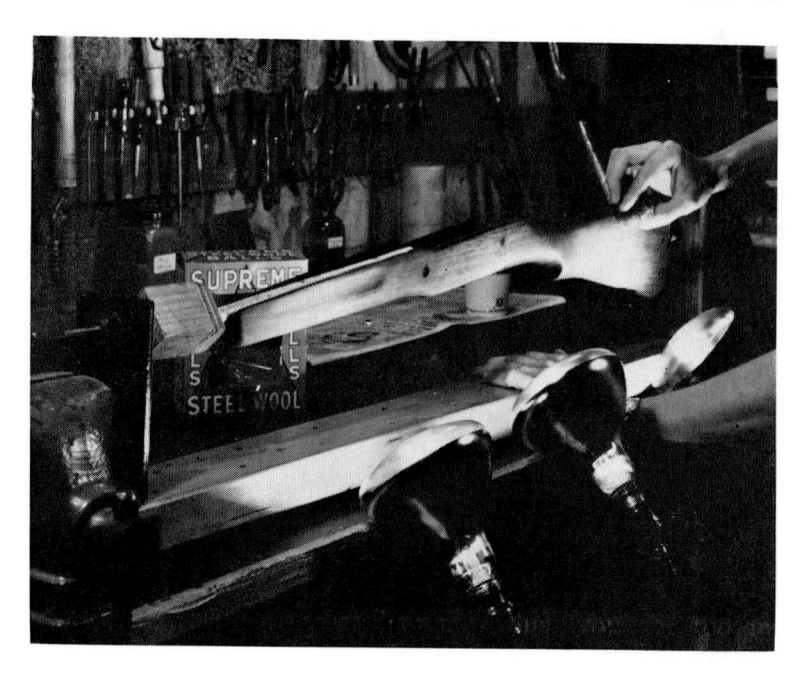

It helps to avoid laps by working from stained areas to unstained sections since the unstained wood will still be cool and errors can be worked over before the heat has a chance to set it up.

When using stains dissolved in a fast-evaporating liquid like alcohol, a great deal of heat will not be needed, since such stains dry quickly even without heat being applied. However, water stains definitely require the use of heat lamps.

The heat lamps are also useful in grain raising, or whiskering. Enough heat is generated to do the job well, and you don't singe your pinkies holding the stock over the kitchen range.

Bring the bulbs up to within 10 or 12 inches of the wood and dampen the wood with a rag. Slowly turn the stock so that the dampened sections pass in front of the lamps. In a very few seconds the wood will be dry and the fibers raised. They can then be removed with fine steel wool as you see being done on the opposite page.

Be careful not to splash water on the face of the heat lamps. The water may possibly cause them to crack and burn out or burst.

If you can get a good lacquer sanding sealer you will find it does a good job of sealing and filling the pores of the wood, yet dries in a very short time.

If, however, you must resort to something else you can use either shellac or the same clear lacquer you use for the final finish. Shellac is OK if nothing else is available, but it doesn't dry as fast as lacquer and becomes brittle with age.

Whatever you use will require more than one coat (unless you have birch or maple wood which have no pores to speak of). Back the lights away from the wood to about 15 inches. Using a lint-free rag or clean brush put a thin coat of sealer material on the wood and rotate the stock slowly as you apply it.

Too heavy a coating will not only run and sag, but will take much longer to dry. It will also be very sensitive to bubbling under the heat.

Keep turning the stock and putting on thin coats of sealer till you think the majority of pores and pits have been pretty well filled. If you have not used very thick coats, each coat should be dry enough to re-coat after passing the lamps. Continue till you have a well filled surface on the wood.

Shown next is what happens when you get too much heat too fast on a wet coat of almost anything. It happens if your bulbs are too close to the wood and/or your coating is too heavy.

Heat from these bulbs can easily raise the temperature of the surface of the wood to 160 degrees or more. If you keep the stock moving slowly, though, you don't allow such heat to concentrate in any one spot. You spread it out and make it work for you instead of against you.

In case you do get this though, go right on with what you are doing, only move the bulbs back a bit. In putting on filler or sealer coats a few bubbles won't hurt anything since you can repair them further on along the line.

Now, when you have done all the filling and sealing you think is necessary give it an extra trip or two through the lamps.

Using a sanding block of some sort (preferably flexible) and fine sandpaper (not coarser than 320 grit) take the dry coating off down nearly to the bare wood. Don't go too close since you may sand into the wood itself and leave light areas where you tore into stained wood. If this happens touch it up with some stain on a rag after sanding.

All you are really after here is to get rid of possible brush or rag marks, or bubbling and the like.

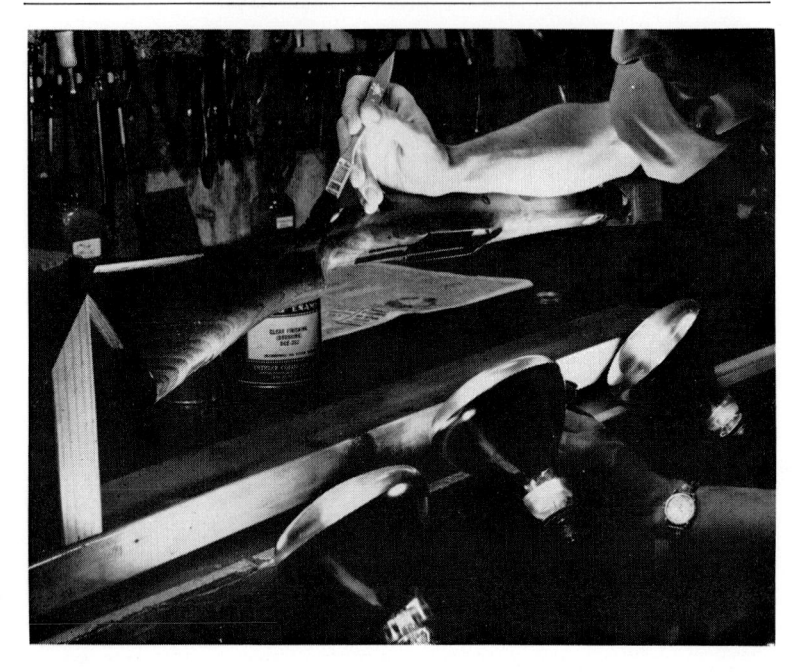

The final finish should consist of a good grade of lacquer. While varnish is equally as good, it requires hours to dry. Even the heat lamps won't help it much.

It is true that you can get Baking Additives, such as are used by automotive repair shops to allow air-dry enamels to be baked, but the heat required will be more than your wood can stand. Over metal it's all right since 180 degrees or so of heat won't hurt anything, but on wood you'll get blistering and bubbling when you get it that hot.

The finish should be applied in the same manner as the sealer coat. Rag or brush it on in *thin* coats. The best tool to use is a *clean* brush, preferably a new one which has been washed with soap and water and dried well. Don't try to economize and get a cheap two-bit one; they lose bristles into the wet surface and cause more trouble than they're worth. Pay a buck for a good one and you can use it around the house for years.

Here you must be very careful about runs and sags. Heavy or thick coats will produce them and they will be very apparent since this operation is the final one. You can sand 'em off, to be sure, but the easiest way is to avoid them in the first place. Keep these coats thin.

Finishing lacquer does not dry as quickly as a lacquer sealer, especially if it is made for brushing. That means you will have to be careful to keep the bulbs about 15 inches from the wet coating. It all depends on the drying time of the particular brand of lacquer you are using and how close you want to cut corners. Sure, you can bring the bulbs up close and hope you don't get blistering, but two to one you will!

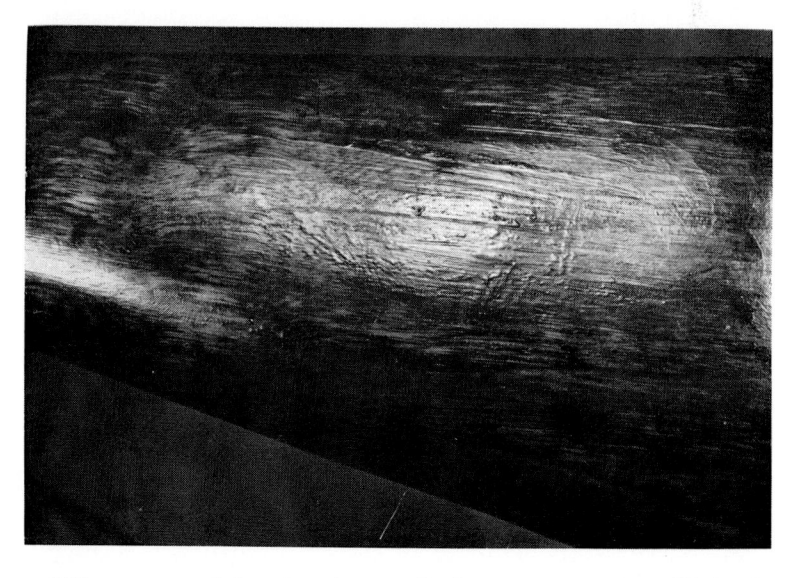

When everything is nice and dry your stock will look something like is shown above. The conditions are exaggerated for sake of illustration, but it usually won't be much better.

The reason, of course, is that generally lacquers dry too fast for all brush marks to be eliminated by the wet flowing of the lacquer. It won't level itself out like enamel or house paint does over a period of time.

This condition is normal. To remove it we must now sand the stock.

This unsavory mess being sanded off on the above stock is sanding mud which has dried on the stock.

If you are using ordinary sandpaper (fine grit) you must dry-sand the surface. Water would dissolve the glue holding the grit to the paper backing. If, however, you can get some Wet-Or-Dry paper (and most places carry it) by all means get it. Used with water it lasts far longer than ordinary paper and gives much better results in terms of appearance.

Start with 320 paper and finish up with 400 grit. One or two sheets of each should be enough for a stock since the water makes it go a long, long way.

Using a flexible sanding block of some sort (even a small,

square rubber eraser from a stationery store will do) dip the paper in a can of water and start sanding. Sand the whole surface evenly and the sanding block keeps the fingers from cutting out troughs in the surface due to unequal pressure.

Sand only deep enough to remove brush marks, laps, and what-have-you. We don't want to cut right on down to the wood, remember.

When you think you've sanded enough, wipe the muddy residue from the wood and look 'er over. Chances are you've got a ways to go yet. Keep on with it, sanding and wiping, till you are satisfied that the surface is as good as you can get it.

If you built up a decent coating on the wood no water or moisture should get down into the wood. Since you are passing the sanded surface in front the bulbs after working on it the water will be evaporated almost at once. The heat is merely insurance that it doesn't get down where it can do damage.

Now a quick rub with a good automobile cleaner-polish will bring up the lustre without actually making it shiny or glossy. You should have little or no need for the buffing wheel/rottenstone process so often needed with ordinary finishing operations.

Incidentally, the average stock can often be completely finished, from stain to final polish, in one evening. This may not hold true with your first try, but a little practise in handling lacquer materials under heat will quickly give you the feel of the thing.

Plain and Quarter Sawed Wood

This shot shows the typical effects from different methods of sawing wood at the tree.

The first method shown in the bottom half of the photograph is called quarter sawed wood. As you can see the radial rings or lines run in such a manner that on a blank they would be from side to side or in a horizontal plane.

The second most common method is called plain sawing. It is shown with a typical pattern from the same board. Such a method produces blanks and stocks with the most beauty, as the figure is accentuated rather than hidden.

The radial lines would run nearly vertical in a stock, or from the heel to the toe of the butt.

For beauty, for strength of grip, and for safety from chipping in the toe and pistol grip the plain sawed blanks will be best.

For accuracy assurance in a target rifle, though, I would specify the quarter sawed blank every time. True, if she warps she is going to warp in a vertical plane, but that can be guarded against by properly waterproofing the stock, inletting the barrel channel to overcome such tendencies, and firing a sighter or two before a match. It is easy to overcome up and down shots, but when the gun is off to right or left *and* up and down then it is a different story.

Anyhow, in my opinion the great majority of weather changes in the stock will be almost completely eliminated if proper care is taken to use a *good* varnish sealer and to apply it as it should be done.

WHISKERING—WETTING DOWN

Here the primary operation of whiskering is being done. This is done by means of wetting the stock with a damp rag or cloth. The wetting of the wood allows some moisture to be introduced into the surface grain ends, just as would happen if sweat or rain water were allowed to penetrate through the finish.

When such a situation develops, the grain ends absorb the moisture and then under the influence of heat, whether it be heat from the hand or from sunlight or any other source, the moisture is forced out of the stock. This swells and forces the grain ends upward and they are then unpleasantly made apparent in two ways.

First, the hand or cheek can readily feel the hundreds of needle-pointed grain ends. Second, if you have a fairly solid finish coat such as varnish or lacquer, it is possible for the grain ends to actually push that finish away from the anchor it has put down into the wood. This will give you peeling and a generally lousy appearance.

The wetting of a stock may be done in small sections as shown, with heat treatment immediately after, or it may be done by wetting the whole stock and then heat treating it as a unit.

I like the small area system. The longer you allow water to remain on and in the wood the deeper it is going to penetrate, and if it goes very far any subsequent heat treatment will not vaporize it and force it out of the wood. It will be there for a long, long time. There is every chance you may have allowed enough to penetrate so that the wood in the relatively thin forearm starts to warp and throws off the careful bedding you have done (presumably, that is). If you gouged out a ditch for the barrel to ride in then you will not hurt anything by soaking it in a bucket, but if you were careful and accurate in the inletting then you certainly are running a big chance of lousing up the whole works.

Whiskering—Raising the Grain

Here is the second operation in whiskering.

The burner that I hold in my hand is being whisked quickly and evenly over the previously dampened wood. The heat from such a flame will force the water out of the wood and with it will come the grain ends. Then a quick rubbing with new steel wool will pull off the raised ends.

Once such an operation has been completed you need have no fear that rain or damp weather will raise the grain on you. What does not come up in this sort of process will never come up under anything you may subject it to.

In using a flame of this sort you must be careful that you do not get the flame so close to the wood that it chars it, or that you leave the flame in one spot for very long. That will char it too, even if it is not actually touching the wood at the time. You can get some fine synthetic graining by doing just that sort of thing, but here we are not interested in graining. We only want to dry off the dampened surface.

The checkering frame or stock holder is the handiest little gadget when attempting almost any work on a stock. You can turn the stock every which way without much handling and you do not have to lay it down on a dirty bench while you change hands.

If you do not have a Meker or Bunsen burner handy (I have both) you could use the flame from the gas plate in the kitchen. Of course, you will not be able to use the holding frame then. You will have to hold the stock in your hands and turn it hither and yon, but it will work just as well.

In such a case, if necessary, you could always send the wife to the local cinema for the evening. Just be sure you operate over the kitchen stove between the time she leaves and the time she gets home!

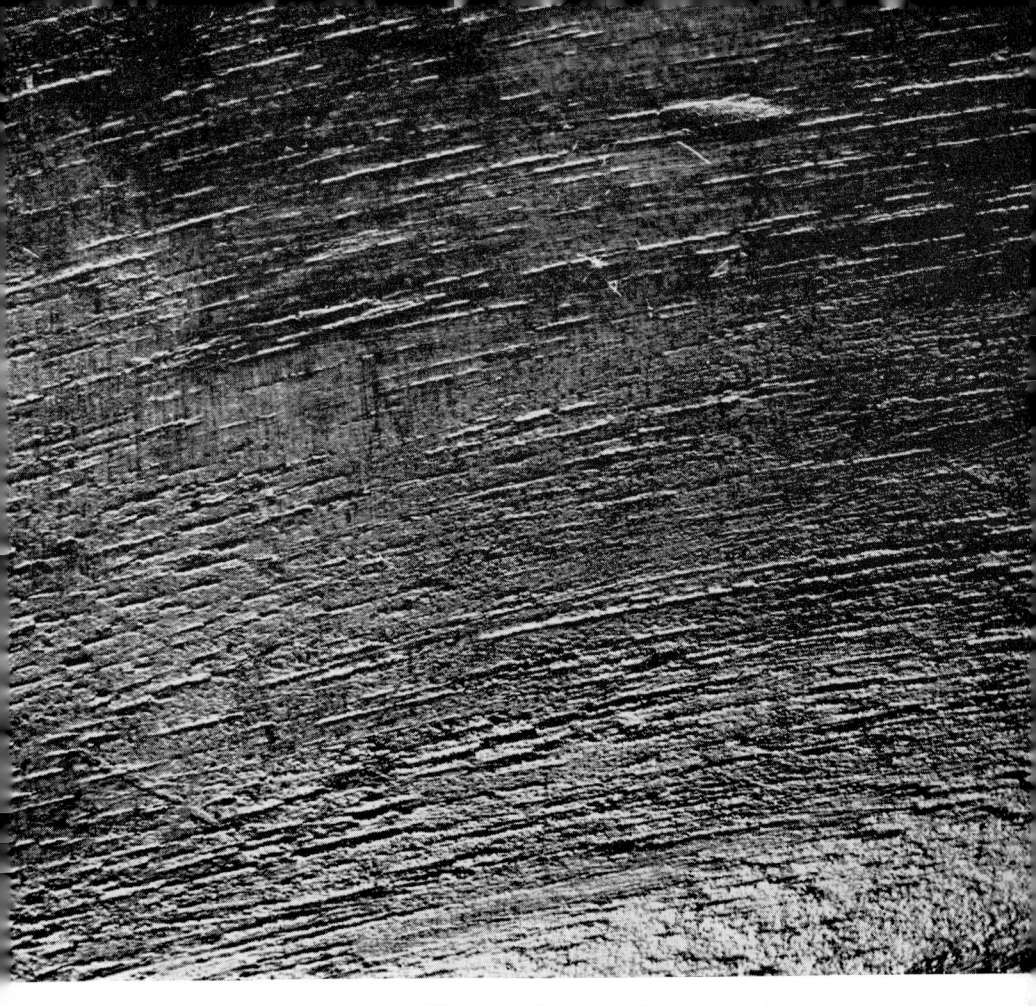

SPRINGFIELD WALNUT—"AS ISSUED"

The stock of which this is an enlarged section was the one present on an issue Springfield from the D.C.M. when I opened the box.

It is impossible to show the generally disreputable appearance of the overall stock in such a small-area shot, but it is certain that the surface of the wood leaves much to be desired. The rest of the stock is in the same condition as this area.

As you can see, the pores of the wood are unfilled and there are many grain ends and rough spots, though they are all so minute that it takes a close examination to detect them in this illustration. The overall effect is rather unpleasing.

There was enough ground-in dirt, perspiration and miscellaneous material so that the general color of the wood was a dirty brown. This, of course, is common with such military arms and detracts greatly from their appearance.

Such a military stock is often considered beyond redemption and thus is taken off and thrown away. By careful workmanship and attention to details the color may be improved considerably and the surface resurrected so that such a stock may do justice to a reblued and refitted action..

Such a stock may be partially cut down to get a sporter effect, or it may be left as issued if that be the desire of the owner.

This same stock is shown on next plate after being reconditioned.

ISSUE SPRINGFIELD—"AFTER TREATMENT"

This is the same section as that shown in the "before" picture.

Conventional methods were used to improve the appearance of the stock; those which are given in this book.

The ground-in dirt and miscellaneous coloring matter was the first target in reworking this stock. Inasmuch as it was an issued gun there is no doubt that some of the discoloration was produced by spilled bore cleaner and lubricating oils.

The whole mess was taken care of by sanding the wood with sandpaper soaked in varnish remover. The varnish remover consisted of toluol and alcohol in equal proportions and did a good job of softening and dissolving those cleaners and oils while the sandpaper took care of the top layer of wood by abrasion. This operation took off maybe a thirty-second inch and brought out the natural color of the wood.

In sanding, the rough surface of the wood was removed, naturally, so that the whiskering operations were simple. Using the traditional water-and-flame process followed by steel wool rubbing gave assurance that future sweat or rain would not bring up the grain ends through the finish to cause unpleasantness.

Following the whiskering, the stock had a thin bath of a reddish-yellow oil stain to enhance the beauty. The natural color of the wood (and most issue stocks will be about the same) was a brown which was nice but nothing special. The red and yellow touch adds a richness which is delightful to see.

Then a lacquer sanding sealer was applied to act as filler.

Over that, three coats of clear lacquer were applied and then rubbed down.

The overall effect on the gun was miraculous. While the metal parts had not been touched it looked like a million bucks.

The surface of this stock is now smooth as a baby's cheek, though it was not polished so much that it looked like glass. Too much of that will be as bad as too little.

The full stock and gun is shown on another plate.

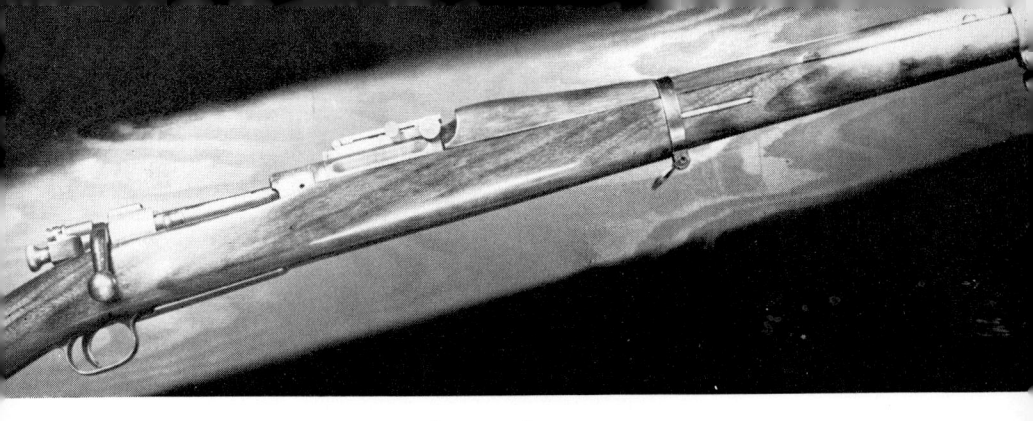

Refinished Service Springfield

This stock is the same as that shown in the "before and after" set in the front part of the book.

It is the issue Springfield which was reworked (stock only).

This larger view of the stock shows the beauty which even such rough guns may assume. Before working over, this was a rather beat-up range rifle with the figure almost entirely obscured due to dirt and oils which had been soaked into it.

The figure which was brought out by proper cleaning and finishing was good, very good, but I added a bit to it by darkening the forend somewhat in spots with flame. This was done by playing the flame of my Meker burner close enough and long enough at the points wanted so that they nearly charred. It was a browning rather than blackening that I achieved. If I had actually burned the wood I would have had to go after those sections with sandpaper and remove nearly all of the burned wood. This, in turn, would have left valleys and ridges in the wood and then I would have had to sand down the remainder of the stock to level the surface.

The metal portions of this rifle were in fairly good shape so they were not even reblued. I was interested only in the wood. However, the rifle is now in such good condition and so attractive that I intend to leave it the way it is, rather than make a sporter out of it, which was my first intention.

Incidentally, this gun has awakened interest in quite a few men as to the possibilities inherent in the rifle as issued. Such a gun in this reworked condition is as attractive, or more so, to the average gunnut as the conventional sporter. To me, at least, there is something about it which is more appealing than the run-of-the-mill restocked rifle. (No, I am not going to carry it on a hunting trip. But it sure looks classy in the gun rack.)

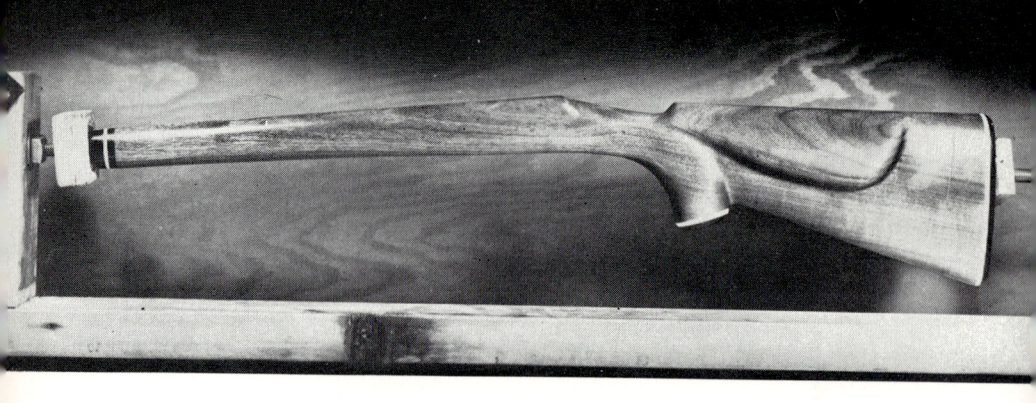

A Varnish Job

The finish on this stock is a varnish which was rubbed and polished to give the gloss shown.

This stock was cut from a halfway decent plank of walnut and finished in the conventional manner.

It was whiskered, stained only slightly with a dash of red to give a little richness, and filled with the finish coat. This was done by applying the varnish in thin coats and allowing them each to dry for 24 hours. It took about four coats before the pores were filled, after which it was sanded down to the wood.

Then the finish itself was applied. This was merely a continuation of the varnishing until another three coats were built up. Then it was polished and rubbed.

It is possible to go too far in this polishing, though. If too much of a gloss is given to the coating it will appear like glass, which detracts rather than adds to the beauty of the gun.

The varnish which was used was a good alkyd varnish. This is what composes the better "clear enamels" or "spar varnishes." (The Marine Spar Varnishes are usually a different type of resin though the name actually means very little. Unless your supplier knows what composes the varnish he sells it is sometimes difficult to determine just what you have to work with.)

Varnish, as a rule, will not polish up as well as the lacquers, though that rule is not infallible. Even poor varnishes (from the rubbing and polishing standpoint, that is) will give a good appearance if handled correctly.

Effect of Coloring a Filler

This is a closeup of a 3″ by 6″ wood panel showing the effect of coloring a filler.

As the uncolored half of the panel shows, the only grain structure visible is that which is forcibly brought to your attention by the light and dark streaks and by the more outstanding grain.

This same effect is evident on a great many stocks, both in the better grades and in the poorer classes. The wood may be good and graining well figured, but under normal methods of handling does not show up too well.

The filler used on this particular specimen was a lacquer sanding sealer. The entire section or panel is finished in the same manner and to the same degree except in the one case the sealer-filler was tinted a bit with burnt umber. Wherever the sealer and umber were retained by the pores, the color remains and thus accentuates the pores and overall grain structure.

Over the sealer was placed a clear lacquer which was then rubbed and polished.

This panel happened to be of mahogany, but any open grained wood will accept such a treatment well. Walnut, being open grained also, will show up in this same manner.

The important thing to watch in such a treatment is that you do not allow the colored filler or sealer to build up above the surface in such a manner that an overall brown cast is given the wood, in the manner of an overcoat. Leave that building up process to the final clear finish, whether it be lacquer or varnish.

The best method is to give the wood a good coat of the colored filler-sealer and then to sand back down until everything but the stuff in the pores is removed. Then go ahead with the finishing coat.

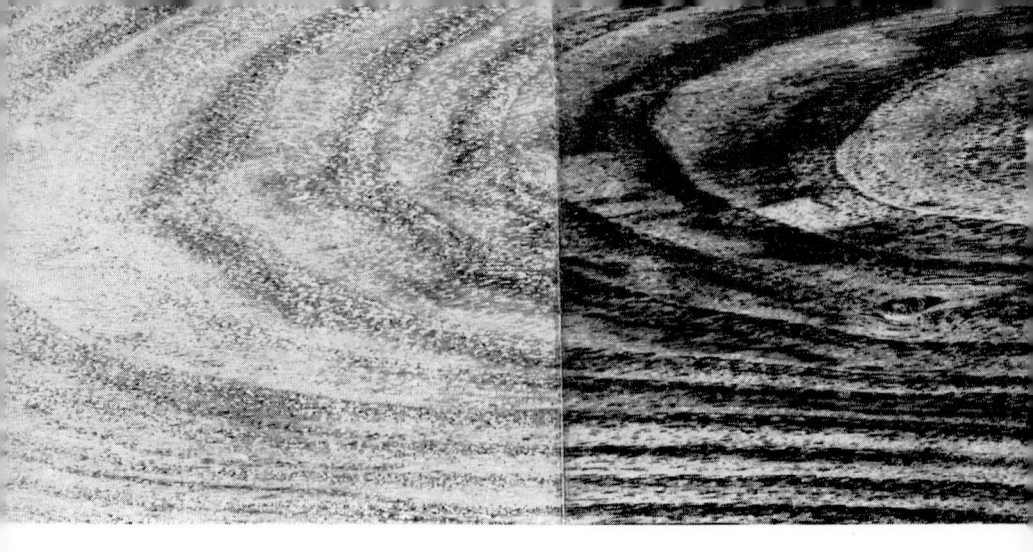

Mesquite

This is a shot of a panel of mesquite wood. This wood is being offered more and more to the trade as a gunstock wood and is found in the southwest part of the United States.

The panel pictured here shows how even a clear coating can bring out figure.

The only thing that has been done to the finished half is to fill the pores with clear varnish and over that to lay a coating of wax. Something to do with index of refraction of the finish and all that sort of thing, you know.

Actually staining is not necessary in such a highly figured piece of wood. It may help if you have a very close grained surface to work with such as birch, maple, or some specimens of myrtle, but for some of the more open grained pieces a plain, ordinary clear (varnish or lacquer) finish will do a great deal.

This was the best piece of mesquite I have seen. The other was a sickly color, soft, open pored (very much so), easily worked wood but one which will take a great deal of work to make into anything.

I understand that a great many of the West Coast stockers go for this wood in a big way and that it is gaining popularity in leaps and bounds. Samworth himself tells me that it really makes up into something to look at. Mebbe so, but I have got to see a whole lot better stock blanks than I have yet seen before I would even get it within hailing distance of a gun.

Understand now, the piece shown here is a whole lot better than the majority of actual blanks. I picked this piece from a lot of others because this one was unusual. The only reason this piece looks so good is that it was plain sawed and with that kind of cutting even soft pine will often take on beauty.

Anyhow, this is what it looks like (if you can choose your specimen). Actually the wood may be better than I have pictured above. Very possibly I have not gotten hold of representative blanks and therefore am prejudiced. Considering the popularity of the stuff in certain circles there must be a lot to recommend it or it would not have achieved the rating it evidently has.

If you can get a blank it may pay you to investigate. I understand that it is being offered to a great extent, especially by the West Coast stockers.

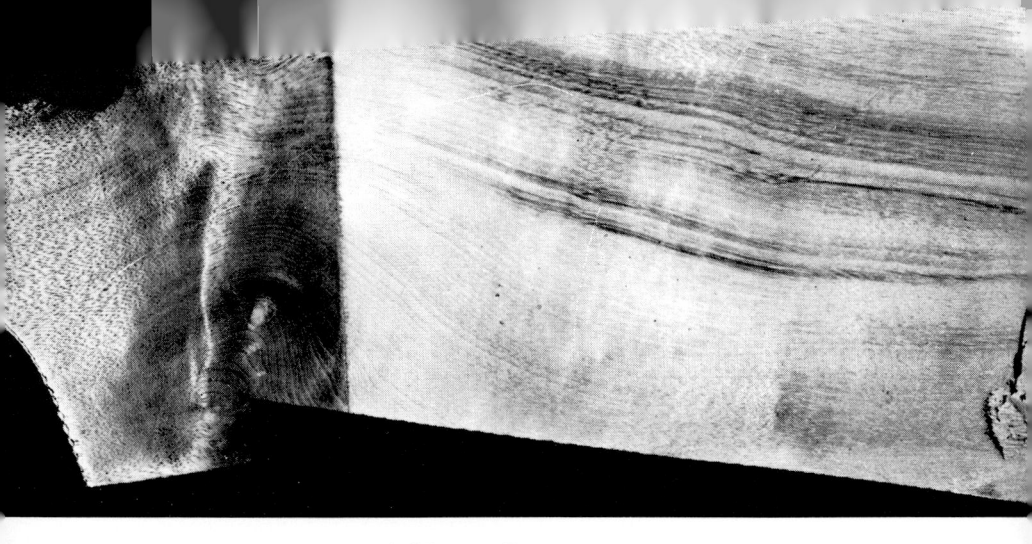

A Myrtle Blank

It is too bad these shots can not be given in color. If so this one would be the pick of the lot.

This shows a very well figured section of Oregon myrtle wood. Of course, the burl or semi-knot configuration leaves a great deal to be desired both in working the stuff and in strength where strength is needed, but for a fireside sporting arm or for a something special it is one of the most beautiful pieces of wood I have seen in a long time.

When you order a myrtle blank you will not always get such a startling specimen. A great many times (most of the time, maybe) you will get a rather straight-grained blank but even then you will be able to get a rather fine looking finished stock.

This piece was sanded smooth and the grain was raised. Then a stain was used to bring out the denser areas as shown. The stain chosen was a thin mixture of about 75% yellow, 20% brown, and just a trace of red. Too much red in this normally light colored wood will ruin it. Actually the ultimate (and most desirable) color is of a golden hue.

Obviously the after section was not treated with anything. This was left bare to show the contrast that proper treatment will give.

After the staining operations, a lacquer sanding sealer was used to fill the pores and then a straight wax finish was applied. The material used was a hard paste wax, similar to that put out for waxing automobiles.

Myrtle is a little harder to work with than walnut. It tends to tear or split more easily (even with very sharp chisels). You must be careful that you do not tear or split out wood when cutting the inletting and barrel channel. The barrel channel at the upper edges is especially touchy.

Once the rough cutting has been done this wood works easily under sandpaper and file. It takes nearly any of the normal finishes well.

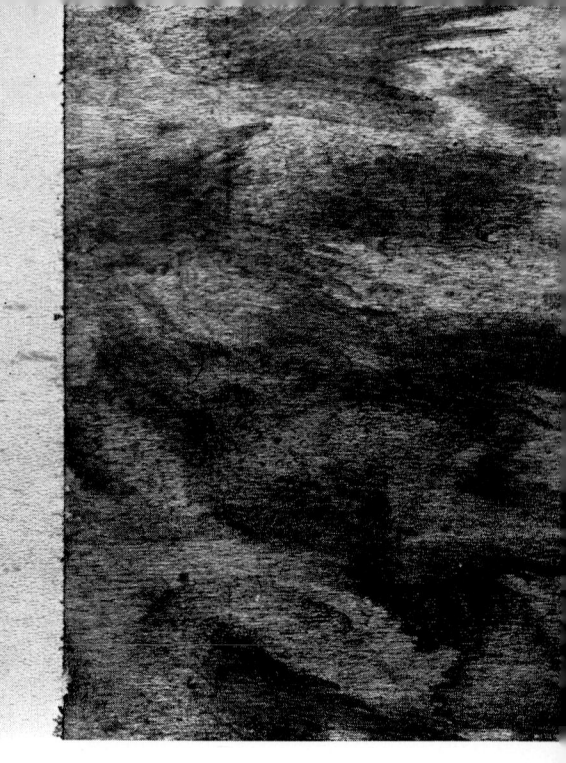

Adding Grain Figure

Here is a bit of faking.

The plain birch panel as shown in the lighter half would not take much of any color or graining treatment. In fact I ruined three such panels trying to develop a successful method of bringing out some figure. There just did not seem to be any.

Sometimes you will run across a stock with the same characteristics. It just will not do much of anything except darken.

The remedy for that is to take some fairly dark, unthinned staining agent. If you use asphaltum dissolve it just enough to make a runny liquid. Do not thin it any more than you can help.

Now take a piece of burlap, excelsior, coarse steel wool or rug padding and wad a little up in your fingers. Dip the wad lightly in the stain, shaking off any excess. Casually slap a few spots here and there on the wood and then feather the edges out so that the blotches are not all round spots. If done correctly and with finesse you will get a swell looking set of grain lines and spots.

The picture is only a small section and a closeup at that, but on an overall stock job you will be surprised at the good looking grain structure you can make out of nothing at all.

I have found that the best thing for this kind of business is some painter's tinting pastes, which you buy at the local paint store for tinting wall paints. They come in a number of different colors and are very thick or heavy. It is easy to thin them to where you will get best results (practice on a board out of the back fence first, though) and the color can be regulated to suit your fancy.

Burnt umber or VanDyke brown pastes seem to work best for most jobs, especially if you have stained the background wood with a bit of red or yellow.

Obviously such a graining job will not have any appreciable penetration. This stuff will stay on the surface and you must build up a fairly decent film over it to protect it from handling abrasion.

I would stick to a varnish finishing coat if I were you. A lot of this stuff is formulated upon a linseed oil base so that it will mix with house paints. In that case a lacquer applied over it would lift that stuff completely away from the stock.

This sort of thing is strictly makeshift, but you would be surprised at the number of times it comes in handy. Even a well figured stock can use a spot or two here and there and be improved 100% for it.

Bringing Out Figure of Wood

This panel is a veneer of bird's-eye maple. The light section shows it in natural condition.

The darker half has been worked over to bring out the bird's-eyes and the natural figure of the wood. The method used in this case was to brush a thin wash coat of asphaltum thinned with turpentine over the half panel. The thin stain soaked in some sections and not so much in others and the difference in the density of the wood gave the effect shown.

Such a staining process will be very useful in many cases where the figure is wanted to stand out, and the slight darkening of the wood not objectionable.

This panel could now be sanded lightly, which would leave the figuring as you see it here and still lighten the overall color to quite an extent.

This same system can be used where flame or wavy grain is actually present but where it needs to be accentuated in some manner. In fact, it can be used over almost any wood where whatever figure present, even if not apparent, is wanted to stand out slightly.

Asphaltum is not the only thing that can be used. Thin solutions of oil or spirit stains will do the same thing.

In a pinch a gob of asphalt from the county highway could be dissolved in turps and used. The asphalt and asphaltum will be the same in properties, except the stuff you pick up off the county highway will have some sand, dirt, and a million and one other impurities in it. Straining it through a cotton cloth will take most of the foreign matter out and leave you with a pretty good dark brown stain, depending upon how much you thin it.

Plastic Forend Tip Details

Here are complete details as to manufacture of plastic forend tips.

The upper left-hand section shows the individual quarter-inch pieces of black plexiglas in proper position for bonding. The one black and one white pieces at the extreme left are the base or stock section before bonding.

The lower right-hand section shows the unit blocks after first bonding. The base or stock section is shown with the two dowels and large wood screw which will be used to fasten that base section to the forend. After that, the large block will be bonded to the small base section.

The center shows the tip fastened in place, shaped and then polished.

The barrel channel (roughly cut to size) was placed in the individual pieces before bonding. This makes it easier to work with when in block form. The plastic is easy to work, but cutting out a channel from the solid block takes quite a little while.

The color design may be changed in any way you desire. It is not necessary to use contrasting colors at all. If you desire you could make the whole thing of black, or even of white. Inasmuch as the tip is built up of quarter- or eighth-inch sections it is a simple matter to place whatever color you wish in any spot you wish.

Pistol grip caps may be made in precisely the same manner. The same goes for buttplates, though it is a bit difficult to place serrations evenly on such a buttplate and not have it look too crude.

Power Sander for Gunstocks

This shot shows the Dremel MotoSander being used to rub and polish down a varnish finish.

This little tool is very, very handy around the gunsmith's establishment, especially for stock work. Not only can it be used for sanding medium to fine work, but it is the cat's pajamas for this rubbing and polishing.

The tool comes equipped with sanding pads and also a sheepskin buff for this polishing.

The big advantage in this machine is that it sands in a back and forward motion, doing away entirely with any cross sanding marks. (The rotary or disc sanders are bad offenders from that standpoint.)

In rubbing or polishing, a dab of the abrasive is placed on the face of the buff, not the stock itself. If you plaster the stock with it and then come along with the polisher you will find that in a great many cases no polishing will be done. The abrasive will cake up on the stock and refuse to be distributed evenly over the wood under the movement of the buff. Always place the compound on the buff.

The big disadvantage of this machine, as I see it, is that you cannot wet-sand with safety. That is, in using waterproof sandpaper (which is always more economical in the long run) you may possibly get some of the water up into the works of the gimmick. Then there is hell to pay. Not only do you buy a new machine, but 110 volts through the trigger finger raises the devil with scores.

GUNSTOCK SPRAYING TOOL

The gun shown here is the Air-Mite, made by the Edmonds Engineering Company.

This little gun has given me complete satisfaction for stock work. It atomizes, varnishes, and lacquers well.

You will note the droplets forming on the stock where it is being sprayed. These droplets immediately flow out upon striking the surface and give a good, smooth finish. I have never had a bit of trouble from orange peel or sagging with this gun.

Normally I do not spray my stocks at the location shown in the picture. That just happened to be the best place to photograph the checkering frame and stock at the time. If I did much spraying as shown, my buffing wheels would have a nice coating of varnish on them. Usually my spraying is done in a separate corner of the shop where I do not care how much spray gets blown around.

INDEX

Abrasives for rubbing, 169
Acetone, 271
Acid graining, 96
Acrylics, 255
Adhesion, 200
African walnut, 9
Airmite, Model AB, 391
Alkyd resin
    drying type, 144
    non-drying type, 144
    phenolated, 145
    rosin modified, 144
Alligatoring, 185
Almond wood, 2
Amaranth, 18
American black walnut, 6
American walnut, 6
Antique stock finishes
    bone polish, 369
    coloring wood, 368
    drying oils, 367
    duplication, 369
    filling agents, 368, 374
    solvents, 368
    spirit varnishes, 368
    waxes and oils, 367
Apple wood, 3
Artificial graining, 84
Ash wood, 2
Auxiliary equipment
    cloth cover, 389
    drying cabinet, 387
    infra-red light banks, 396
Avodire, 18
Baking accelerator, 258
Baking varnishes, 258
Beechwood, 3
Beeswax, 277
Benin, 18
Benzine, 270
Benzol, 270
Benzol, 90%, 270
Binks, 391
Birch, 4

Bleached shellac, 231
Bleaching, 97
Blown oil, 106
Blushing, 226
Boea resin, 142
Boiled oil, 105
"Bois d'arc" wood, 5
Bone polish finish, 369
Brazil wax, 278
Brush keeper, 405
Brush marks, 224, 250
Brushes, 155
    bristle types, 400
    cleaning, 401, 404
    types, 399
Bubbles and bumps, 225
Bubinga, 18
Bumpy surface, 184
Burgess Vibro-Sprayer, 392
Butyl acetate, 271
Butyl alcohol, 271
Candelilla wax, 279
Care of finished stocks, 332
Carnauba wax, 278
Ceresine wax, 278
Checking, 185, 252
Checkered and carved areas, staining, 96
Checkering and carving, 56
    in refinishing operations 327
Chemical stains, 65
Cherry, 4, 18
Chia oil, 114
China wood oil (tung), 111
    permeability, 112
Chlorinated rubber, 255
Circassian walnut, 8
Coke oven distillates, 269
"Cold checking," 223
Cold pressed raw linseed oil, 102
Color combinations in staining, 73
Color graining, 89
    formulae, 91
Coloring wood, 368

INDEX

Combinations of wood for laminating, 20
Compressor equipment, 393
Congo copal, 146
Congo copal ester, 146
Congo ester gum, 142
Congo resin, 142
Converter, 258
Copal, phenolated, 146
Cottonseed oil, 115
Coumarone-indene resin, 146
Cracks, shellac filling, 334
Curtains, 185
Dammar resin, 141
Dehydrated castor oil, 115
Dents, removal, 36
DeVilbiss, 391
Diluent, lacquer, 191
Dremel Moto-Sander, 395
Driers, 263
  effects on durability, 265
  history, 263
  in varnish, 138
  Japan, 264
  properties of metal, 264
  reaction, 263
"Drip" viscosity test, 418
Drying, definition, 262
Drying oils, 100
  blown, 106
  bung hole, 106
  history, 100
  processing, 102
  refining, 103
  types, 106
  uses, 117
Drying oils, application, 122
  drying time test, 121
  over fillers, 119
  over varnish sealer, 119
  preparation of wood, 118
  viscosity test, 121
Drying oils, finishing
  Dull London oil finish, 135
  formulae, 128
  polishing, 124
  suitability, 132
Drying oils in antique work, 367, 377
Drying oils, lists, 132
  chia, 114
  cottonseed, 115
  dehydrated castor, 115

Drying oils, lists (*Continued*)
  experimental synthetic, 115
  fish, 115
  hempseed, 114
  Japanese wood oil, 115
  linseed, 108
  oiticica, 112
  perilla, 113
  poppyseed, 114
  safflower seed, 114
  soybean, 113
  sunflower seed, 114
  tung (china wood), 111
  walnut, 114
Drying time list, 422
Dull London oil finish, 135
Dulling, 252
Duplicating antique finishes, 369
Durability, drier effect on, 265
Dust particles, 250
Dyewood stains, 73
Earth wax, 278
East India resins, 143
Ebony, 18
Electric sanders, 158
Electric Sprayit, 391
Elemi resin, 143
English walnut, 7
Equipment
  care, 402
  cleaning, 403
Equivalents formulae, 423
Esparto wax, 279
Ethyl acetate, 271
Ethyl alcohol, 271
Ethyl cellulose, use in waxes, 280
Evaluation of blanks, 12
Evaporation rates, solvents, 422
Filler
  composition, 47
  "hard," 46
  manufacture, 47
  reason for, 44
  "soft," 44
Fillers
  application, 50
  finish coat as, 53
  finishing faults, 55
  sanding, 54
  touching up, 55
Filling agents, antique, 368

INDEX

Finishing faults
  fillers, 55
  lacquer, 224
  shellac, 250
  varnish, 184
Finishing operations
  preliminary, 28
  shaping, 28
  sanding, 29
  (de) whiskering, 34
  staining, 37, 60
  sealing, 39
  filling, 44
Finishing systems
  drying oils, 117
  lacquer, 208
  lacquer sanding sealer, 205
  shellac, 236
  varnish, 152
  wax, 281
Fish oils, 115
Flame graining, 85
Flatting (flattening), 185, 252
"foots," 105, 109
Ford cup, #4, 419
Forearm tips, plastic, 299
  composition, 299
  forming, 303
  fitting, 305
  clamping, 308
  inletting, 309
  shaping, 310
  polishing, 310
  faults in bonding, 312
  time of application, 312
Forearm tips, rare woods, 313
French polish, original formula, 386
French polish, shellac, 246
French polishing, varnish, 175
French walnut, 9
Fusel oil amyl acetate, 271
Glossary of words, 426
Gluing laminated blanks, 22
Graining, artificial, 84, 89, 93, 96
  flame, 85
Grip caps, plastic, 299
Grit, 251
Hardness list, resins, 422
Heat lamps (infra-red), 259
Hempseed oil, 114
High boiling point solvents, 271
High flash solvent, 270

High solvency naphtha, 269
Holly, 18
Hot application, 177
Humidity in varnishing, 180
Infra-red heat lamps, 259
Italian walnut, 9
Isopropyl acetate, 271
Japan tallow, 278
Japan wax, 278
Japanese wood oil, 115
Kauri resin, 143
"Keeper," brush, 405
Kerosene, 268
Kingwood, 19
Lacewood, 19
Lacquer (see lacquers)
  history, 186
  application, 208, 213
  desirability, 224
  effect of temperature change on, 222
  finishing faults, 224
  "lifting" of undercoat, 212
  over shellac, 221
  over wax, 295
  rubbing, 219
  thinner (mist) coating, 217
  time of application, 220
  wet sanding, 209, 216
  viscosity, 193
Lacquers
  composition, 187
    solvent and thinners, 189
    diluent, 191
    latent solvent, 191
    plasticizer, 189
  equipment
    spray guns, 194
  finishing types, 198
  moisture resistance, 202
  sanding sealer, 199
    application, 205
    composition, 204
Lacquer thinning, 270
Laminated blank
  combinations of wood for, 20
  gluing of, 22
Laminated stocks, 16
  advantages of, 23
  manufacture, 21
  woods for, 17
LD Naphtha, 269
Lighter lacquer diluent, 269

INDEX

Lignite wax, 279
"Lifting," 212, 225
Linseed oil, 108
  cold pressed raw, 102
  alkali or acid refine, 105
  permeability, 110
Liquid measures, standard, 423
Low bake converter, 258
Lucite, 299
Lye, 272
Magnolia, 19
Mahogany wood, 4
Maintenance refinishing, 330
Maple, 6, 19
Mastic resin, 141
Measure, standard liquid, 423
Melamine, 258
Methyl ethyl ketone, 271
Mineral spirits, 268
Mineral wax, 278
Mist coating lacquer, 217
Moisture resistance, 409
  lacquer, 202
  sealer, 411
Montan wax, 279
Naphthas, 268, 269
Natural resin list, 421
Natural resins
  boea, 142
  congo, 142
  congo ester, 142
  dammar, 141
  East India, 143
  elemi, 143
  kauri, 143
  mastic, 141
  pontianak, 143
  sandarac, 142
  soluble manila, 142
NGR stains, 63
Nitrocellulose in lacquers, 187
Non-drying oils, 107
Oil rubbing varnish, 174
Oil stains, 70
Oiticica oil, 112
Orange peel, 224
Orange shellac, 231
Osage orange, 5
Ouricury wax, 278
Oxidizing type varnish, 140
Ozokerite, 278
Padouk, 19

Paint removers, 272
  application, 274
Paraffin wax, 279
Paste colors, 79, 95
Penta resin, 145
Perilla oil, 113
Permeability, 189
  lacquer, 202
Permeability tests, 409
Peroba, 19
Petroleum thinners, 268
Phenolic resin
  modified, 145
  pure (100%), 145
Phenolated copal, 146
Phenoplast, 257
Pigment graining, 93
Pigment stains, 72
Pinholding, 185
Pitting, 185, 227
Plain sawing of stock blanks, 10
Plastic finishes, 253
  acrylics, 255
  chlorinated rubber, 255
  definition, 253
  melamine, 258
  phenoplast, 257
  urea, 258
  vinyl, 254
Plastic tips and grip caps, 299
Plasticized shellac, 236
Plasticizers in lacquer, 189
Plexiglas, 299
Polishes
  formulae, 286
Polishing
  lacquer, 219
  oil finish, 124
  varnish, 167
Polishing, final high gloss, 171
  machine polishing, 173
Polishing plastic, 310
Polishing varnish, 167
Polymerization type varnish, 140
Pontianak resin, 143
Poor adhesion, 226, 252
Poppyseed oil, 114
Porter-Cable Sander, 396
Prima Verde, 19
Pyroxylin, 188
Quarter sawing of stock blanks, 10
Quick stock finish (30 minutes), 288

INDEX

Refinishing factory guns, 325
Refinishing military stocks
  model 1898, 7.9 MM Mauser, 340
  model M 1917, Enfield, 349
  model M 1903, Springfield, 356
  Japanese Arisaka '38 and '39, 361
Refinishing operations, 315
  removal of old finish, 317
  carved and checkered areas, 327
  sanding, 320
  sealing, 322
  staining, 322
Removal of dents, 36
Removal of old finish, 317
Resins, hardness list, 422
Resins, source of natural, 421
Rock maple, 5
Rosewood, 19
Rubber, chlorinated, 255
Rubbing
  lacquer, 219
  shellac, 243
  varnish, 167
    abrasives for, 169
    use of oil, 174
Rubbing compounds
  abrasives, 296
  composition, 296
  formulae, 297
Safflower seed oil, 114
Sagging, 184
Sandarac resin, 142
Sanders, electric, 158, 395
Sanding, 29
Sanding block, 31
Sanding machines
  Dremel Moto-Sander, 395
  Porter-Cable, 396
Sanding, method of, 32
Sanding over flame graining, 87
Sanding sealers
  lacquer, 199
  composition, 204
  application, 205
  tinting, 207
Sandpaper, Wet-Or-Dry, 31, 32
Sandy surface, 184
Satinwood, 19
Scratching, 227
Sealers
  varnish, 39
  lacquer, 199

Sealing in refinishing, 322
Secondary amyl acetate, 271
Semi-drying oils, 107
Semi-gloss lacquers, 199
Shaping, 28
Shellac, 142
  history, 228
  manufacturing, 229
  commercial classification, 230
  strength of solutions, 234
  properties, 231, 233
  water resistance, 231
  base coats, 233
  plasticized, 236
Shellac, filling of cracks, 334
Shellac finishing
  brushing, 236
  spraying, 245
  sanding, 239
  use under lacquer, 221
  "spiriting" off, 240, 241
  polishing, 241, 242
  rubbed finish, 243
  sanding and waxing (polish), 242
  French polish, 246
  finishing faults, 250
  desirability, 250
Shellac washcoat, 75
Silky oak, 19
Soluble manila chips, 142
Solvents
  lacquer, 189
  antique, 368
Solvent evaporation list, 422
Solvent type paint remover, 273
Solvent release varnish, 140
  spirit varnish, 141
  sources of supply, 432
Soybean oil, 113
Spanish walnut, 9
Spermaceti, 279
Spirit varnish, 141
  antique, 368, 381
Spray gun
  care and cleaning, 403
Spray gun types, 300
  Binks, 391
  DeVilbiss, 391
  Airmite, AB, 391
  Electric Sprayit, 391
  Burgess Vibro-Sprayer, 392
  Miscellaneous, 392

INDEX

Spray gun, compressor equipment, 393
Spray gun, operating principles, 390
Spray gun, use with varnish, 177
Staining, 37
Staining agents
  water stains, 62
  spirit stains, 67
  chemical, 65
  oil stain, 70
  varnish, 72
  pigment color, 72
  dyewood, 73
  tinting colors (paste), 79
Staining checkered or carved areas, 96
Staining in refinishing, 322
Staining over old varnish, 80
Staining varnishes, 82
Stains, 60
  type of agents, 61
  characteristics of, 62
  preparation of wood, 74
  application, 75
  color combinations, 73
  in varnish, 82
Stains, antique, 368, 371
Standard liquid measures, 423
Steam raising, 37
"Stick test" for viscosity, 418
Sticky film, 185, 251
Stock blanks, 10
  plain sawing, 10
  quarter sawing, 10
  warping, 10
  evaluation of rough, 12
  storage of, 14
Stock curing box, 158
Streaking, 227
Sugar maple, 5
Suigi finish, 85
Sumac wax, 278
Sunflower seed oil, 114
Sweating, 185
Synthetic varnishes, 143
  alkyd resin, drying, 144
  alkyd resin, non-drying, 144
  alkyd resin, rosin modified, 144
  alkyd resin, phenolated, 145
  congo copal, 16
  congo copal ester, 146
  coumarone-indene, 146
  ester gum, 146

Synthetic varnishes (*Continued*)
  penta resin, 145
  phenolated copal, 146
  phenolic resin, modified, 145
  phenolic resin, pure (100%), 145
Tack rag, 159
Teak, 19
Tenite plastic, 299
Thinners, lacquer, 189
Throw out, 225
Time of application
  forearm tips, 312
  lacquer, 220
  varnish, 183
Tinting colors, 79, 95
Tinting sanding sealers, 207
Toluene, 270
Toluol, 270
Touching up factory stocks, 325
Tulip, 20
Tung (china wood) oil, 111
  permeability, 112
Turpentine, 267
Urea, 258
Varnish, 136
  history, 137
  early types, 139
  modern types, 139
    solvent release, 140
    oxidizing, 140
    polymerization, 140
    synthetic, 143
Varnish, hot application, 177
Varnish over wax, 295
Varnish remover, 80, 272
  application, 274
  removal of old finish, 317
Varnish sealers, 39
  composition, 39, 41
  reason for, 40
  application, 42
  manufacture, 41
Varnish stains, 72
Varnish, storage of, 154
Varnishing
  application, 160
  use of sealer, 153
  brushing, 160
  sanding, 164
  preparation of wood, 152
  rubbing and polishing, 167
  French polish method, 175

INDEX

Varnishing (*Continued*)
　as a filler, 163
　humidity effects on, 180
　time of application, 183
　finishing faults, 184
Varnishing equipment
　brushes, 155
　cloth cover, 389
　curing box, 158, 387
　electric sanders, 158, 395
　spray gun, 177, 390
　tack rag, 159
Vermilion wood, 20
Vinyl, 254
Viscosity
　definition, 416
　importance, 416
　determination, 417
　drying oil test, 121
　lacquer test, 193
　varnish test, 417
Viscosity cup, 419
VM & P naphtha, 268
Walnut
　American, 6
　English, 7
　Circassian, 8
　Italian, 9
　French, 9
　Spanish, 9
　African, 9
Walnut oil, 114
Warping tendencies of stocks, 10
Wash coat, 295
Waterproof sandpaper, 31
Water resistance, shellac, 231
Water stains, 62
Watin, early varnish maker, 139
Wax
　application, 281
　formulae, 283
　30 minute stock finish, 288
Wax finishes, 291
Wax in paint removers, 275
Waxes
　beeswax, 277
　candelilla, 279
　carnauba, 278
　ceresine, 278
　earth wax, 278
　esparto, 279
　Japan, 278

Waxes (*Continued*)
　lignite, 279
　mineral, 278
　montan, 279
　ouricury, 278
　ozokerite, 278
　paraffin, 279
　spermaceti, 279
　uses, 280
Waxes in antique work, 367
Wet-Or-Dry sandpaper, 31, 32
Whiskering
　wetting phase, 35
　heat phase, 35
Wood, desirable types, 2
　ash, 2
　almond, 2
　apple, 3
　beech, 3
　birch, 4
　cherry, 4
　mahogany, 4
　Osage orange, 5
　maple, 6
　walnut, 6
Woods, rare
　amaranth, 18
　avodire, 18
　benin, 18
　bubinga, 18
　cherry, 18
　ebony, 18
　holly, 18
　kingwood, 19
　magnolia, 19
　maple, 19
　padouk, 19
　peroba, 19
　prima verde, 19
　rosewood, 19
　satinwood, 19
　silky oak, 19
　teak, 19
　tulip, 20
　vermilion, 20
　zebra, 20
Wrinkling
　varnish, 184
　lacquer, 225
Xylol, 270
Zebra, 20